North Yorkshire County Council Library Service

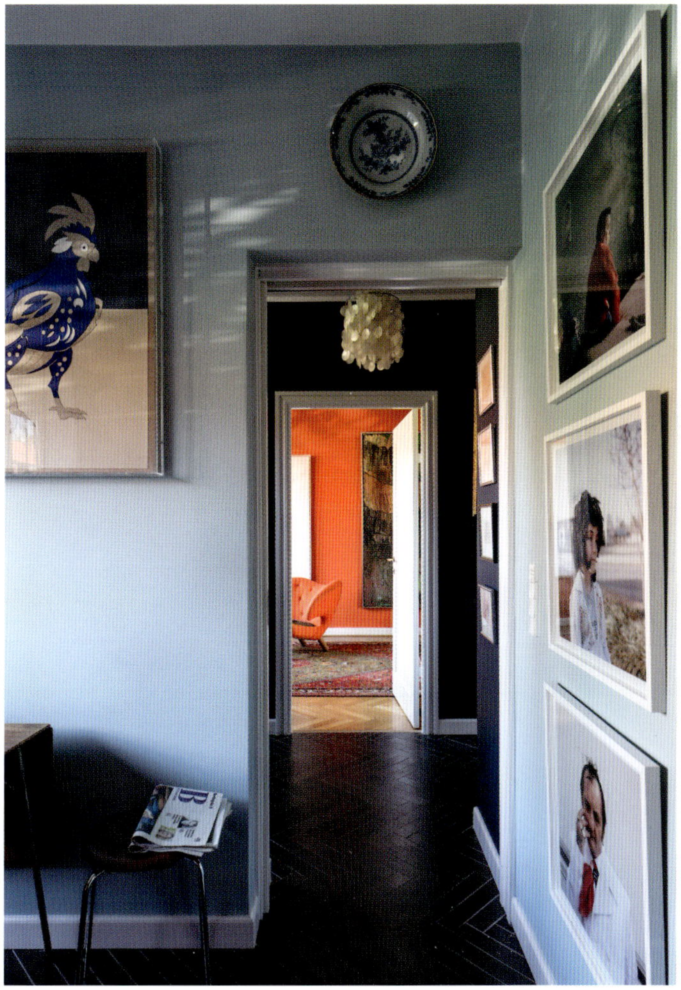

Farrow&Ball

RECIPES FOR DECORATING

JOA STUDHOLME

MITCHELL BEAZLEY

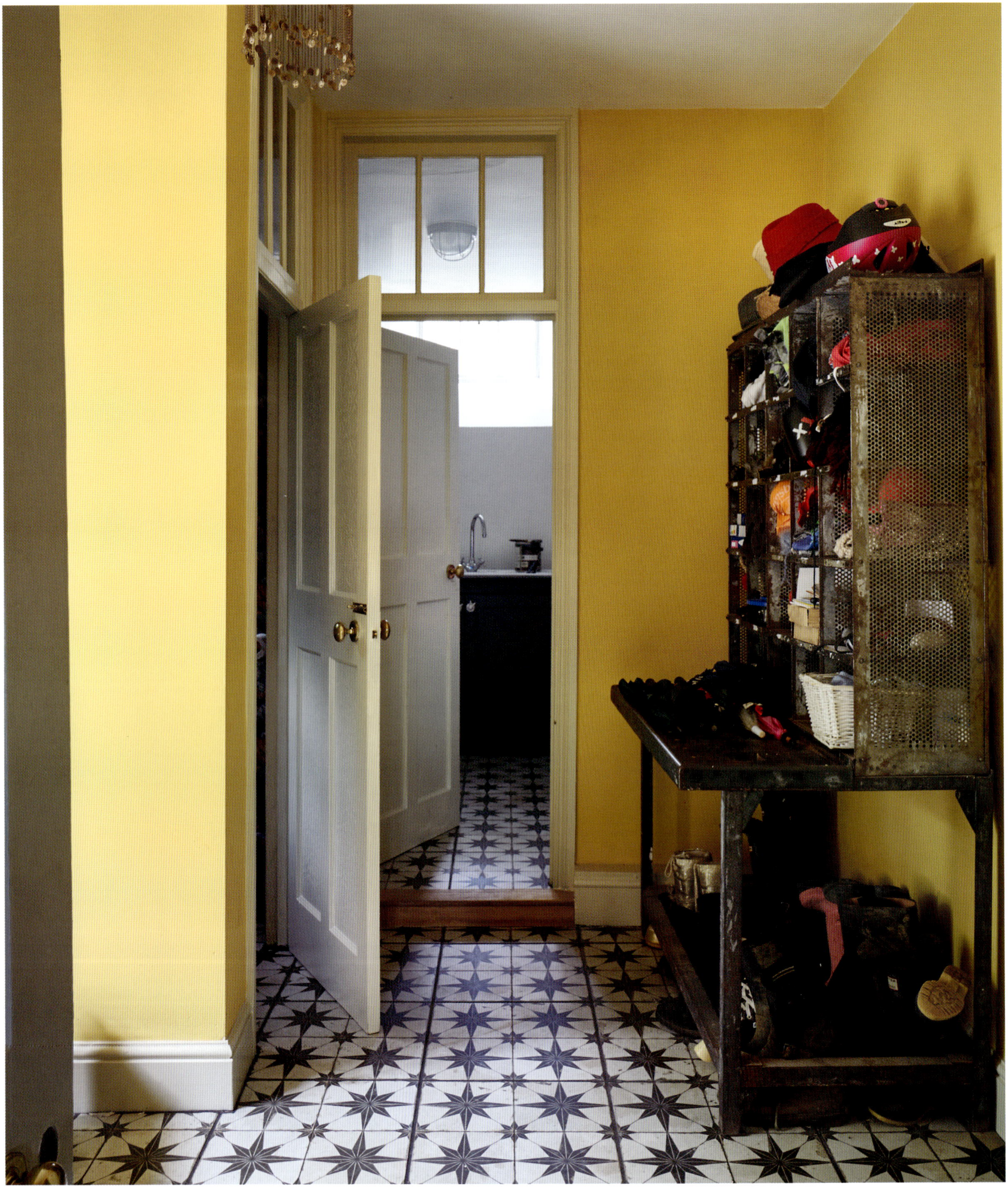

CONTENTS

8 Introduction
12 A Hand-picked Palette
14 Three Different Recipes
16 Style, Flow and Light
18 Taster Menu
20 The Naming of Names
22 Tried-and-tested Tips

24 **PART ONE: CASE STUDIES**

26 Be Your Own Consultant
28 Which Order?
30 Case Study 1:
   Danish Contemporary
40 Case Study 2:
   Understated Grandeur
52 Case Study 3:
   Copenhagen Art House
64 Case Study 4:
   Manhattan Chic
76 Case Study 5:
   Georgian Classic
88 Case Study 6:
   Modern Family
98 Case Study 7:
   Old Schoolhouse
110 Case Study 8:
   East London Elegance
122 Case Study 9:
   Quintessentially Country
134 Case Study 10:
   Easy Modern
146 Case Study 11:
   Industrial Reborn
154 Case Study 12:
   Light-filled Brownstone
162 Case Study 13:
   Upstate Oasis

172 **PART TWO: ROOM RECIPES**

174 Store Cupboard
176 Neutral Recipes
178 Halls
186 Kitchens
196 Sitting Rooms
208 Bedrooms
216 Bathrooms
226 Children's Bedrooms
236 Exteriors

240 **PART THREE: COLOUR SOLUTIONS**

242 Which Finish?
244 Quantities and Coverage
246 Small Rooms
248 Big Rooms
250 Light and Dark
252 High and Low
254 Tried-and-tested Recipes

262 Farrow & Ball Showrooms
264 Index
268 Acknowledgments

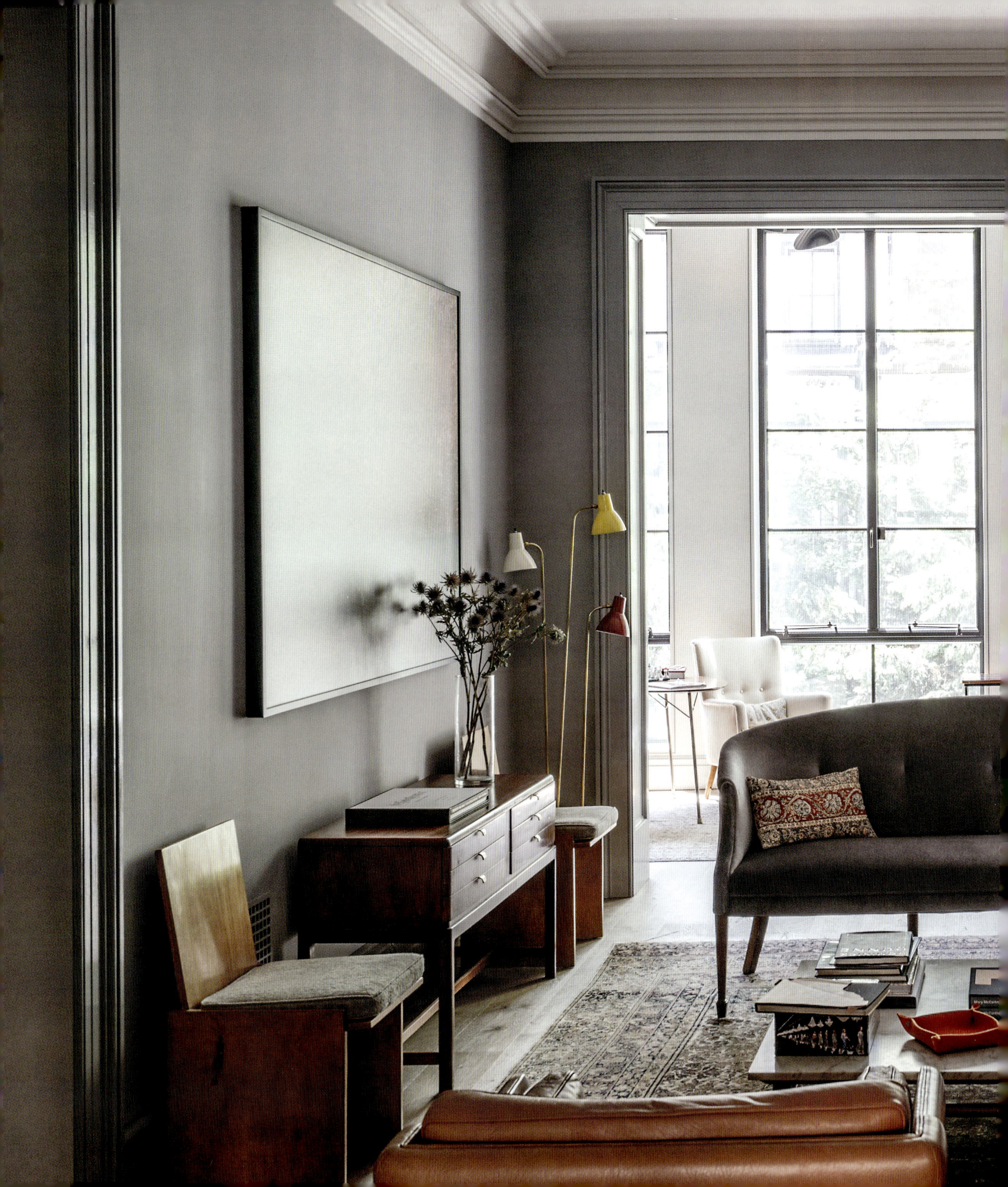

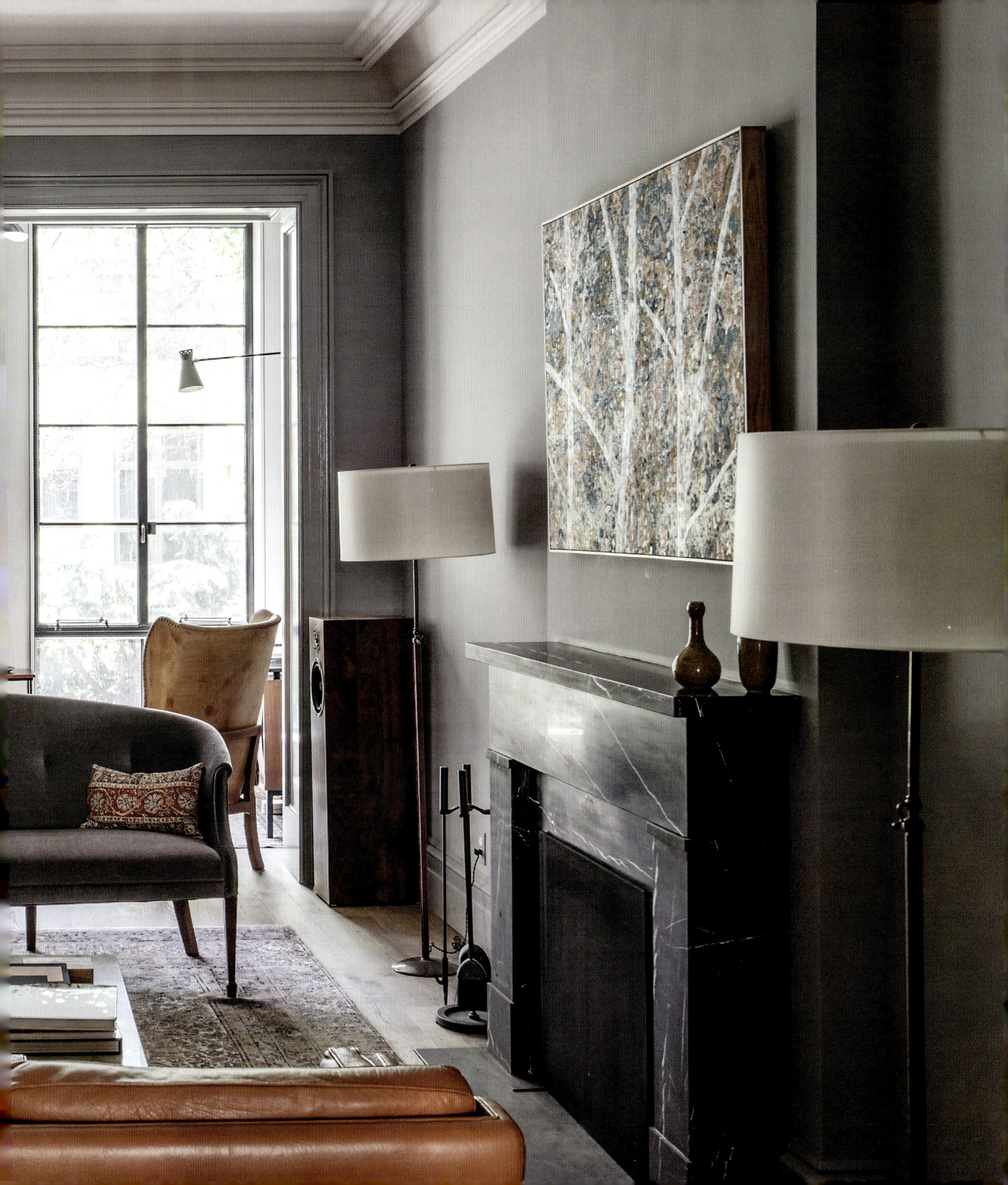

INTRODUCTION

You don't have to be a chef or even a particularly good cook to experience proper kitchen alchemy. The same can be said of decorating because, like cooking, it is not a science but an art. It is fine to make mistakes and to experiment because the joy is in creating a scheme then sharing the result.

Decorating your home should be a process of pure pleasure – your home is, after all, where you nurture both yourself and your family. Without doubt, colour is closely related to emotion, and my children have grown up surrounded by colour and, more specifically, by Farrow & Ball colour. They were resigned to me using their rooms to test colours that I was developing – the paint on their walls changed monthly, if not weekly. As they grow older, I am fully confident that their own recipes for decoration will not be insipid or flavourless, but altogether more appetizing. Colour nurtures the soul, but even the most perfectly decorated room is empty without people to love it. As you will discover in this book, the most interesting homes are those that reflect the occupants' tastes and personality as much as the decoration.

At Farrow & Ball, we believe that there are no firm rules when it comes to decorating. There are a few basic things to think about, as outlined in our previous book *How To Decorate* (Mitchell Beazley, 2016), but, above all, your home should tell the story of who you are and contain what you love. So in this book we bring you the decorative recipes that have been used to create 13 very different homes, ranging from Manhattan town houses to country cottages.

Of course, one of the most important ingredients in any home is colour. Many years ago I began to think about how paint colours are like ingredients in a recipe. They need to be combined and balanced, just like any ingredients are when being made into a culinary dish, to create something that is far greater than the sum of its parts.

I confess that I am not the most natural cook in the world but, like most people, I can follow a recipe pretty well. To make the techniques in this book as easy as possible to follow, we have included lists of all the ingredients in the form of detailed colour specifications for each house. To be honest, my lack of culinary prowess is quite often disguised by the careful presentation of food at my table, using a range of multicoloured bowls and an abundance of different garnishes. In the same way, colour can help to disguise a multitude of problems. When ceiling heights are compromised, light is lacking or joinery is unsophisticated, colour can come to the rescue – as you will discover. Changing everything to make a room perfect may simply be impossible – budgets might be tight, planners may heap on restrictions or we just might not be inclined to do the work – and this is when colour becomes your greatest asset, in the same way as my bowls and garnishes.

Since starting my role as Farrow & Ball's original Colour Consultant over 20 years ago, I have chosen colours for more than 4,500 rooms a year. That's a lot of rooms. Of course, it is much easier to do this for other people than for oneself. This was made all the more clear when recently, for the first time in 25 years, I got a new home of my own. It has given me more joy than I could have imagined. My budget was strict, and I wasn't my easiest client, but the use of Farrow & Ball colours has transformed a lovely but rather tired and bland house into a little jewel – a feast for the eyes. Everyone has a favourite recipe, whether it be for a culinary masterpiece, such as magnificent Deans Court on pages 122–33, or for the simplest of dishes, like my house on pages 98–109.

Many contemporary chefs are returning to age-old trusted recipes. Similarly, at Farrow & Ball we are very proud of our historic roots and certainly have trusted combinations. Nothing gives me more pleasure than seeing a colour that was inspired by the grand hall of a historic house being used in a space-restricted bathroom of a contemporary high-rise. Some of our favourite combinations are included at the end of this book (see page 254).

As well as presenting case studies of particular homes, I wanted to look at how people from all over the world treat specific rooms.

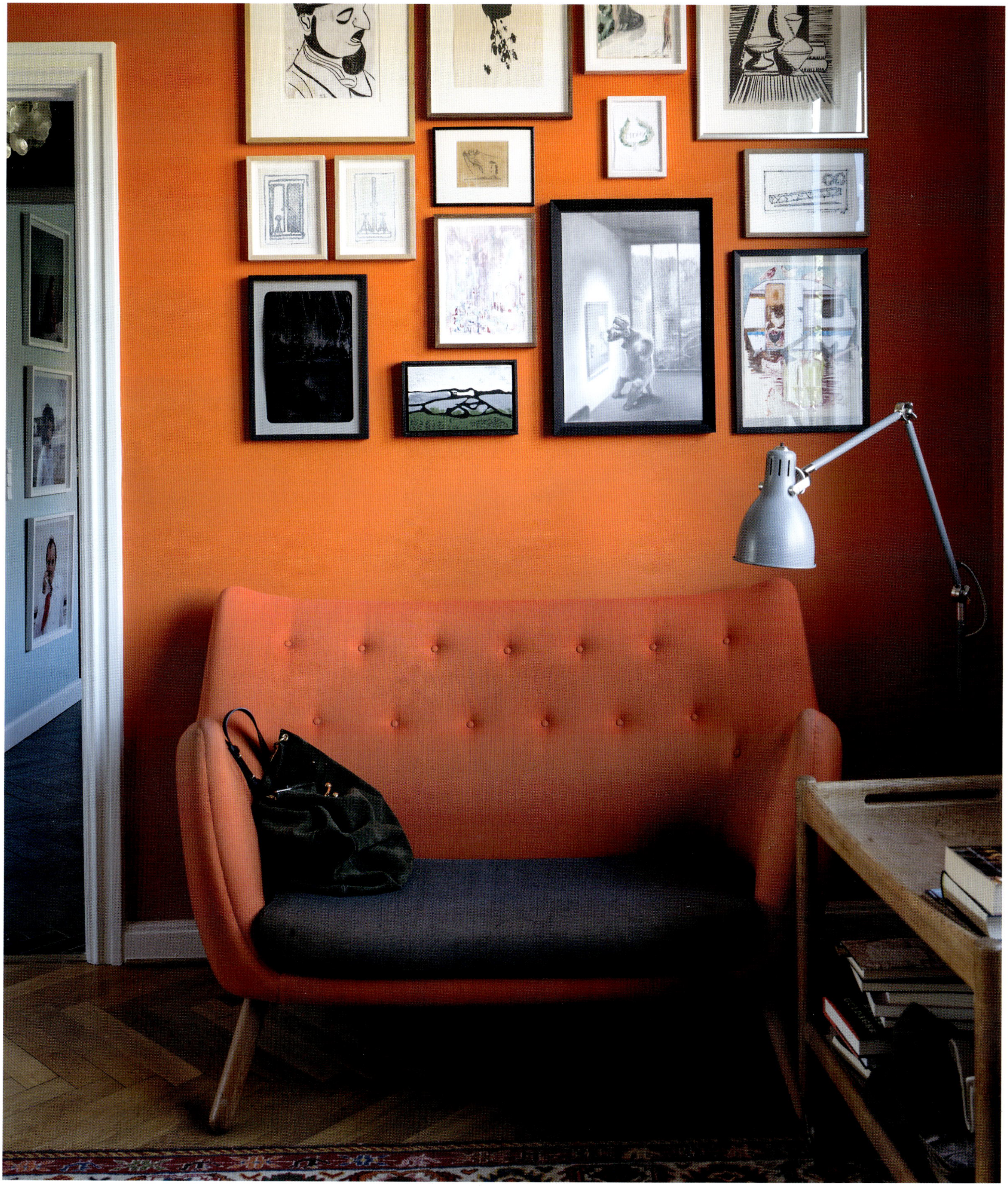

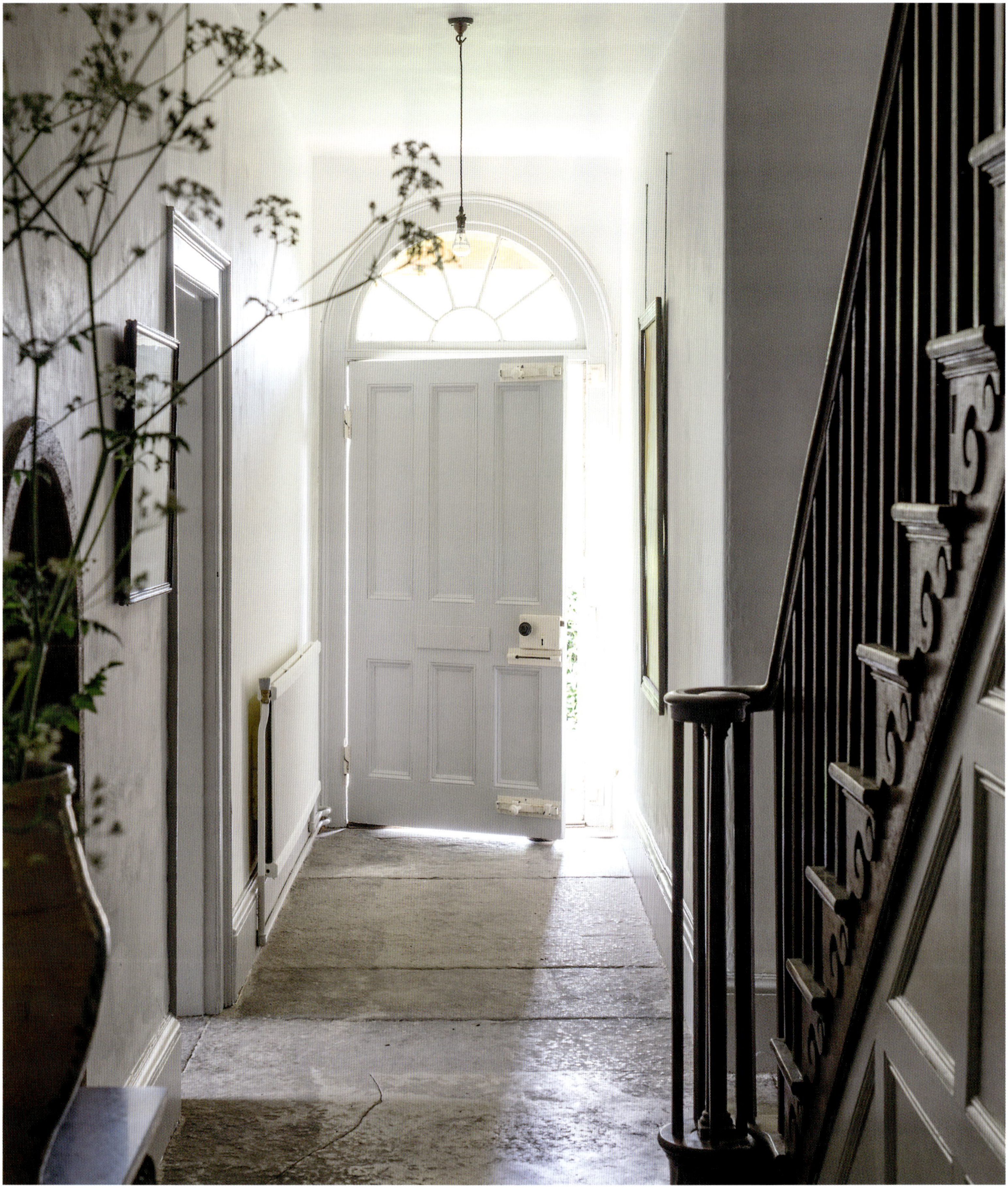

PAGES 6/7
Both walls and woodwork in this Manhattan town house are painted in Manor House Gray, creating a dramatic room that still retains a sense of calm.

PAGE 9
Charlotte's Locks brings this eclectic art grouping to life. A sofa in the same colour is an inspired choice, keeping the pictures as the main focus.

FACING PAGE
Sometimes you need only one ingredient. All White on the walls and trim acts as the perfect foil to an age-old floor and beautifully restored staircase.

BELOW
Although not a scheme for the fainthearted, Cinder Rose on the walls and Railings on the woodwork is often a favourite combination for those with bohemian tastes.

The different choices that people make in their decorating never cease to amaze and delight me. And thank goodness for that – the world would be a far duller place if we all liked the same things. So we have included sleek, ultra-modern rooms, farmhouse rooms, diminutive and huge rooms – all very personal in style but all decorated with love.

Our aim with this book is to provide as much useful information as possible, so in our recipes for successful decorating we have also included some classic colour combinations – the mac and cheese or the tea and cake of the colour world.

Just as there are many ways to cook an egg, from a simple egg-white omelette to opulent eggs Benedict, there are countless ways to decorate a room. Over the following pages we cover both the simple and the opulent in decorating, because the right room, like the right recipe, will nourish one's well-being.

Joa Studholme
Farrow & Ball Colour Curator

INTRODUCTION

A HAND-PICKED PALETTE

COLOUR CARD

Because we are so passionate about colour at Farrow & Ball, we would love to offer you as many as possible, but we know how overwhelming a chart of hundreds of computer-generated tones can be. Instead, we would rather give you our very carefully considered and edited colour card of just 132 hand-picked colours. These are painstakingly curated to help you shape your home and make your decorating choices easier. Loosely split into six colour families, they start with our famous neutrals and drift through our reds, yellows, greens, blues and darks. Although it would be convenient to arrange the colours so that each one works perfectly with its neighbour, this is just not possible when dealing with such subtle tones, so it is best to refer to our website (and, indeed, this book) to see perfect colour pairings. And don't forget that there are short explanations about each colour, and sometimes its name, on the back of the colour card.

ARCHIVE

When new colours are created, we have the sad task of retiring some still much-loved paint shades from the chart in order to make way for some new young blood. However, they are not rendered obsolete – far from it. Instead, they become part of our Archive range, and all of them are available in any finish.

Although not held in stock, they can be viewed and ordered in all our showrooms, or shown on site by a Farrow & Ball Colour Consultant. Some customers consider them hidden jewels, classified colours that fewer people use, which makes them doubly appealing, while others take comfort in knowing that an old friend used to decorate one's home over many decades is still readily available. To date, there are more than 100 colours in our Archive, all of which are loved as much today as they were when first created. In this book, Archive colours are marked with an (A).

NEW COLOURS

Where do new Farrow & Ball colours come from? Well, although their recipes are closely guarded secrets, they are born from a combination of factors.

First, despite our historic roots and the many shades that are perfect for more traditional homes, we like to be able to offer colours that are on trend and appeal to the contemporary home owner. We are certainly not led by fashion, but we do like to think that we lead the way when it comes to colours used in the home.

Second, it sometimes becomes apparent that there is a gap between two popular colours, or we make a darker and lighter version of an existing tone. Many of our famous neutral groups have been created in this way, as gradations of the same tone, such as those from Cromarty through to Pigeon. Occasionally colours are simply removed and tinkered with to make them more appealing to the modern market.

Finally, creating new colours is a very exciting process but it is far from an exact science. However, once you are immersed in the fabulous world of Farrow & Ball, it becomes almost instinctive. It is an innate sense that tells us what feels right and sits seamlessly in our palette. We like to think that we are in the great position to build on the original and the best.

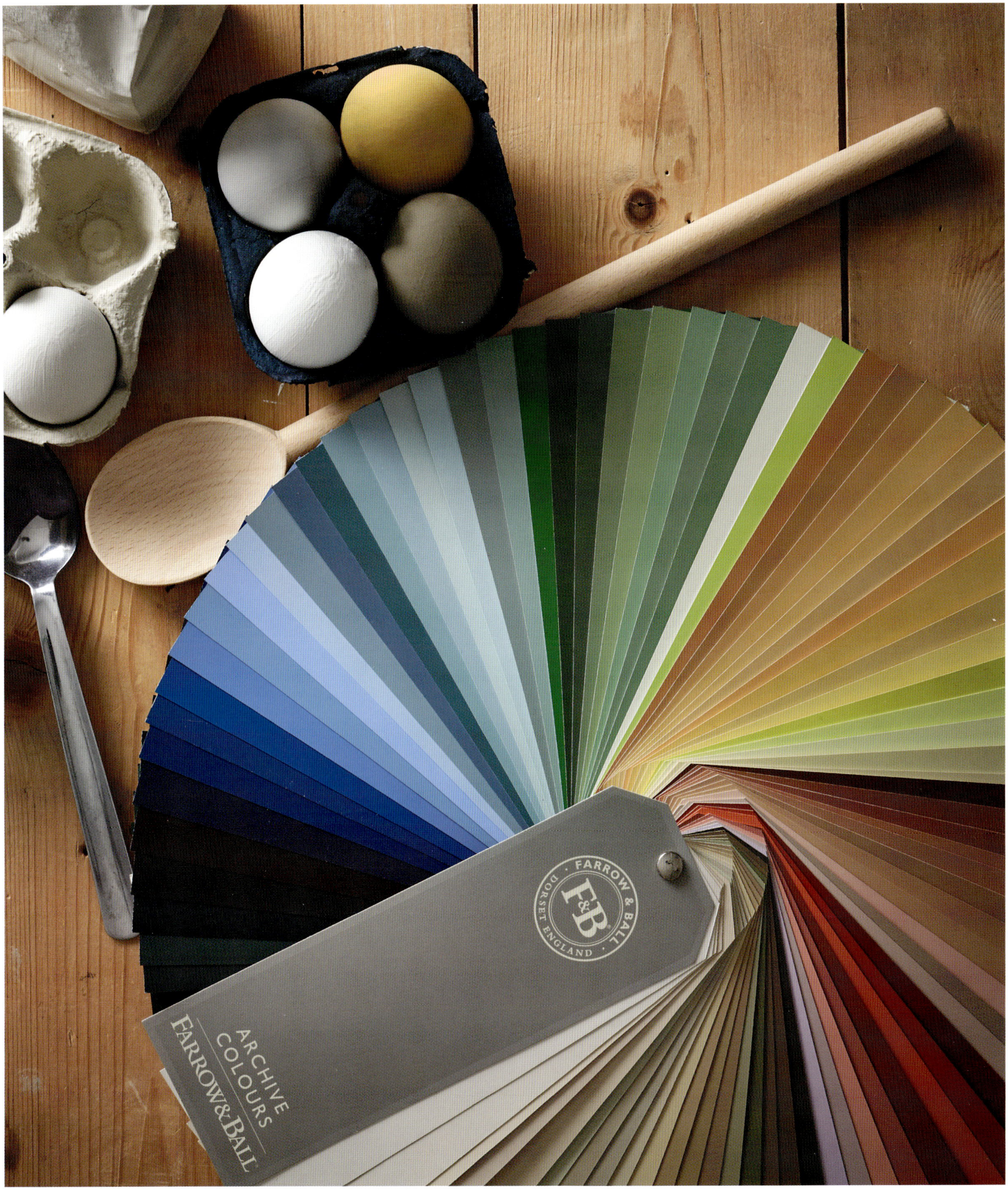
FARROW & BALL
F&B
DORSET ENGLAND
ARCHIVE
COLOURS
FARROW&BALL

THREE DIFFERENT RECIPES

Food ingredients can be served up in different ways. Potatoes, for example, can be mashed, boiled or made into skinny fries, but these dishes are all still made from the same ingredient. Similarly, a room can be painted in three different ways using the same colours. The woodwork can be picked out in white or it can be painted darker than the walls, or just one colour can be used on both walls and trim. The main ingredient, the wall colour, remains the same, as with the humble potato, but the look of the room, like the cooked potato, will be totally different.

DARKER WALLS WITH WHITE WOODWORK
- Creates a fresh and uncomplicated look.
- Can be used throughout the home to unify all the rooms.
- The crisp contrast between the elements defines the shape of a room.
- Choosing a white that is sympathetic to the colour of the walls, rather than a stark white, creates a bigger, calmer space.
- The classic choice for traditional rooms, where there is a presumption that the woodwork should be painted lighter than the walls.

RIGHT
Classic Elephant's Breath has been used on the walls of this hall, with complementary Strong White on the woodwork and delicate plasterwork, to make sure that all elements sit seamlessly together.

FACING PAGE, LEFT
The windows are a huge feature here, so their frames (along with the skirting) have been painted in bold Railings, which complements the Peignoir walls.

FACING PAGE, RIGHT
Inky Stiffkey Blue is an inspired choice for this well-used and much-loved room at the heart of this home. Using the same colour on both the walls and trim creates a calm backdrop for a busy family life.

TRIM DARKER THAN WALLS

- A stronger colour on the woodwork than on the walls makes a room feel lighter.
- Delivers a decorative twist without overwhelming the space.
- A slightly darker tone-on-tone woodwork gives an interior a feeling of calm.
- Very strong woodwork draws the eye to architectural elements that you may want to highlight.
- Works in any style of room, in the same way that woodwork does when left in its natural, unpainted state.

SAME COLOUR ON WALLS AND WOODWORK

- It is difficult to read the confines of a room when everything is one colour, which makes it seem bigger.
- Rooms feel tranquil and elegant.
- Using one colour covers up a multitude of sins, such as making an ugly trim disappear.
- A bridge between the interior and exterior can be established when you don't have to register a second colour on the trim.
- Particularly suited to contemporary rooms because it is more conducive to minimalist living.

STYLE, FLOW AND LIGHT

When preparing a menu for a grand feast, you would obviously consider how all three courses work together. Maybe the starter should be fresh and light, the main course rich and exotic, with a palate cleanser to follow. Whatever your taste, the courses should come together to create a balanced meal. Planning your decorating menu should be done in the same way, by thinking about how the different rooms sit together. If you have the luxury of redecorating your entire home, embrace the three elements of style, flow and light to help you to create your own nourishing thread of colour.

STYLE

Decide if you want an unchallenging environment, where you can drift seamlessly from room to room, or a riotous kaleidoscope of colour – or maybe something between the two.

It is impossible not to be influenced to some degree by fashion, but you don't have to be a slave to colour fads. Don't be afraid of your instincts when it comes to selecting colour. Make choices that reflect your personality. You are in charge in your own home, and while it's not so easy to control what's going on in the world, you can create a home where you feel comfortable and secure.

RIGHT
Nothing gives me more pleasure than to see a room that has had so much love and imagination invested in it. Aranami wallpaper, with the pattern in uplifting St Giles Blue, has been paired with Yellowcake (A), to create a scheme that might not be to everyone's taste but can't help but make you smile.

FACING PAGE, LEFT
The flow from clubby Studio Green in the sitting room to lighter Calke Green in the kitchen makes each room feel inviting. The spaces are unified by an All White trim.

FACING PAGE, RIGHT
The simplicity of soft Wimborne White, which is only a shade away from a pure white, is perfect in a light-filled space such as this.

FLOW

Start by choosing a colour for the hall, as this is the most important space for establishing a sense of flow. This colour can unify the house because it is visible from the greatest number of rooms.

Consider how you usually move around your home. Most people naturally gravitate to their kitchens, so if you make this the lightest space, you will be drawn to it like a moth to a flame.

If you feel more comfortable with a neutral scheme, then different tones can shift your focus and create a visual destination. Start with the darkest tone and progress to the lightest in order to create a sense of flow. If you prefer a more compelling colour story, think about the colours floor by floor so that adjacent rooms will complement each other and feel harmonious.

LIGHT

It is always wise to consider the direction your room faces because our highly pigmented paints change in different light conditions, which is what makes them so special. It is best to work out when you spend most of your time in a room.

Spaces that you want to relax in at the end of the day are often more alluring when painted in a deeper tone that won't be affected by a lack of light. Rooms that you work in and spend most of your time in during the day are best kept lighter and brighter, making the colour selection more dependent on the character of the natural light. And don't forget that while paint colour can be considered a work of art in itself, the colours of your pictures should also be considered when planning your decorating menu.

TASTER MENU

Sampling paint feels like a chore to many people, but it can actually be a lot of fun. Think of it as a tasting menu. With the Farrow & Ball range, you have the opportunity to try 132 morsels of delicious colour. Each one has its own individual flavour, and you need to take your time discovering those you like best. Sampling also allows for mistakes and experiments as well as for shifts in mood.

Unfortunately, you cannot appreciate the true essence of these colours unless you test them in your own home. Each one reveals its own peculiarities depending on the light conditions and the size of the space you intend to decorate.

Although it is tempting to get a sample pot, open the lid and simply look at the paint inside, the colour will change significantly when it is dry on the wall. You could also paint a piece of paper and leave it on a table to occasionally glance down at, but it is impossible to appreciate the nuances of a colour unless you see it vertically on the wall in the room for which it is intended. And although it may be fun to pick up a paintbrush and start testing a colour directly on a wall, this, too, will give a false impression because you will inevitably compare it to what is there already.

It really is worthwhile sampling colours properly. Paint up two large samples on the back of some old wallpaper or card and put them on the wall in two different parts of the room. Then look at them throughout the day, as well as in the evening when there is no longer any natural light. You will discover how different the colours look at different times. This is their magic, when you see them come alive, but you will never be blessed with this knowledge unless you make a little effort.

ABOVE AND FACING PAGE
While we do not recommend painting straight onto a wall when sampling colours, sometimes we find it just impossible to resist. This is especially true when contemplating a tone for a room such as this idiosyncratic hall in a spectacular Glasgow villa (facing page), which had fallen into disrepair over many years of neglect. Here, the rich mix of natural stone and wood is the starting point for the entire decoration. For other rooms, it may be a mix of furniture, art or personal mementoes that determines the choice of colour (above).

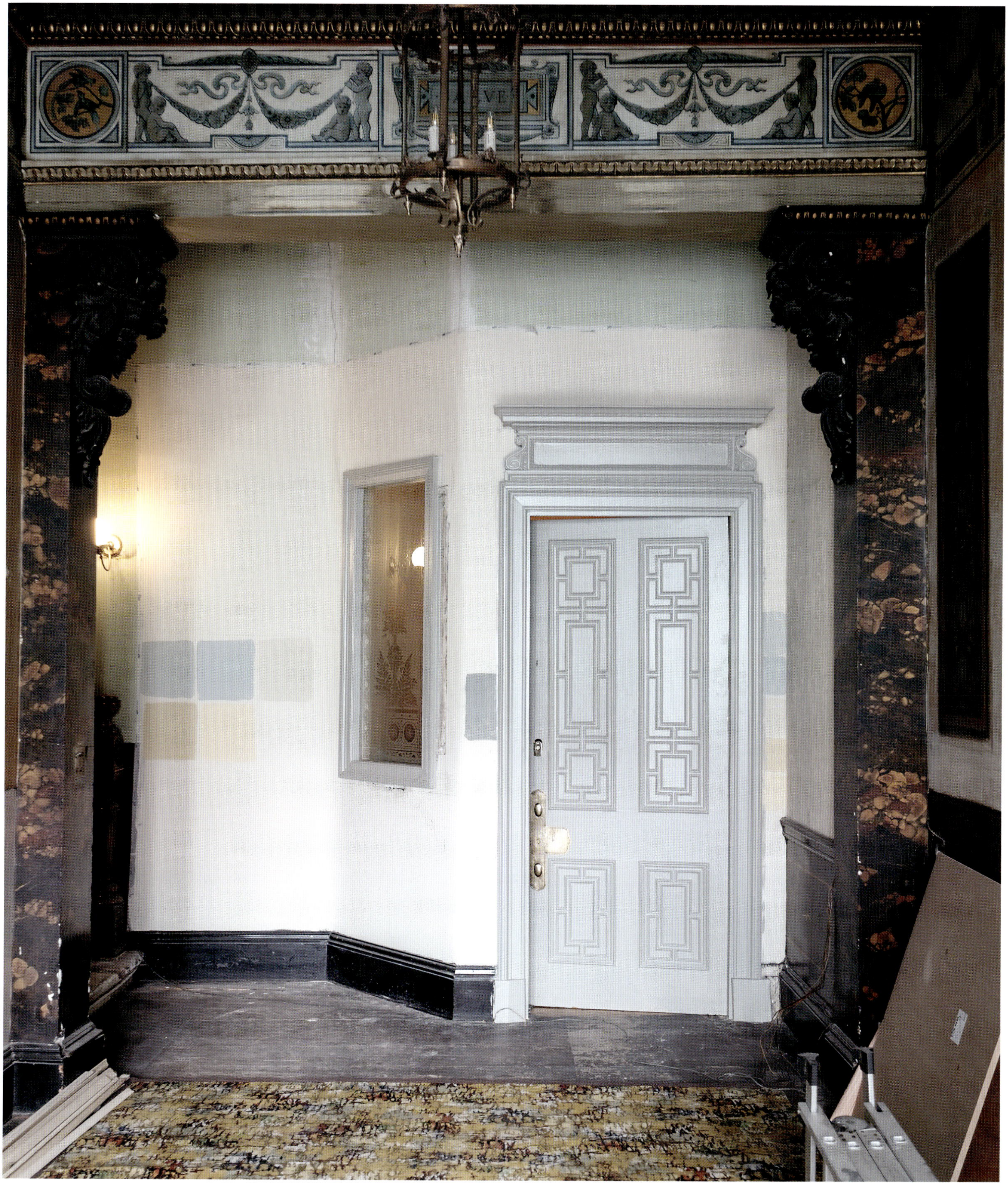

THE NAMING OF NAMES

Farrow & Ball is renowned for its quirky colour names. Here is an insight into the naming of some of our latest colours – and an old favourite.

SULKING ROOM PINK

This colour was inspired by the shade used for traditional boudoirs. Although we have named many colours after rooms (Eating Room Red, Oval Room Blue, Print Room Yellow (A)...), Boudoir Pink just didn't sound like a Farrow & Ball name. So we spent time considering the boudoir and how it got its name, only to discover it comes from the French *bouder*, meaning "to sulk", hence Sulking Room Pink. As with all our "room-named" colours, it can also be used in other rooms.

TRERON

Pigeon is one of Farrow & Ball's most enduring colours, being the darkest accent in a very well-established group that includes Blue Gray. In the same way, this much-requested new dark green-based colour works perfectly as a stronger tone with French Gray in the same group. So it seemed appropriate, if a little esoteric, to name it after a species of green pigeon: Treron. There is a great Farrow & Ball tradition of linking colours that work together by name – String and Cord, Vert de Terre and Lichen, Shaded White and Shadow White – but perhaps you need to be a real connoisseur of the Farrow & Ball colour chart to recognize them.

RANGWALI

The inspiration for Farrow & Ball colours comes from many sources, often nature or historic houses, but occasionally from somewhere or something altogether different. The Hindu ceremony of Holi, or Rangwali Holi, also known as the Festival of Colours, is a kaleidoscopic event when vibrant-coloured powders are thrown across all and sundry with gay abandon. To suit the particularly exotic nature of our new pink, and be true to its inspiration, we named it Rangwali.

DE NIMES

This is one of our favourite new colours. Inspired by the colour of workwear, this down-to-earth indigo feels a little more utilitarian than our other strong blues. Once the domain of the worker, denim is now loved by hipsters all over the world. It was first woven in the French town of Nîmes, so our name is simply derived from *serge de Nîmes* ("serge from Nîmes").

PREFERENCE RED

We are very proud of our historic roots at Farrow & Ball. Back in 1946, Richard Ball and John Farrow started a paint factory in Wimborne, Dorset, where we still are to this day. The company was called Farrow & Ball but the paint range was known as Preference Paints, and we have a much-treasured paint chart from that time in our library. In honour of that original name, and the fact that we feel it is the preferred red of the moment, we have named this colour Preference Red.

PAEAN BLACK

There is a cherished and evocative Archive colour called Bible Black, which brings to mind old bibles bound in a very particular tone of leather. Paean Black is a Georgian-inspired bohemian dark, another chic black, packed with red. Like Bible Black, it conjures up the colour of old leather tomes, and we named it after the songs of praise so often included in hymnals.

ELEPHANT'S BREATH

No, we'll never tell!

TRIED-AND-TESTED TIPS

I thought it might be fun to share my favourite decorating tips – tricks that I have used in my own home and, most importantly, that have made me smile. My original intention was to decide on one technique and discuss it in depth, but this proved simply impossible. There are so many inspiring and innovative ways of using paint and wallpaper – and they all make me clap my hands with glee – that I couldn't possibly restrict myself to just one. After all, what could be more exciting than introducing rich colour and pattern to the most unexpected places?

MY CURRENT FAVOURITE TRICKS

- Make doors and windows look bigger by extending the paint colour onto the walls and ceiling around the frame. Extra decoration can be added in the form of a thin coloured line.
- Paint window surrounds in a contrasting colour to the window frame and walls, to create depth.
- Paint the bottom half of walls in Full Gloss, for a very durable surface, and the top half in Estate Emulsion, using the same colour to create a magical decorative effect.
- Never leave the interior of a cupboard undecorated. Strong colour or bold wallpaper will always make you smile when you open the door. Wallpapers with metallic patterns look particularly sensational in drinks cupboards.
- Use paint in a Full Gloss finish for a ceiling. This will bounce light around the room during the day and be glamorous at night, especially when lit by candles.
- Let your imagination run wild when it comes to painting floors. You can emulate a patchwork of geometric tiles, create a rug effect or just paint simple borders to frame a room.
- Painting a bedhead shape directly onto a wall has long been a favourite trick – easy, economical and stylish.
- Paint the spindles of a staircase in a dark tone, to give a really chic twist to the look of your home – so, so popular at the moment but for very good reason.

FACING PAGE, TOP LEFT
A neutral-coloured Tessella wallpaper on the walls of this room feels poised and elegant, but the addition of the same wallpaper on the ceiling in this dynamic colourway of Vardo and Inchyra Blue totally changes the atmosphere.

FACING PAGE, TOP RIGHT
This Green Smoke door has been given added impact by the outsize frame painted around it with a contrasting line of Charlotte's Locks running through it – both of which continue up onto the ceiling for an extra decorative twist.

FACING PAGE, BOTTOM LEFT
One of our favourite tricks is to wallpaper inside cupboards and shelves. Here, the colours of the Tourbillon wallpaper — Purbeck Stone background and Stone Blue pattern — are used on the walls and trim respectively in the adjoining room.

FACING PAGE, BOTTOM RIGHT
Dark spindles on a staircase, such as these in Railings Estate Eggshell, create a striking spine running from the top to the bottom of the house. This adds a modern touch as well as introducing some strong colour without being overwhelming.

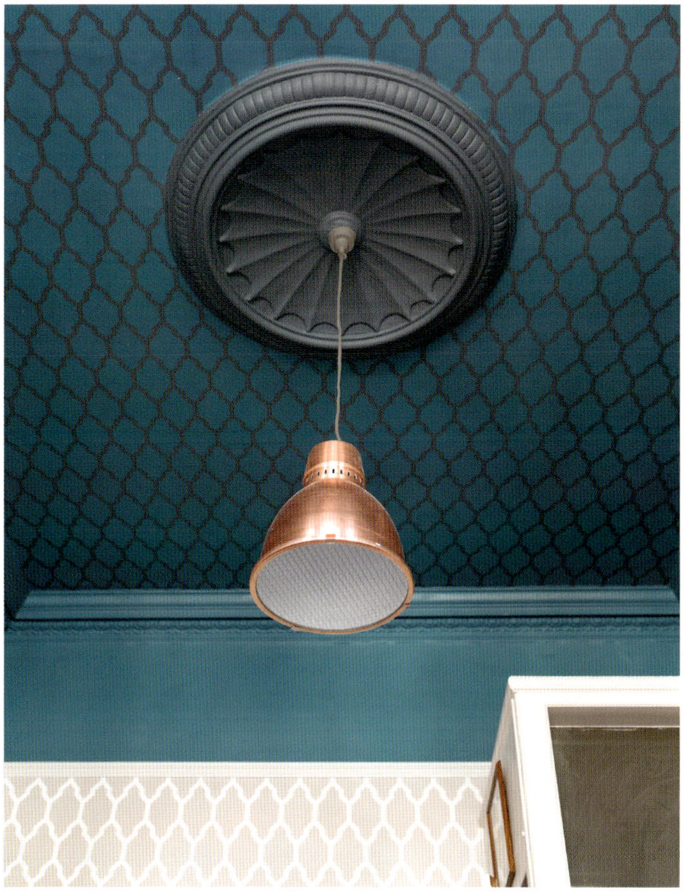
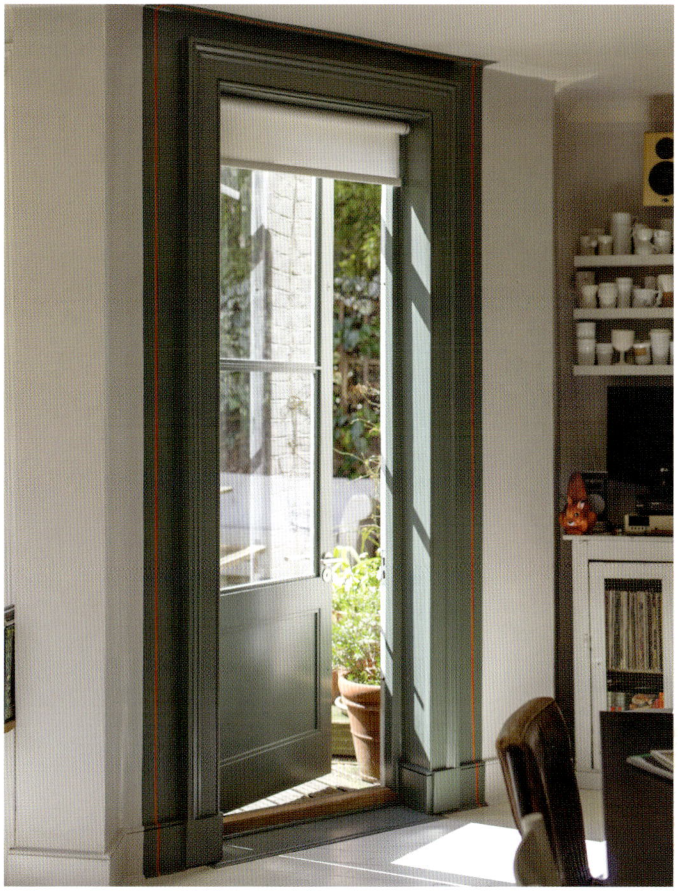
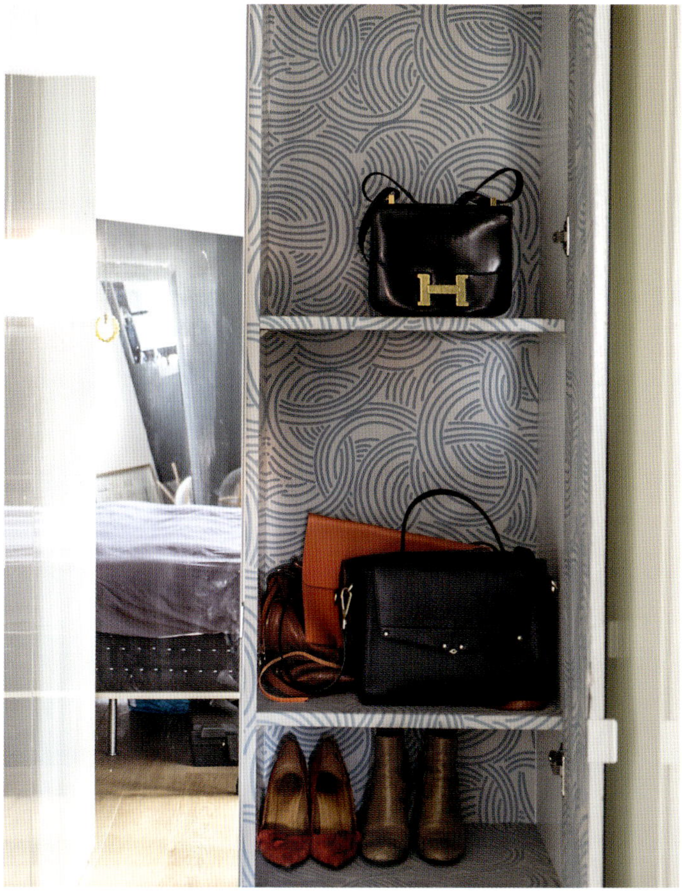
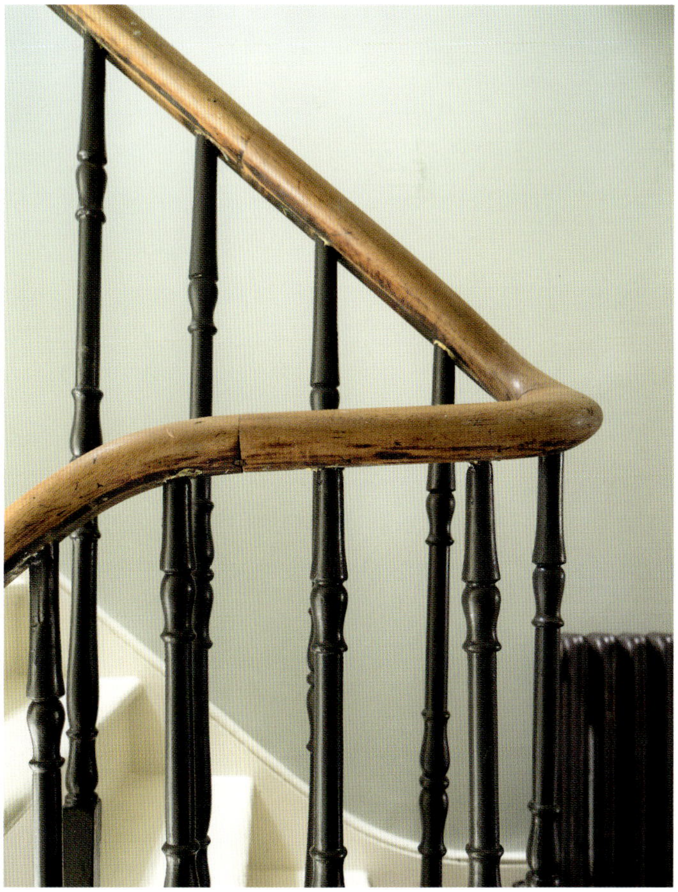

GREENWICH
CARD GAMES
COLERIDGE
IAN McEWAN
MICHAEL PALIN
DAVID SEDARIS
SCHAMA

PART ONE

—

CASE STUDIES

FACING PAGE
Surely the best way to spend
a few lazy hours in the sun
is on a settee that perfectly
matches the beguiling Octagon
Yellow (A) walls of the room.

BE YOUR OWN CONSULTANT

When our first showroom opened in 1996 I was lucky enough to be involved. It was a privilege to see how much excitement Farrow & Ball colours provoked. People could not wait to decorate their homes with intriguing Mouse's Back and curious Dead Salmon. As we discussed the peculiarities of these subtle shades with customers, it became apparent that a service to help people in their homes would be very helpful. It would give them time to appreciate particular shades on site and see the colours, which change according to the light conditions, in situ. Thus the Farrow & Ball Colour Consultancy was born.

For the next ten years, I took on this monumental task myself and had a very happy time decorating houses all over the world, but now there are in-home Colour Consultants on hand in every showroom to help you transform your home. They will suggest cohesive schemes that suit your lifestyle and a palette that complements the period of your home. It is the perfect service for anyone who is a little daunted by choice, short on time or simply hoping for the confidence to try something bolder than they would on their own. If, however, you would prefer to take this work on yourself, here are some pointers for how to approach the decoration of your home.

1.
Work out which direction each room faces: east, west, south or north, as this will affect the way a colour appears in the space. South-facing rooms will always make colours appear lighter and brighter while north-facing rooms tend to make colours look a little more green. Colours that are in rooms that face either east or west will change dramatically throughout the day.

2.
Think about how you use your home and the flow of traffic through it. In many houses there is an obvious axis that runs from the front door to the kitchen, which you should consider. Do you wish to move from the darkest area to the lightest? Is there an accent colour that you could carry throughout the house, maybe on spindles on the staircase, units in the kitchen and shelves in the living room?

3.
List your rooms floor by floor and work out which ones you would like to be light and those you can afford to make more intimate. Think about creating a harmonious view into all the rooms from the hall on each floor.

4.
Would you prefer to have a single woodwork/trim colour throughout the house or are you happy for it to change on either side of any doors in order to complement the wall colour in the room?

CASE STUDIES

5.
Do you want the hall to be as light and spacious as possible or are you yearning for something more dramatic that will make the rooms off it look lighter?

6.
If you are considering selling your house in the near future, it is often best to keep your colour schemes fairly neutral. But do include some strong colour somewhere (perhaps a downstairs cloakroom), to give the house some vitality and make it memorable.

7.
A guest room or a rarely used dining room might be an opportunity to be more adventurous with colour and pattern – you probably spend little time in such rooms and your guests will be made to feel extra special in a richly decorated space.

8.
Analyse the room. Do you want to make it look longer, squarer, higher, lower? This can all be achieved with paint colour (see Colour Solutions page 241).

9.
Do you use the room during the day or only at night? Evening rooms benefit from richer tones, while daytime spaces often suit being light and bright.

10.
Make a list of every element you need to paint or wallpaper. Remember that the colour of the trim/woodwork can be as important as that on the wall, and all these elements have to work together. Think of them as ingredients in a recipe that need to balance correctly.

11.
The Farrow & Ball Colour Fan is available to purchase in showrooms or on the website and is a great investment when choosing colours. You can remove the pages of the colours that interest you and stick them on the wall to sample them in situ (see page 18). Alternatively, you can buy little sample paint pots.

12.
When you have decided on your colours, consider the paint finishes (see page 242).

WHICH ORDER?

One of the most perplexing aspects of decorating is the order in which to choose things for a room. Some people like to start with the paint colours, but this can make life complicated when you then have to choose everything else to work with them. It is better to decide on the less flexible elements first, such as flooring, and rely on our comprehensive colour chart to find a complementary tone.

We would suggest the following order:

FACING PAGE
What could be more chic than this view from an Eating Room Red hall into an Inchyra Blue sitting room? Both of these colours have that special Farrow & Ball depth, making them sit seamlessly together, while the All White trim brings dynamism to the scheme. And how clever to link the two rooms by reprising the red on the sofa.

FLOORING
Whether your floor is old limestone, engineered wood or vintage parquet, it is essential to decide on it first so you can make sure the wall colour is complementary.

TILES
These may be anything from subtle marble to adventurous Moroccan tiles, but it is best to choose them before your paint colours to make sure that they remain the stars.

WORKTOPS
Due to long lead times, kitchen units are often the first thing one has to choose a colour for, but it is preferable to have already decided on the worktop colour to ensure there is no clash.

FABRICS
Have the luxury of choosing fabrics you adore without having to match them to pre-chosen wall colours. Gather all your fabric samples together in readiness for choosing wall coverings.

WALLS AND TRIM
Now comes the time to choose paint colours and wallpaper. Spend time with our colour cards and wallpaper patterns, and read the advice in our book *How To Decorate*. Remember to test the colours at home, as described on page 18, or have a Farrow & Ball Colour Consultant come to help you in your home.

CARPETS
It is easier to find a carpet armed with your chosen wall colours, unless you are going for a particularly spectacular carpet colour, which would require specific choices for the walls.

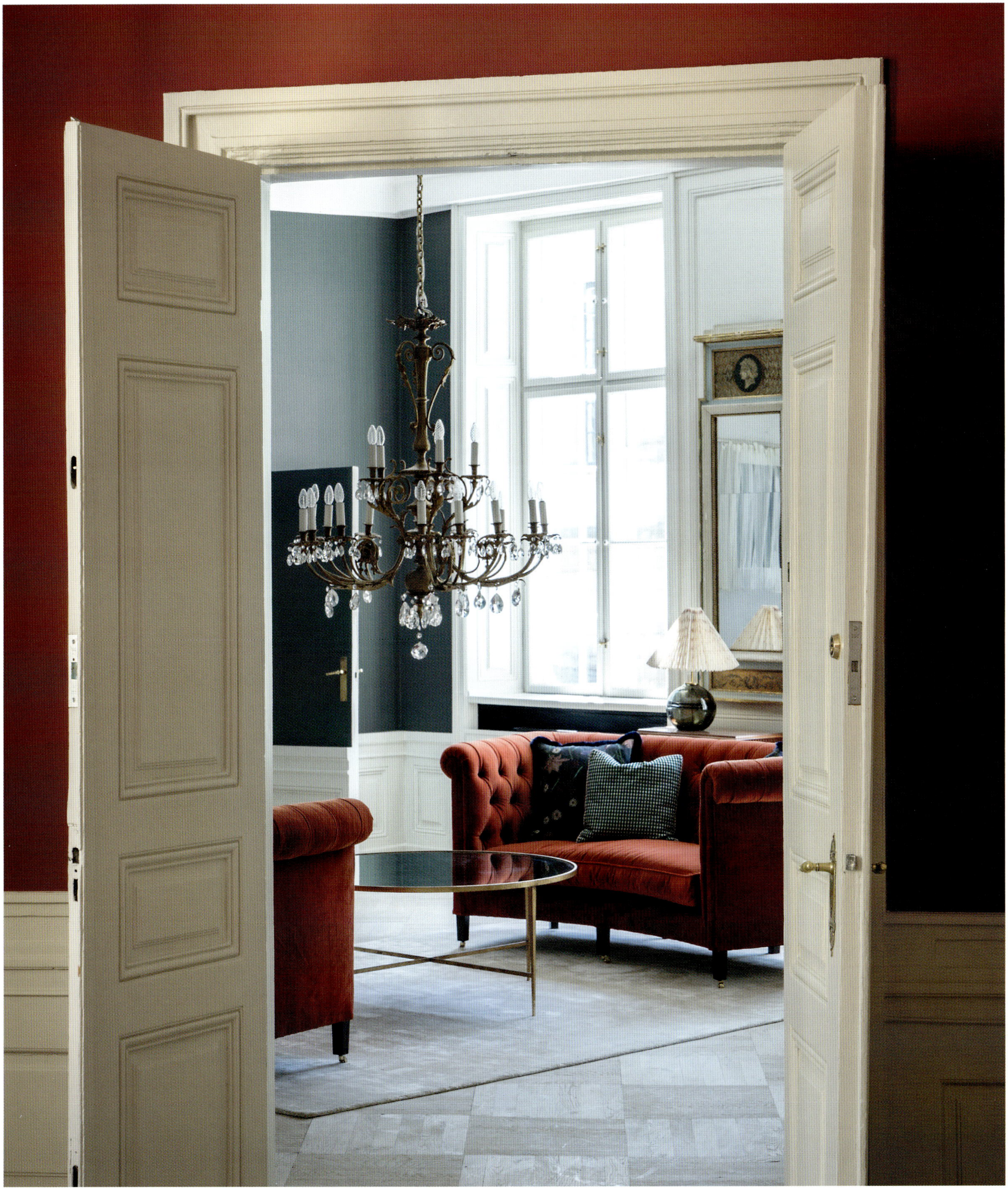

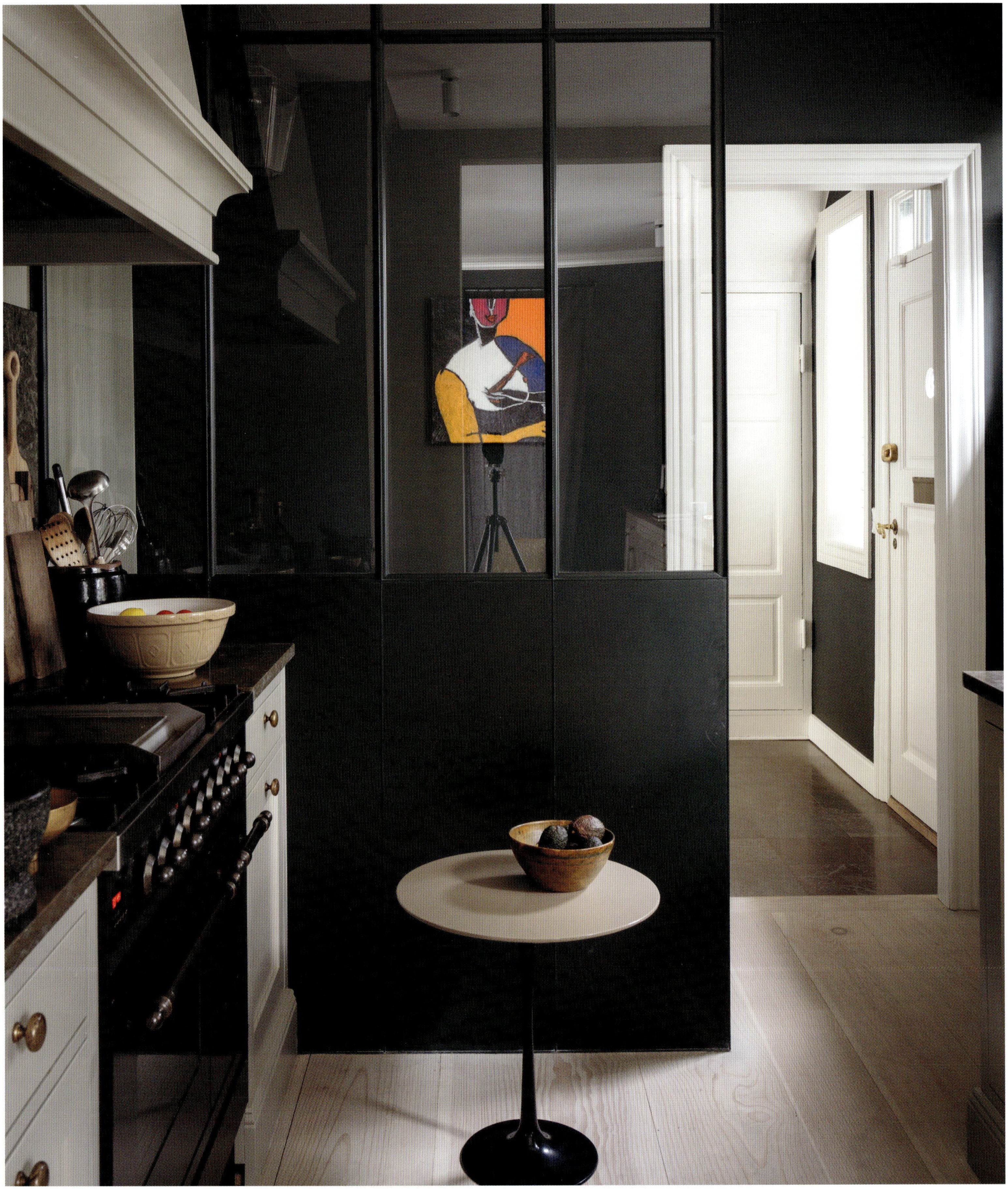

CASE STUDY 1

DANISH CONTEMPORARY

The Danish mastery of interior design is very much in evidence in the home of the owners of Tapet-Café, one of Copenhagen's top interior design houses and a long-term partner of Farrow & Ball. Everything in this house feels considered, with all the interior design decisions being of equal importance, whether that is the choice of paint colours on the walls or the fabrics and rugs, which the owners designed. They gave themselves free rein to exercise their great passion for analysing every element of their home, starting by paying respect to the original character and architecture of the building.

Built in 1922 in Hellerup, a seaside suburb to the north of Copenhagen, the house is unusual for Denmark in that the ground and first floors have similar proportions (traditionally, the first floor tapers in much more), which makes the bedrooms upstairs surprisingly light and airy. The exterior is painted white but it has been embellished with Railings on both the window frames and doors. Using Exterior Eggshell, which has a mid-sheen finish, on the windows creates a slightly more relaxed look, while Full Gloss, a traditional high-gloss finish, on the doors garners more attention and gives them a greater sense of importance.

FACING PAGE
Studio Green looks majestic in this dramatic hall and is wrapped around the glazed panelling into the kitchen, to marry the two areas together. Strong White on the woodwork enhances the urban, contemporary look. Art by Bentemarie Kjeldbæk.

INSET ABOVE
For a handsome entrance, paint the front door in Full Gloss, but leave the windows and frames a little more relaxed by using Exterior Eggshell. Railings on both elements here gives a hint of the wonderful colours to expect inside the house.

ABOVE
The colour nuances in Studio Green are more apparent when contrasted with Strong White, in which the underlying grey appears deceptively clean and crisp in contrast. This deliciously modern recipe gives a dynamic quality to the hallway.

CASE STUDY 1

Energy levels soar on entering this home. In the hall you are greeted by intense Studio Green, which travels throughout the house, creating a striking core in the middle of the building. This dark colour is made all the more dynamic by being contrasted with Strong White on the woodwork, which, despite its underlying grey, lends a crisp, clean look to the space.

The kitchen, off the hall, has a slightly quieter atmosphere. Here, the design for the units was inspired by old English kitchens, and they do seem as if they have been whisked in from another age, particularly as they are painted the same colour as the wall they sit against, creating a feel that is both seamless and timeless. Hardwick White, with its unsurpassed depth of colour, is really a traditional grey that doesn't seem very white to most, unless it is contrasted with a much darker shade. So, in the dining room area, off the kitchen, we are reintroduced to some strong colour in the form of Down Pipe, which also provides the perfect dark backdrop for some art. As well as suiting the architecture and the family living here, many of the colour choices were determined by the art.

ABOVE LEFT
Lead-grey Down Pipe appears softer when contrasted with the intensity of Studio Green. It is used here to define the dining area and some carefully curated art by Tal R. The chalky hue of Hardwick White on the kitchen units sits as well in a contemporary room as it does in a historic house. This is a fine example of three carefully balanced colours used to great effect in a small space.

ABOVE
You could be forgiven for thinking that you have been transported from 21st-century Copenhagen to below-stairs 19th-century England. The design of the units is key to this look, but painting them the same colour as the walls (Hardwick White) makes the traditional design look right on trend.

FACING PAGE
One of the joys of Studio Green is how it responds to different light conditions. In a room flooded with light, it is obviously green, but in a darker space, such as this, it becomes very intense, creating a velvety surface close to black.

CASE STUDIES

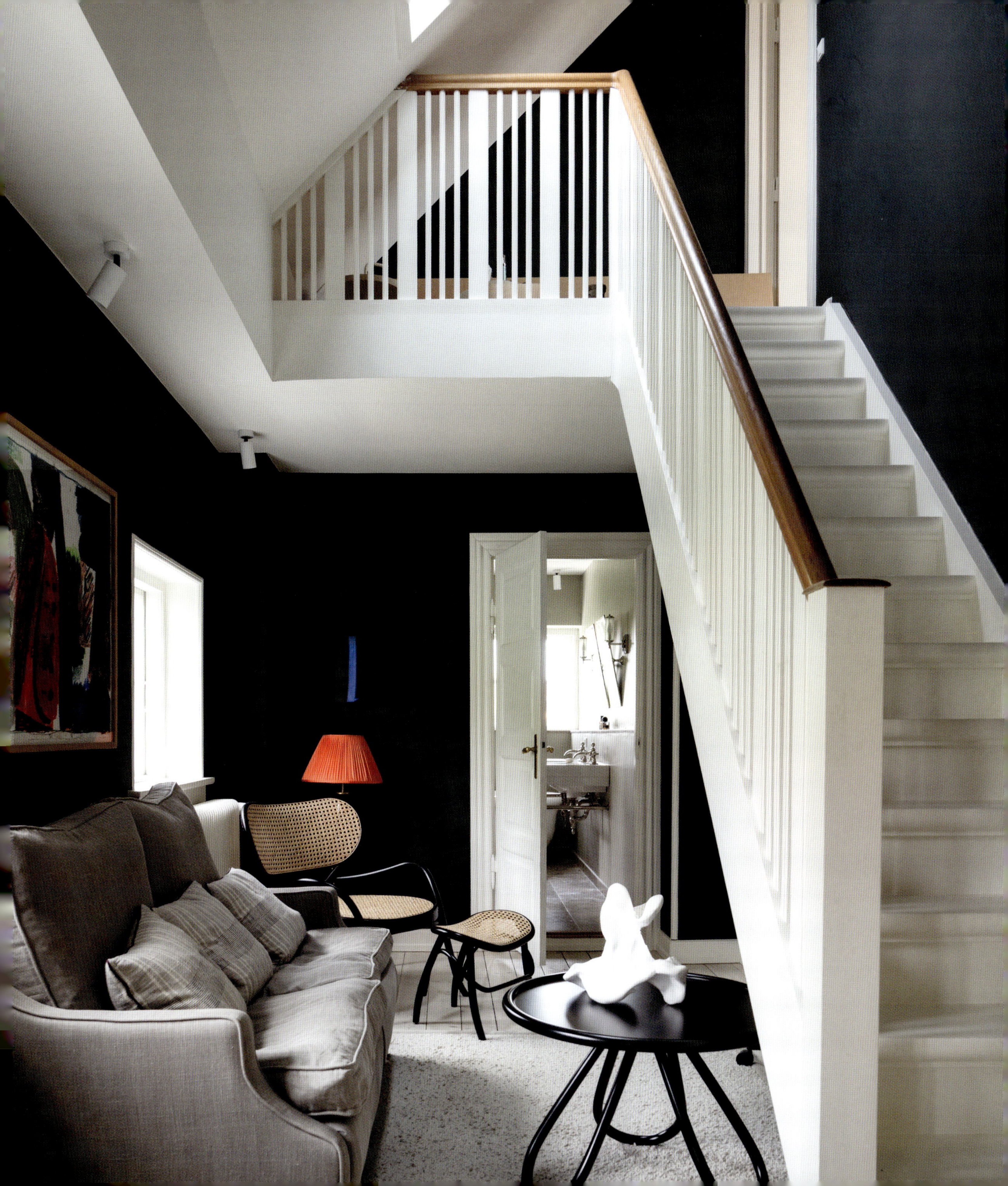

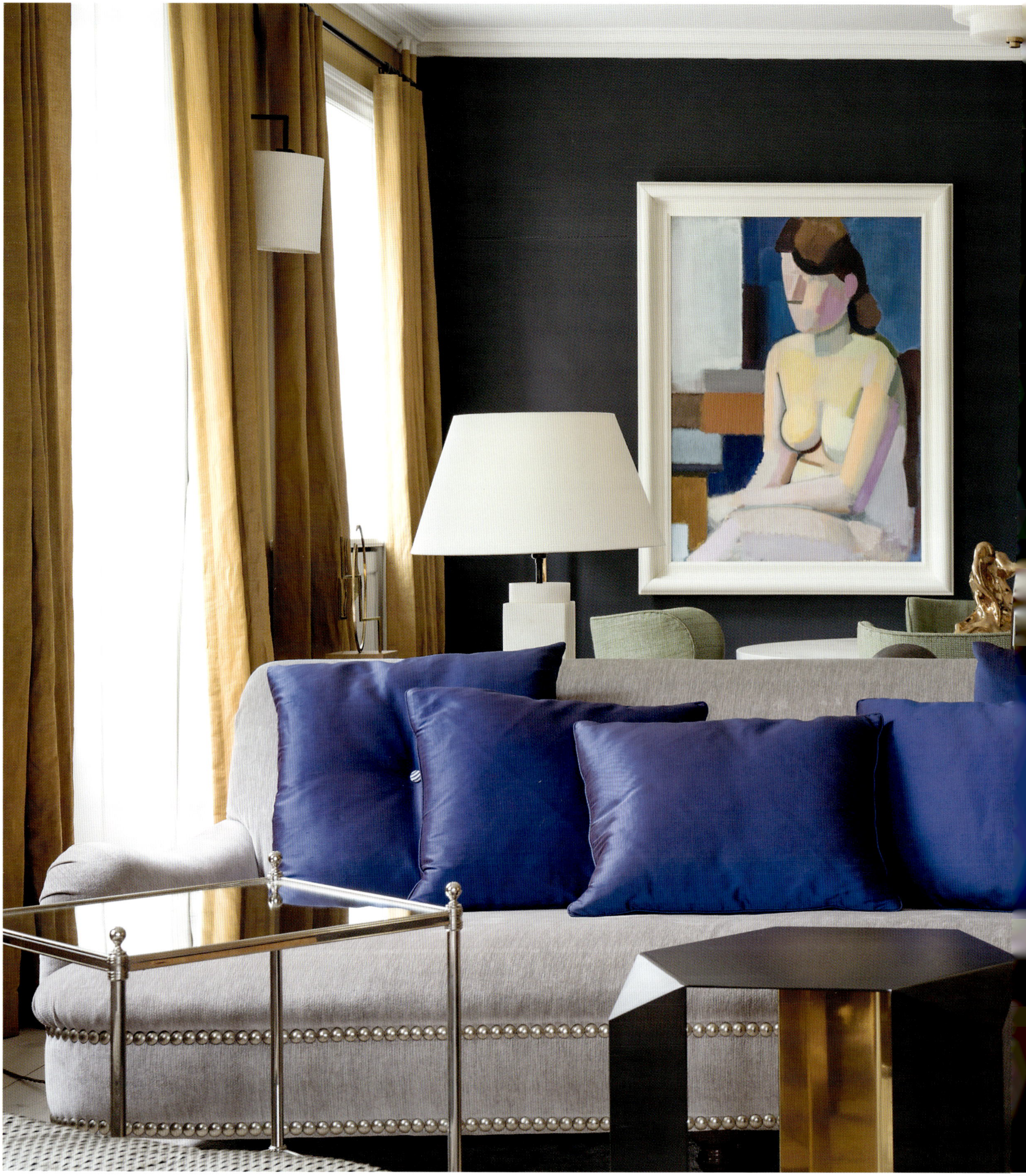

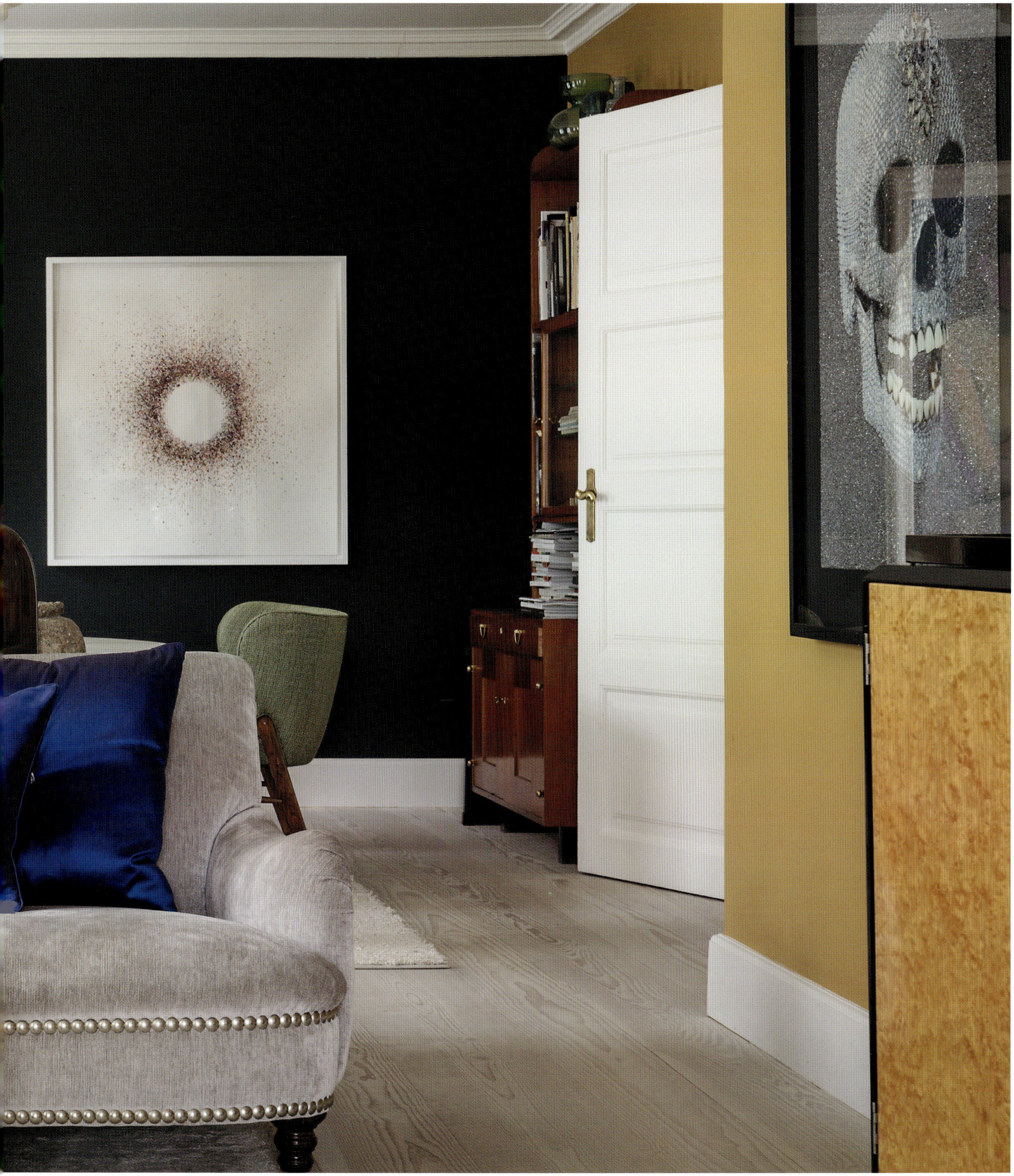

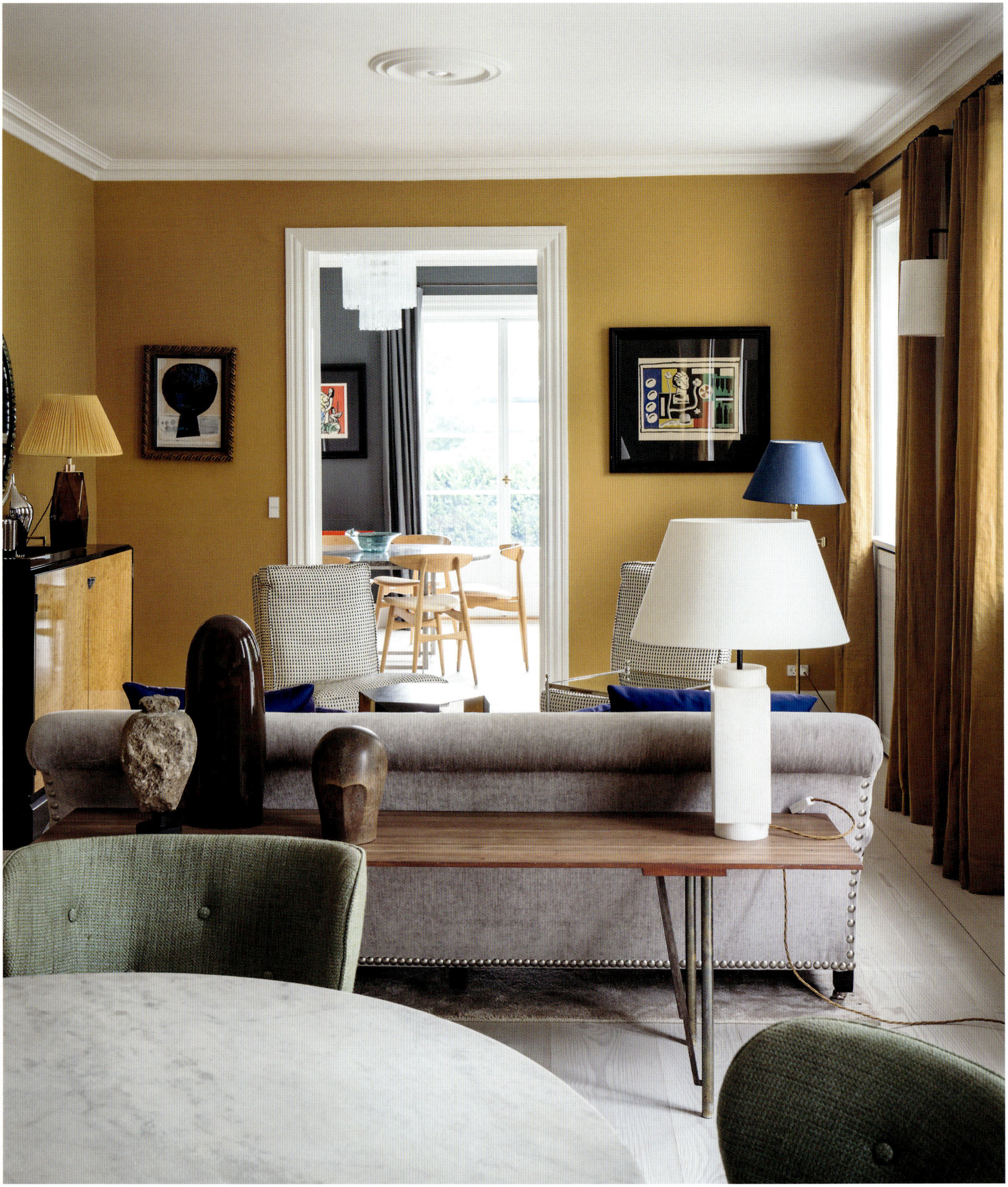

CASE STUDY 1

PAGES 34–5 AND FACING PAGE
The combination of Railings and mustardy India Yellow is a rich dish. Here, they work in harmony to create a glamorous sitting room. Colour drastically adjusts our sense of space, and the darker Railings wall creates a dramatic and enveloping area in which to sit and eat (see pages 34–5) and helps steal some of the focus away from the windows. Deep India Yellow on the other walls heightens the moody intensity. At the other end of the room (see facing page), a glimpse of leaden Down Pipe in the dining room reflects the Railings feature wall, lending familiarity and creating visual symmetry. Art on pages 34–6 by Vilhem Lundstrøm, Jeppe Hein, Damien Hirst and Fernand Léger.

RIGHT
In the children's bedroom, tucked into the eaves of the second floor, subtle and modest Cromarty feels like the perfect antidote to the plethora of powerful colour in the rest of the house. Its purity and simplicity make it the perfect choice for promoting calm and sleep, especially when the colour is taken over the ceiling. The beams in Wimborne White add to the charm.

Moving through from the open-plan kitchen/dining room, there is more than a touch of glamour in the adjacent sitting room but it is without ostentation, and nothing is without interest. Inspiration for the palette for this room came from Copenhagen's Thorvaldsen Museum. The moody intensity of India Yellow creates a sumptuous effect. Railings on the far wall (see pages 34–5) creates both depth and balance by reflecting back the stronger tone of Down Pipe in the dining room beyond (see facing page). The sitting room is about visual unity, something that can often be upset with the use of a different colour on just one wall, but here it is executed to perfection because Railings, India Yellow and Down Pipe all have the same intensity and so sit together harmoniously.

The brave colour choices reflect the exuberant personalities of the owners. Their enthusiasm for dressing their home in textiles as well as art is at its greatest in the sitting room. The fabric for the curtains was specially woven in Lake Como, Italy. With fantastic attention to detail, the curtains are just half a tone darker than the walls to allow for the light that may filter through them. When fabrics and walls are so close in colour, it means that no focus is stolen from the windows and the eye is drawn to the garden beyond.

The colour journey through the ground floor of this house is certainly exciting, but continuity is established by the use of Strong White on all the trim and ceilings. On reaching the first floor, this changes to the slightly softer and less grey Wimborne White, which was felt to be a better match for the timeless wallpapers designed by the owners and used in all the bedrooms. Only a shade away from a pure white but with the addition of the smallest amount of warm yellow pigment, Wimborne White is an incredibly versatile shade and it sits perfectly alongside Cromarty in the children's bedroom on the top floor. Cromarty, which is neither too blue nor too grey, is an inspired choice here, creating a muted softness that sits seamlessly against the big sky. It is also suitably neutral alongside the charming rug, also designed by the owners. However, its atmospheric tone brings just enough personality when used in rooms set in the eaves.

This house is very much a platform for its inhabitants, and their interior choices express the intermingling of different personalities. Two very talented designers, who are leading the way in embracing colour, have created a life-enhancing home for their family, and one that is full of soul.

CASE STUDY 1

DANISH CONTEMPORARY PALETTE

RECIPE TIPS

* When using several strong colours, look at them as a group to make sure that they sit together seamlessly, as Railings, Studio Green and India Yellow do here.
* Make strong tones look crisp by establishing a "white" that can be used throughout. In this home Strong White was chosen.
* A feature wall could change the proportions of a room if its colour is a lot stronger than the other walls.
* Colours used on both walls and ceilings in rooms in the eaves should be atmospheric but not overpowering. Cromarty contains the perfect amount of colour to achieve this.

HALL

STUDIO GREEN
walls

STRONG WHITE
trim/ceiling

DINING ROOM

DOWN PIPE
walls

STRONG WHITE
trim/ceiling

SITTING ROOM

INDIA YELLOW
walls

RAILINGS
feature wall

STRONG WHITE
trim/ceiling

KITCHEN

HARDWICK WHITE
walls/units

STRONG WHITE
trim/ceiling

CHILDREN'S BEDROOM

CROMARTY
walls/ceiling

WIMBORNE WHITE
trim

CASE STUDIES

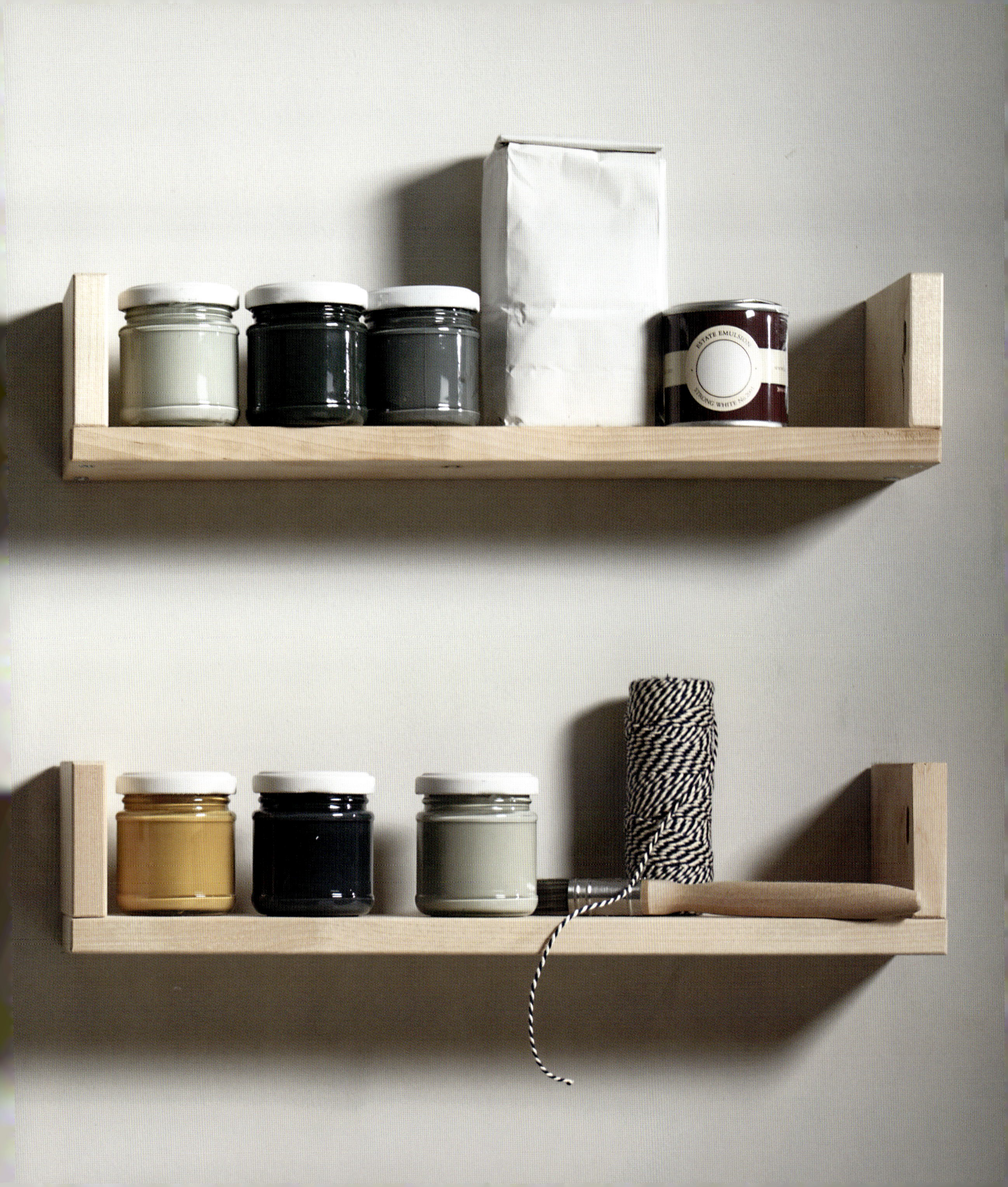
ESTATE EMULSION
STRONG WHITE

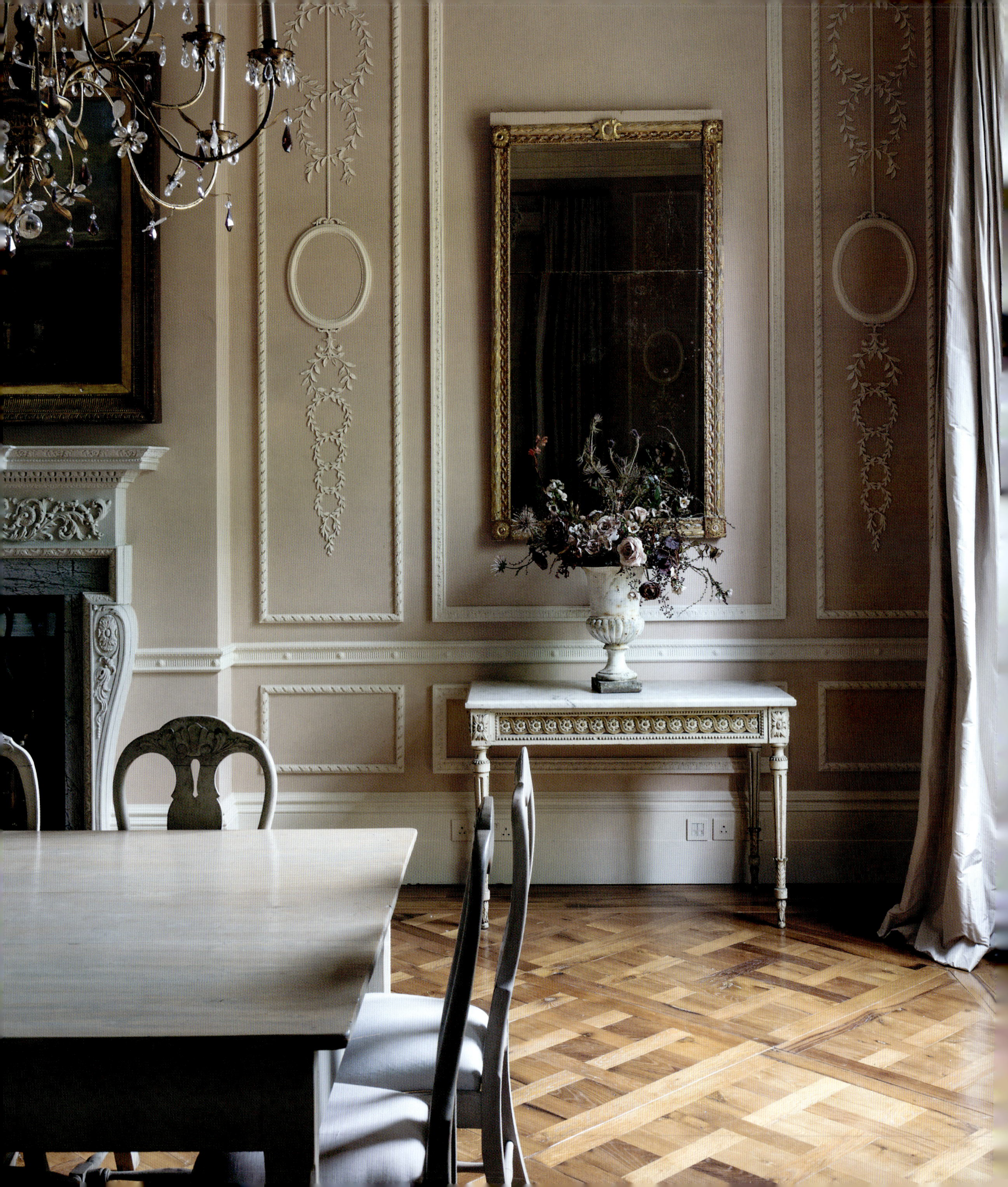

CASE STUDY 2

UNDERSTATED GRANDEUR

Occasionally there is a rare and treasured opportunity to decorate an entire house in one go, rather than piecemeal over a period of time. This can be slightly overwhelming in an average home – and this property, with its 66 rooms, is by no means average. Templeton House is a Grade II Georgian country mansion that just happens to be in London.

My task was to find colours that flattered the proportions of the building, giving more than a nod to its historic roots, while creating a home that was comfortable for a modern family and that reflected the owners' style and personality: a taste for opulence and comfort, as well as balance and restraint.

Elephant's Breath and Strong White, colours often associated with contemporary houses, might be considered an odd choice for a classical building such as this, but they are totally at home in the many halls and corridors, creating a calm, neutral thread that runs throughout the house. Here, you travel through the Elephant's Breath front entrance hall to the slightly lighter Skimming Stone back entrance hall, which creates the impression that the house opens out and becomes brighter. This effect is enhanced by using the more deeply coloured, but sympathetic, Dead Salmon in the entrance reception that adjoins the front hall. Although a subtle

FACING PAGE
Choosing colours for this dining room was a little daunting because it is just as likely to be used in the day, when it is flooded with natural light, as it is at night, when candles and chandeliers are the primary light source. The owners favoured a pink palette and, after much sampling, we fell upon Potted Shrimp (A), which works in both light conditions. We resisted picking out the plasterwork in bright white and used red-based Dimity, for softness against the wall colour.

INSET ABOVE
You could not get a higher gloss finish than that of the bespoke colour on the front door to Templeton House — the result of true craftsmanship.

ABOVE
Dead Salmon is teamed with Oxford Stone and Joa's White in the entrance reception. These colours, each with a red base, sit seamlessly together and provide a link to the warm Contemporary Neutrals group of colours used in the main hall beyond.

CASE STUDY 2

BELOW
In the exuberant games room, created not only for games but also for general merrymaking, every surface, except for the Dove Tale ceiling and Elephant's Breath windows, is painted in Full Gloss Radicchio.

BELOW RIGHT
Surprisingly contemporary colours were selected for the classical Georgian hallways. The warm tones of Elephant's Breath sit perfectly with the rich parquet floors, and its colour changes delightfully as the light does during the course of the day. Strong White on the trim retains the traditional feel appropriate to such a grand setting.

FACING PAGE
Ornate decoration requires subtle colours. In the Churchill room, Old White, the darkest of the historic Traditional Neutrals, is used on the walls, with Lime White on the plasterwork and Off-White on the trim.

shade, Dead Salmon creates a serene but rich environment that is truly welcoming, especially when teamed with Red Based Neutrals on the ceiling and trim.

The main drawing room, known as the Churchill room, is a dignified space. The Traditional Neutrals used here feel suitably restrained, while reflecting the green tones of the imposing gardens and lake, glimpsed through the vast windows.

In contrast to the Churchill room is the deliberately pretty Lady Templeton Parlour, the smallest and most elegant of the reception rooms. It has been decorated accordingly in the soft green-blues and pinks so often associated with calmness and serenity. The unusual combination of Pale Powder and Joa's White on the walls and cornice respectively has been used alongside Green Blue, which has transformed the magnificent plasterwork.

The visual unity of these important rooms in the centre of the house is matched in a somewhat different way when it comes to the more everyday rooms. Alchemy is at work once again but this time using more saturated colour to sumptuous effect.

The decoration of the games room on the lower ground floor is deliberately provocative. Bright, contemporary Radicchio, a colour that is cleverly tempered with magenta, confidently fills this room with energy without having the brashness of a true, clean red.

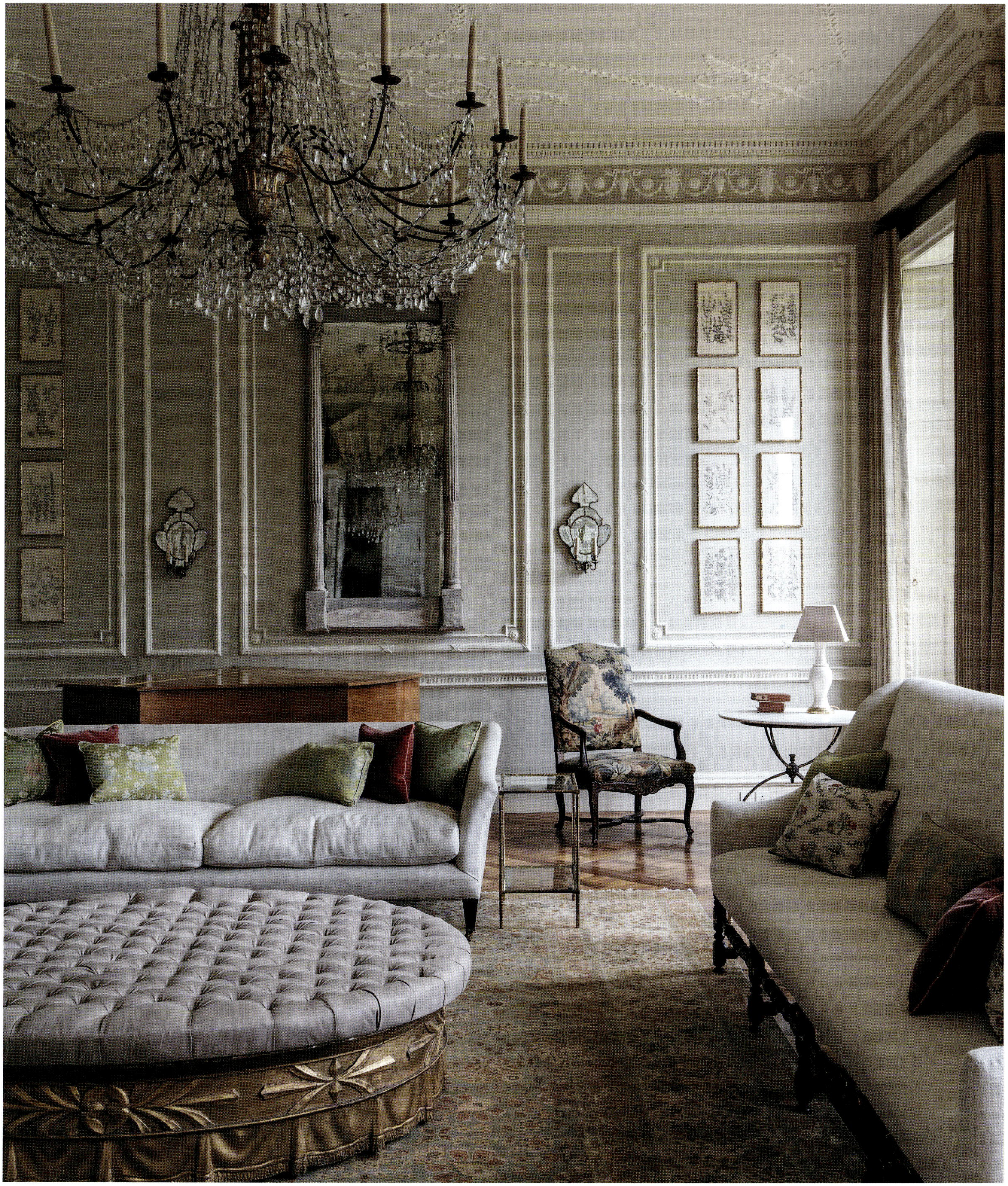

CASE STUDY 2

BELOW
Inspiration for the colours in the powder room come from the marble floor. Elegant Cornforth White on the panelling sits below Ammonite walls and moulding. Mole's Breath, the strongest tone, is used on the domed ceiling.

FACING PAGE
Huge windows dominate this kitchen. Ammonite keeps their appearance traditional and complements the marble. For a more contemporary feel, the walls and the units have been painted in alluring Oval Room Blue.

PAGES 46-7
This bedroom has to be one of the most inviting in London. The complex pink and grey tones of Peignoir create a chalky look and make the walls seem as if they have been this colour forever. To retain a tranquil feel, we refrained from picking out the panelling but painted the trim in sympathetic Skimming Stone.

Using a Full Gloss finish on every surface of this room makes it feel distinctive and inviting. It is a brave choice and one that cannot fail to excite.

Close to the games room is the equally rich cinema, where everything (including the furniture) is also in one tone – this time, the unapologetically clubby Studio Green – another luxurious triumph. This colour was chosen as much for entertainment as for intimacy. When confronted with a dark room such as this, it is often better to dismiss any natural light and create a dramatic space instead.

As in most family homes today, the kitchen is at the heart of this house. Its decoration duly bridges the gap between the highly saturated colours of the lower ground floor and the more elegant and distinguished decoration of the reception rooms. With no less than eight glorious Georgian windows, the kitchen is flooded with natural light. Oval Room Blue, the most blackened of our blues, which has a subtly aged feel, creates the required depth and balance. As there is so much white trim in this room, it worked best to use one colour on both the walls and the kitchen units, to prevent an over-fussy look. An enormous kitchen island painted in ever-enduring Railings grounds the space.

In the bedroom suites (see examples on pages 46–7 and 49) we return to softer tones. Among some of the colours used in them for evoking calm and serenity are Peignoir, Light Blue, Shaded White, Mizzle, Cornforth White and Pavilion Gray, often complemented by richer tones in the adjoining bathrooms and dressing rooms. Although the bases of these colours are far-ranging, they sit together seamlessly because they all have the same depth of colour, meaning that one room never feels more important than another.

So often in the past, paint colour has played a subsidiary role in a room's decoration, serving as a neutral foil or background. This was also the desired effect in the historic reception rooms of this house.

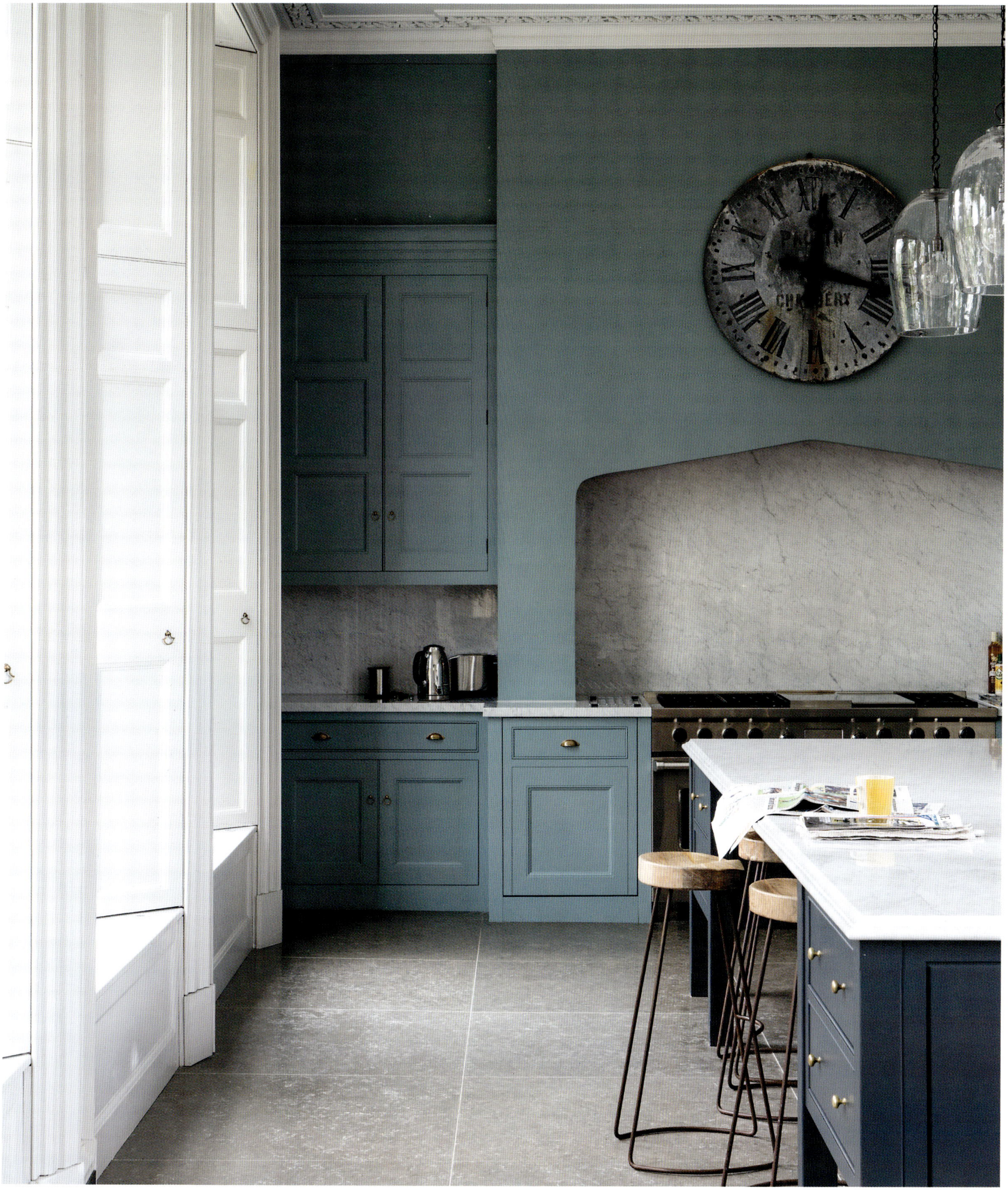

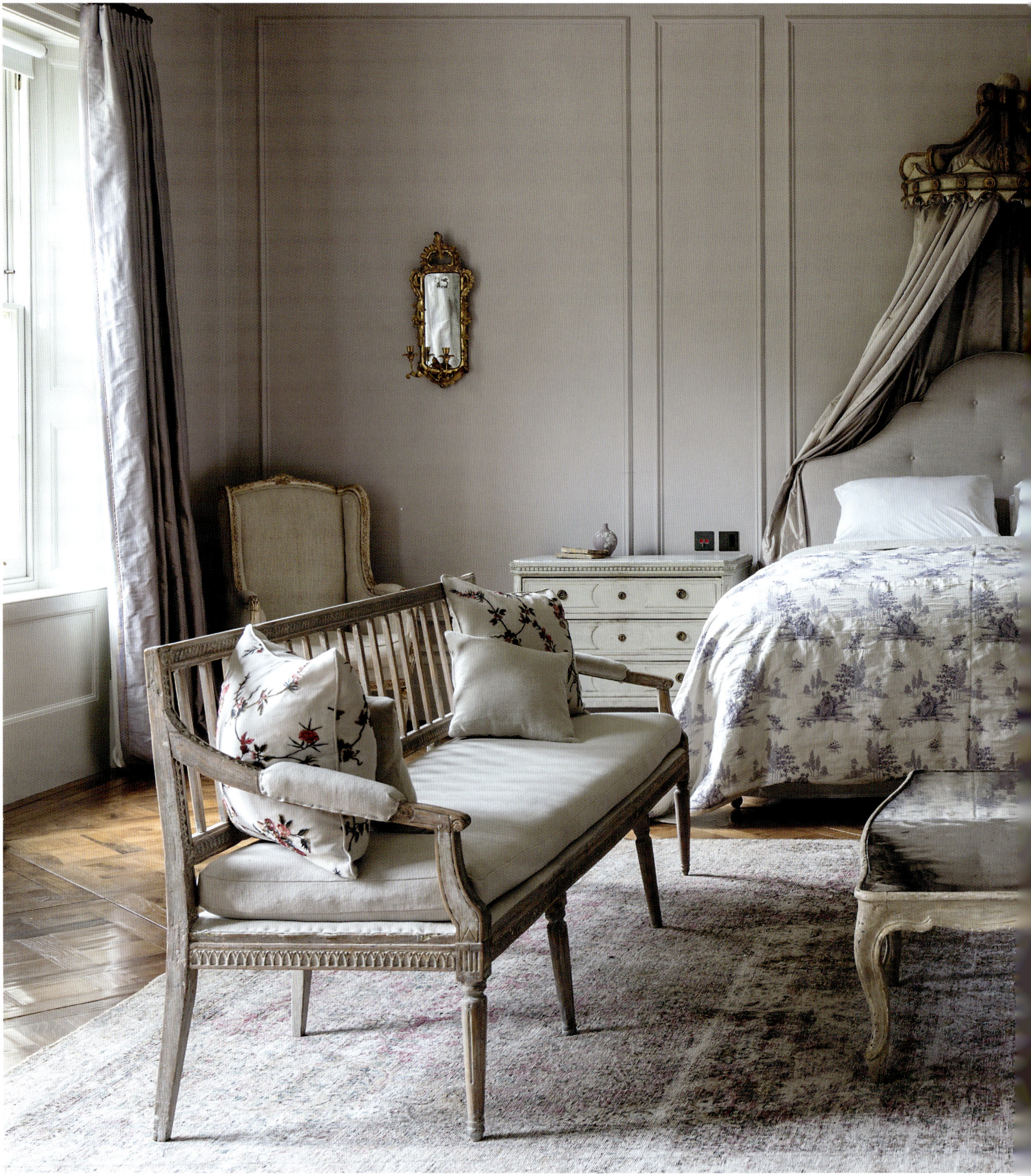

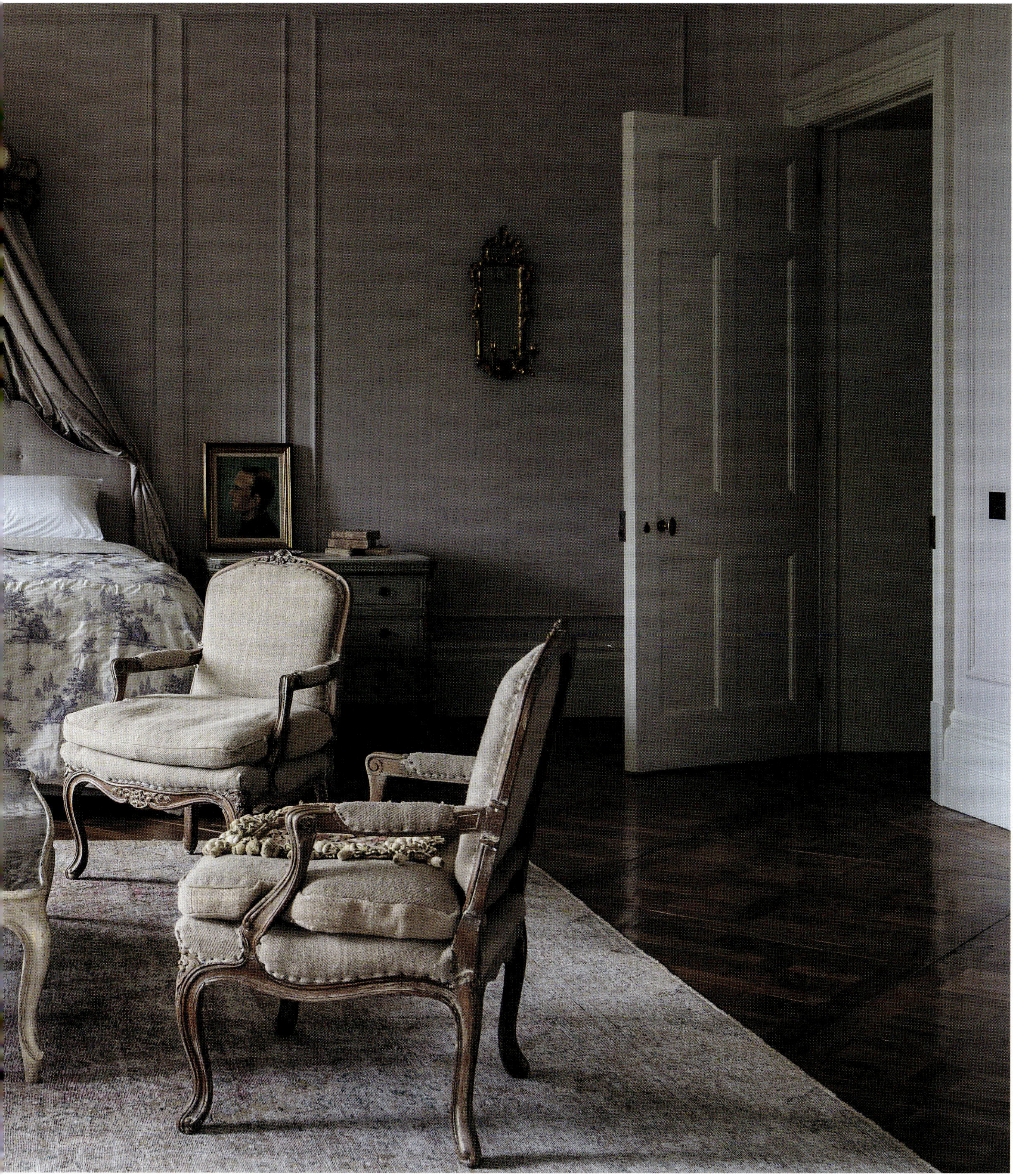

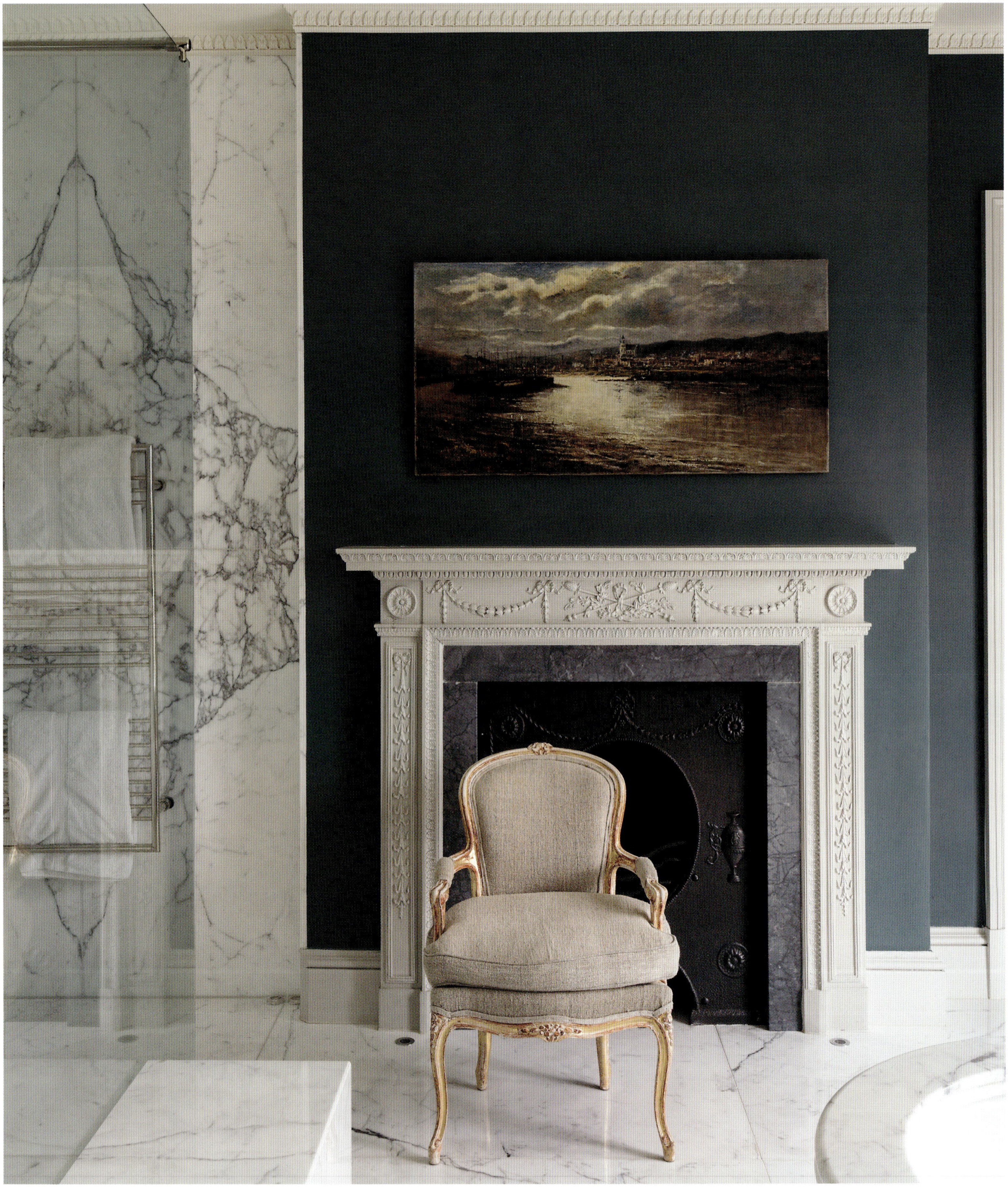

CASE STUDY 2

FACING PAGE
It is a treat to drift through to the rich atmosphere of the master bathroom from the calm of the Light Blue bedroom (left). Far larger than many bathrooms, it benefits from being painted in Inchyra Blue whose moody tone creates a more intimate area and complements a treasured piece of art.

LEFT
The outsized master bedroom is an elegant oasis of calm, with Light Blue on the walls and the trim. This magical colour becomes more silver in tone in the shaded area where the bed sits, but in this well-lit reading area it feels peaceful and calming.

Creating a sense of flow between the rooms was paramount, as was the appreciation of the architecture of the building and the way that light plays in each room. But it was almost more important to create a house that could be lived in happily by a family. The colours chosen for the reception rooms are gracious and dignified but there is more than a little fun introduced in the games rooms.

Despite, or perhaps as a result of, the exceptional attention to detail, this house has a dignified simplicity – an understated elegance that is the perfect backdrop for what must be one of the most sophisticated homes in London.

UNDERSTATED GRANDEUR

CASE STUDY 2

UNDERSTATED GRANDEUR PALETTE

RECIPE TIPS

* Use Full Gloss, especially in a rich colour such as Radicchio, on walls and panelling to create unrivalled glamour.
* Paint a dark colour on a domed ceiling, as seen in the powder room, to draw the eye up and accentuate a room's curves.
* If your house is big enough, zone groups of rooms with strong or delicate colour.
* Use the same colour on kitchen units and walls while leaving the trim neutral, to link to strong-coloured and subtle areas.
* Keep to one colour in each bedroom suite, as has been done in the master bedroom, using the lightest tone (in this case, Light Blue) in the bedroom and the darkest (Inchyra Blue) in its adjoining bathroom.

EXTERIOR
- MOUSE'S BACK *window frames*
- RAILINGS *ironwork*

ENTRANCE RECEPTION
- DEAD SALMON *walls*
- JOA'S WHITE *cornice/trim*
- OXFORD STONE *ceiling*

CHURCHILL ROOM
- OLD WHITE *dado/walls/frieze*
- OFF-WHITE *trim*
- LIME WHITE *wall detail/cornice*
- SLIPPER SATIN *frieze detail/ceiling*
- WIMBORNE WHITE *ceiling detail*

CINEMA
- STUDIO GREEN *all*

DINING ROOM
- POTTED SHRIMP (A) | *walls*
- DROP CLOTH *trim*
- WIMBORNE WHITE *cornice*
- SHADOW WHITE *ceiling*
- DIMITY *plaster detail*

MASTER BATHROOM
- INCHYRA BLUE *walls*
- STRONG WHITE *ceiling/trim*

LADY TEMPLETON PARLOUR
- PALE POWDER *walls*
- AMMONITE *trim*
- JOA'S WHITE *cornice*
- GREEN BLUE *frieze/ceiling coins*
- ALL WHITE *frieze detail*
- STRONG WHITE *walls*
- MOLE'S BREATH *ceiling*
- CORNFORTH WHITE *trim*

HALL, STAIRS AND LANDING
- ELEPHANT'S BREATH *walls*
- STRONG WHITE *trim/ceiling*
- SKIMMING STONE *cornice*

GAMES ROOM
- RADICCHIO *walls/trim*
- DOVE TALE *ceiling*
- ELEPHANT'S BREATH *windows*

KITCHEN
- OVAL ROOM BLUE *walls/units/frieze*
- ALL WHITE *cornice/ceiling*
- AMMONITE *trim*
- RAILINGS *kitchen island*

POWDER ROOM
- CORNFORTH WHITE *panelling*
- AMMONITE *walls*
- MOLE'S BREATH *ceiling*

BEDROOM SUITES
- LIGHT BLUE *walls*
- MIZZLE *walls*
- PEIGNOIR *walls*
- CORNFORTH WHITE *walls*
- PAVILION GRAY *walls*
- SHADED WHITE *trim/ceiling*

CASE STUDIES

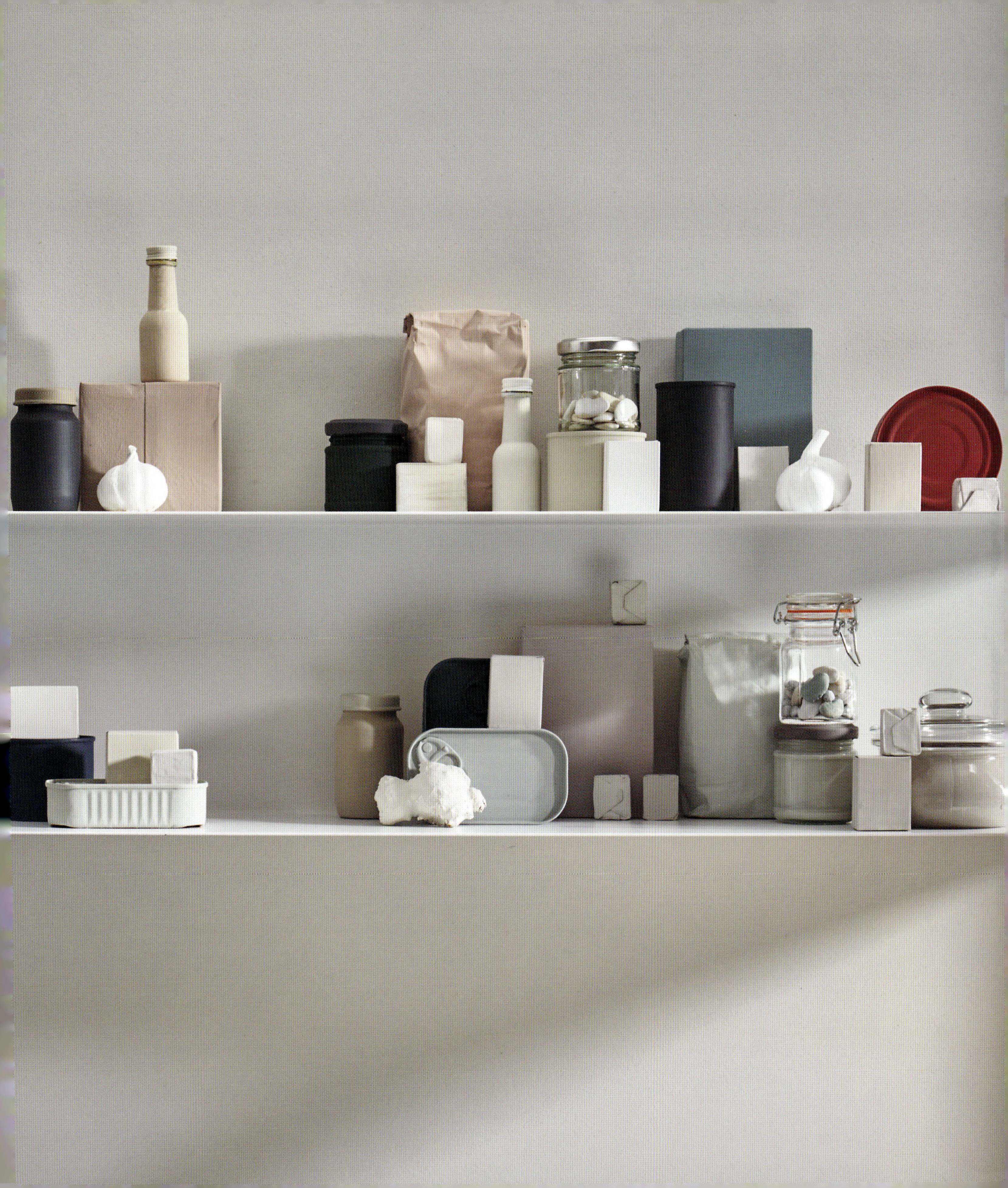

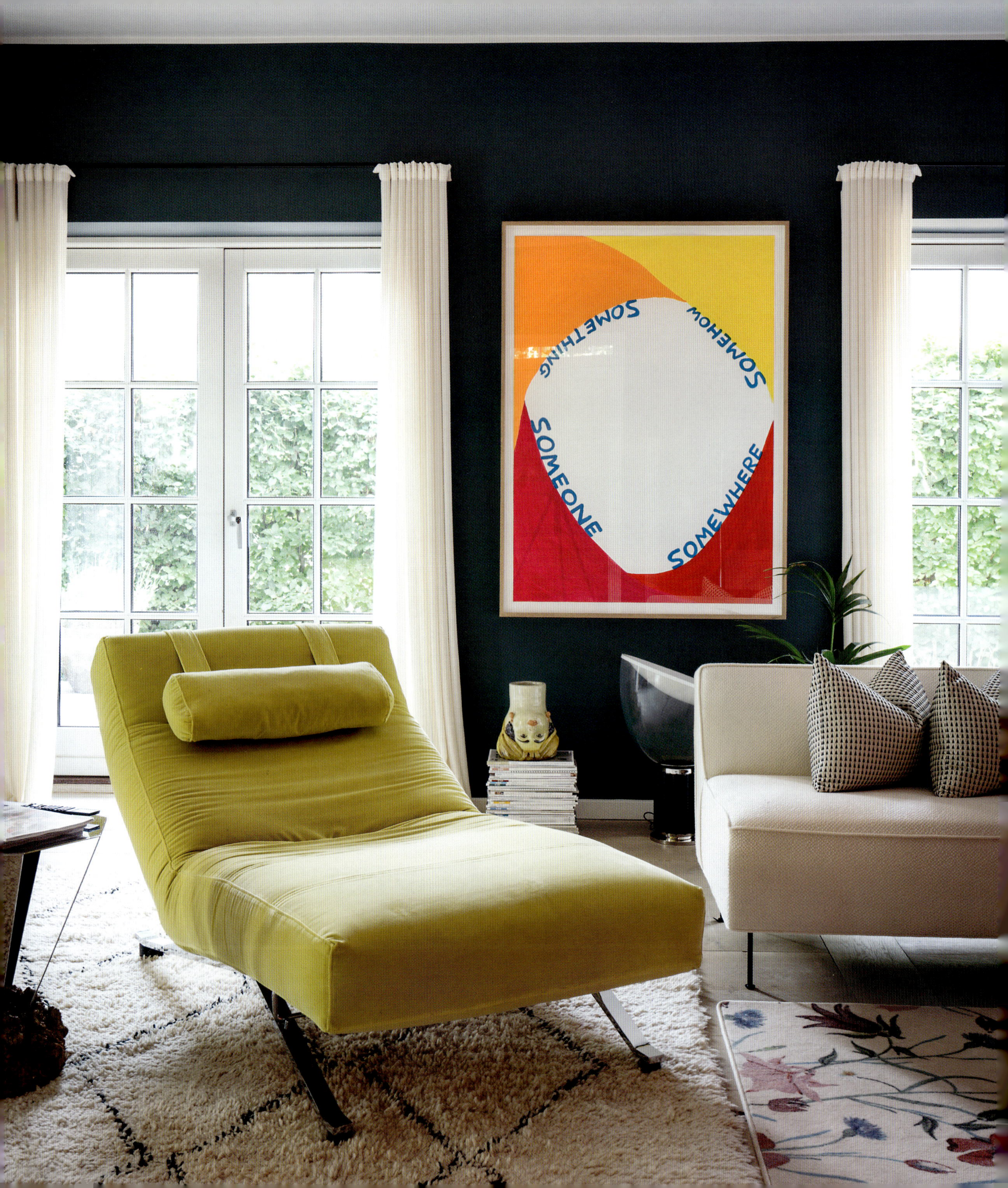
SOMETHING
SOMEHOW
SOMEONE
SOMEWHERE

CASE STUDY 3

COPENHAGEN ART HOUSE

The owner of this house clearly has a huge passion for art, and she has filled her home not only with an extremely diverse collection, but also with vibrant colour on the walls. She admits that the house was once painted in a moderate Nordic palette, but this has changed as her colour aesthetic has developed over the years. Now she refuses to be bound by any prescribed rules, whether it comes to paint colours or to art.

There is no intention of establishing a colour flow through the house – quite the opposite, in fact. It is about choosing colours to play to the strengths of each space and the art that it houses, and creating wildly different experiences in spaces that are used in wildly different ways, jolting the senses and keeping you on your toes. But, most importantly, it is about making you smile. The choices are bold and each colour makes a statement. The journey through this house is dynamic but never discordant.

One cannot help but feel that the unsurpassed depth of colour from the heavily-pigmented Farrow & Ball paints plays a big part in achieving these aims. The quality of the paint becomes paramount in such a setting, and the flatter the finish, the better the paint is at highlighting art. In this house, Estate Emulsion, with its minimal sheen and chalky finish, has been used so that the light reflection will come from the art, not the walls. The selection of these colours, though bold, is a subtle art in itself.

FACING PAGE AND PAGES 54-5
The living area is full of bold gestures. Distinctive Inchyra Blue walls provide a perfect backdrop for the contemporary art. All White on the trim becomes an accent colour, making it just as important to the scheme. Art by David Shrigley, Tom Humphreys, Elmgreen & Dragset, Henry Krokatsis, and Torbjørn Rødland.

ABOVE
The rich pigmentation in Farrow & Ball paints means that a colour looks different depending on where it is used. In this intimate dining corner, Inchyra Blue has a seductive feel, contrasted with the crisp All White ceiling. Art by Gun Gordillo.

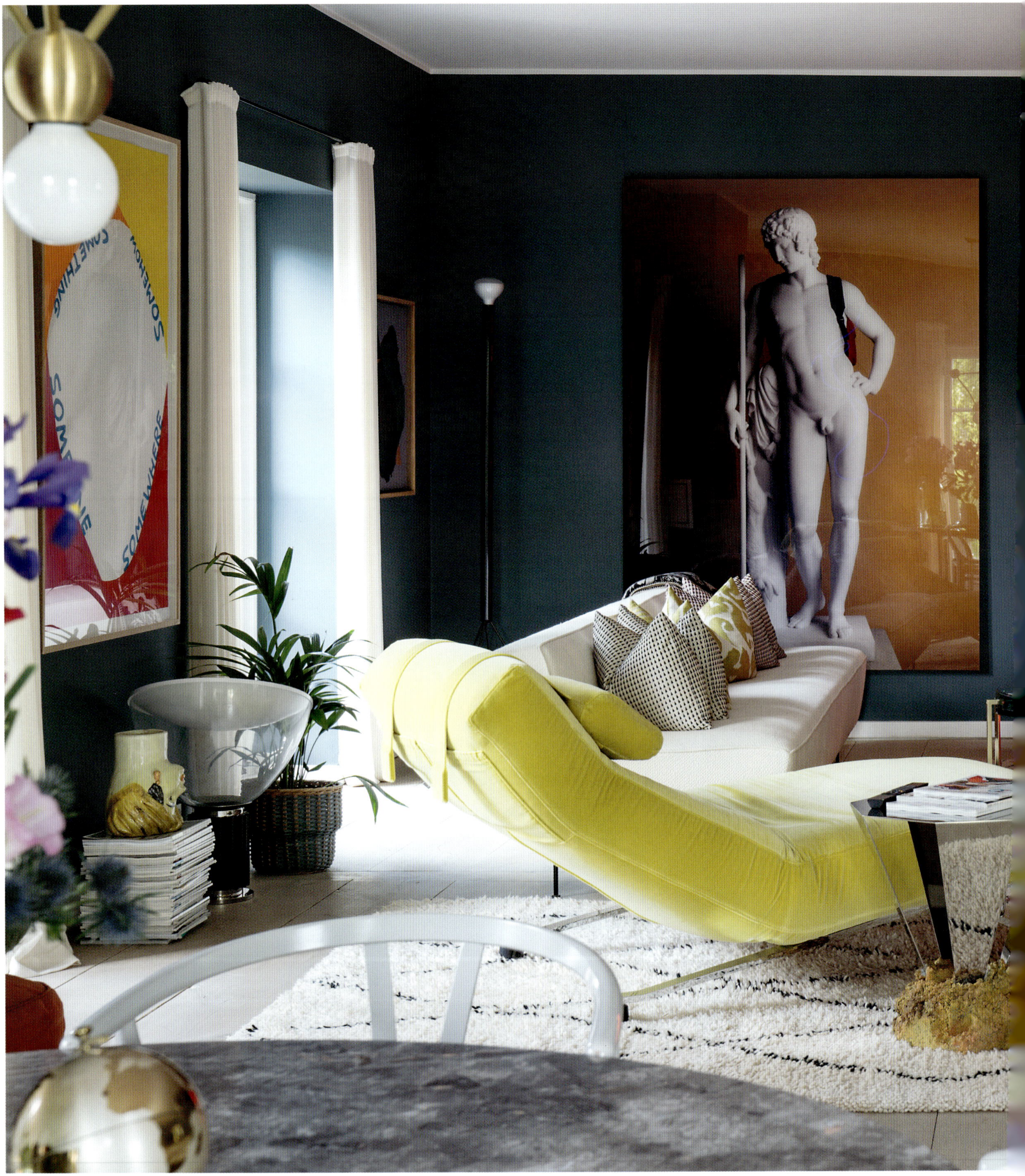
SOMETHING
SOMEHOW
SOMEWHERE

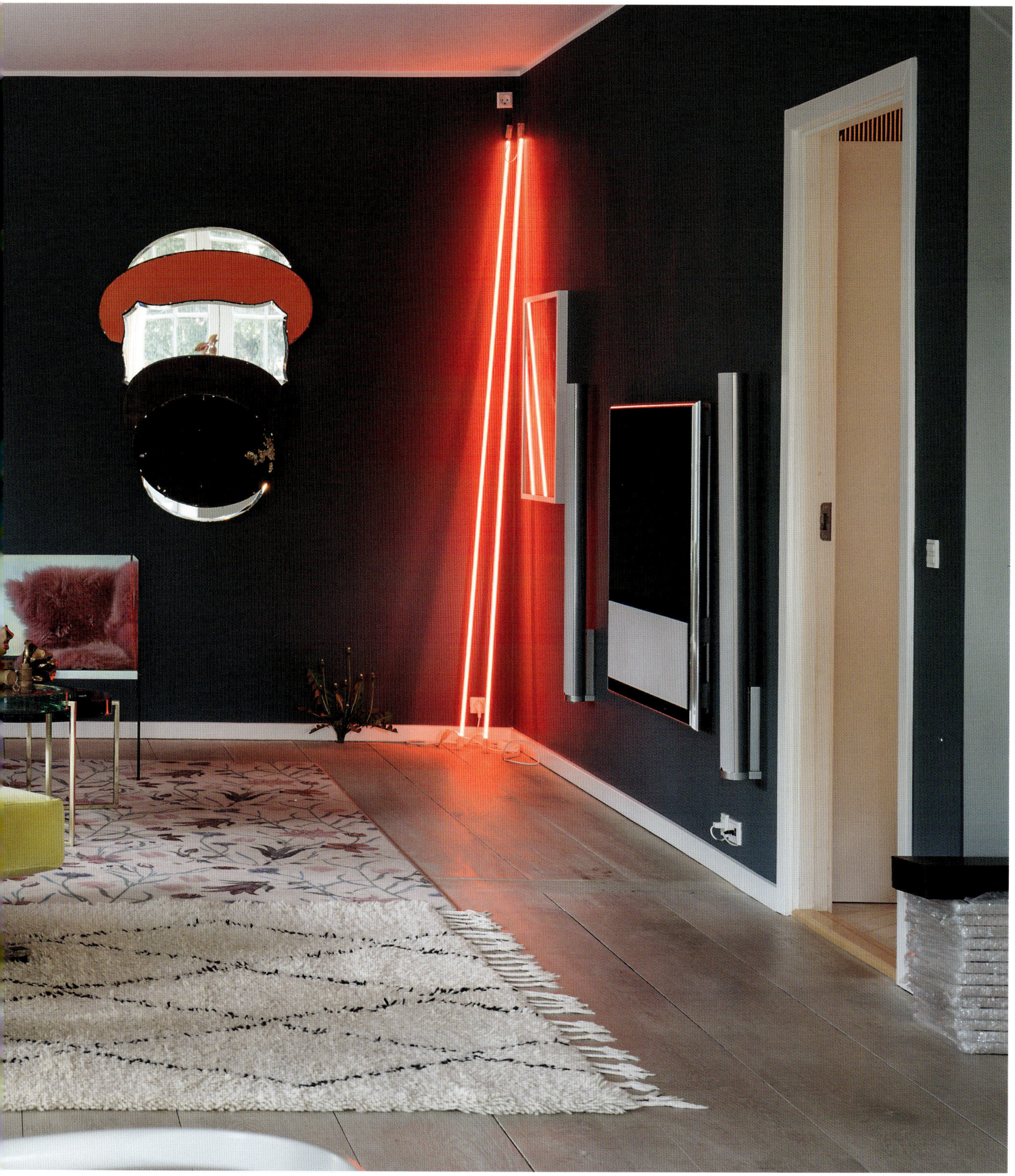

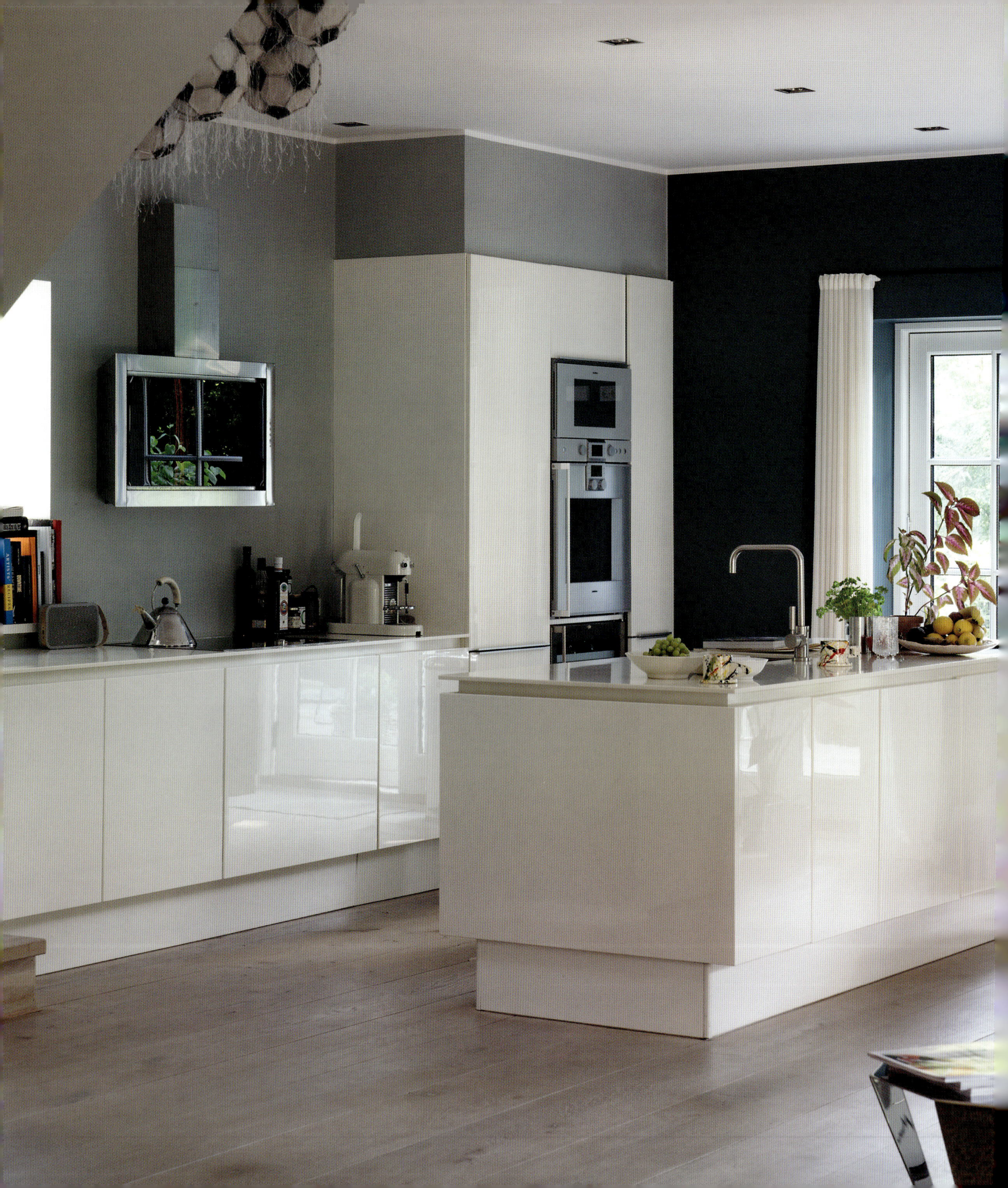

CASE STUDY 3

FACING PAGE
Having different colours on adjacent walls can look jarring, but in this kitchen it appears considered and harmonious. Moody Inchyra Blue meets silvery Light Blue, creating a fresh, modern take on a classic colour combination. Glossy white kitchen units distract the eye from where the two colours meet, while the unadorned floor has a suitably grounding effect.

RIGHT
Light Blue is a mysterious colour, which becomes a little more silver in tone when used in shaded areas, like this corner of the kitchen. Here, it has a luxurious, velvety effect, but changes to feel more peaceful and calming in the well-lit corridor upstairs (see page 58). Art by Darío Escobar.

COPENHAGEN ART HOUSE

RIGHT
Light Blue flows up the stairs into this corridor and provides respite from the strong colours used on the floor below. Natural light hits these walls from varying angles, changing how their colour reads. This is a perfect example of why sampling colours on every wall and viewing them at different times of the day is advisable.

FACING PAGE
Setting Plaster is a perfect pairing with the artwork in the bedroom. All the elements here combine to create a sensual experience. The wall colour is far from incidental but one is less aware of its strength because it has been taken onto the ceiling. Had the owner defaulted to a white ceiling, this would have detracted from both the art, by Michael Bevilacqua, and the pendant lights.

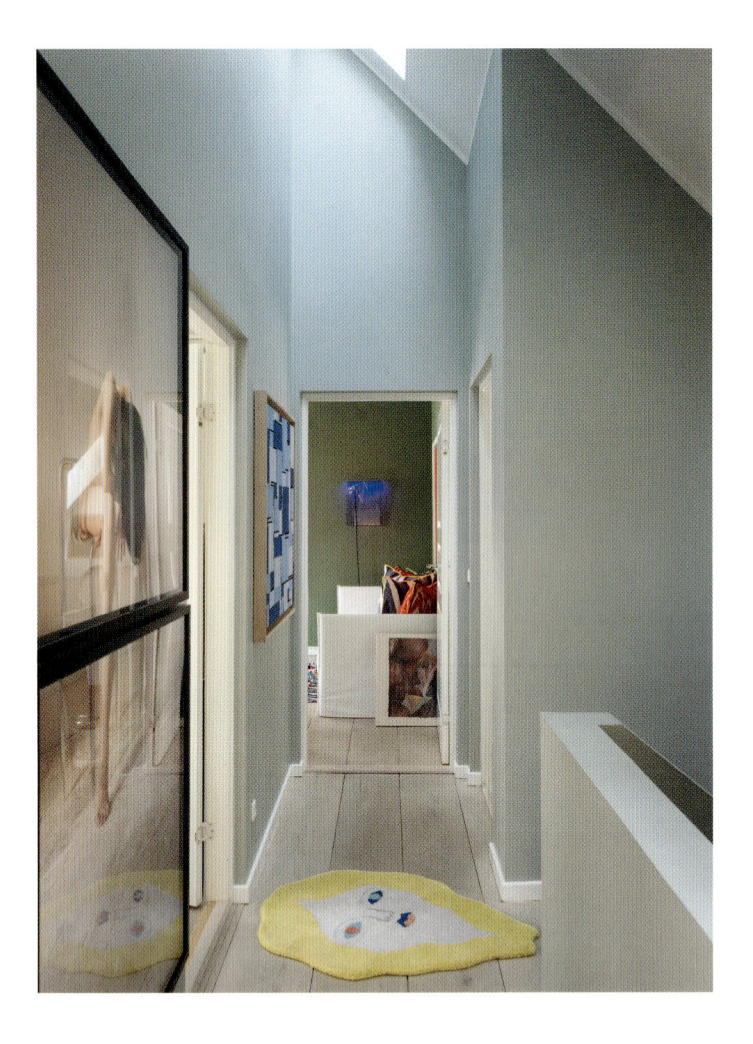

Inchyra Blue in the main living area (see pages 52–5) works to great effect, its deep, dark colour drawing attention to the pictures and sculptures while disguising the confines of the room, making it feel bigger. Had the owner taken the obvious route and used an "art gallery" white as a backdrop, the room would have felt like a clinical box.

The skirting, coving and architraves, picked out in All White, frame the room and act like a picture mount, making the space resemble an installation. This simplicity is reflected in the crisp silk curtains framing the five large glazed doors. The curtains have been selected to match the colour of the trim exactly and are instrumental in drawing attention to the art that sits between them. High-gloss kitchen units bounce light around at the other end of the room, where the wall colour has been changed to Light Blue. Many people would have opted for white here, but this silvery blue has just enough gravitas to sit sympathetically with the stronger Inchyra Blue, yet still feel peaceful and calming in the well-lit landing on the first floor.

The journey around the rooms upstairs is made all the more compelling because there is a move away from the cooler blue tones on the ground floor to an altogether warmer environment. Setting Plaster taken over both the walls and ceiling softens the bedroom but the overall effect is far from sugary. This dusty pink is named after the blushing walls we often admire in newly plastered houses, and its softness is down to the inclusion of yellow pigment. The magnificent white pendant lights serve to emphasize the colour of the walls, which, in turn, complements the artwork exquisitely. The result is an oasis of calm modernity.

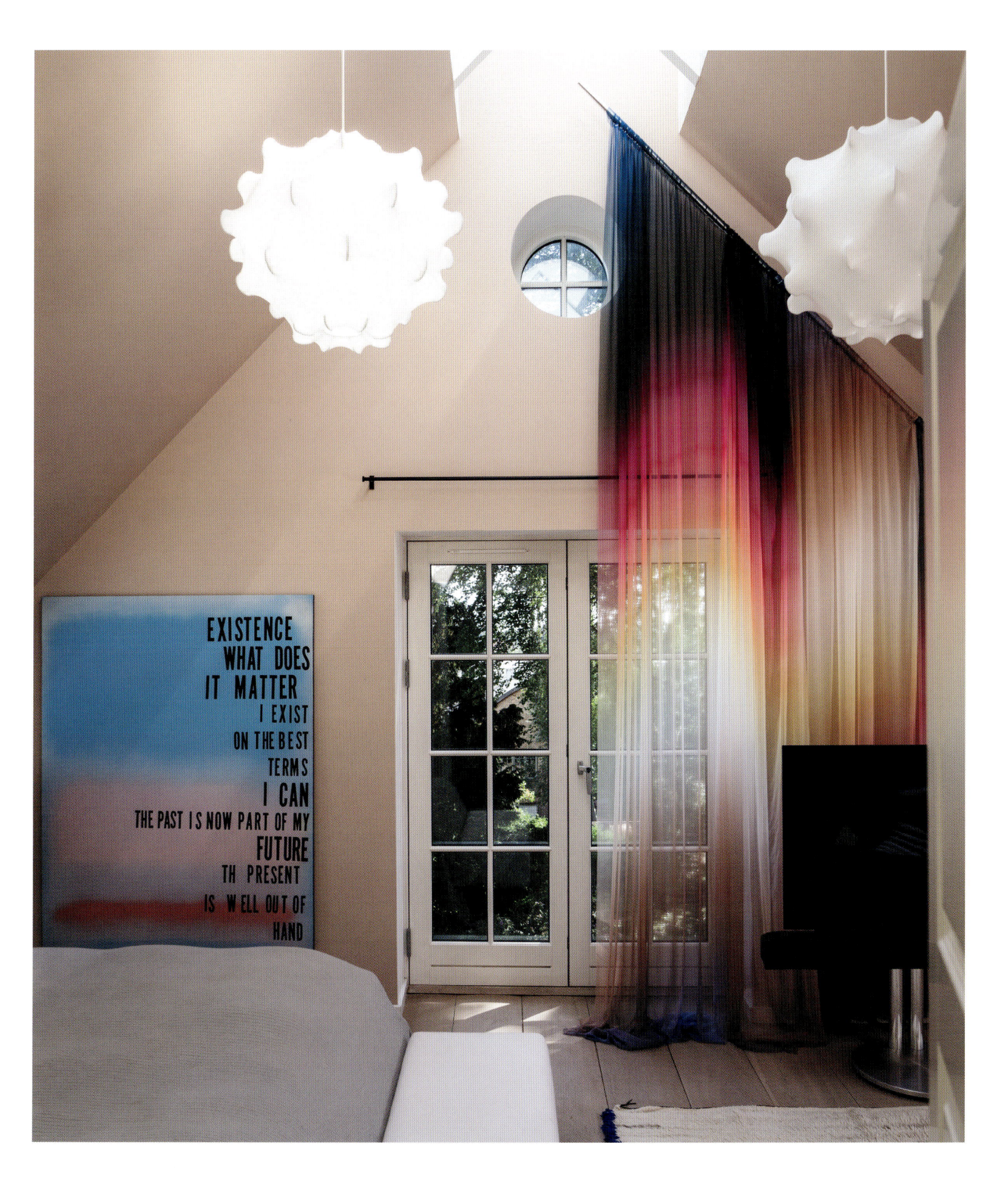

EXISTENCE
WHAT DOES
IT MATTER
I EXIST
ON THE BEST
TERMS
I CAN
THE PAST IS NOW PART OF MY
FUTURE
TH PRESENT
IS WELL OUT OF
HAND

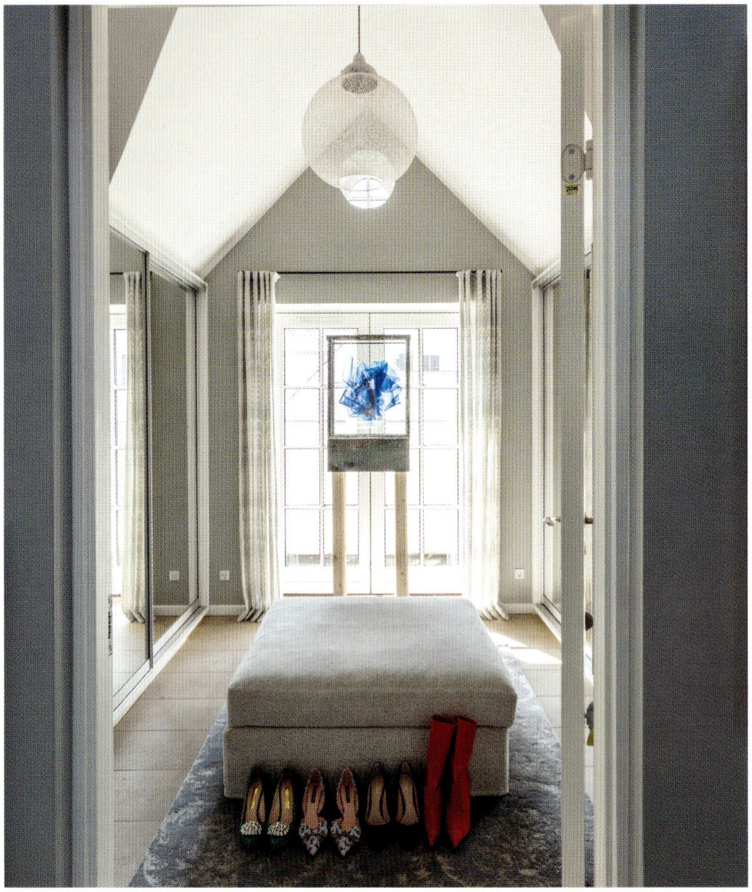

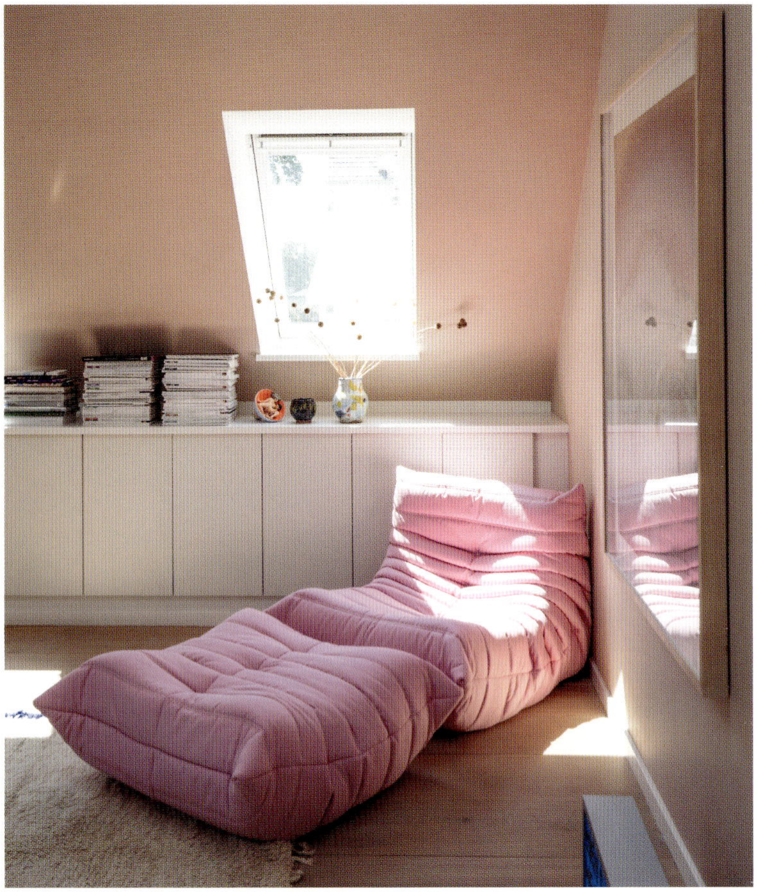

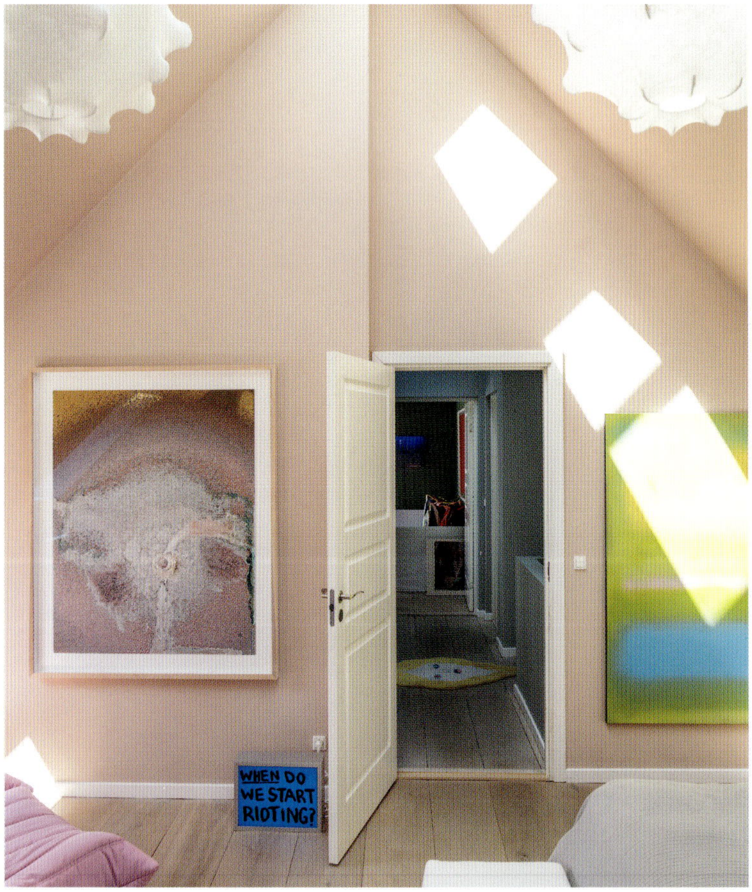
WHEN DO WE START RIOTING?

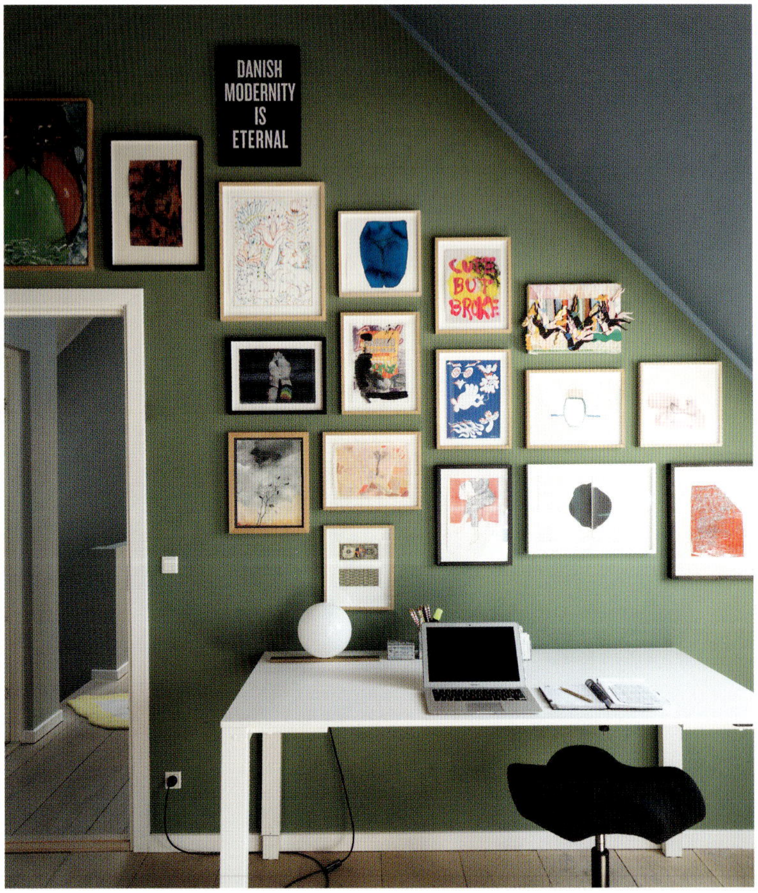
DANISH MODERNITY IS ETERNAL

CASE STUDY 3

At the other end of the upstairs corridor, there is a smaller space used as both a study and a guest room, and the colours have been selected accordingly. The rich, traditional qualities of Calke Green, with its deep sage notes, has a certain soberness, making it ideal for a study. Not surprisingly, there is an unexpected twist to the decoration, with saturated Stone Blue on the ceiling introducing a measure of liveliness.

The dressing room has a totally different atmosphere. It is all about order, a feeling augmented by the crisp contrast between the wall and ceiling colours. Here, the architecture is highlighted to give structure to the room and make it feel a little more formal than the bedroom or study. The room is dominated by huge mirrored wardrobe doors along two sides, making the Pavilion Gray on the other walls seem almost incidental, but the subtle blue undertones of the paint do help create a sense of space and make a suitably understated backdrop for a wardrobe of clothes that must surely be as flamboyant as the art.

To conclude this colour adventure, Charlotte's Locks has been used in the typically diminutive bathroom. Its deep, dramatic orange tone is spectacular in small areas such as this, especially so when used with sharp contrasts. This is just about as perfect a use of this tone that you could find. The question is, which came first, the art or the colour choice?

Many of the colours included in this house have historic roots, including those that were first discovered in an 18th-century Baroque mansion (Calke Green) and a Scottish Regency estate (Inchyra Blue), so it is inspiring to see them being used in such a diverse way. It is also exciting to see the owner's aesthetic unfold through a large set of references, whether from the art world or the ever-evolving world of colour. In this house you are surrounded by alluring, provocative and compelling art, but the pieces sit together harmoniously, and because they are so diverse, they don't battle for attention. In much the same way, the contrasting colours are part of the experience, too, and they take nothing away from each other or the art. In fact, they very often enhance it. The colours on the walls reflect the overall look of the collection, allowing it to be experienced in a more powerful way.

FACING PAGE, TOP LEFT
There is a formality to this dressing room painted in Pavilion Gray, a colour that sits flawlessly with the mirrors stretching the length of the room. A sense of order is achieved by the contrast between the walls and the All White ceiling.

FACING PAGE, TOP RIGHT AND BOTTOM LEFT
Setting Plaster is a fabulous colour to come home to. Its blushing tone feels like the antithesis to the busy world outside. The pink chair positioned in a well-lit corner of this bedroom proves that discordant tones *can* work together. Art by Sven Dalsgaard and Matilde Duus.

ABOVE
Charlotte's Locks feels tailor-made both for the art hanging in this bathroom and for completing the edgy but cohesive colour journey through the house.

FACING PAGE, BOTTOM RIGHT
Calke Green in the study provides a rich backdrop against which pictures and treasures can stand out. It also has a slightly serious air, making it a good choice for workspaces. In this dynamic house it has been teamed with lively Stone Blue on the ceiling, for a suitably modern twist.

COPENHAGEN ART HOUSE

CASE STUDY 3

COPENHAGEN ART HOUSE PALETTE

RECIPE TIPS

* Crisp white woodwork and ceilings emphasize the colours on the walls. In this home, All White was the natural choice to frame each room.
* Don't be afraid to use strong colours – they will enrich your life.
* When a room has a dual purpose, such as a combined study and guest room, think about how the colours impact on the different uses of the room.
* A Stone Blue ceiling in a guest room will delight its occasional occupants.

LIVING AREA

INCHYRA BLUE — *walls*
ALL WHITE — *trim/ceiling*

KITCHEN AND STAIRS

LIGHT BLUE — *walls*
ALL WHITE — *trim/ceiling*

BATHROOM

CHARLOTTE'S LOCKS — *walls*
ALL WHITE — *trim/ceiling*

BEDROOM

SETTING PLASTER — *walls/ceiling*
ALL WHITE — *trim*

STUDY/GUEST ROOM

CALKE GREEN — *walls*
ALL WHITE — *trim*
STONE BLUE — *ceiling*

DRESSING ROOM

PAVILION GRAY — *walls*
ALL WHITE — *trim/ceiling*

CASE STUDIES

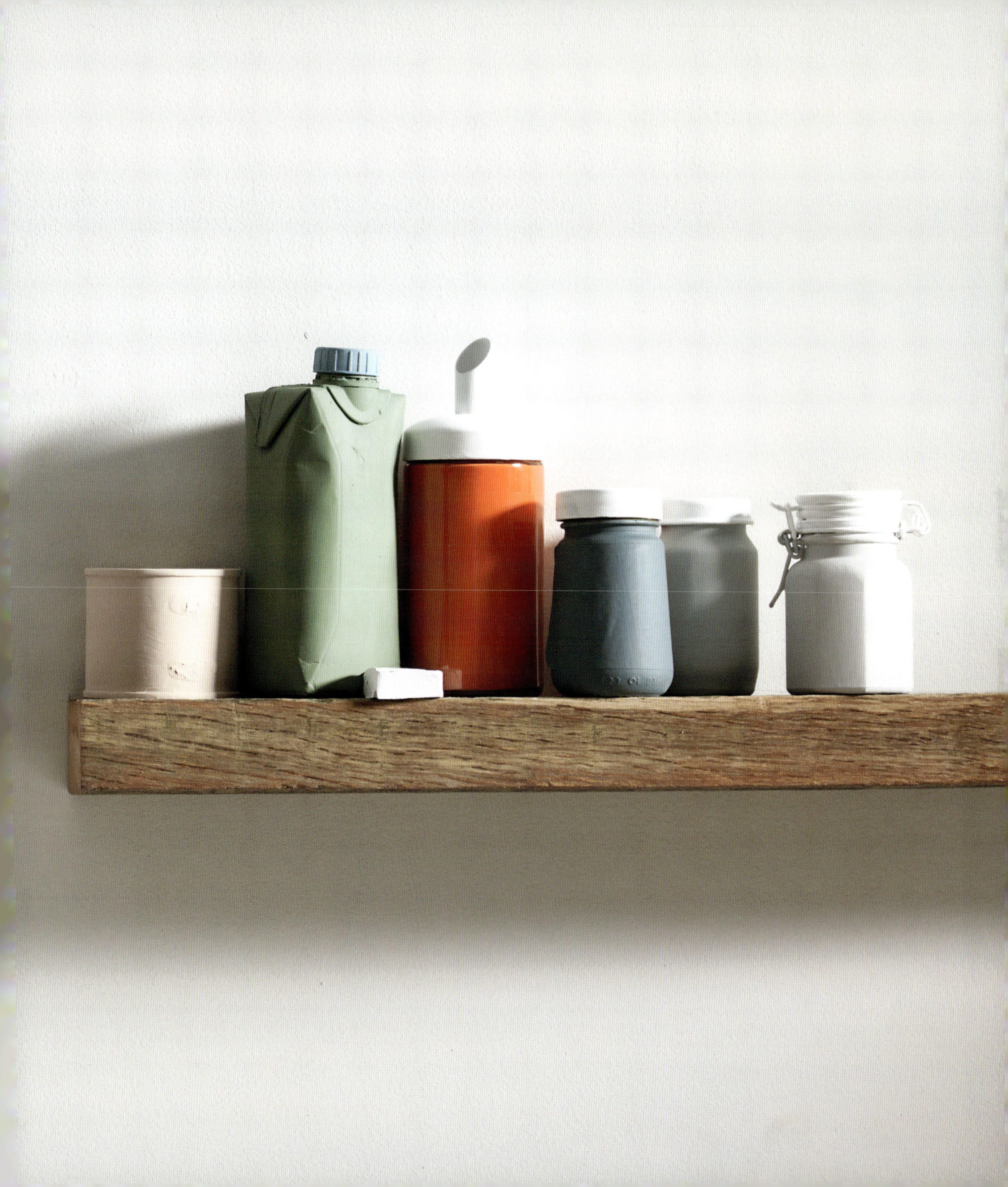

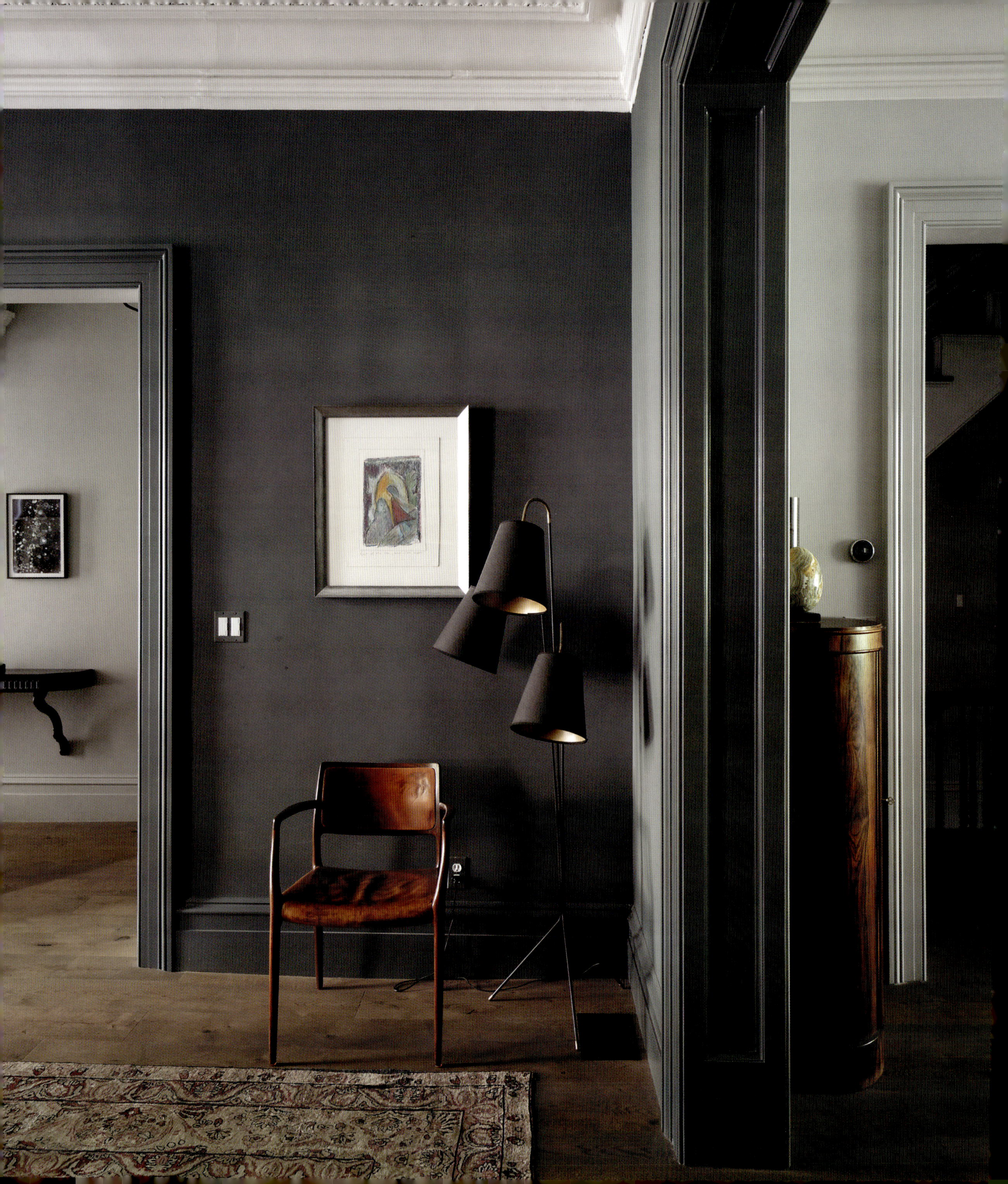

CASE STUDY 4

MANHATTAN CHIC

It would be difficult to find a better example of everything you need for urban living than this stylish, historic town house in New York. The first thing you sense is a hushed formality, which permeates the house, but it is the calmness that makes it so attractive and welcoming. This is the ultimate study in restraint. However, things that look simple usually aren't, and it takes a lot of love to create a home like this. Luckily, the owners not only have a passion for interiors, but also were keen to live in a space that fits the vernacular of the city. The carefully curated palette of greys could not be more Manhattan, and the look is unique and sophisticated. The flow between rooms is second to none, proving that you do not need to use one trim colour to provide continuity.

Stepping into the hall you are greeted by the cool tones of Pavilion Gray. This classic mid-grey works perfectly as an antidote to the bustling city streets. The atmosphere is serene and all is perfection. The staircase banister is given more importance by being painted in Pitch Black, creating a grounding central spine through the house, and the Full Gloss finish here and on the stair treads provides an understated element of chic (see page 70).

From the dignified hall you can drift unhindered into the dining room at the front of the house or the sitting room in the centre. Crucially, there are no doors between any of these spaces, but the architraves have been retained, so you get the sense of an open-plan space without losing the pleasure of the original architecture.

FACING PAGE
The perfect example of a cohesive palette. Lead-grey Down Pipe adorns the walls of the dining room, while the slightly lighter Manor House Gray is used in the adjoining sitting room. The lightest tone, Pavilion Gray, decorates the hall beyond.

ABOVE RIGHT
Down Pipe may feel daringly dark but the colour-saturated corners that it creates in this dining room are hard to read, making the room feel bigger. All White, a cool white, was chosen for the ceilings and mouldings throughout the house.

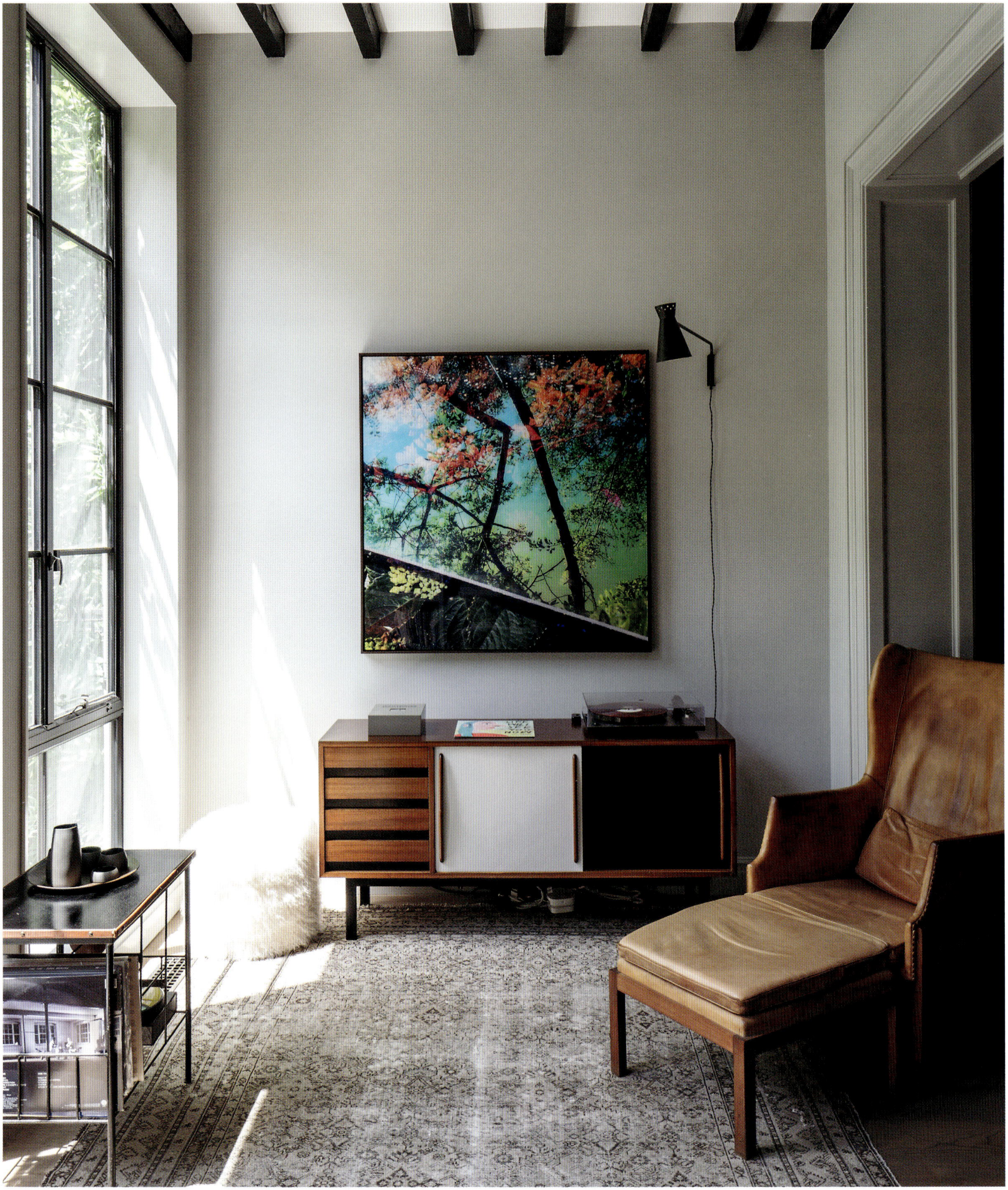

With every space so connected, it was vital to use the right colours. Each one has been chosen not only to complement its neighbour but also, more importantly, to create a definite atmosphere in each room. The Architectural Neutrals in the Farrow & Ball range were originally created to give an edgier feel than the other neutral groups, and they form the ideal palette for those wanting a strong architectural or modern, industrial feel. Purposely cool, with a blue undertone, they bring a slightly more hard-edged look, but when combined with the warm wood floors and leather-clad furniture in this home, the overall effect is softer.

The strongest tone is in the dining room, a wise choice because this room is used mainly in the evening when there is no natural light. Dramatic, lead-grey Down Pipe is just sensational here. A daringly dark hue for interiors, it is fabulous as a background for art, and extremely effective in creating a space full of drama. The fact that as much importance has been given to the corners of the dining room as to the centre stage makes it a satisfying space – everywhere you look, there is a carefully selected piece of furniture that acts almost as a sculpture. There is no sense of overcrowding, but neither does the room feel stark. This is luscious minimalism.

The central sitting room, which opens into both the darker dining room and the lighter hall, has been painted in Manor House Gray. The colour works perfectly as a visual bridge between the two spaces. A clean, definite grey, it retains its colour in all lights, making it the perfect choice for a room used throughout the day. Nothing has been overlooked in the decoration of this house, and how and when rooms are used is an extremely important factor to take into account – rooms that are decorated purely for a sense of drama or with no consideration of the amount of natural light that they receive can be very uncomfortable to live in. Like the other rooms in the house, the sitting room retains its own serene spirit, as well as helping to enhance the sense of flow between the spaces.

In both the dining room and the sitting room, All White has been used on the ceiling and the cornice. This gives structure to the rooms and makes the perceived ceiling height drop a little, so when you pass through to the library, with its more simple beamed ceiling, that space feels higher as well as lighter. This light-filled space on the garden side of the house must be one of the best spots in the whole of Manhattan to relax with a book.

FACING PAGE AND ABOVE
Much thought has gone into the light–dark contrasts in this home. Pavilion Gray has been used in the library to take advantage of the light conditions and be a mood-changer from the stronger sitting room and dining room. In this fairly contained space, it was wise to take the wall colour over the joinery, leaving the Pitch Black beams and doors as the stronger elements. Had a contrasting colour been used on the joinery, the room would have appeared smaller. Art by Karine Laval.

PAGES 68-9
Ever-popular Down Pipe makes any room feel sophisticated, and it is both dramatic and elegant in this dining room. The Architectural Neutral palette may be inspired by the city, but the result here is a room that feels both chic and tranquil. Art by Raymond Pettibon.

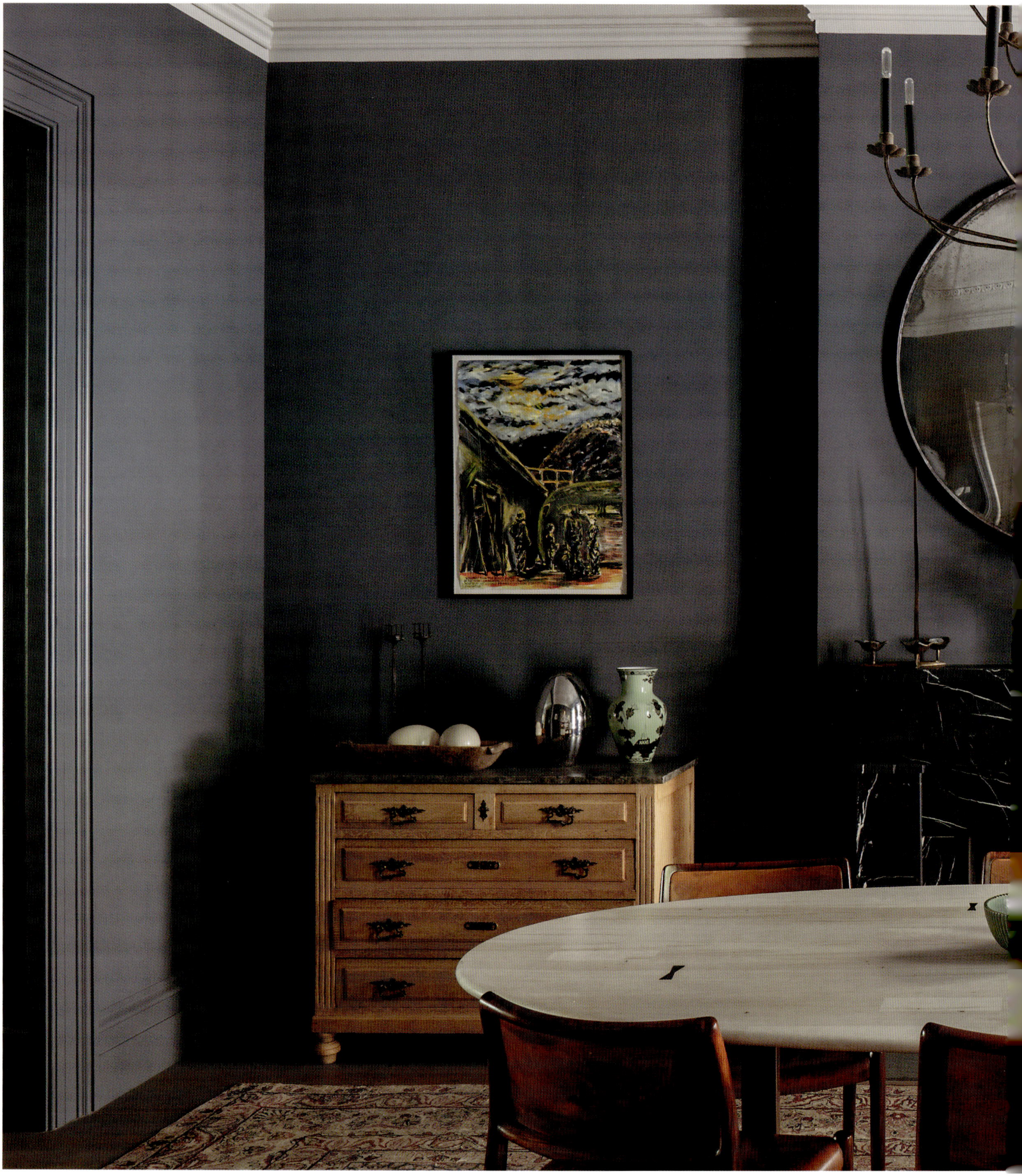

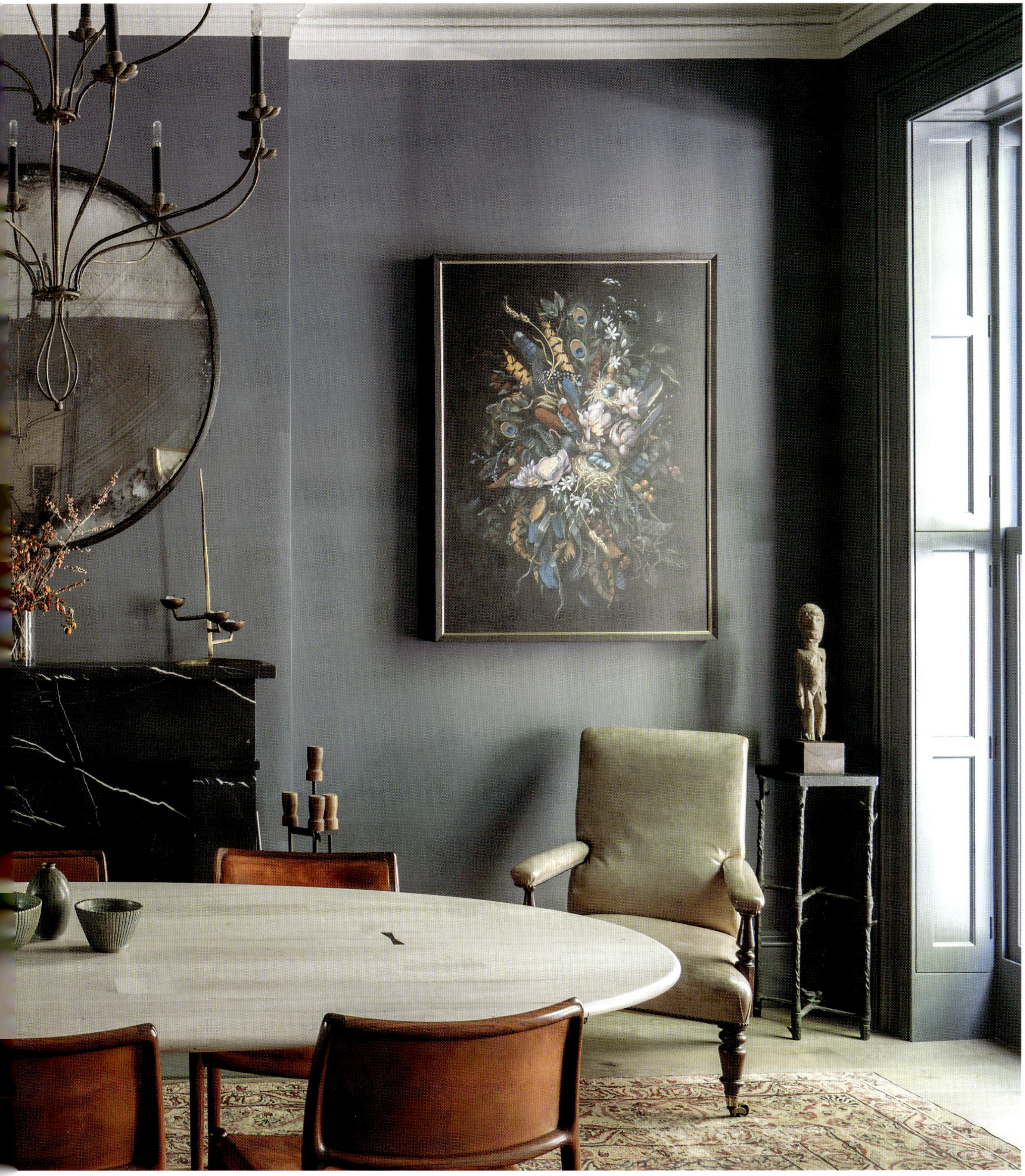

CASE STUDY 4

The palette changes to one of the Farrow & Ball Easy Neutrals for a slightly softer feel in the kitchen, which opens invitingly into the garden. Purbeck Stone avoids an unforgiving clinical look and takes advantage of all the available light and space. This calming grey, which resembles the colour of stone, takes on a personality that a plain white would lack. It works brilliantly in this room, particularly because it has been used not only on the walls and trim but also on the kitchen units. This decorative trick makes spaces seem bigger, and by underplaying the colour of the joinery, the room feels more like a living room and less like a purely utilitarian space.

Upstairs, there is a momentary break from grey. The bedroom has been painted in Hague Blue, to complement the imposing fire surround and create an enticing atmosphere. Unsurprisingly, there is a return to more sober greys in the spacious bathroom (see pages 72–3). Care has been taken, however, to use a warmer one. Dove Tale is a little softer than the shades used in the living areas, and its lilac undertone flatters both the flooring and the leather stool to perfection. Down Pipe has been reintroduced from the dining room walls onto the outside of the bathtub, making it look positively regal standing in the centre of the room.

This house may bear little frivolity, but it undoubtedly feels like a home. The design fits the personality of its owners, who relish perfection, and they have created an urban masterpiece in which to escape the crazy life of the city.

ABOVE
An elegant combination of understated Pavilion Gray in an Estate Emulsion finish on the walls and Pitch Black in Full Gloss on the banister and stair treads creates a grounding dark spine that runs down through the house.

FACING PAGE, TOP LEFT AND BOTTOM
The kitchen is also grey but in a warmer tone. Muted Purbeck Stone on the walls and cabinets brings a sense of calm, while the paint's stony properties connect with the garden walls outside.

FACING PAGE, TOP RIGHT
Blackened has been used on the walls of this study, where it feels cool without being cold. Pitch Black in a Modern Emulsion finish is a simple yet inspired choice for the floor.

CASE STUDIES

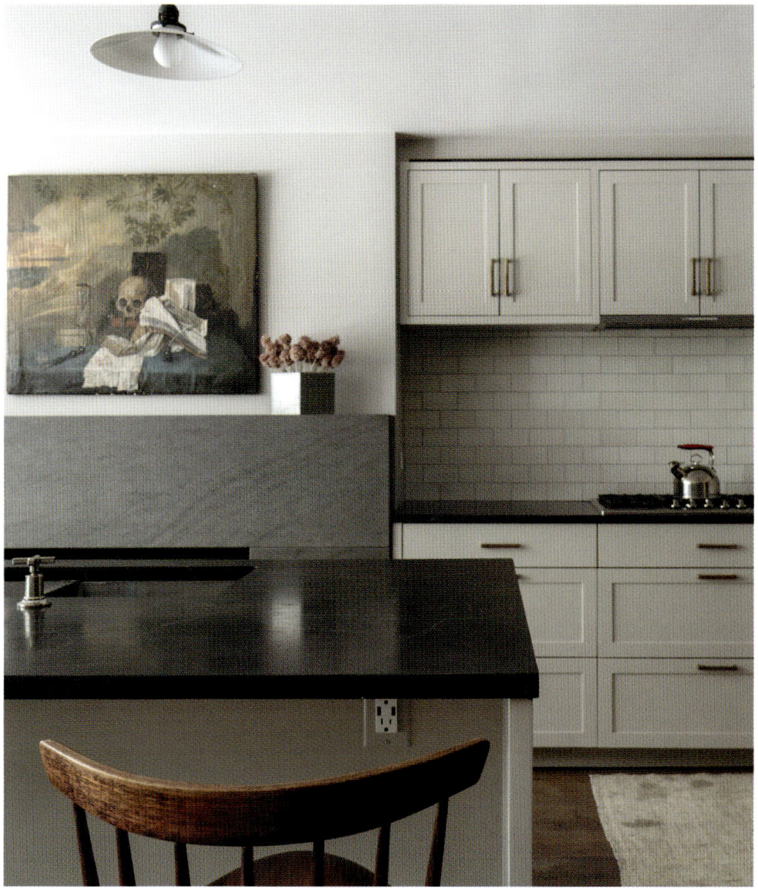
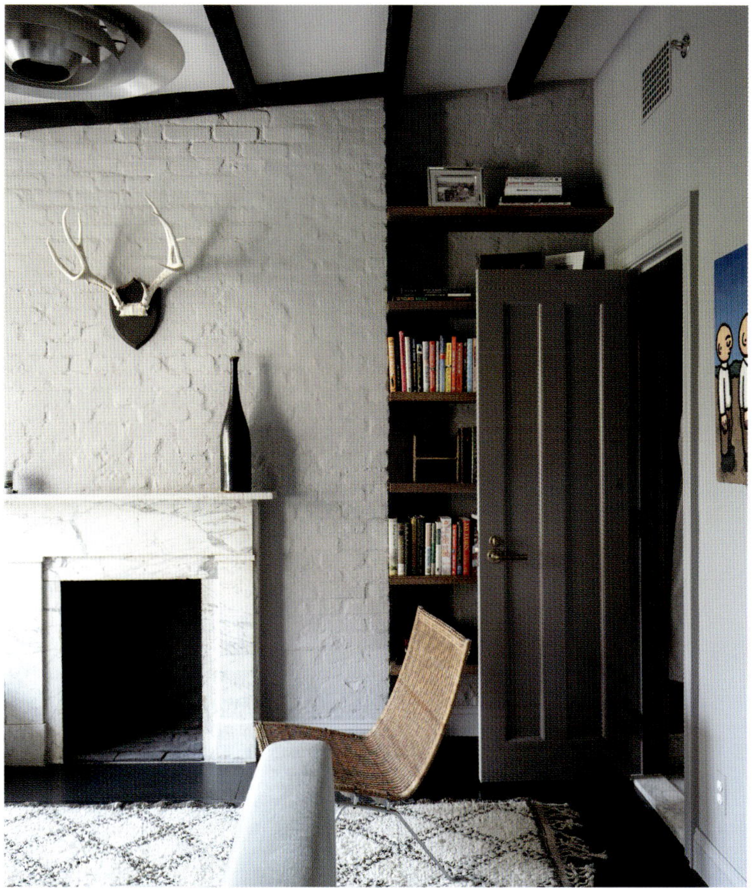
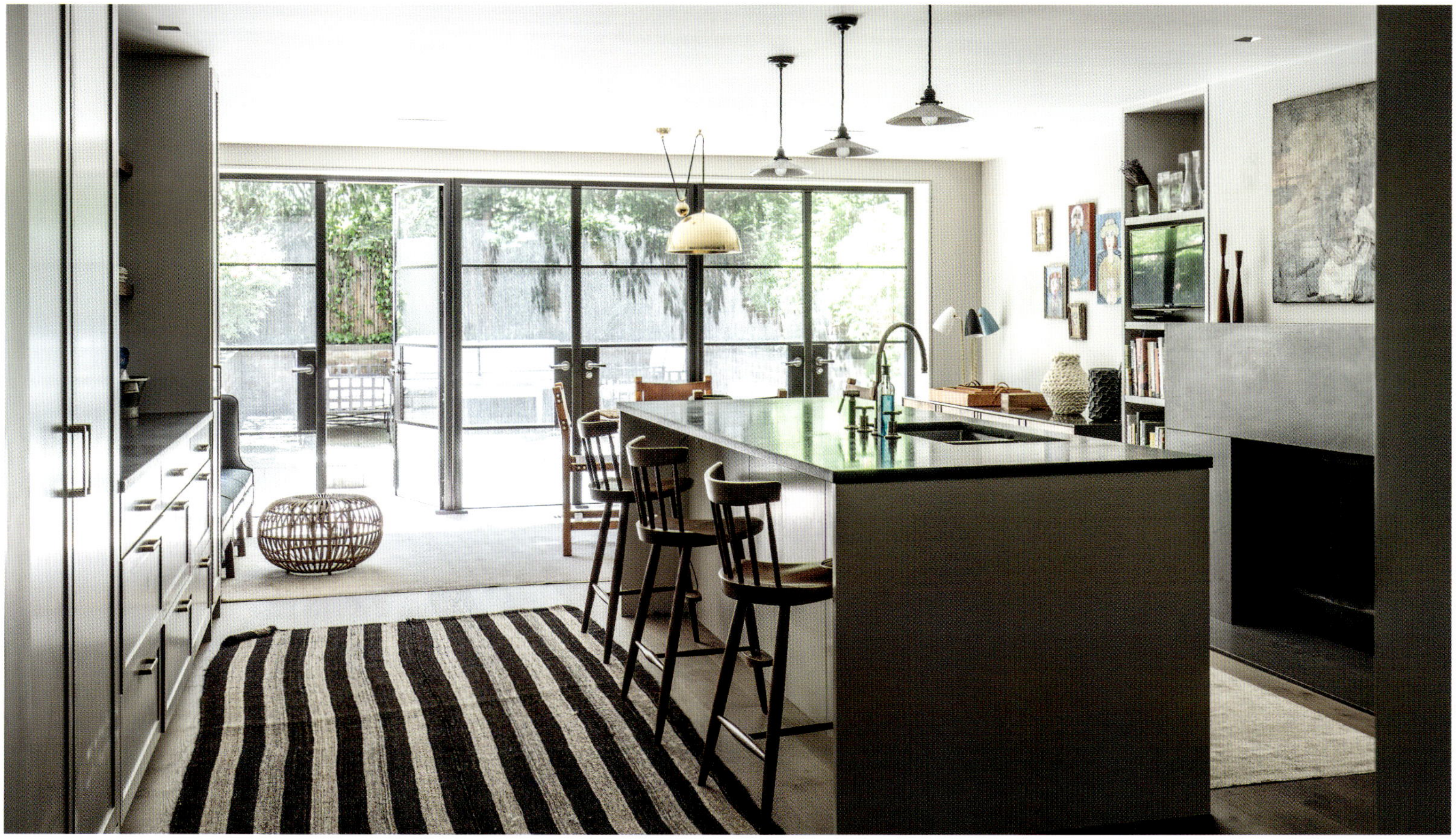

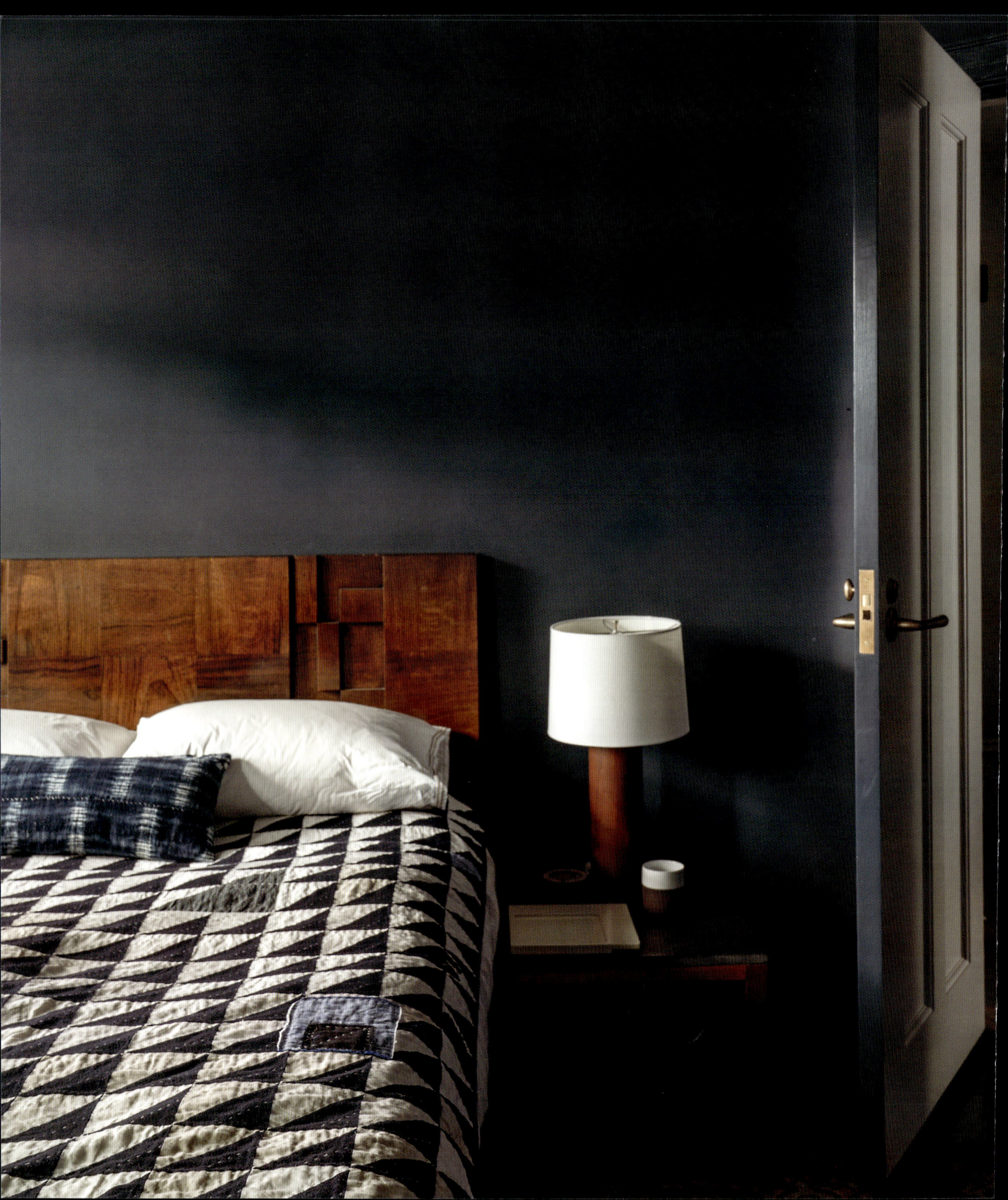

CASE STUDY 4

FACING PAGE
Chic Hague Blue has a therapeutic quality about it, making it perfect for bedrooms. The calm feel of this room is achieved by using the same colour on the walls and trim. It is a truly enveloping space.

BELOW
The walls of this sophisticated bathroom have been painted in warm grey Dove Tale. The stronger shade Down Pipe on the bathtub, set in the centre of the room, makes the space feel both bigger and lighter.

BELOW
This Hague Blue corner of the bedroom feels perfect to relax in — both for the owners and an urban friend.

MANHATTAN CHIC

CASE STUDY 4

MANHATTAN CHIC PALETTE

RECIPE TIPS

* By choosing a neutral group in the Farrow & Ball range, you can decorate with total confidence, knowing that the colours will work harmoniously together.
* Use the strongest tone, in this case Down Pipe in the dining room, in the room where you spend least time during daylight hours.
* Pitch Black in a Full Gloss finish on stair treads and banisters adds a chic twist.
* If the same colour is used on both the units and the walls, the kitchen will expand in size and feel less utilitarian.
* Graduate colour through open-plan spaces, just as Down Pipe, Manor House Gray and Pavilion Gray have been here.

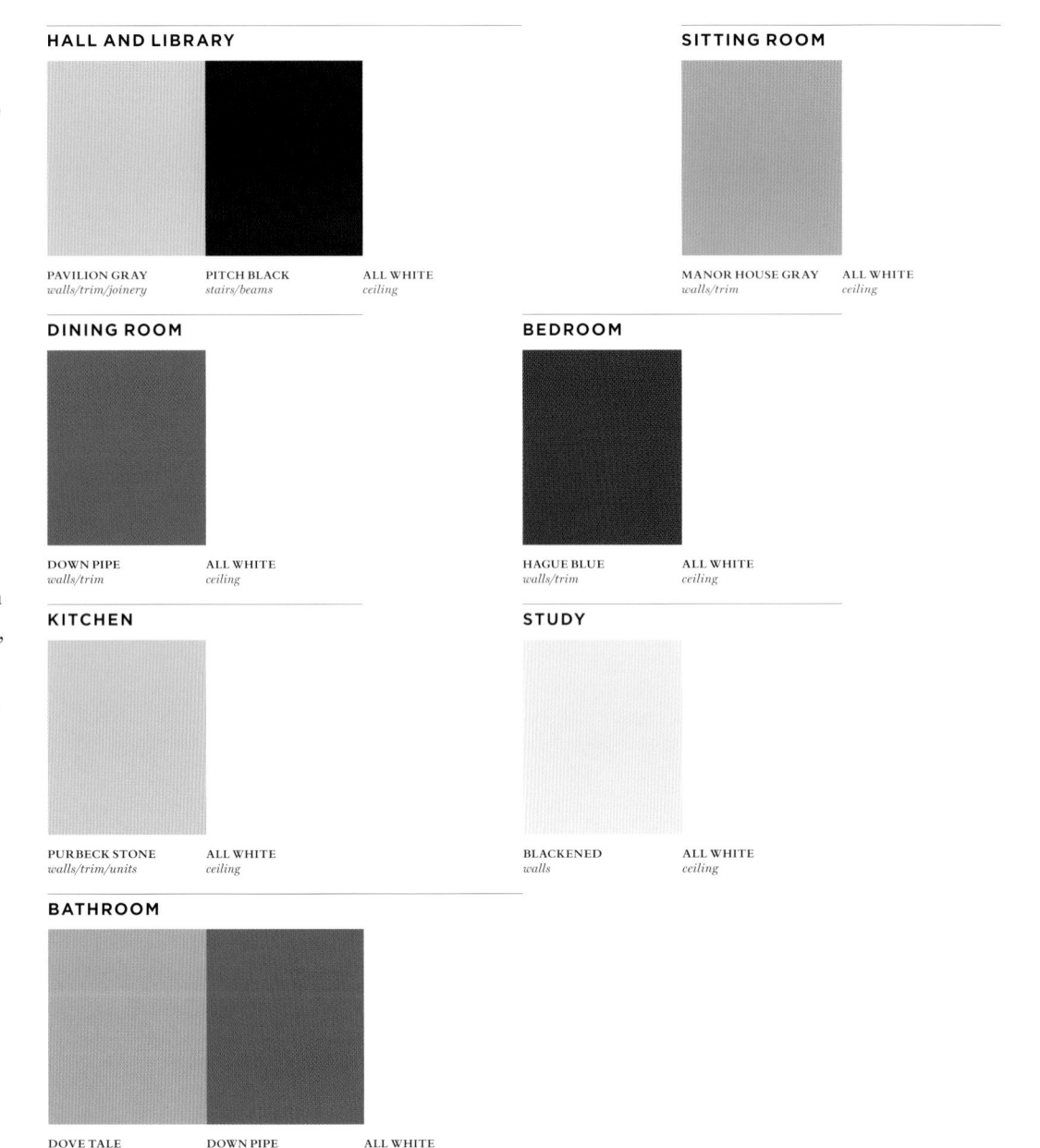

HALL AND LIBRARY

PAVILION GRAY — *walls/trim/joinery*
PITCH BLACK — *stairs/beams*
ALL WHITE — *ceiling*

DINING ROOM

DOWN PIPE — *walls/trim*
ALL WHITE — *ceiling*

KITCHEN

PURBECK STONE — *walls/trim/units*
ALL WHITE — *ceiling*

BATHROOM

DOVE TALE — *walls/trim*
DOWN PIPE — *bath*
ALL WHITE — *ceiling*

SITTING ROOM

MANOR HOUSE GRAY — *walls/trim*
ALL WHITE — *ceiling*

BEDROOM

HAGUE BLUE — *walls/trim*
ALL WHITE — *ceiling*

STUDY

BLACKENED — *walls*
ALL WHITE — *ceiling*

74

CASE STUDIES

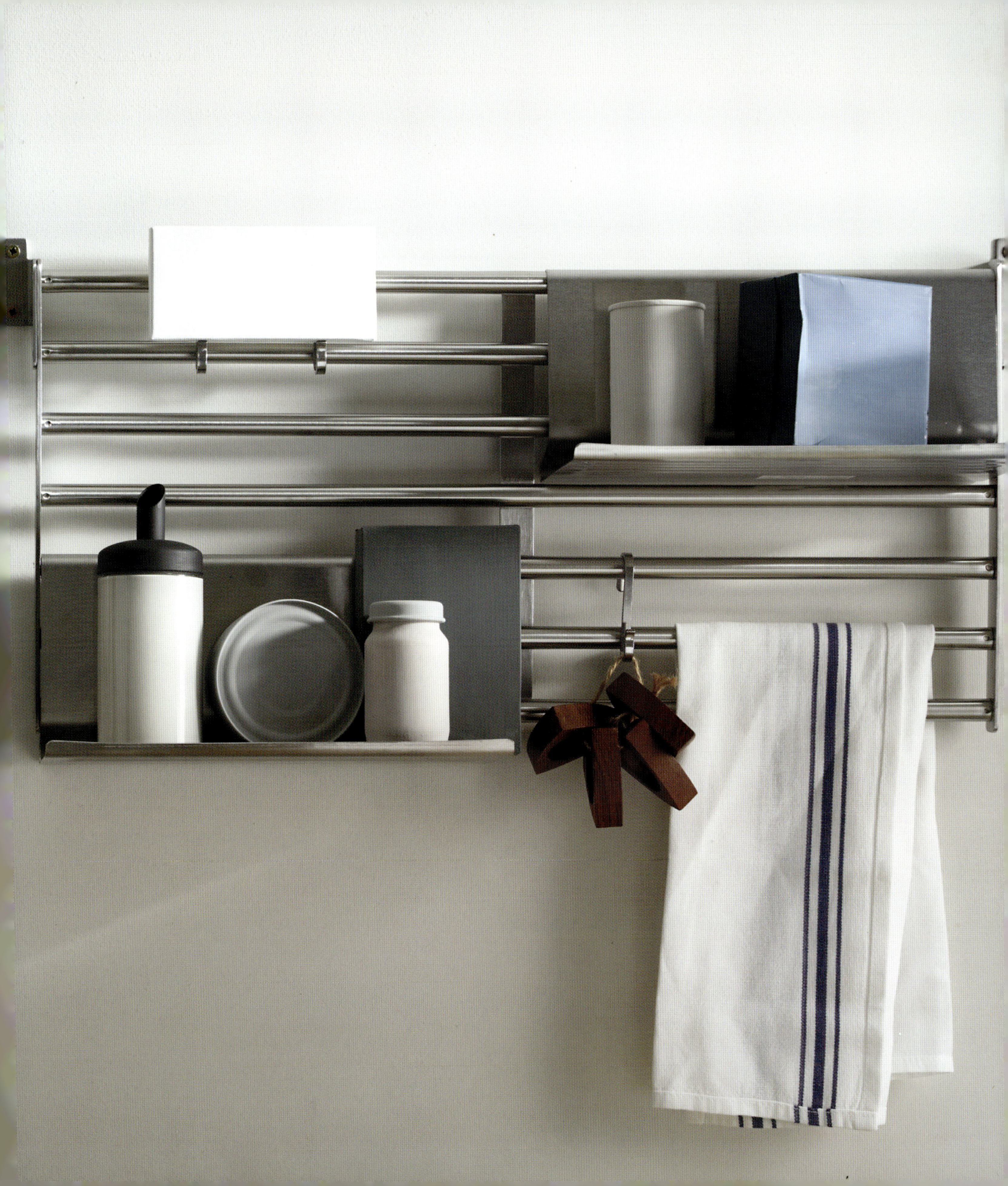

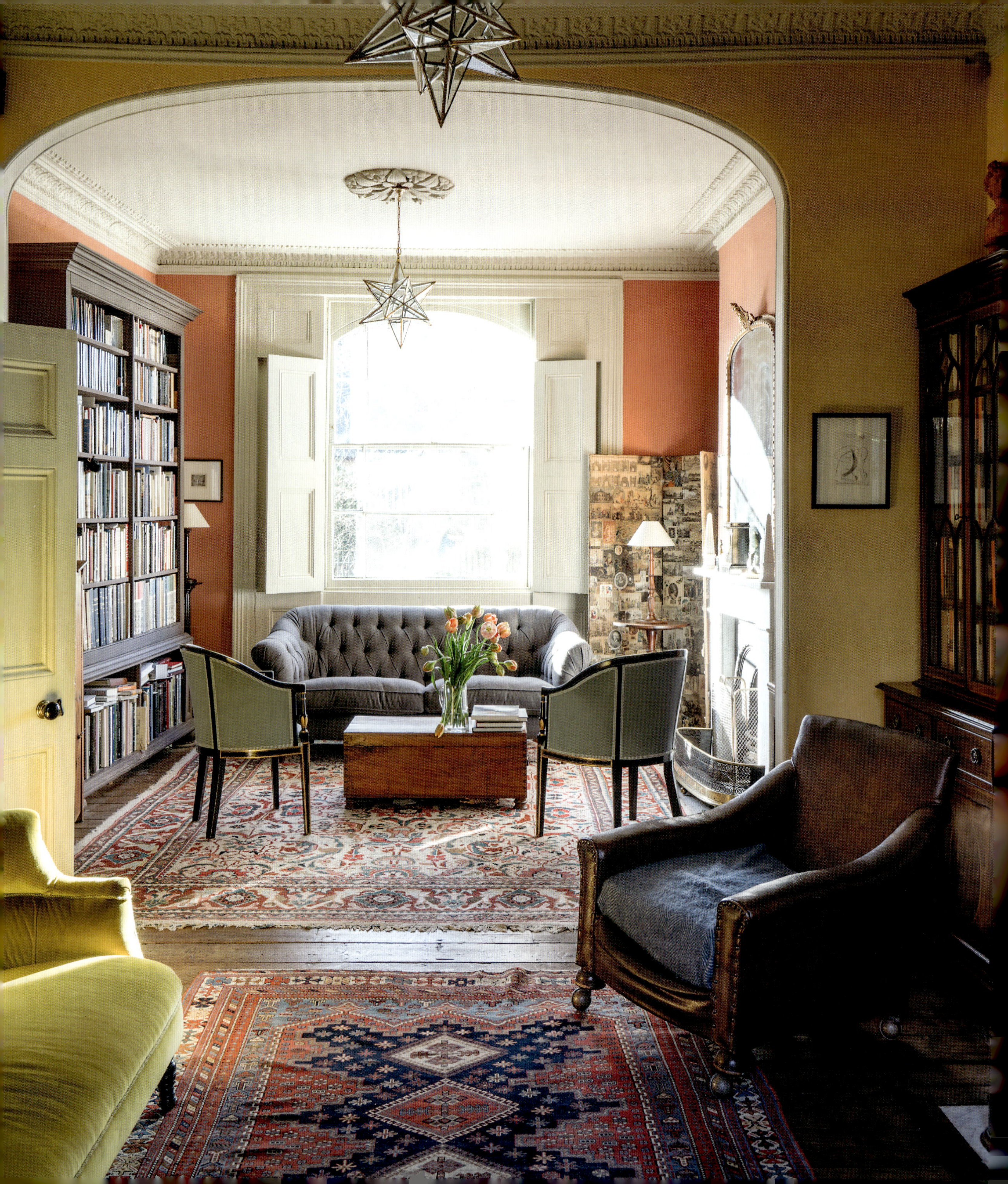

GEORGIAN CLASSIC

The dignified exterior of this Georgian house in north London encapsulates the owners' sensitive approach to decorating. The Shaded White walls, Light Gray woodwork and Black Blue (A) front door feel utterly authentic and tempt us inside to catch a glimpse of one of the most significant restored residential houses in the city.

Period features such as panelling, shutters, fireplaces and cornices have been reintroduced, yet the house retains a remarkable lived-in intimacy. The owner has used Casein Distemper, with its organic feel and very matt finish, on the walls, and Dead Flat on the woodwork, for an extremely tactile surface. They look sublime.

There is a certain modesty to the Cord walls in the hall but they provide enough warmth to be inviting, while Mahogany on the stair spindles and skirting provides depth and drama. It is delightful to see this approach, so loved by contemporary decorators, included several times in this book but being used in its original way.

The deeply coloured walls of the sitting room – beguiling Octagon Yellow (A) and seductive Book Room Red – create an irresistible vista from the hall, which is decidedly understated in comparison. This surprising combination of colours works to perfection.

FACING PAGE AND PAGES 78-9
Sensitive decoration at its best. The choice of Old White on the woodwork, cornices and ceiling is equally important as that of Book Room Red and Octagon Yellow (A) on the walls of this sitting room. Authentic colours that retain the owner's historic style.

INSET ABOVE
This house has been so sensitively restored that even the exterior colours are typical of the time when the house was built. The walls in Shaded White, with Light Gray woodwork and a Black Blue (A) front door feel dignified.

ABOVE
The understated hall, painted in stone-coloured Cord, is as refined as the exterior, and it is likely that its original colour would have been very similar. The magic here comes from the use of Mahogany on the beautifully restored staircase spindles.

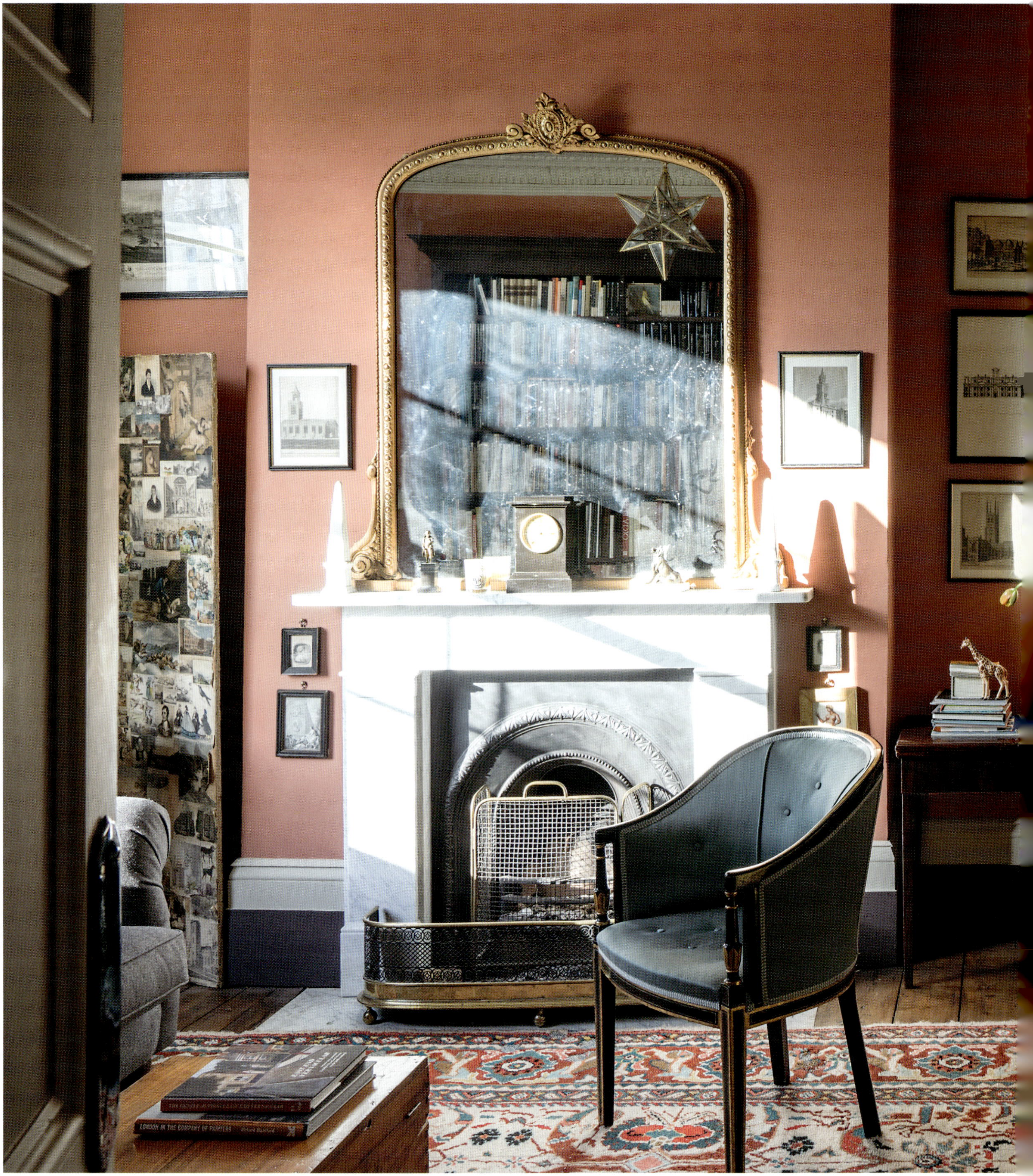
LONDON IN THE COMPANY OF PAINTERS

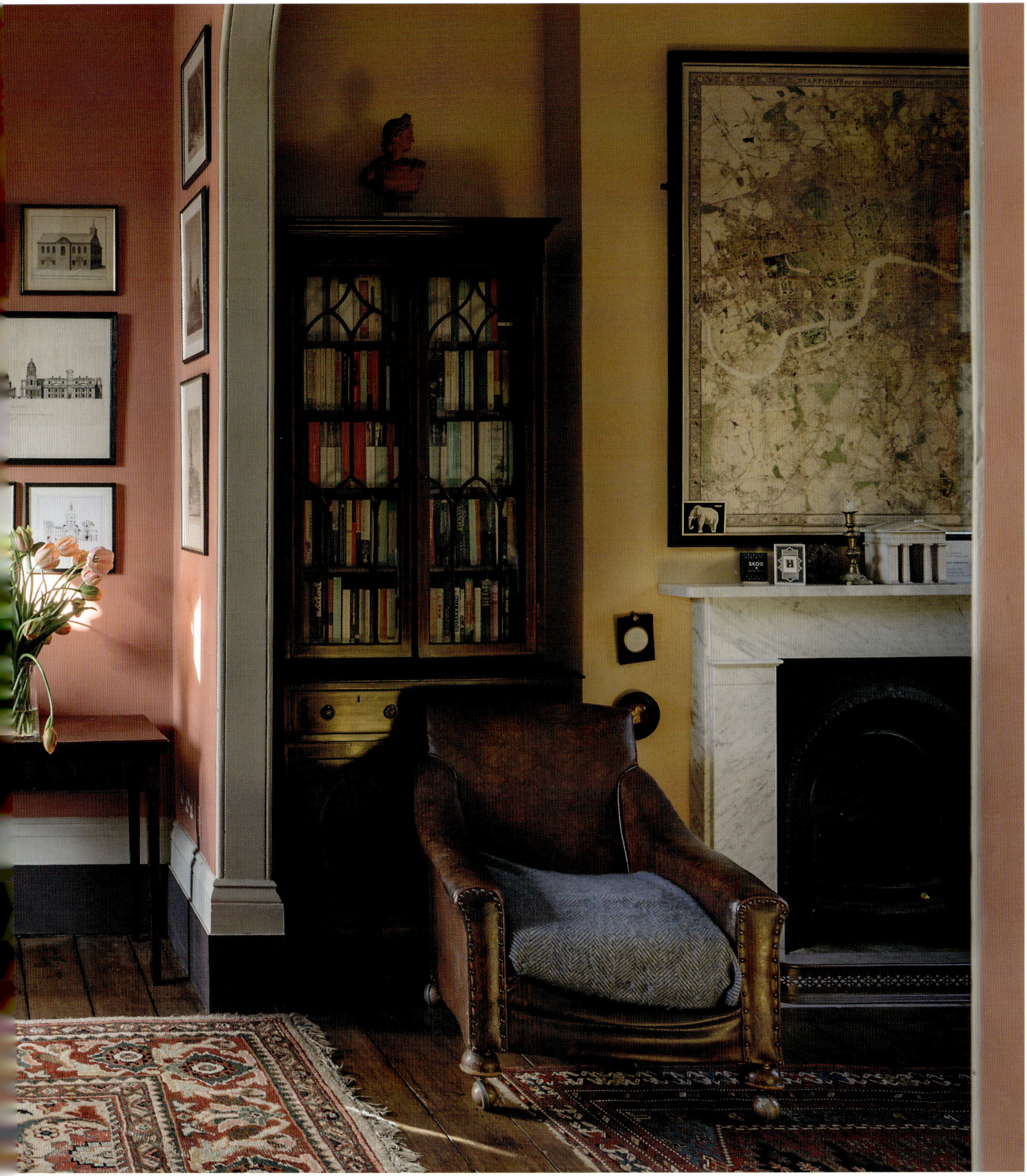

CASE STUDY 5

ABOVE LEFT AND RIGHT
It is hard to believe this kitchen was only recently created. It feels weathered in all the right ways and has a charming modesty. There is something familiar about the Lime White, which is used on both the walls and ceiling to disguise the slightly compromised ceiling height, and the contrasting Off-Black skirting, fire surround and door finger plates, which are both practical and authentic.

CASE STUDY 5

ABOVE
Off-Black appears again on the simple fire surround in the playroom area of the kitchen. This remarkable soft black has the ability to look as if it has never been new.

ABOVE
Stone Blue feels a little more contemporary in style but it has been chosen to inject a bit of fun into this boy's bedroom. Although a little brighter, it still sits seamlessly in the house, having the same saturated nature as the colours in the other rooms. Old White on the ceiling and woodwork maintains continuity.

GEORGIAN CLASSIC

CASE STUDY 5

Despite being from totally different colour families, they both have the same depth of colour, which means that they work seamlessly together. They both also have the ability to change depending on the quality of the light, creating spaces that never fail to surprise. The south-facing part of the sitting room in Book Room Red is filled with light for most of the day, but becomes suitably intimate at night, while the Octagon Yellow (A) part of the room benefits from the light of both south and north aspects, making the character of the space change throughout the course of the day. Mahogany is used again, here on the lower part of the skirting, which grounds the room and gives authenticity.

The north light enters via a lovingly reconstructed Georgian plant room on the back of the house, which brims with light, making it the perfect place to work. Painted in Old White, chosen for its "ready-weathered" look, as is the woodwork throughout most of the house, it appears to have been there forever, a characteristic unique to the Farrow & Ball Traditional Neutrals group of paints.

Another of these Traditional Neutrals has been used in the kitchen (which can seen on page 80), on the lower ground floor, to the same effect. Lime White on the walls, ceiling and woodwork, including the kitchen cupboards, results in a space that feels as if it could be located deep in the country and has remained unchanged for a couple of centuries, despite the fact that it is newly created. There is no trace of following a trend here, just the use of simple colour embellished with Off-Black finger plates, which were painted on the doors by the owners, to match the skirting and fire surrounds. These are a testament to the owners' ability to put together a room in a way that feels nonchalant yet very special. The use of just one colour in this lower ground floorspace makes it feel spacious and light, as well as helping to disguise the slightly compromised height of the ceiling.

Upstairs on the first floor, a lucky little boy has had his bedroom painted in Stone Blue by his discerning parents, a colour that fits perfectly with the palette of the rest of the house but still delivers a nod to childhood. In contrast, the master bedroom is much more serene. Breakfast Room Green feels as if it has been lifted from a pastoral watercolour and is used here to echo the garden square visible through the magnificent windows, with their perfectly renovated shutters and boxes, while the master bathroom, in somewhat moodier Calke Green, has a more functional feel.

ABOVE
On entering this room you might be surprised to discover that it is the master bathroom, where the decoration has the same sensitivity and authenticity as every other room. Sober Calke Green walls result in a really intimate space and are the perfect foil for treasures collected over many years.

FACING PAGE
A restful quality pervades the entire house, but never more so than in the master bedroom, where Breakfast Room Green was selected to reflect the colour of the garden square that it overlooks. The shutters and boxes have been restored and painted in Old White, giving them a weathered look.

82

CASE STUDIES

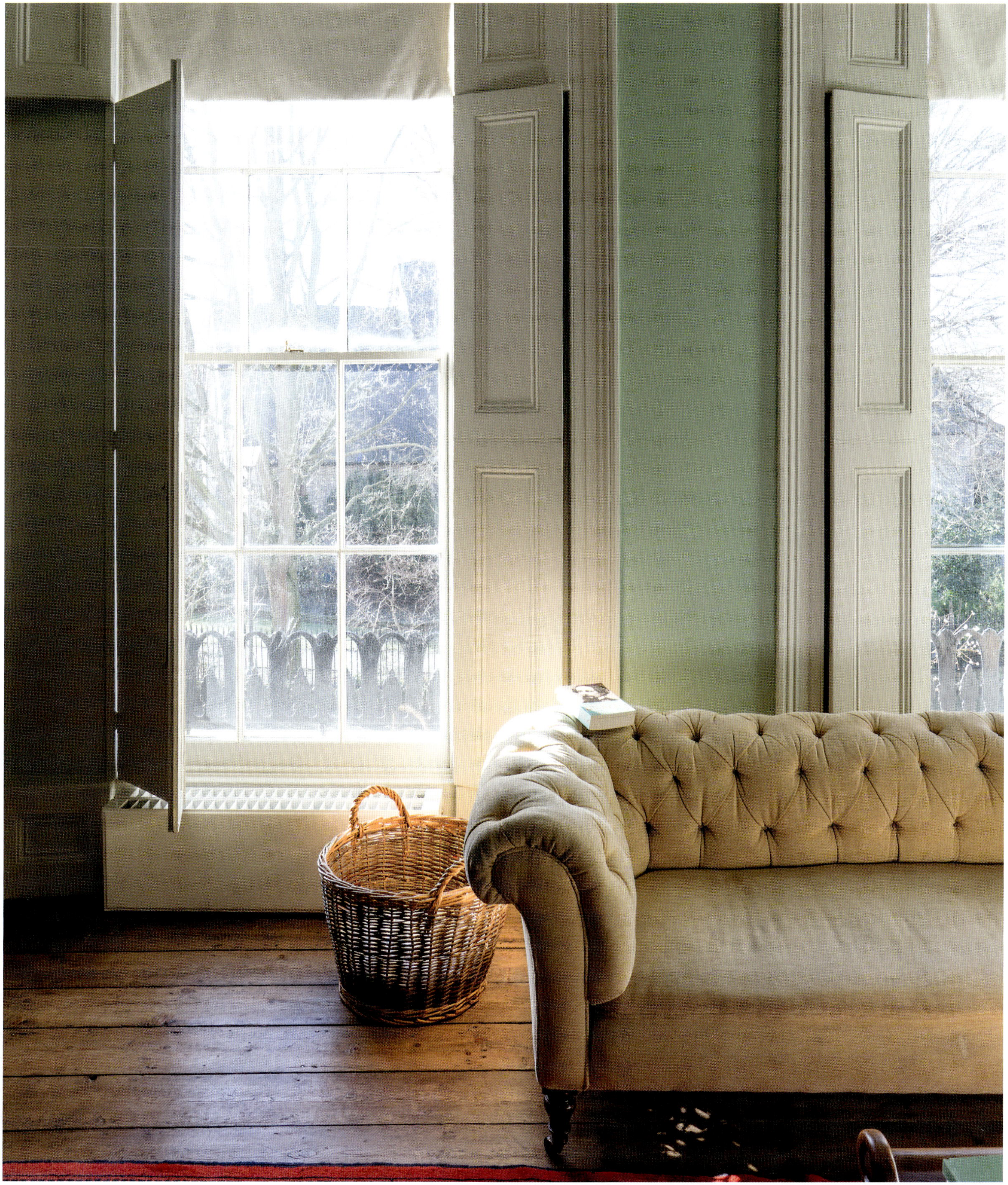

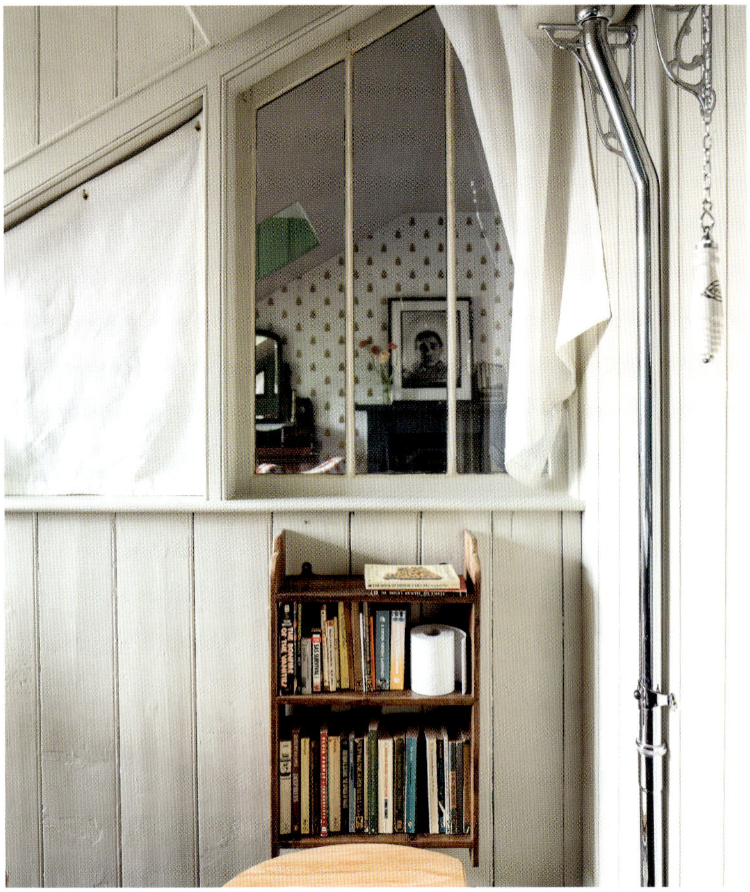

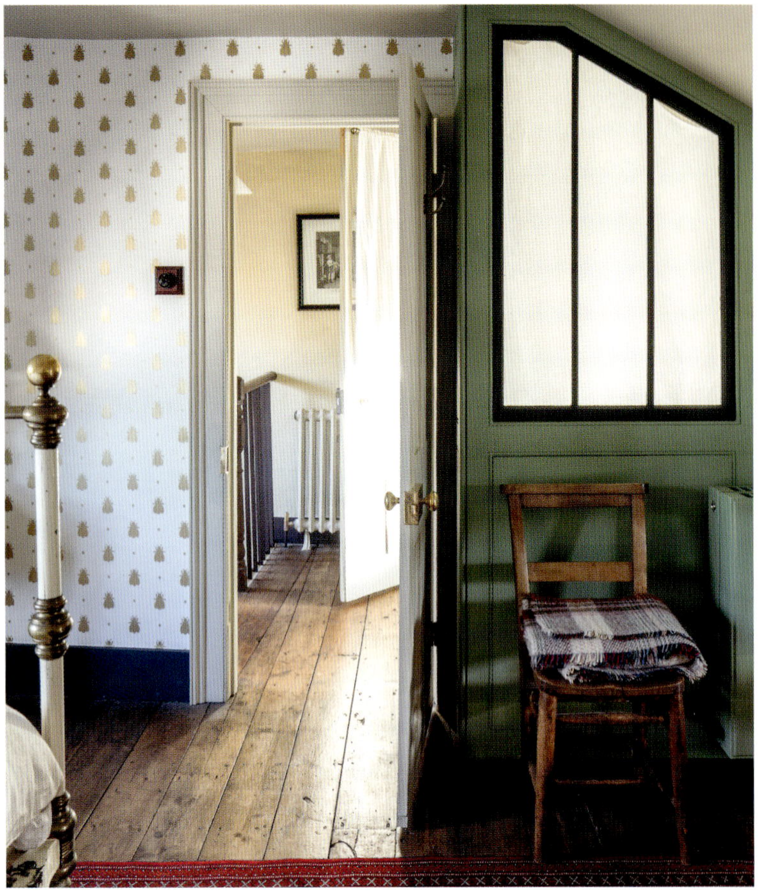

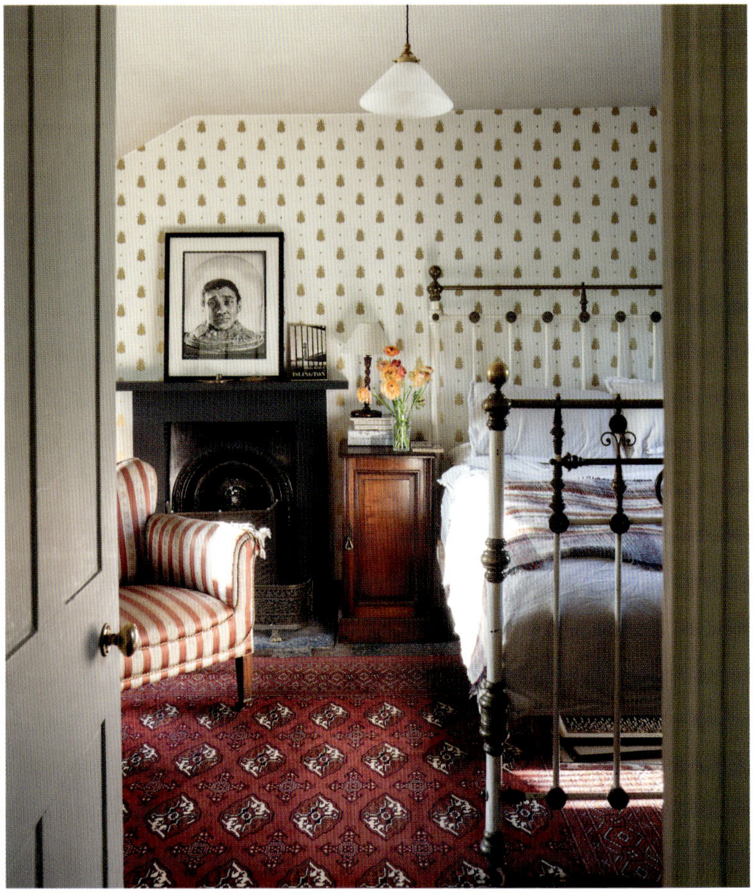

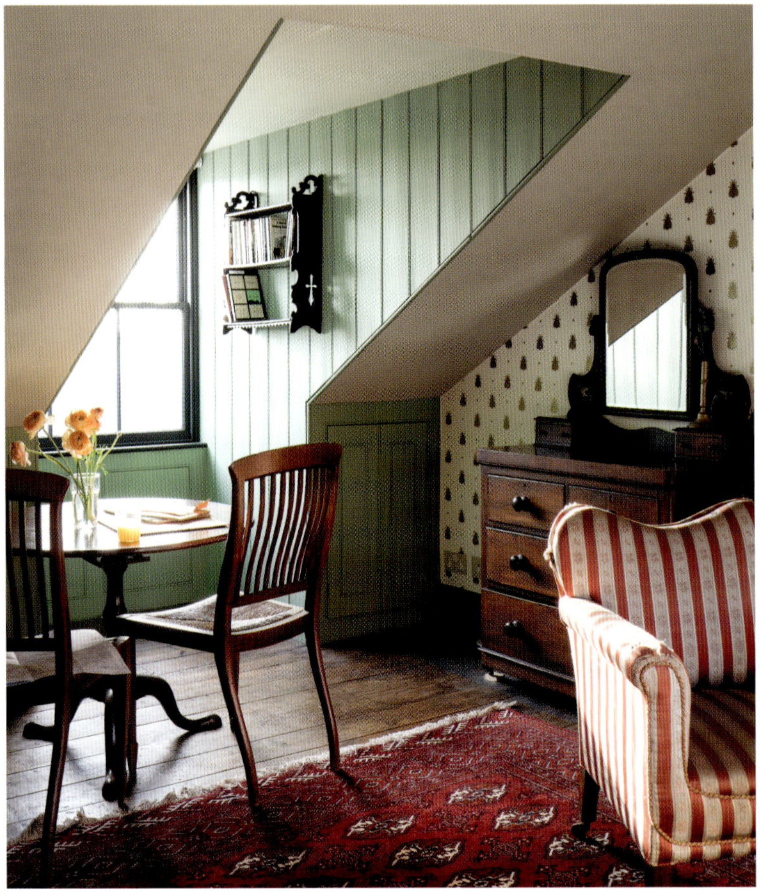

One of the greatest treasures lies at the very top of the house, where a giddy mixture of paint colours and wallpaper in the guest bedroom create an enchanting room that looks totally authentic. Pea Green (A), an old favourite of the owners', has been painted on the panelling, while stronger Studio Green works perfectly on the windows and frames to enhance the garret feel. These have been teamed with a Bumble Bee wallpaper, the pattern of which was originally found on a silk fabric in Joséphine Bonaparte's bedchamber. The playfulness of the wallpaper design, as well as its light background colour, lifts the room and makes it all the more welcoming for guests. An intriguing internal window looks through to the guest bathroom where Stone Blue has been reprised on the walls and Off-Black on the underside of the bath. There is something very comforting about recycling colours in different ways in different rooms, and even in different homes – this owner has reused his favourite colours from a number of previous homes and woven them into a new story.

This house feels like a series of colour events as you wander from one room to another, yet it still feels totally cohesive. And although everything here is deeply considered, it manages not to feel as if every detail has been obsessed over. The decoration in this house is imbued with the heart and soul of a true enthusiast, aesthete and lover of colour – colour that has become a key creative element and not just a trimming.

FACING PAGE
The guest bedroom in the garret is a theatrical space. Pea Green (A) panelling and Studio Green woodwork enhance the old-world feel, but it is the much discussed addition of the Bumble Bee wallpaper that makes this room so charming. Everywhere you look there is an enchanting combination of pattern and colour.

ABOVE
This delightful guest bathroom has an internal window to the guest bedroom (visible in the top pictures on the facing page) so its Stone Blue wall becomes part of the whole tantalizing colour mix. The Off-Black underside of the bathtub looks particularly wonderful in combination with the polished floorboards.

GEORGIAN CLASSIC PALETTE

RECIPE TIPS

* Use a dark colour, such as Mahogany, on skirting throughout the house to unite rooms and give an increased sense of flow.
* Use two different colours of the same depth in interconnecting spaces, as in this sitting room.
* Don't be afraid to use a dark colour on woodwork in some rooms but not others.
* Farrow & Ball have many specialist paint finishes to suit different tastes and locations. Dead Flat has been used on all of the walls in this house to enhance its historic feel.
* Our Archive colours, of which Pea Green (A) is one, are always available to order – discover them in your nearest showroom (see page 262).

EXTERIOR
SHADED WHITE *walls* | BLACK BLUE (A) *front door* | LIGHT GRAY *woodwork*

FRONT SITTING ROOM
MAHOGANY *skirting* | BOOK ROOM RED *walls* | OLD WHITE *wood/cornice/ceiling*

KITCHEN
LIME WHITE *all* | OFF-BLACK *skirting/fireplace/finger plates*

MASTER BATHROOM
MAHOGANY *skirting* | CALKE GREEN *walls* | OLD WHITE *wood/cornice/ceiling*

HALL
MAHOGANY *skirting/spindles* | CORD *walls* | OLD WHITE *wood/cornice/ceiling*

BACK SITTING ROOM
MAHOGANY *skirting* | OCTAGON YELLOW (A) *walls* | OLD WHITE *wood/cornice/ceiling*

MASTER BEDROOM
MAHOGANY *skirting* | BREAKFAST ROOM GREEN *walls* | OLD WHITE *wood/cornice/ceiling*

BOY'S BEDROOM
MAHOGANY *skirting* | STONE BLUE *walls* | OLD WHITE *wood/cornice/ceiling*

GUEST BEDROOM AND BATHROOM
MAHOGANY *skirting* | BUMBLE BEE 507 *walls* | STUDIO GREEN *woodwork* | PEA GREEN (A) *panelling* | LIME WHITE *walls/ceiling* | STONE BLUE *walls* | OFF-BLACK *bath*

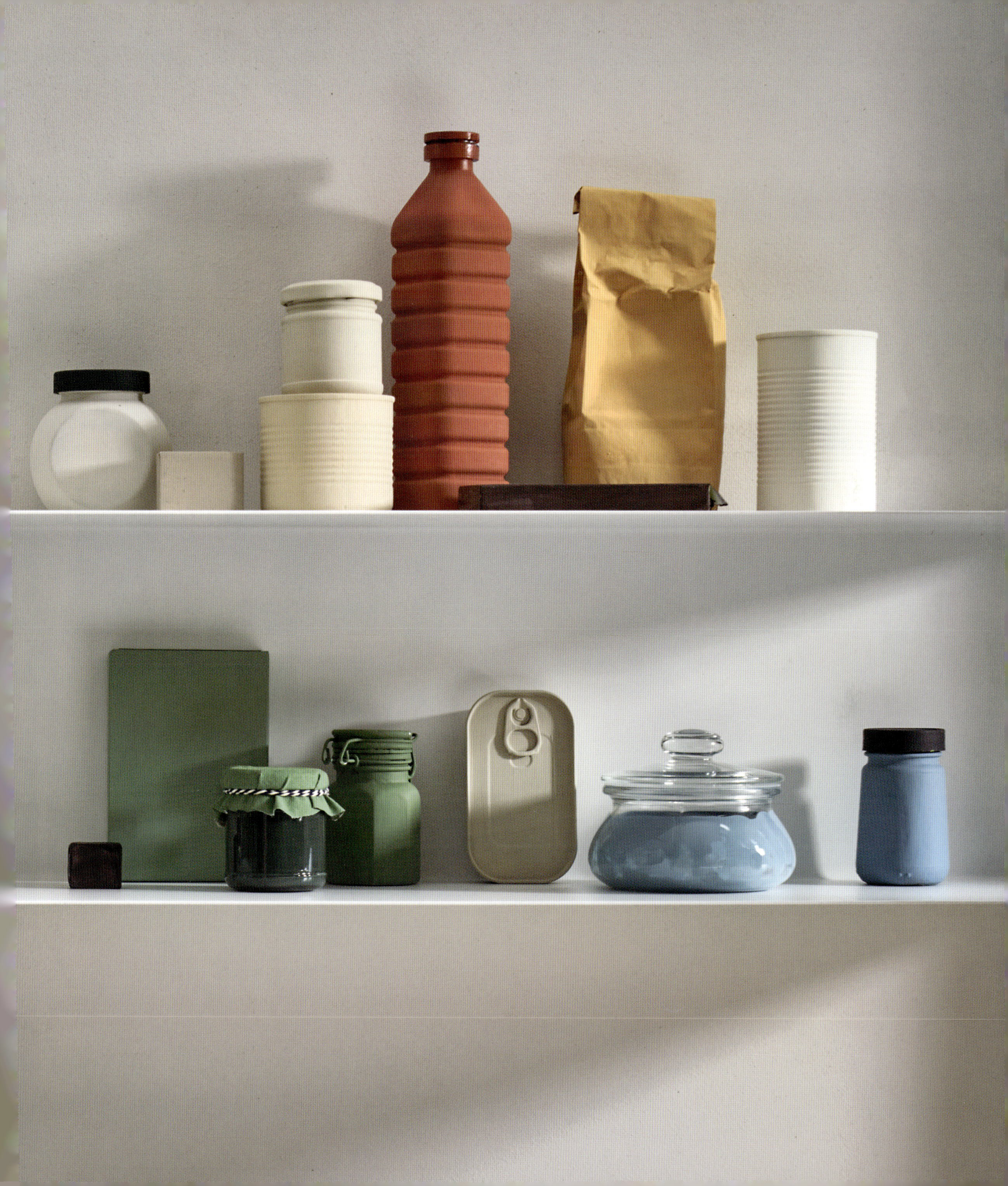

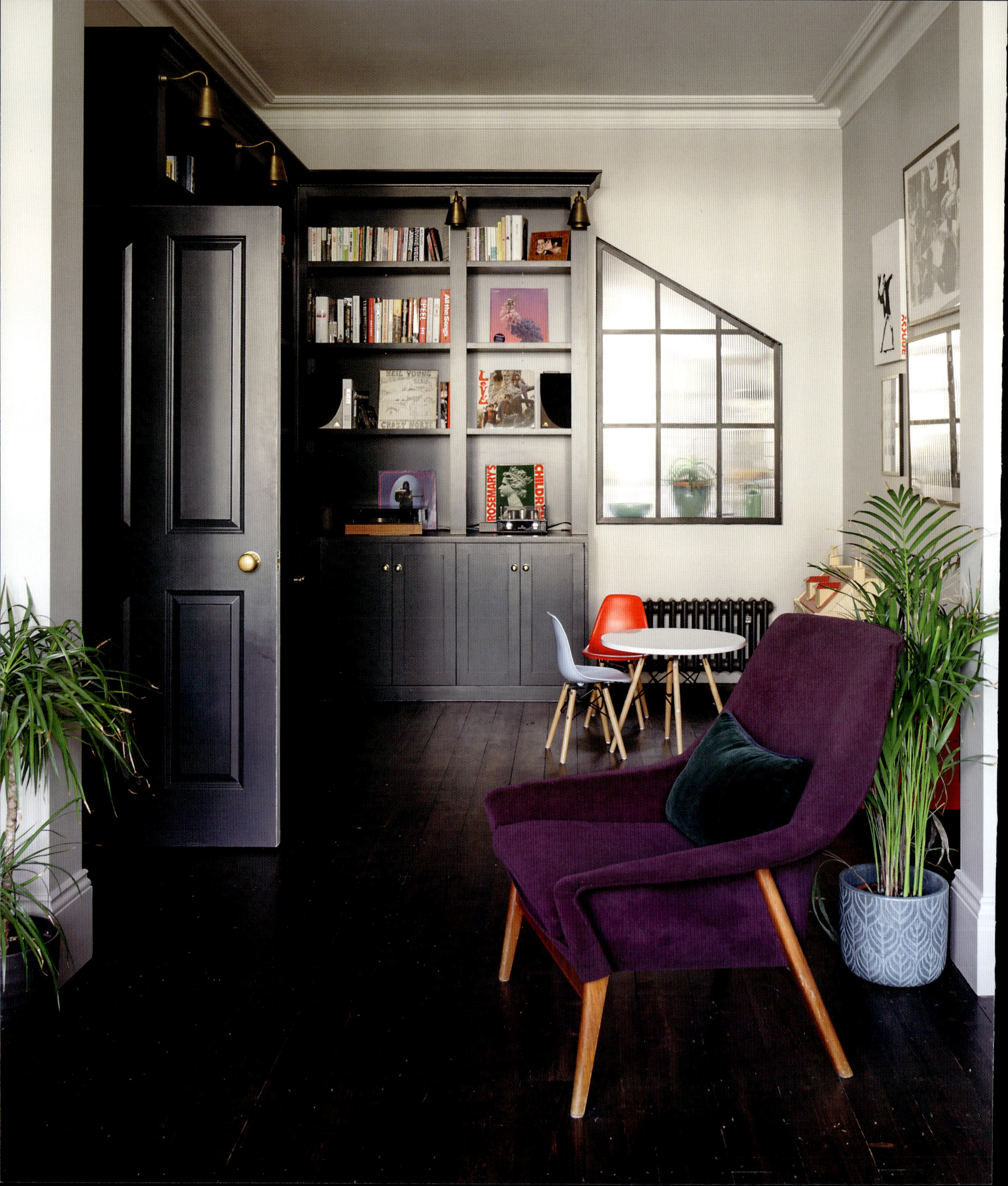
All the Songs
NEIL YOUNG
CRAZY HORSE
ROSEMARY'S

CASE STUDY 6

MODERN FAMILY

One of the joys of working as a Farrow & Ball Colour Consultant is that every house, and every client, is different. Some people want reassurance that the colours they are considering are going to work for their space and light. Others want the responsibility of making the colour decisions taken away from them altogether. For me, the best jobs are when the client has a keen design sense but is also open to all the wonderful things that colour can achieve. This client was interested in a kaleidoscope of colour, and this has resulted in a home that is full of fun yet effortlessly stylish.

It was a bold decision to paint the entrance hall in strong colours, but one that has resulted in an exceptionally special space. Inchyra Blue, with its complex mix of blue, green and grey, has been used in two finishes on the walls. Full Gloss on the bottom half creates an extremely durable surface for the boisterous young family, as well as serving to bounce light around in a typically narrow space. Swapping to chalky matt Estate Emulsion on the top half creates a little design twist and feels super-stylish. The drama continues with Railings on the trim. With its underlying blue tone, this is the perfect complement to both Inchyra Blue and the original floor tiles, where a solid black would feel too hard.

FACING PAGE
Understated and cool grey Dimpse on the sitting room walls is brought alive when combined with dramatic Railings, which is used as an accent all over this house, creating a pleasing link between rooms.

INSET ABOVE
You know you are in for a decorative treat when greeted with this exuberant, bespoke-coloured front door.

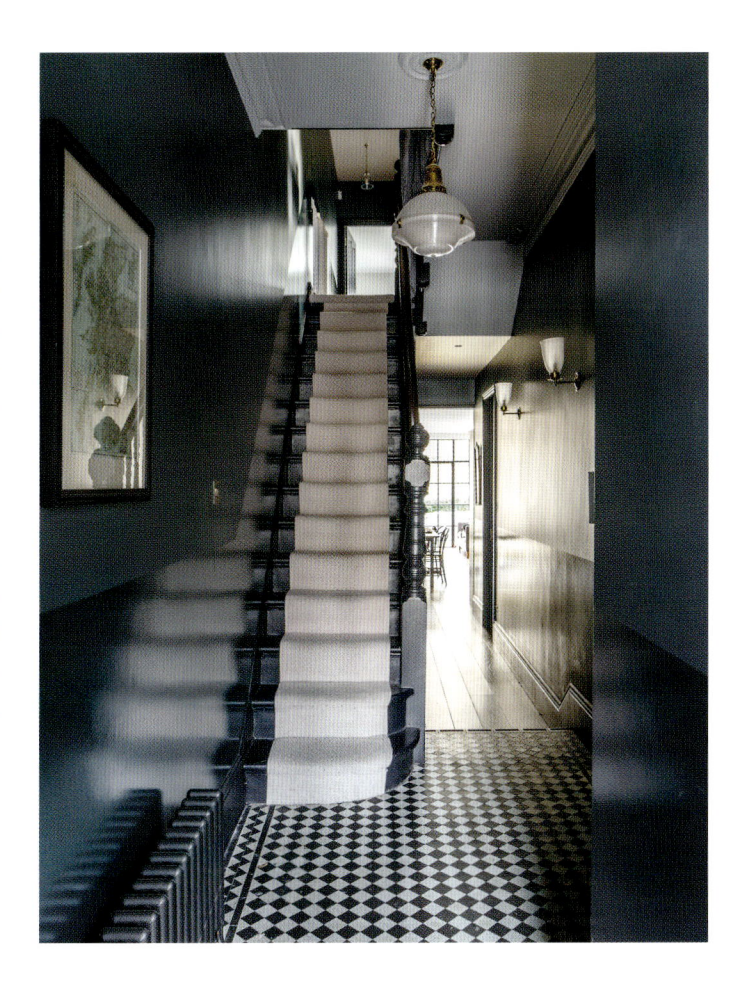

ABOVE
Moody Inchyra Blue on the walls of the hall creates drama, while Railings on the woodwork reflects the colour of the Victorian floor tiles. One of the joys of having such a densely coloured entrance is that when you pass into the rooms leading off it, they feel full of light. Here, the bright kitchen draws you through the house like a moth to a flame.

89

MODERN FAMILY

CASE STUDY 6

The strong-coloured hall draws you through the house to the light of the kitchen. As you pass by Railings on the cupboards under the stairs, you catch a glimpse of the same colour on the kitchen units – a perfect way of creating flow in a house. As in most families, the majority of time at home is spent in the kitchen, so we wanted to make it as light as possible, without defaulting to white. Peignoir, a colour created to prove that pink is not just for girls on account of its underlying grey tone, covers walls, trim and ceiling. By taking the colour over the ceiling, it disguises the slope of the side extension and therefore makes the space feel bigger. Although not overtly pink in this light-filled space, the colour adds both warmth and interest alongside the metal doors and brass fittings. The moody units are not only perfectly on trend, but also make the room feel lighter due to their extreme contrast with the walls.

At the back of the kitchen, a small space has been cleverly moulded into a pantry area, where an internal window (painted in Railings to match the units) allows light to spill through into the part-library, part-playroom end of the sitting room (see page 88). The walls at this end of the sitting room are painted in cool Dimpse,

ABOVE LEFT
Such bold decorating is practical and bang on trend, perfect for a fashionable house with a lively young family. Inchyra Blue in a Full Gloss finish is used on the bottom half of the walls in the hall while the same colour in Estate Emulsion is painted above. There is no need for a dado rail — the look is far too modern.

LEFT
This rather awkward space, made into a pantry, is one of the family's favourite areas. It benefits hugely from the borrowed light flooding through the internal window to the sitting room, which has been painted in Railings in an Estate Eggshell finish, to match the units and retain a slightly industrial feel.

FACING PAGE
It is brave to choose pink for your kitchen when it is presumed that the walls should be white, but it is fabulous twists such as this that make this home so special. Peignoir is used on the walls, trim and ceiling, so as not to compromise the height of the room and to prevent the overall look from becoming jarring.

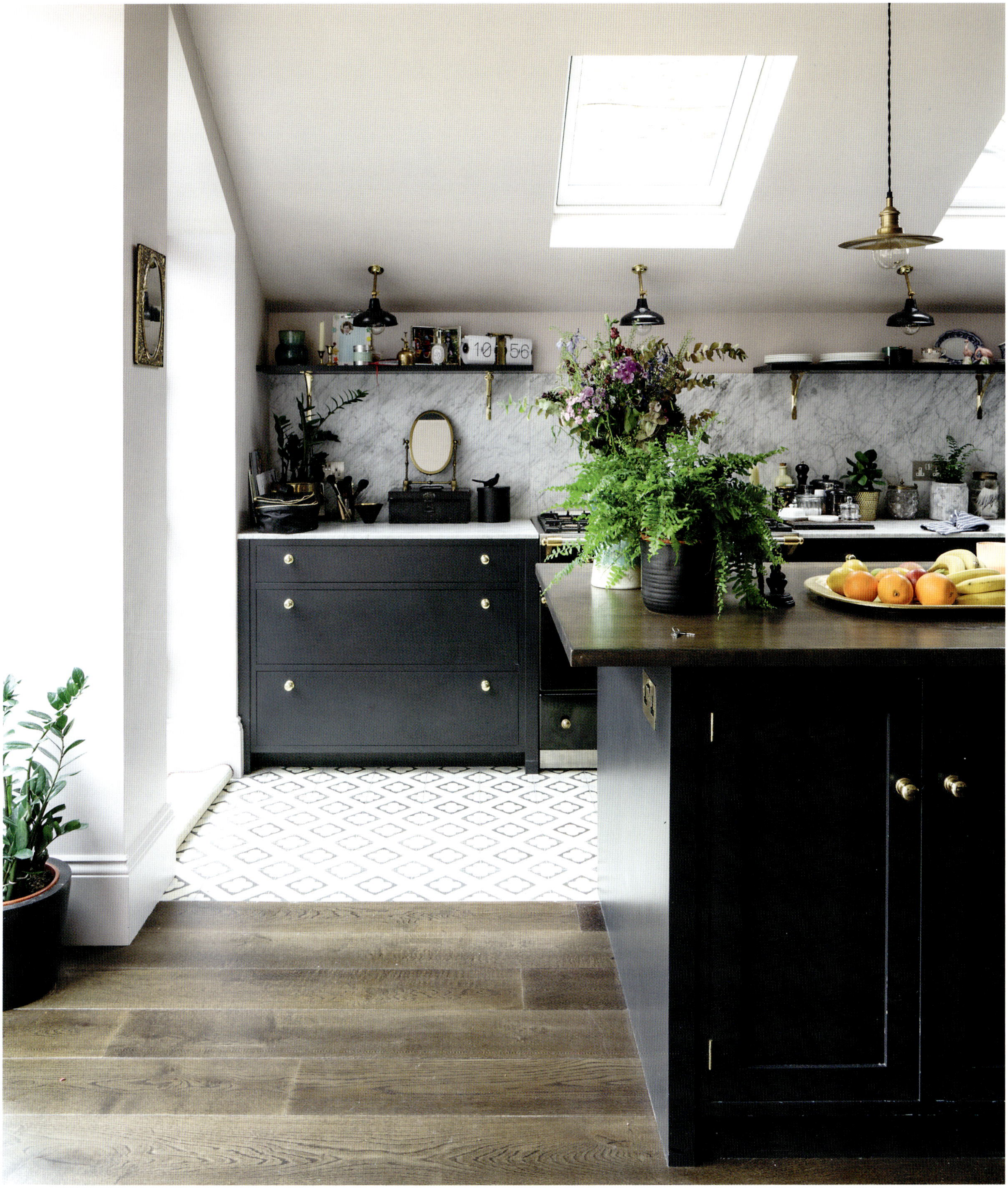
10 56

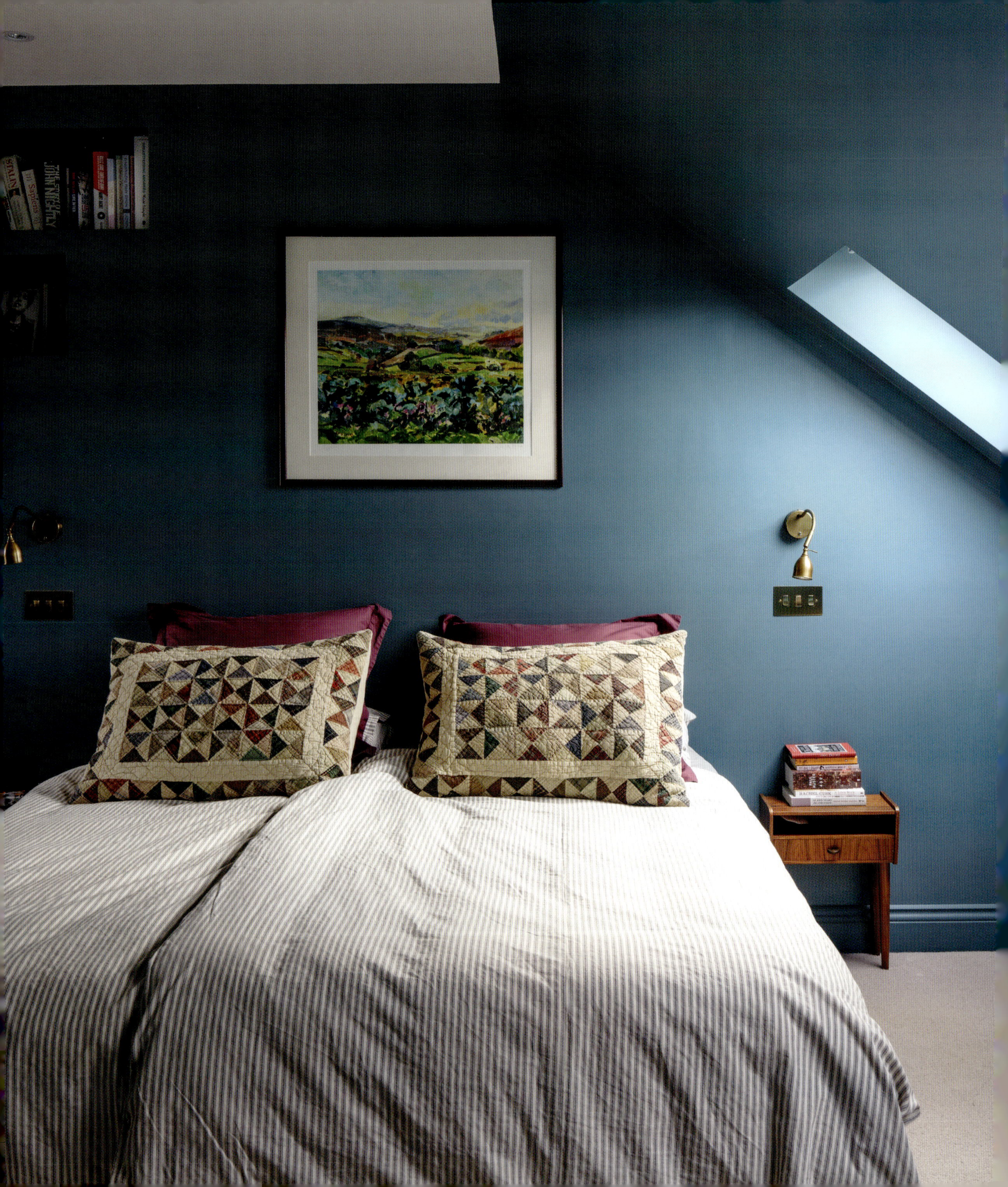

the colour of twilight, according to West Country dialect, while in the front part of the room the complementary but stronger Pavilion Gray creates a little more impact. Many people would be wary of using two different colours in this way, worrying that it would break up the space, but here it is seamless and evens out the light conditions to perfection. Again, Railings has been used on the joinery at both ends of the room to tie the two areas together and connect them to the rest of the ground floor.

The master bedroom has been cleverly carved out of an attic space. Here, once more, the colour of the walls does not disappoint. Archive colour Claydon Blue (A) makes the room feel like a natural extension of the hall, being a lighter version of Inchyra Blue. Although it has been taken over the trim for a contemporary feel, the ceiling has been left a crisp white so as to bounce light entering through the skylight windows around the room.

The drama continues with a study painted in Archive colour Olive (A), resulting in a protective and soothing environment in which to work. It is also the perfect colour adjoining the hall. The door to this room is always left open to make use of all available light, and a glimpse of Olive (A) inside cannot fail to make you curious about the room. Used on both the walls and the trim, it makes the room feel both bigger and calmer.

FACING PAGE
The master bedroom has been painted in Claydon Blue (A), chosen for its cocooning effect. It also flows naturally from the slightly darker Inchyra Blue hall. The ceiling in Strong White reflects any available light.

RIGHT
The view from the master bedroom into the en suite bathroom brings some well-deserved calm. Worsted, an accent from the ever-popular Easy Neutrals group of paints, looks elegant and uncomplicated on the walls.

CASE STUDY 6

BELOW
Stopping the wall colour shy of the ceiling reduces the perceived height of a room. In this bedroom, Brassica is accompanied by Ammonite over the ceiling, moulding and onto the walls.

FACING PAGE, TOP
Skylight is always a popular choice for children's rooms. Here, it benefits from west-facing light and feels soft and inviting. A wall-to-wall run of cupboards in Stiffkey Blue acts as a feature wall.

FACING PAGE, BOTTOM LEFT
A band in Oval Room Blue flows at low level around the guest bedroom. Taken over the doors, walls and joinery, it adds a decorative twist and makes the Ammonite above it appear lighter.

FACING PAGE, BOTTOM RIGHT
Sometimes choosing paint colours is easy. These floor tiles were simply crying out to be combined with Setting Plaster, a colour which is also always flattering in a bathroom.

The lucky children who live here are certainly not deprived of colour. Brassica is used in the girl's bedroom, where its lavender tones feel charming, and its warmth lifts the cold north-facing light without being overtly red. This time we stopped the colour a small distance from the coving in order to reduce the perceived ceiling height and make the room feel cosier.

The tried-and-tested combination of Skylight and Stiffkey Blue has been used in the adjacent boy's bedroom. Having the darker Stiffkey Blue on the floor-to-ceiling cupboards, which stretch the full width of the room, creates, in effect, a striking feature wall.

The guest bedroom has purposefully been left a little less colourful to give guests the opportunity to escape the exciting tones featured elsewhere in the house. However, it felt too sad to leave it totally neutral, albeit it in stylish Ammonite, so Oval Room Blue has been introduced to the bottom of the room and taken over both the walls and woodwork. Although a fairly strong colour, it does not darken the room, because it is used below the eyeline; instead, it opens the room out and makes it feel lighter than if it had been left in one neutral tone. And, of course, it introduces a quirky decorative element that feels perfect in this house.

In the family bathroom, the client had already chosen some stylish floor tiles that just begged to be used with the dusty pink-coloured Setting Plaster on the walls. Together, they have created another little oasis of perfectly paired colour.

There are many, many decorating tricks used in this house, the most significant being painting the walls of the hall in dramatic Inchyra Blue and the woodwork in Railings, so that the rooms leading off the space feel large, bright and inviting. The wall colour also acts as the perfect strong spine to ground the sensational tones used elsewhere. Although not everyone would want to live in such highly coloured surroundings, this house cannot fail to make you smile because it perfectly reflects its equally colourful occupants.

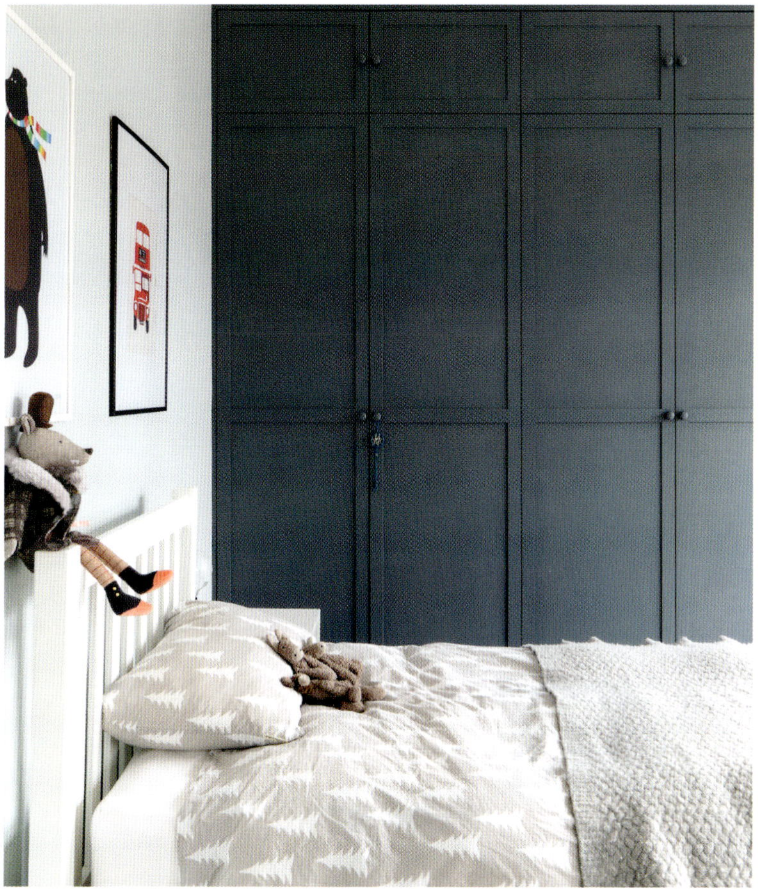
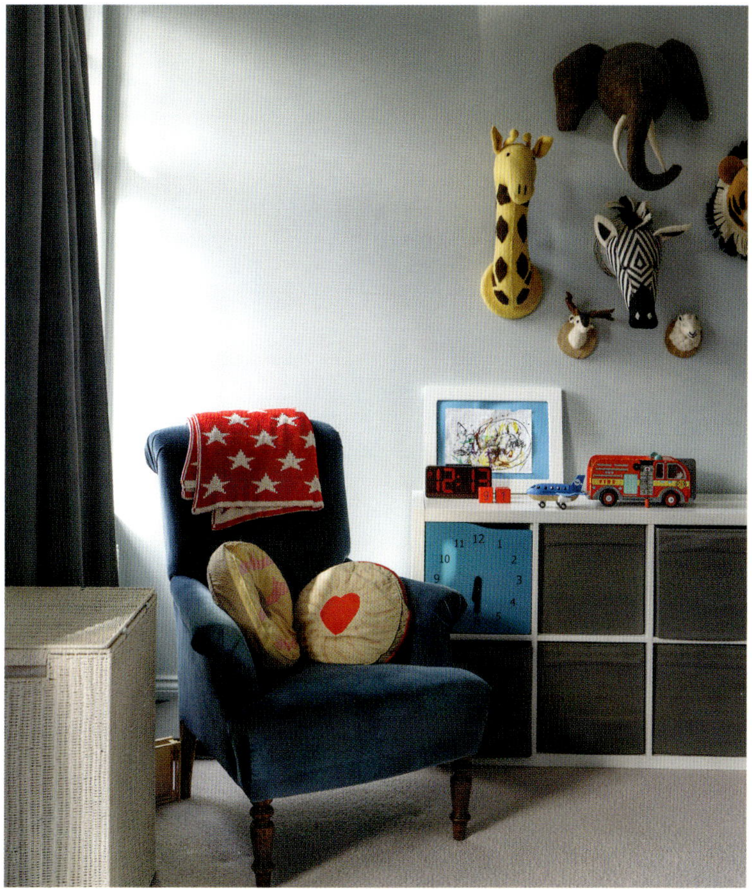
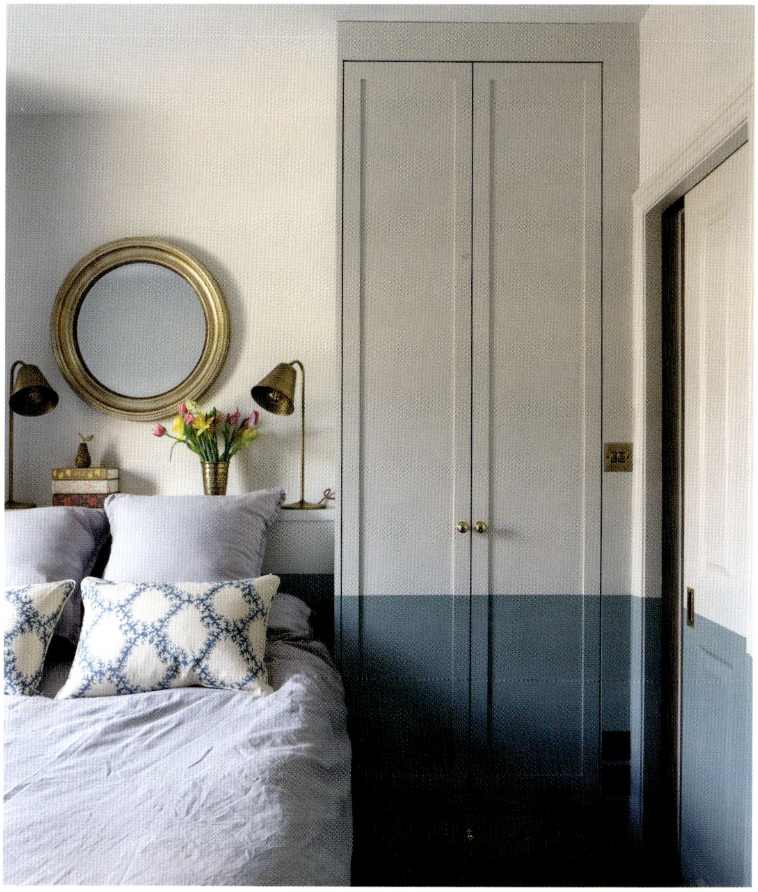
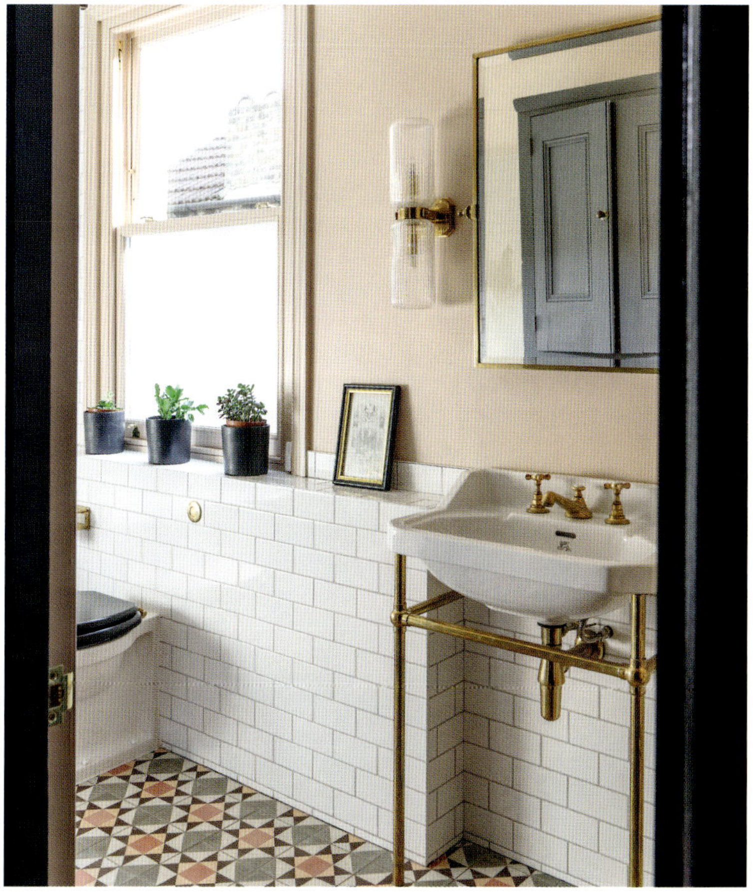

CASE STUDY 6

MODERN FAMILY PALETTE

RECIPE TIPS

* A strong colour, such as Inchyra Blue, used in a hall will make the rooms leading off it look huge and filled with light.
* Using Full Gloss on the bottom half of a wall is both stylish and practical.
* Repeat one colour as an accent throughout the house, just as Railings has been here, to create a sense of flow.
* Extend the ceiling colour onto the top part of the walls to make a child's room feel more intimate.
* Run the same colour over walls and woodwork for extra design appeal.

HALL, STAIRS AND LANDINGS

INCHYRA BLUE
walls

RAILINGS
trim

STRONG WHITE
cornice/ceiling

SITTING ROOM

DIMPSE
walls (back)

PAVILION GRAY
walls (front)

RAILINGS
woodwork

STRONG WHITE
ceiling

KITCHEN

PEIGNOIR
walls/ceiling/woodwork

RAILINGS
units/island/internal window

FAMILY BATHROOM

SETTING PLASTER
walls/wood

STRONG WHITE
ceiling

GUEST BEDROOM

OVAL ROOM BLUE
walls to dado

AMMONITE
walls above dado

STRONG WHITE
ceiling

GIRL'S BEDROOM

BRASSICA
walls/wood

AMMONITE
ceiling/moulding/walls

MASTER BEDROOM

CLAYDON BLUE (A)
walls/trim

STRONG WHITE
ceiling

BOY'S BEDROOM

SKYLIGHT
walls/wood

STIFFKEY BLUE
cupboards

STRONG WHITE
ceiling

MASTER EN SUITE

WORSTED
all

96

CASE STUDIES

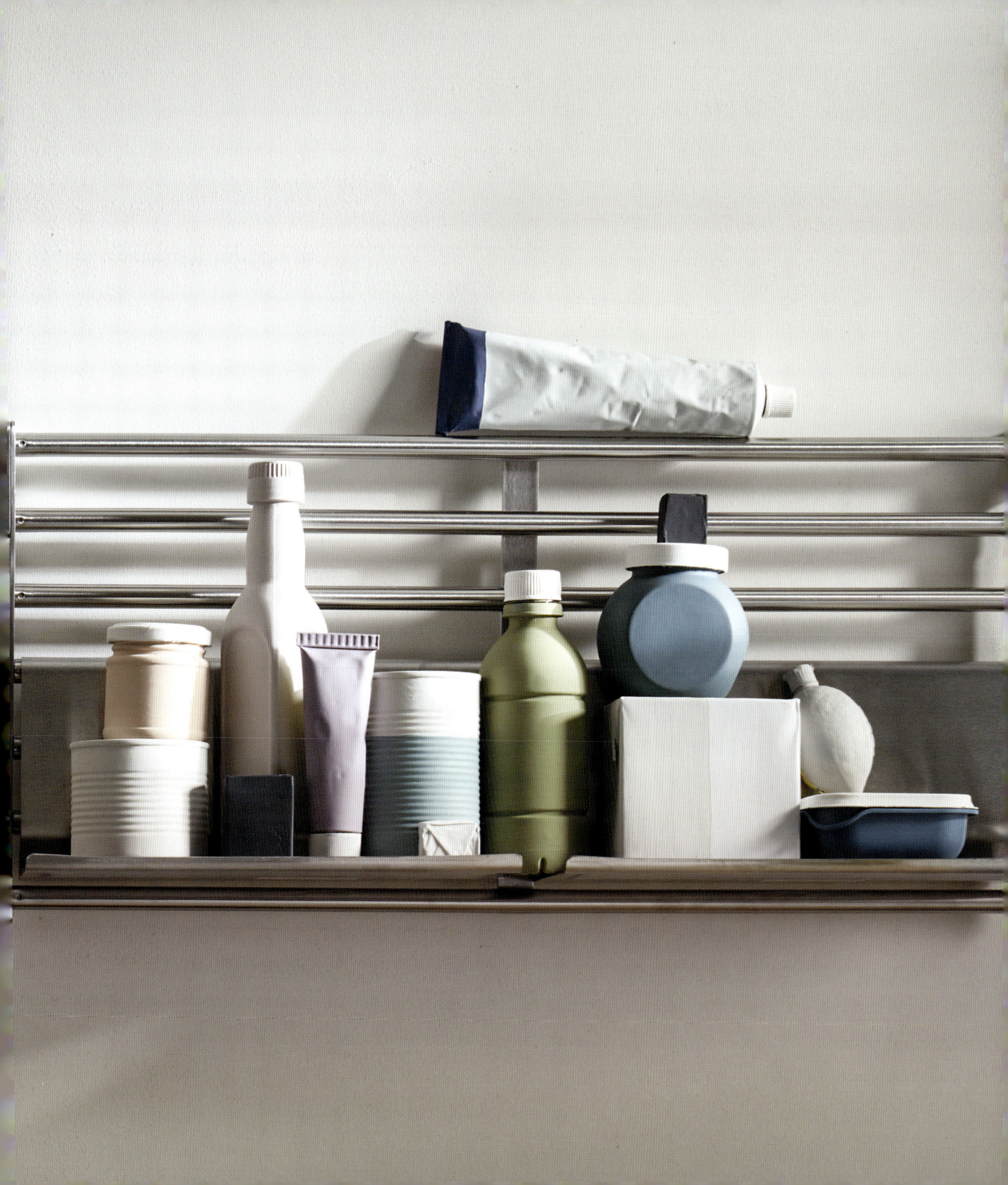

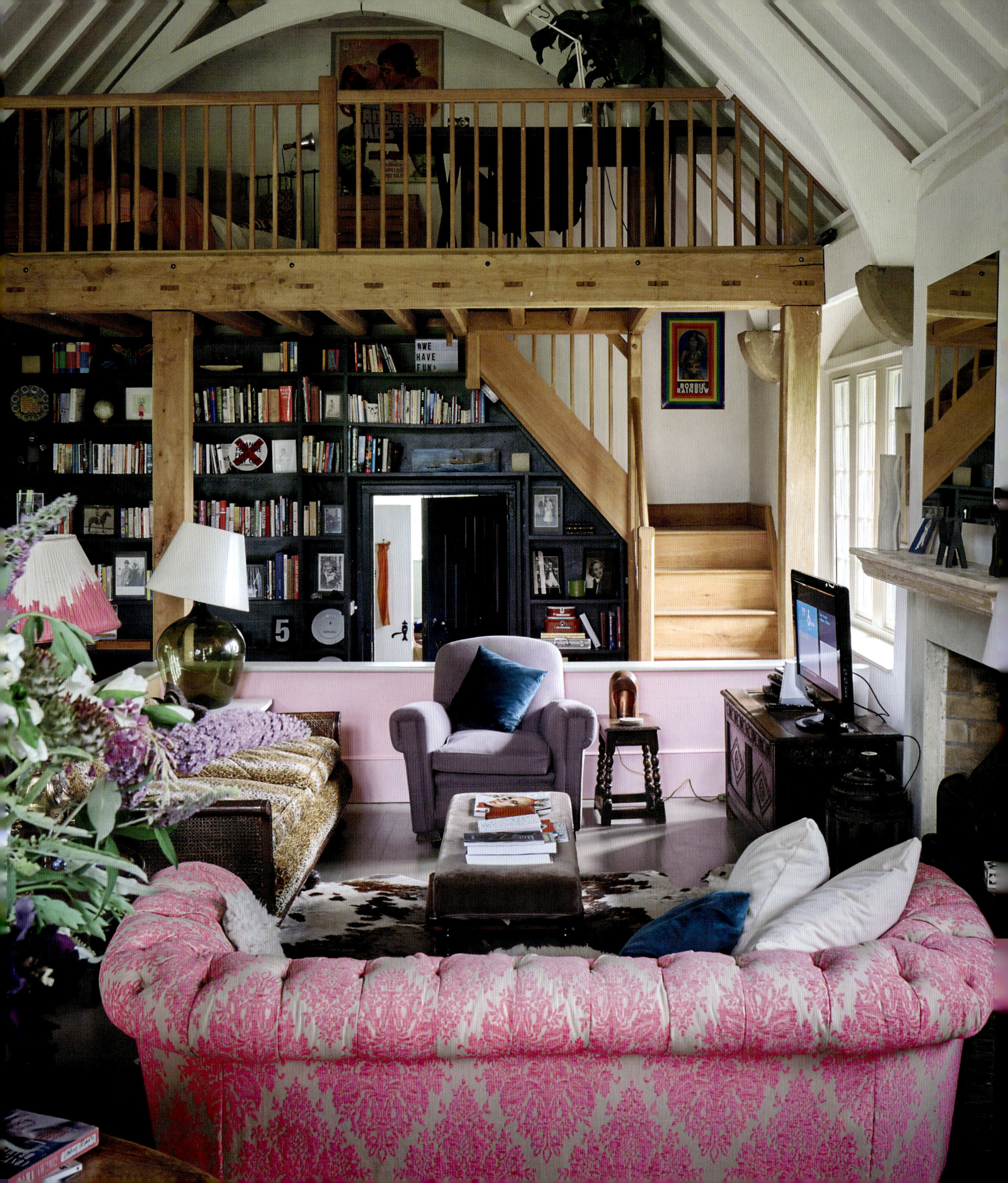
#WE HAVE FUN
BOBBIE RAINBOW

CASE STUDY 7

OLD SCHOOLHOUSE

The exterior woodwork of this old schoolhouse has been painted to reflect the colour of the cows in the surrounding fields. Soft Black Blue (A) is undeniably the perfect match. It also hints at the colour treasures that await inside. It was originally painted throughout in an unstimulating white (albeit fitting for a schoolhouse), but now the smaller rooms have been transformed into little jewel boxes of colour, which not only satisfy the owner's – my – insatiable appetite for colour but also make the most of each individual space.

On entering the house, one is greeted by rich green Olive (A) on the entrance hall walls, which echoes the hues of the lush garden. This strong-coloured space exudes drama, which makes the living room leading off it feel large and light in comparison.

The entrance to the living room sits beneath the gallery and has also been kept dark to continue the sense of intrigue. Railings, a softer alternative to black, has been taken over the door and bookcase. It contrasts with the rest of the walls and ceiling, which are painted in a soft white akin to their original colour – appropriately, School House White. This emphasizes the size and light of the room and also retains the spirit of the building. There are, though, a few colourful embellishments here.

FACING PAGE
The living room bookcase, tucked under the gallery, has been painted in eye-catching Railings. Incorporating the door into the bookcase wall increases the overall dramatic effect.

INSET ABOVE
Black Blue (A) on the front door is the same colour as the cows in the surrounding fields. The silk sheen of the Exterior Eggshell finish contributes to a relaxed country atmosphere.

ABOVE
Rich green Olive (A) perfectly complements the garden and the original stone floor. It also creates a surprisingly bold hall and makes the rooms leading off it seem bigger and lighter.

CASE STUDY 7

A low wall around the seating area surprises in Nancy's Blushes (named after my daughter's rosy cheeks when she was a child). This helps achieve a quirky and snug atmosphere, which can be difficult in a large, open-plan space.

The floor was originally much lower in order to prevent the school children from being distracted by looking out of the window. In its raised form, it has a simple painted wood finish, which makes the space feel remarkably relaxed. Mouse's Back, one of the original Farrow & Ball drabs (colours with no brightness), was chosen to create warmth as well as to disguise muddy boot marks.

The windows are undoubtedly the stars of this space. To draw attention to them, they have been picked out in Drop Cloth, which also reflects (but, importantly, does not mimic) the colour of the stone architraves. This use of colour may be subtle but it has transformed the space from being bland and a little unloved to feeling cherished and considered.

ABOVE LEFT
The interior of this sitting room bookcase, created from a long-defunct window, has been painted in Drop Cloth to match the windows and doors and echo the stone corbels. The contrast with the walls is very subtle — when the room is bathed in light, you can barely notice the difference — but the stone colour is invaluable in linking the original values of the house with its more contemporary style of decorating.

ABOVE
Nancy's Blushes on the low walls surrounding the seating area creates a place in which to relax.

FACING PAGE
The bookcase tucked under the gallery has been painted in arresting Railings so as not to fight the lack of light at this darker end of the room. It was vital to paint the door within the bookcase and the ceiling underneath the gallery in the same colour to enhance the dramatic effect.

WHO'S WHO
TONY BLAIR
AMERICA
RECKLESS
WILLIAM BOYD
GILBERT & GEORGE
5

LEFT
The colours of the boot room and pantry add to the decoration of the kitchen, as their doors have been cut in half to create tempting glimpses of their more upbeat colours. Oval Room Blue in the boot room and Rangwali in the pantry are used on every surface in these rooms, including the ceiling, to create brilliant gem-like antechambers that beg you to enter them. Poster by Ed Ruscha.

FACING PAGE
The school room for the younger children is now a kitchen, with the units painted in Studio Green to fit the rustic setting. As in the main living area, the walls and ceiling retain their historic roots by having been painted in School House White (as have the majority of mismatched chairs and the table legs). Sunny Babouche in the window recess provides an uplifting twist.

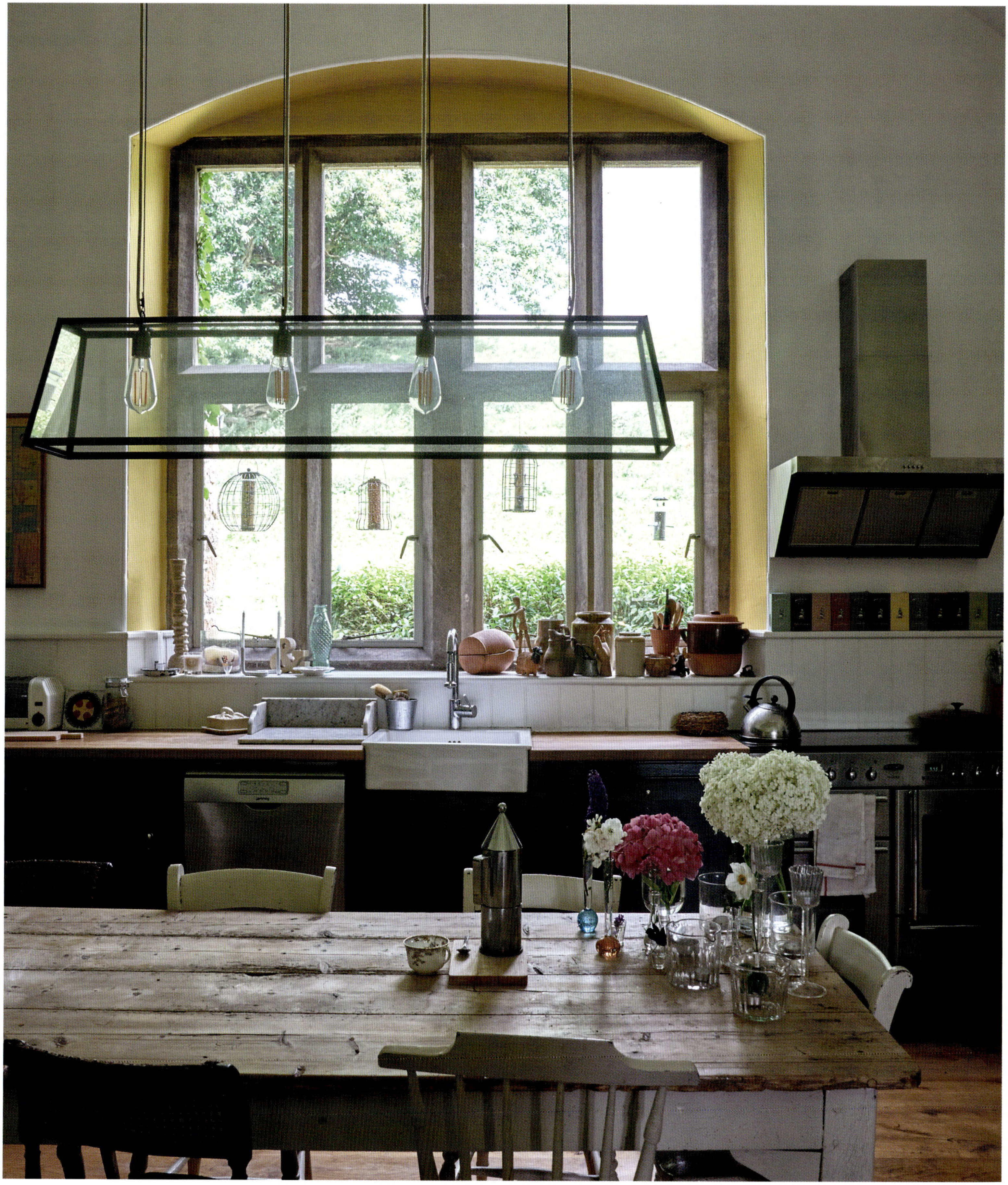

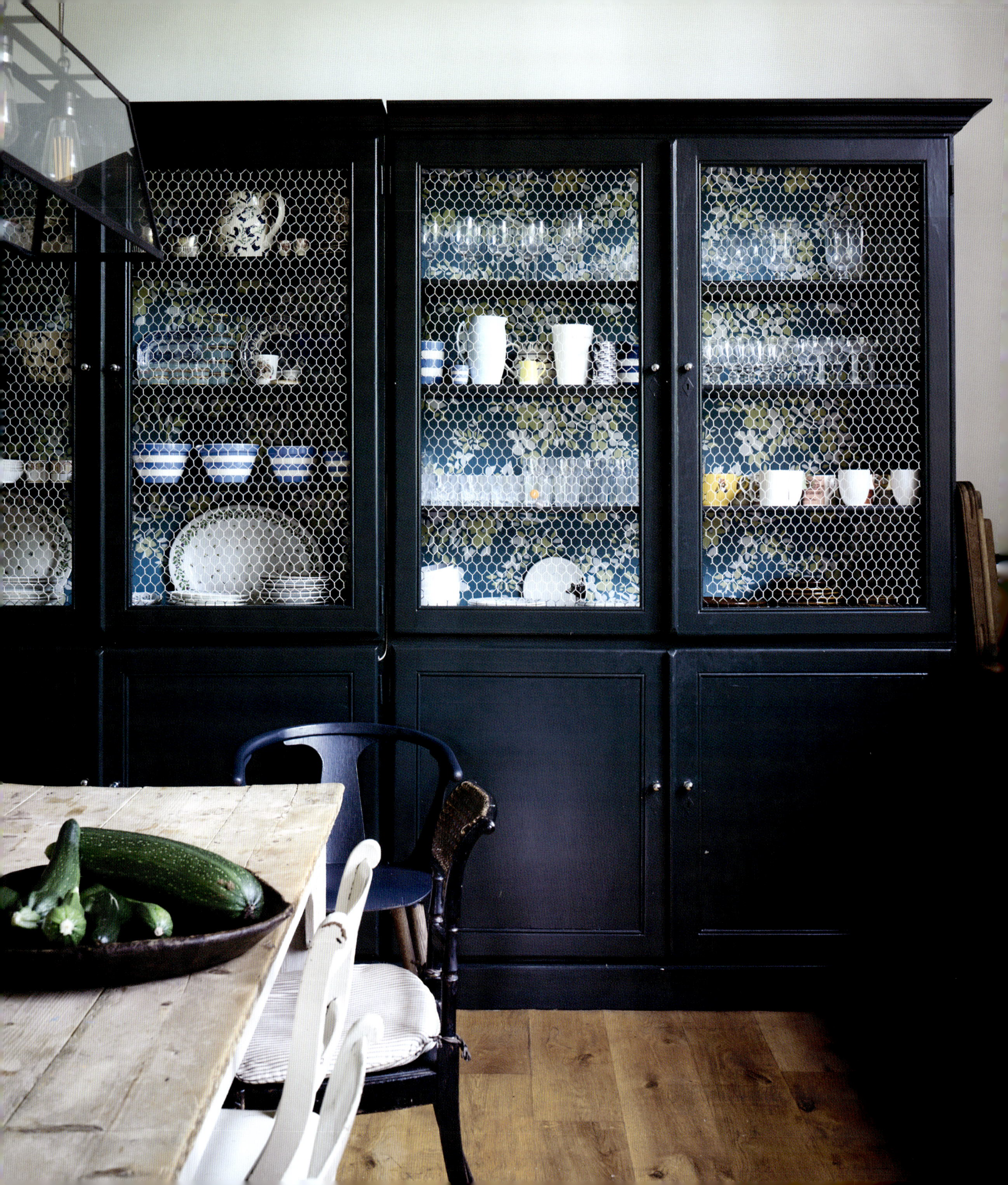

The kitchen, once the school room for the younger children, has also been painted in School House White, but the window recess has this time been picked out in unexpected Babouche, to reflect the colour of the forsythia hedge outside. This simple use of colour creates a happy glow in the kitchen, even on the gloomiest of days. Studio Green on the units feels suitably modern, while still being totally appropriate in the heart of the countryside.

The introduction of stable doors adds extra excitement to the kitchen, allowing tantalizing glimpses of the colours in adjacent rooms. Upbeat Rangwali and Oval Room Blue have been used in the pantry and boot room respectively (see page 102), even though they are exceptionally small working spaces. Leaving them white would have resulted in disappointing and insignificant rooms, but now they are a pleasure to use. In order not to draw attention to their small size, one colour has been used on every surface – walls, ceiling and trim – which means you cannot read the confines of the room. The trick of using just one colour has been used in every bedroom, too, although these diminutive rooms are in much softer tones, reflecting the characteristics of each one.

The corridor to the bedrooms (see page 106 left) is a dark, compromised space but it has been transformed with Inchyra Blue on the lower part of the walls and doors, and School House White on the top half of the walls and the ceiling, which makes the space open out and feel wider. Using School House White here as well as in the kitchen and living room creates a link between the recently built bedroom extension and the main part of the house. The same colours and decorative device also appear in the more traditional cloakroom situated off the entrance hall, to achieve the same effect.

With its doors opening straight onto the garden, the master bedroom (see page 106 right) begged to be painted in a restful green, making the connection between the interior and exterior practically seamless. French Gray looks enchanting and is the perfect shade here.

Similarly, the second bedroom, with windows on three sides, was only ever going to feel right painted in Light Blue. This colour's magical qualities mean that, like French Gray, it appears to change according to the different intensity of light at various times of the day. It is positively blue in strong morning light and then becomes greyer as the evening progresses. Perfect for a bedroom.

FACING PAGE
Hegemone wallpaper on the interior of this dresser makes it feel less formal and adds a whimsical touch to the kitchen. The colours of the paper reflect both the window recess and the boot room. For those wary of using bold colours or strong patterns, this is the perfect way to be a little braver.

ABOVE
Moody Inchyra Blue has been used on the cloakroom walls to an intriguing eye level. The colour was chosen to enhance the proportions of the room and to make the lofty ceiling height feel lower. The upper walls and ceiling are painted in School House White to link with the woodwork colour in the hall.

CASE STUDY 7

ABOVE
By using rich Inchyra Blue on the bottom half of the walls and refreshing School House White above, the corridor no longer feels dark and gloomy. The delight here is that this treatment continues across the doors and frames — a simple way to totally transform a space.

ABOVE RIGHT
Not many bedrooms open onto such an abundant garden. To magnify the pastoral feel, French Gray, with its underlying green, has been used on every surface in the master bedroom, including the doors to avoid creating a barrier between the interior and exterior.

FACING PAGE
The smallest bedroom has been painted in intimate Setting Plaster. The colour has been taken over the ceiling, to disguise its low height, and over the woodwork, to create the ultimate calm space. This room proves that good things do come in small packages.

The features of the smallest and most intimate third bedroom have been embraced by cocooning it in delicate Setting Plaster, which makes it feel soothing, as if it is giving you a hug.

There is a tendency to think that only big, light-filled rooms are able to "take" strong colours, and that small, dark rooms should be restricted to light shades. This house demonstrates perfectly that this is not necessarily the case. The large rooms, in which the most time is spent, are kept light and airy, while the smaller bedrooms have been enriched with colour and embrace you in their walls. It is a recipe for happy living.

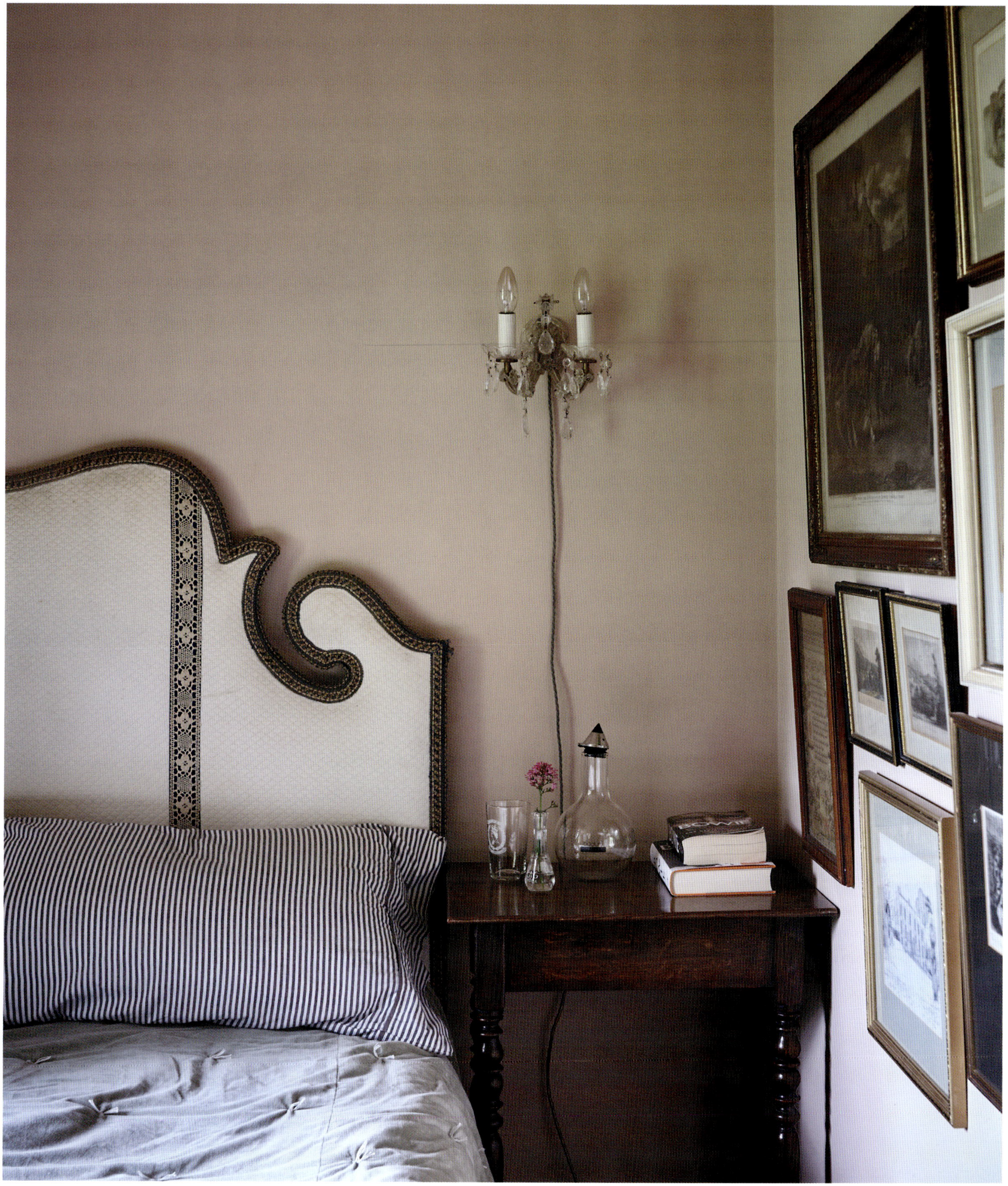

CASE STUDY 7

OLD SCHOOLHOUSE PALETTE

RECIPE TIPS

* Keep big, airy rooms light but add some colour accents for extra interest.
* Enrich small, dark spaces, such as the boot room and pantry here, with just one strong colour.
* Choose colours to enhance the main attributes of a room, such as the low wall in the living room here, painted in Nancy's Blushes to create a more intimate space for watching TV.
* Keep light-compromised areas dark at the base and lighter at the top, to open out the space.
* Introduce stable doors to allow intriguing glimpses of colour in other rooms.
* Link different parts of a building by using the same decorative scheme and repeating a colour, as with Inchyra Blue in this home.

ENTRANCE HALL

OLIVE (A)
walls

SCHOOL HOUSE WHITE
woodwork/ceiling

CLOAKROOM

INCHYRA BLUE
lower walls

SCHOOL HOUSE WHITE
upper walls/ceiling

LIVING ROOM

SCHOOL HOUSE WHITE
walls/ceiling

DROP CLOTH
woodwork

MOUSE'S BACK
floor

RAILINGS
bookcase/door/ceiling

NANCY'S BLUSHES
low wall

KITCHEN

SCHOOL HOUSE WHITE
walls/ceiling

STUDIO GREEN
units

BABOUCHE
window recess

HEGEMONE 5705

CORRIDOR

INCHYRA BLUE
walls

SCHOOL HOUSE WHITE
walls/ceiling

BOOT ROOM

OVAL ROOM BLUE
all

MASTER BEDROOM

FRENCH GRAY
all

SECOND BEDROOM

LIGHT BLUE
all

THIRD BEDROOM

SETTING PLASTER
all

PANTRY

RANGWALI
all

EXTERIOR

BLACK BLUE (A)
woodwork

108

CASE STUDIES

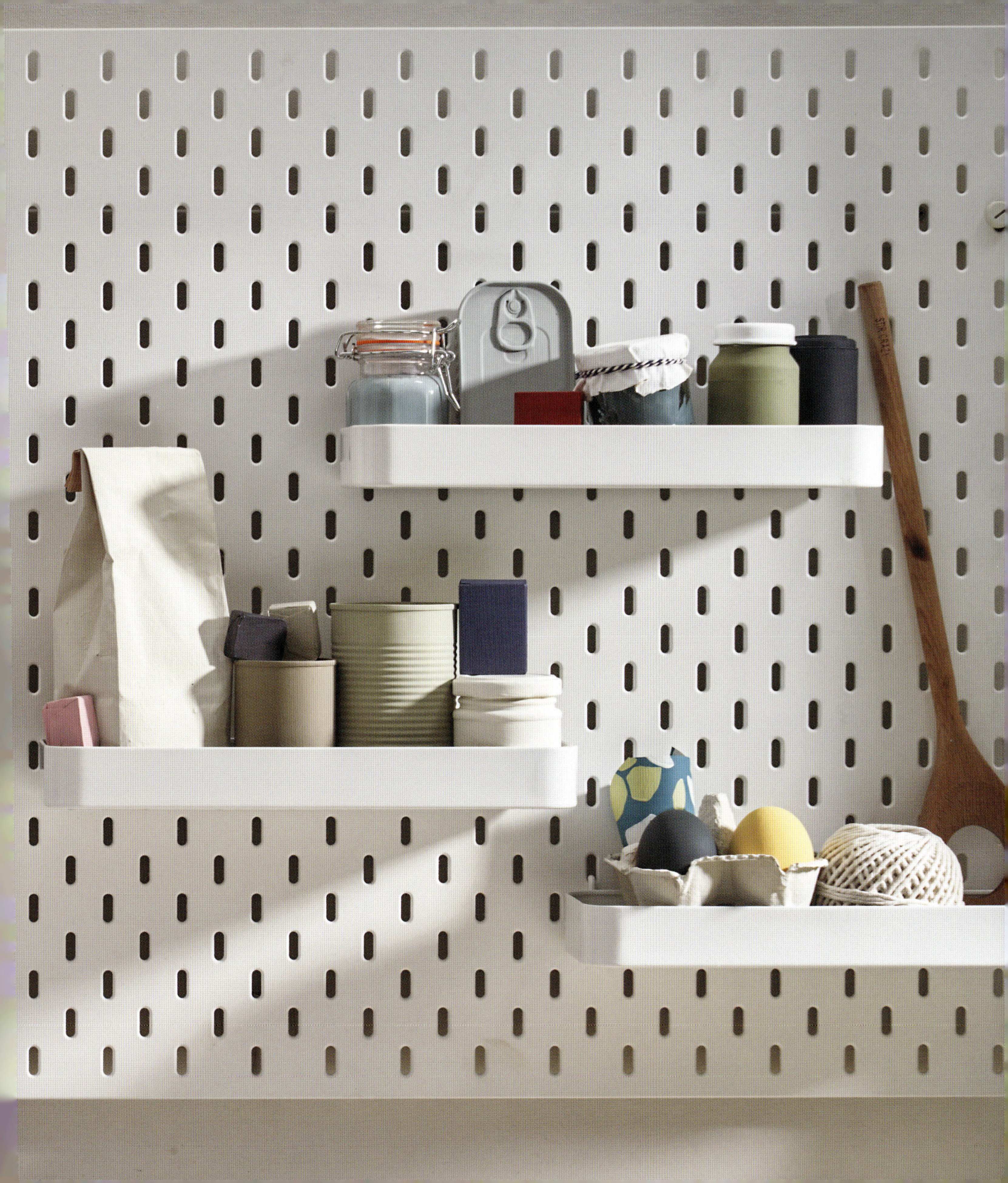

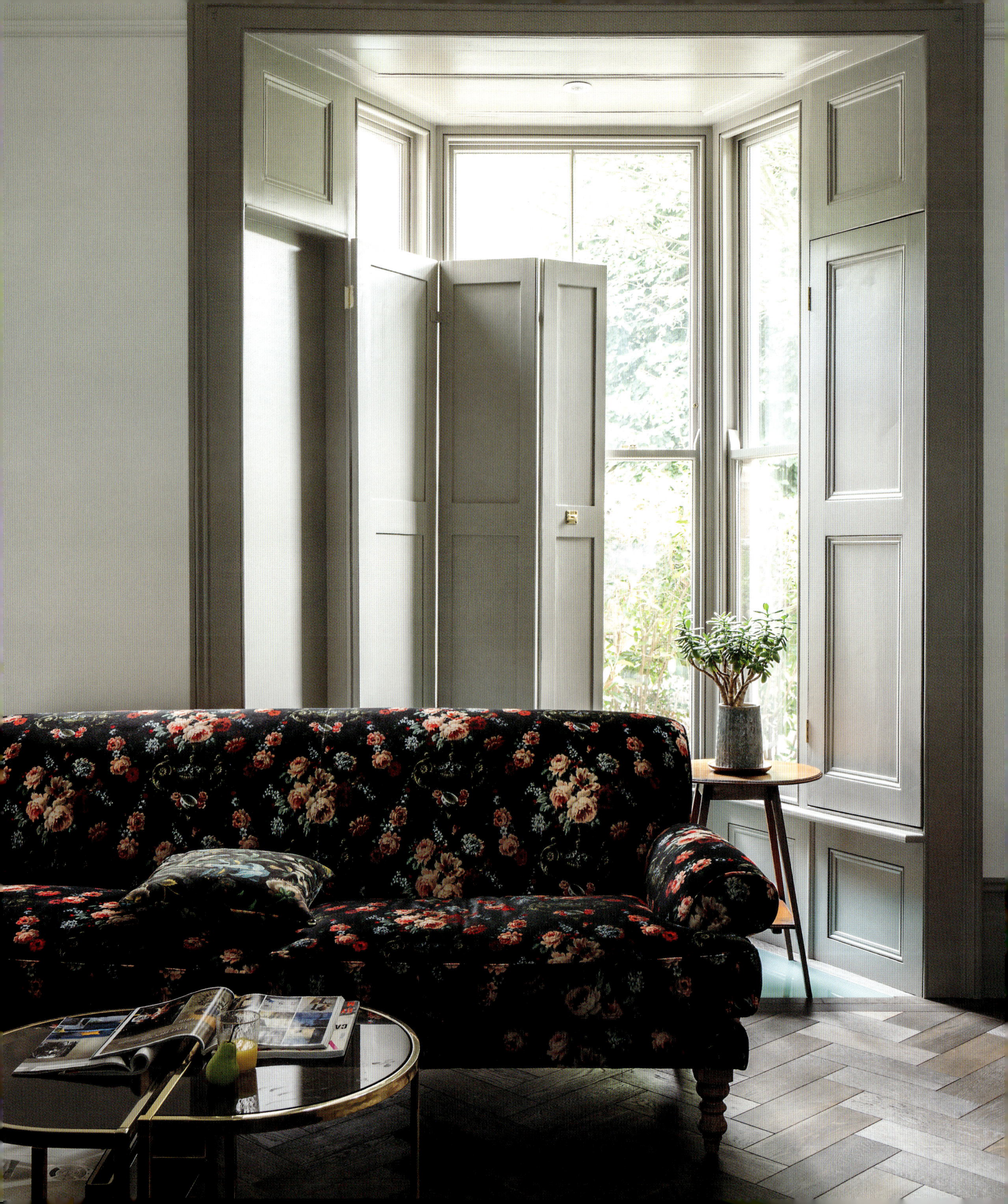

CASE STUDY 8

EAST LONDON ELEGANCE

Colour allows us to be brave, to try new combinations and then enjoy the unexpected results, as seen in this London house, which oozes glamour while maintaining the nurturing demeanour of a family home.

The occupants are certainly hooked on colour, and this includes their choice for the front entrance of their house, which stands loud and proud in a Victorian terrace. Painted in London Clay, a warm brown loaded with magenta pigment for a rich, earthy hue, it packs a punch while being far from garish. This moody exterior creates a sense of drama on arrival at the house and when you pass through the front door, the interior feels much lighter in comparison. Making spaces feel bigger and brighter in this way is one of our favourite tricks and it works perfectly here as we enter the hall painted in Ammonite. Neither too warm nor too cool, its subtle grey tone creates a calming feel. The colour of the walls is intensified somewhat by clean and delicate Wevet on all the trim, including the original dado rail. This form of decorating – a classic choice for traditional rooms where it is presumed the woodwork should be painted lighter than the walls – feels fresh and uncomplicated in an area of the house where the architecture is as it was more than a hundred years ago.

FACING PAGE
The Strong White walls in this east-facing front living room maximize the light. Rich grey Worsted on the woodwork not only gives an extra edge but sits sympathetically with the floor and creates a warmer feel when the windows and shutters are closed at night.

INSET ABOVE
London Clay on the front door gives instant high impact. Taking the colour over the architrave makes the entrance look as big as possible.

ABOVE
Viewed from the middle living room, with its intense Inchyra Blue walls, understated Ammonite on the walls in the hall appears delightfully simple — a breath of fresh air that links the highly coloured spaces together.

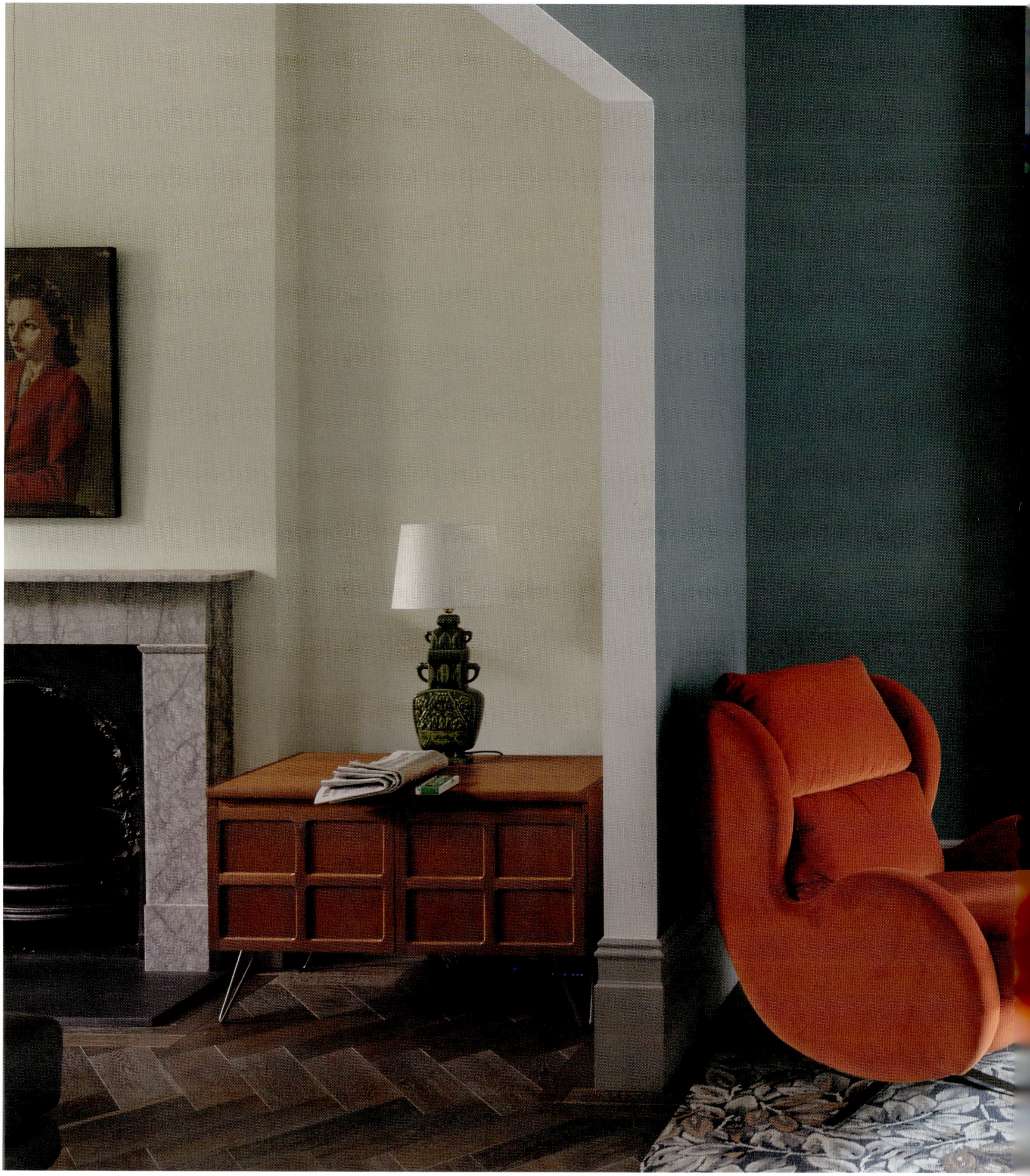

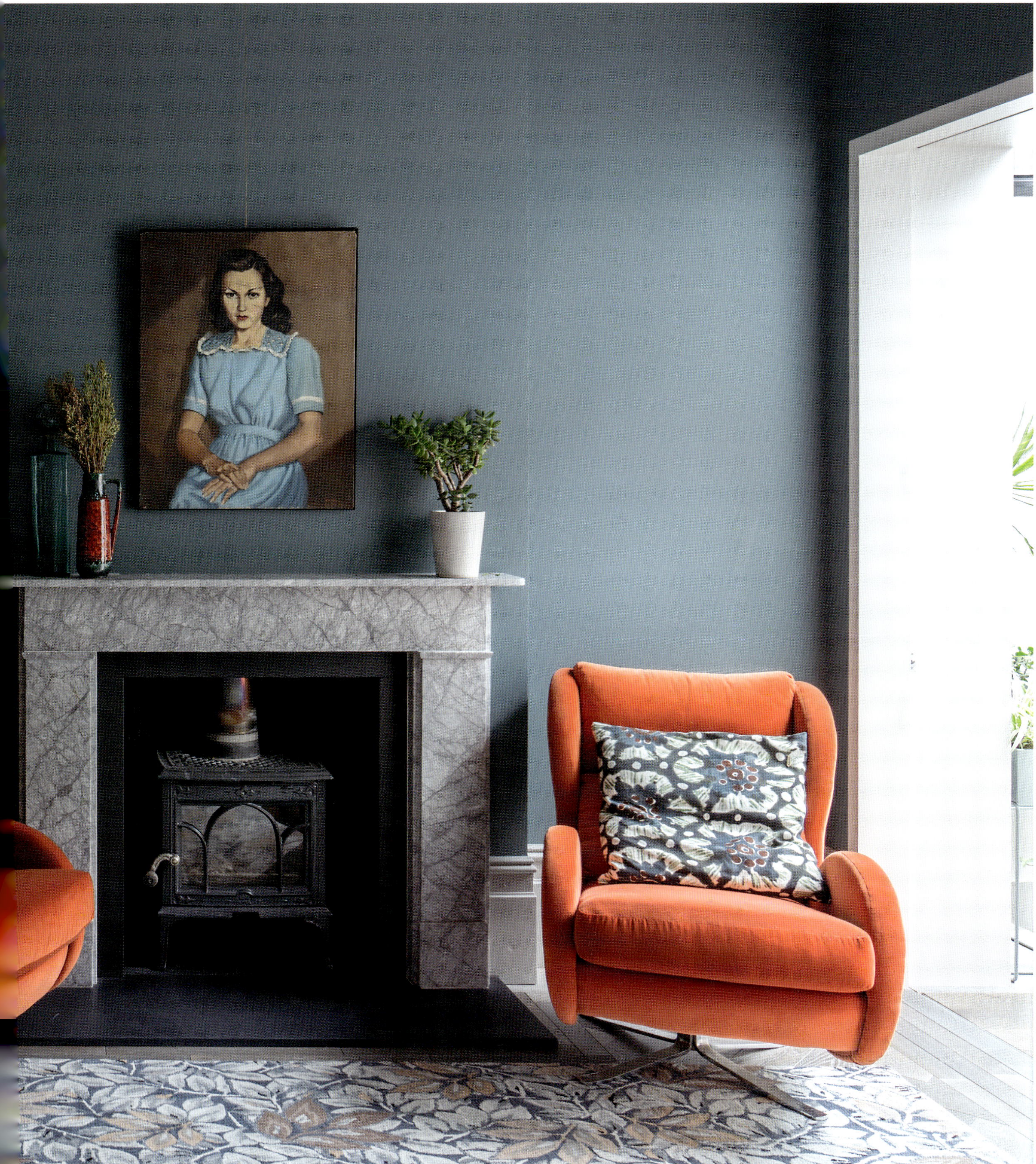

CASE STUDY 8

PAGES 112–13 AND BELOW
The living rooms are linked by woodwork in Worsted, which appears neutral in the middle room in contrast to the strong Inchyra Blue walls, but makes more of a statement in the front room against the simple Strong White walls.

FACING PAGE
Ammonite on the walls in the hall and Worsted on the woodwork in the living rooms have been carried through to the kitchen. Subtle grey Ammonite stops the walls from appearing stark, while rich grey Worsted adds intrigue.

In other areas the original architecture has changed considerably to accommodate modern family living. The open-plan living rooms are proportionally similar but they have been coloured in totally different ways, to make contrasting but still elegant rooms. The middle room, which only benefits from light borrowed from adjacent spaces, is painted in magical Inchyra Blue. This moody hue reads grey, blue or even green, depending on the light and time of day, keeping it charismatic and alive. A pale colour would have felt cold here, and this dramatic interlude means that the connecting front room, with walls and ceiling painted in neutrals, appears bathed in light. Architecture of this nature can be difficult to live in. Everyone craves bigger spaces but if they knock through, they often end up underusing the middle room. However, this middle living room has been remodelled as part-hall, part-reading room, and coloured with a beguiling dynamism. It stops us in our tracks and serves to decorate all the adjoining rooms.

The two living spaces are, however, united by rich grey Worsted on the trim. This adds gravitas to the original shutters and boxes against the Strong White walls of the front room, and looks suitably understated with the Inchyra Blue of the middle room. Two charmingly similar portraits hang over identical fireplaces, one standing proud against a dark backdrop, the other allowing the painted wall to dominate. Although these pictures are recent additions to the home, it feels as if the wall colours have been specially chosen to show them at their best.

The approach to the kitchen from the middle room painted in Inchyra Blue is made all the more exciting by coming from such a strong colour. This contemporary-styled room sits seamlessly

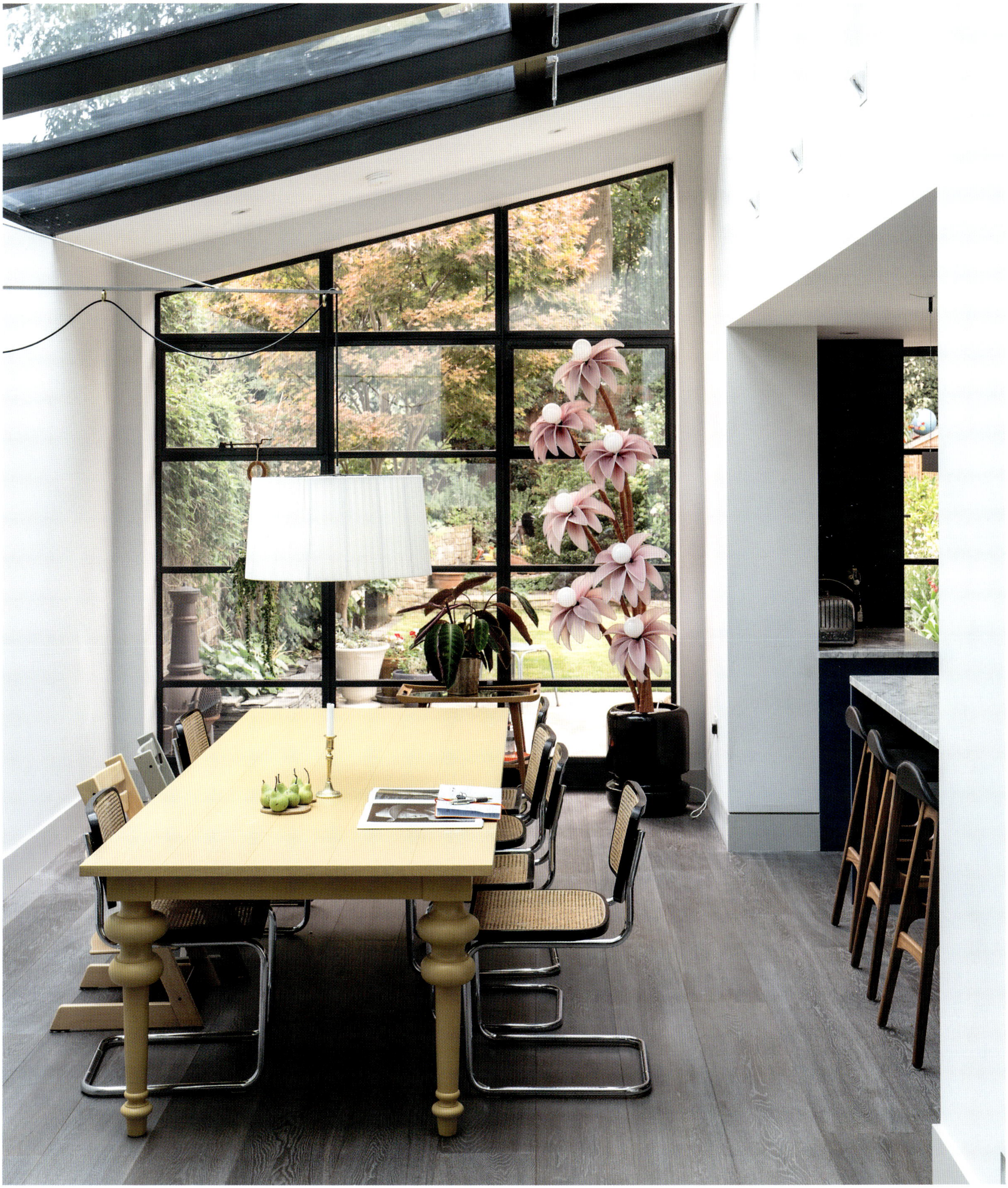

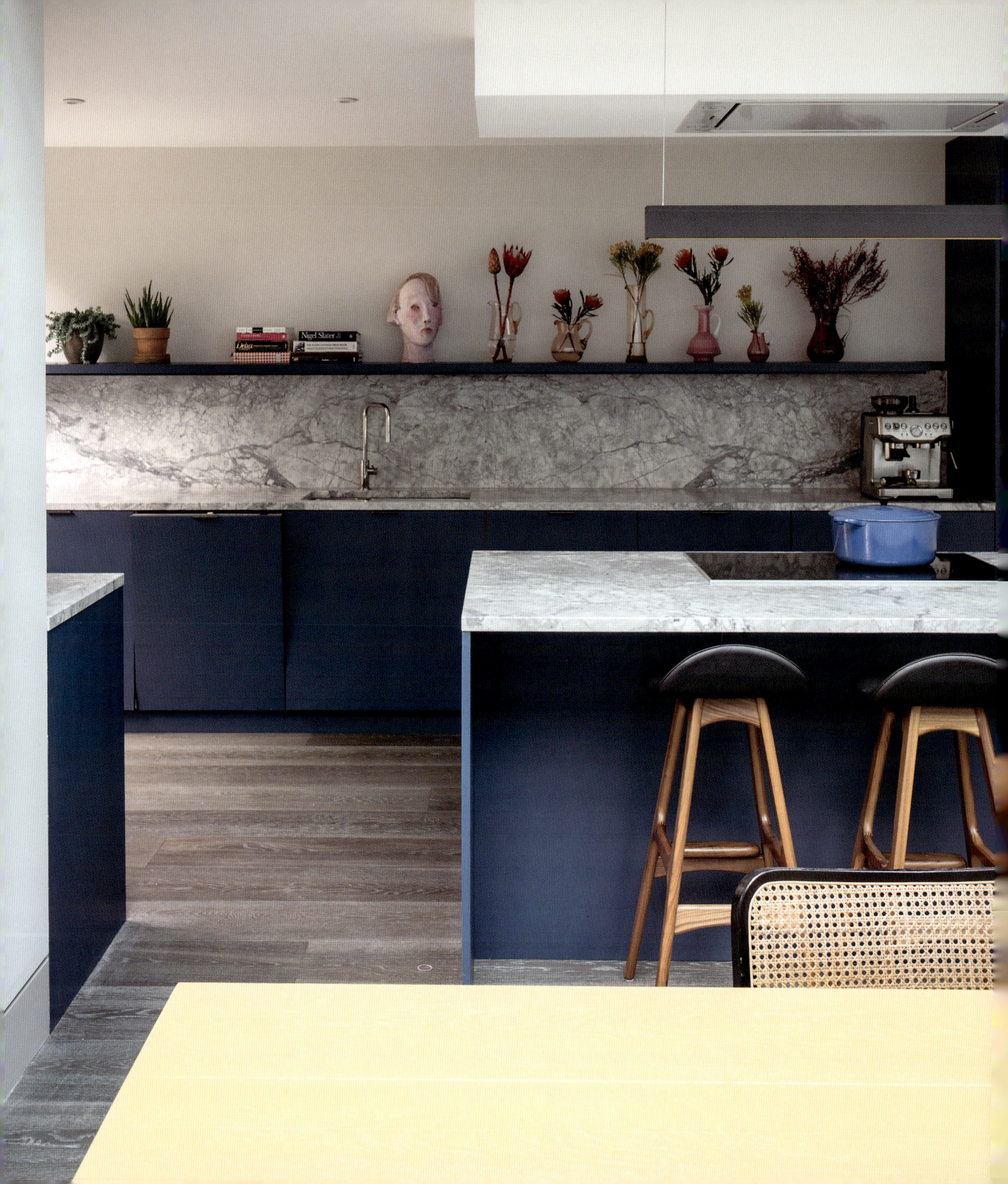
Nigel Slater

CASE STUDY 8

FACING PAGE
Stiffkey Blue appears upbeat in this light-filled kitchen. Using a strong colour on work surfaces below eye level makes everything above them feel lighter. Wall-hung units in this colour might have felt oppressive but the eye-level shelf is perfect.

BELOW
The Stiffkey Blue staircase, which ties in with the kitchen units on the ground floor, is the star of the understated Ammonite hall and acts as a grounding backbone to the entire house.

BELOW
Black Blue (A) in Full Gloss has been used on the underside of this reclaimed Victorian bathtub, in contrast to the very matt tiles. The joy of adding colour to small areas such as this is that it is easy to change on a whim.

with the rest of house simply because no new colours have been introduced: Ammonite on the walls transitions from the hall, Worsted on the woodwork from the living room trim and Stiffkey Blue on the units from the stairs. In this well-lit area, Stiffkey Blue appears much bluer and more upbeat than it does in the hall, and it contrasts wonderfully with Ammonite. Although the palette is the same here, the different light conditions make the colours look more modern and uplifting. This brings a dynamism to the newly created kitchen, while maintaining the bond with the main body of the house. Clever decorating, indeed.

The traditional architecture of the house has been given a powerful contemporary twist by reinventing the original staircase in Stiffkey Blue. This colour was named after a Norfolk beach where the mud and cockles that can be found there are intriguingly dark navy in colour. This is a brave colour choice to introduce into a traditional space, but the drama is tempered by the dark inky colour being used only on the treads, risers and spindles. This allows the hall to retain a gentle sense of order, where everything has its place, with the dark stairs acting as a strong core to ground the whole building.

EAST LONDON ELEGANCE

LEFT AND FACING PAGE, TOP
The master bedroom is a picture of quiet glamour. Dead Salmon feels totally on trend here because it has been taken over all the walls and trim, creating an oasis of warm calm. The Oxford Stone cupboards in the dressing area at the back of the room create an intriguing contrast with the walls and help to maximize the natural light available.

FACING PAGE, BOTTOM LEFT
Stone Blue on every surface in the children's bedroom creates a calm backdrop for toys and treasures.

FACING PAGE, BOTTOM RIGHT
Setting Plaster softens the architectural lines in this guest room up in the eaves. This colour never fails to result in a tender space, even when contrasted with strong-coloured furnishings.

Upstairs, the bedrooms appear a little softer than the rooms on the lower floors. Dead Salmon in the master bedroom is enchanting, at times looking like a buff neutral, at others, a strong mushroom. This colour is steeped in history, but here it appears on trend all over again in a different guise. Taken over all the walls and trim, including the fire surround, it is the perfect earthy tone to warm up a room deprived of light, making it feel quietly glamorous yet settled and comfortable at the same time.

Another timeless colour, Stone Blue creates a captivating vintage feel in the children's bedroom and is again taken over every surface in line with current fashion, making it feel just as loved and considered as every other room in the house, as it should be.

A small guest room in the eaves illustrates how paint allows us to update and rejuvenate even the smallest of spaces. Dusty pink Setting Plaster is often favoured to create subtle and serene environments. Used here, it softens the angular nature of the roof space, creating another room that feels comfortable and lived-in.

A bold colour palette has made this sophisticated cosmopolitan home fantastically inviting. Every room has its own jewel-like personality, and they all sit effortlessly together, resulting in a refined way of living that inspires and delights.

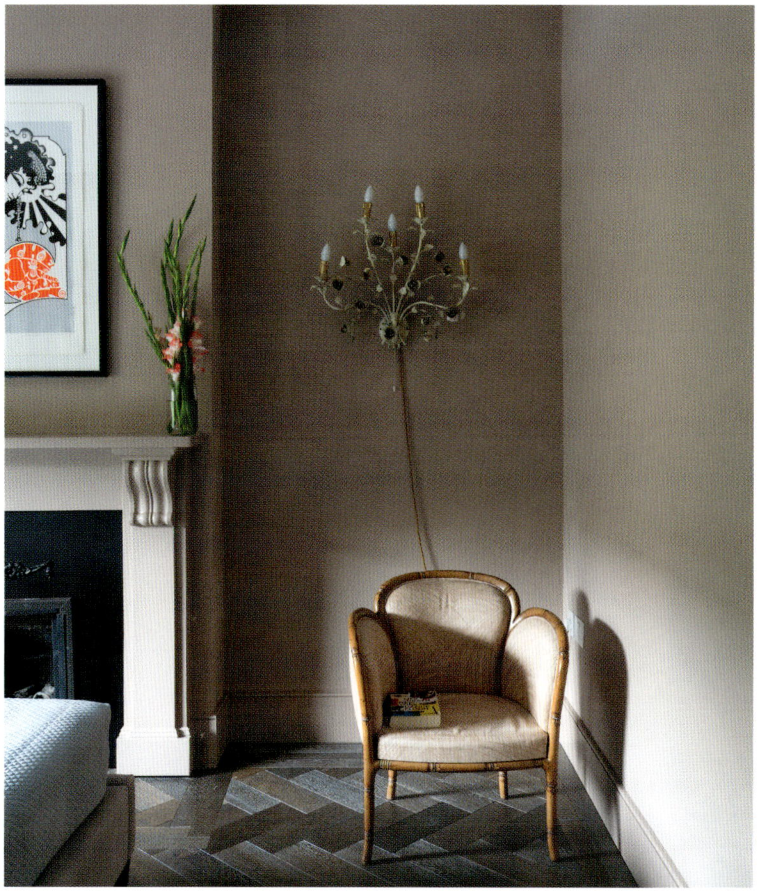
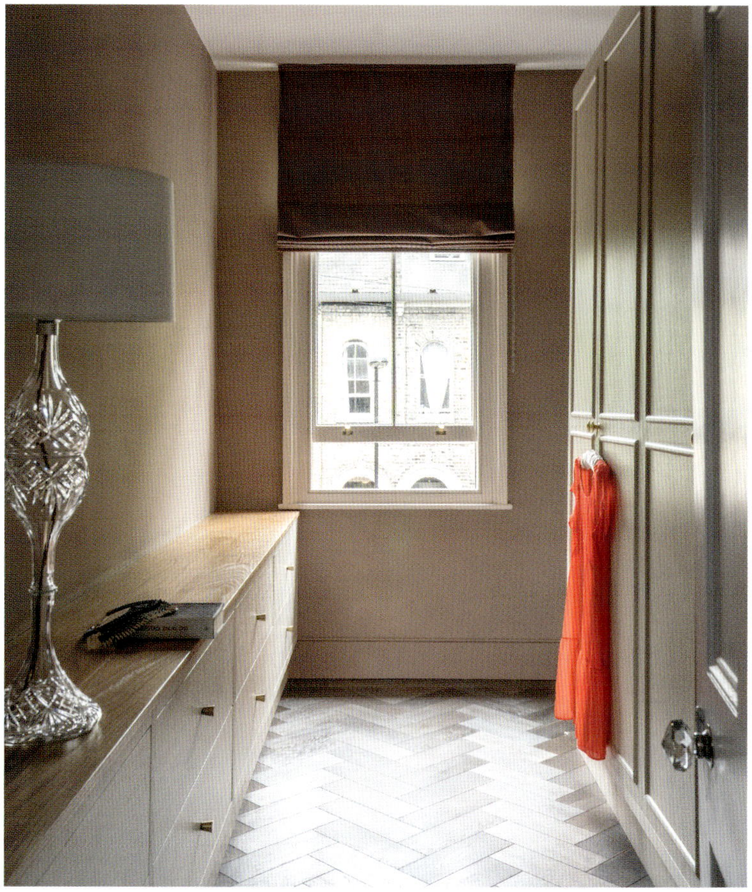
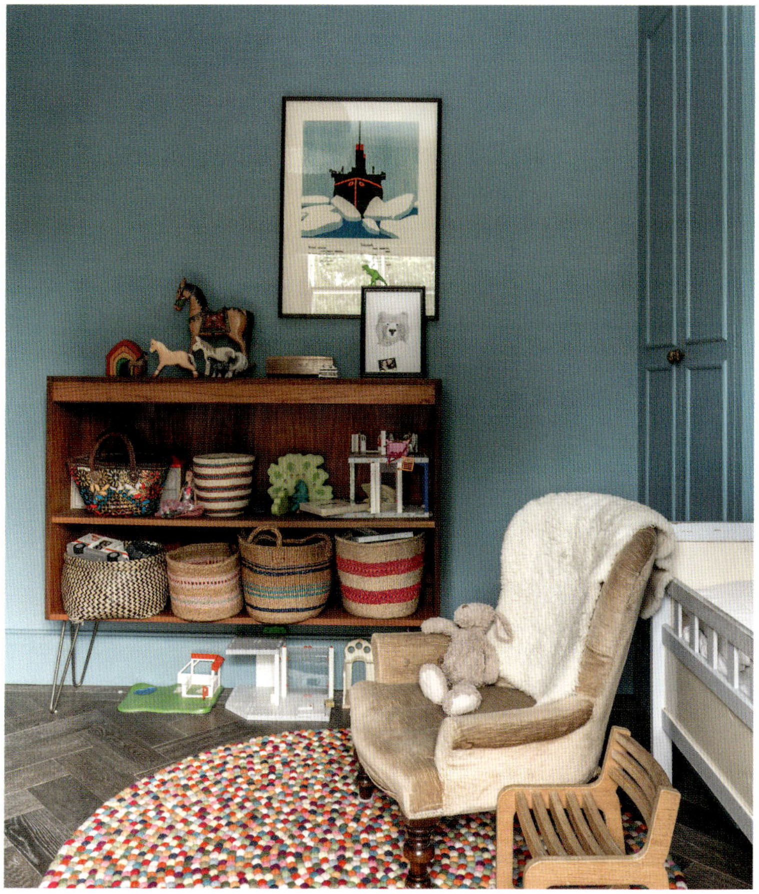
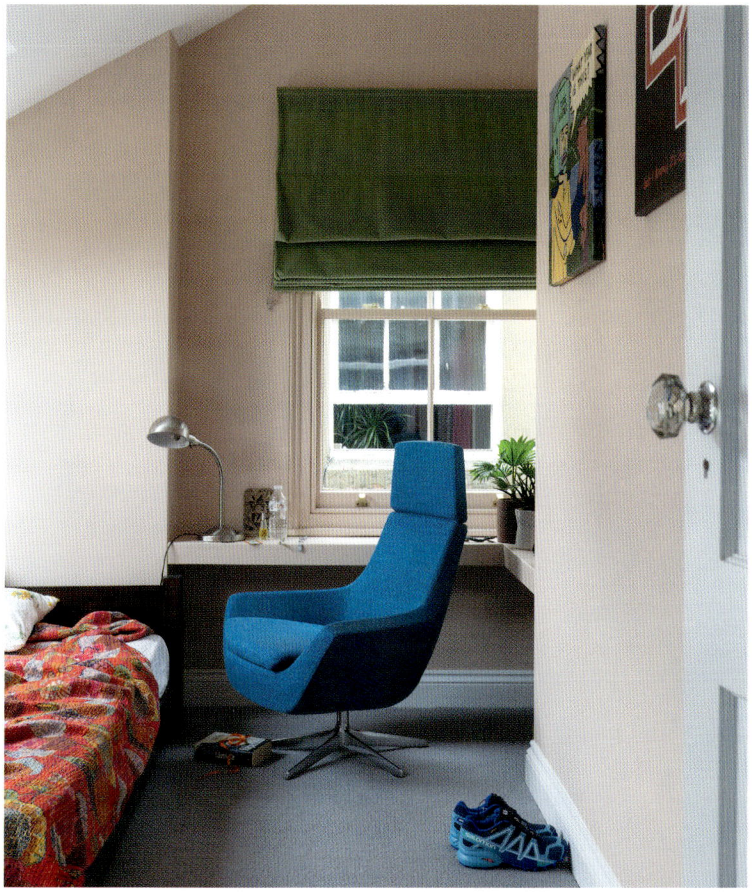

CASE STUDY 8

EAST LONDON ELEGANCE PALETTE

RECIPE TIPS

* A dark and brooding exterior will make the interior feel brighter and lighter – the transition from London Clay to Ammonite is particularly effective in this house.
* Use the same palette in different rooms – in this case, Stiffkey Blue and Ammonite. The change in light conditions will make them appear quite different.
* Unite rooms by using the same strong colour on the trim, as Worsted has been used in this house.
* Let your big rooms expand with light, and your smaller rooms envelop you.
* Decorate children's bedrooms in line with the rest of the house.

HALL, STAIRS & LANDING

AMMONITE *walls*
WEVET *trim/ceiling*
STIFFKEY BLUE *stairs*

FRONT SITTING ROOM

STRONG WHITE *walls*
WORSTED *trim*
WEVET *ceiling*

MIDDLE SITTING ROOM

INCHYRA BLUE *walls*
WORSTED *trim*
WEVET *ceiling*

KITCHEN

AMMONITE *walls*
WORSTED *trim*
WEVET *ceiling*
STIFFKEY BLUE *units*

MASTER BEDROOM

DEAD SALMON *walls/trim*
OXFORD STONE *cupboards*
WEVET *ceiling*

CHILD'S BEDROOM

STONE BLUE *walls/trim*
WEVET *ceiling*

GUEST BEDROOM

SETTING PLASTER *walls/trim*
WEVET *ceiling*

EXTERIOR

LONDON CLAY *front door/frame*

CASE STUDIES

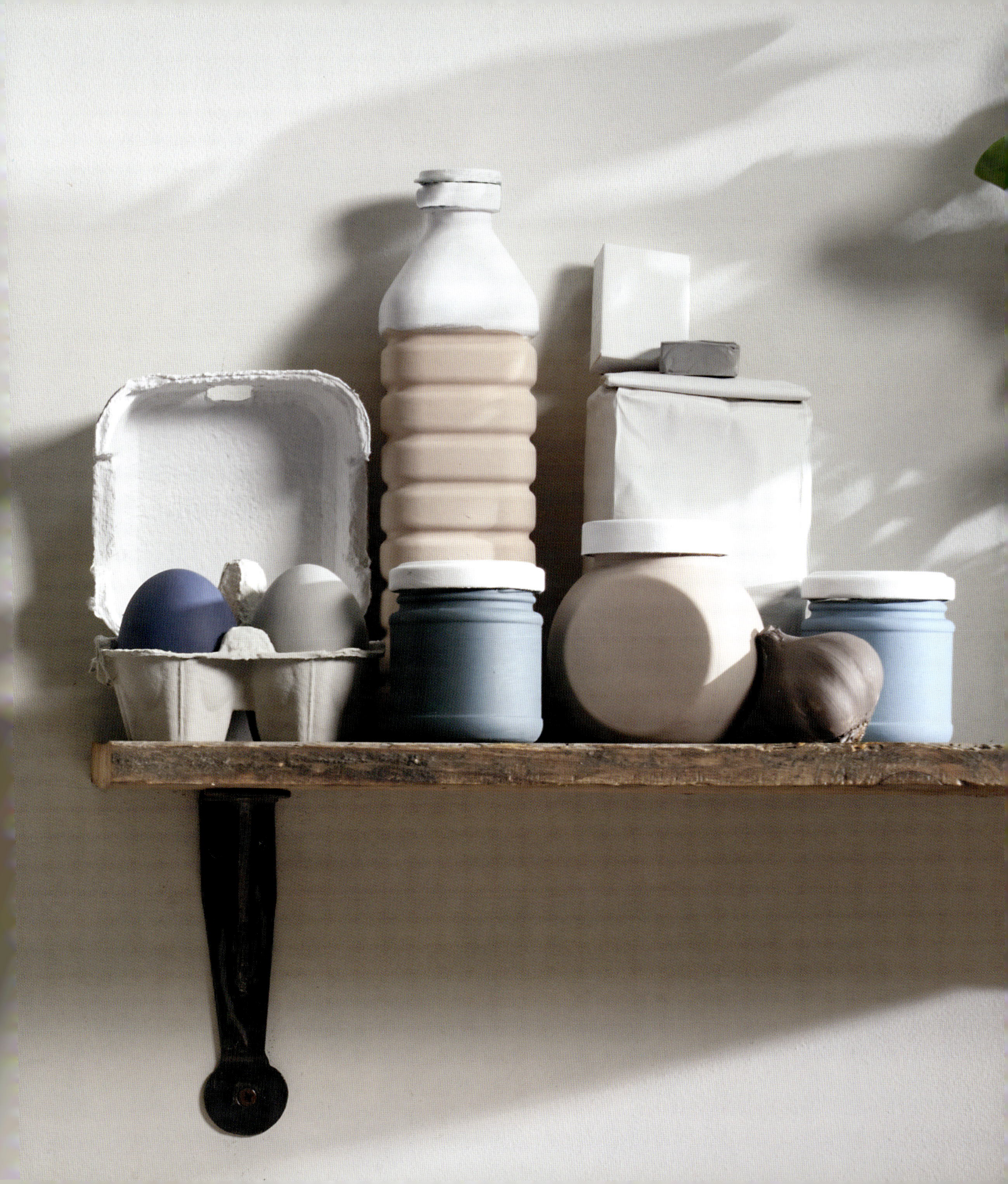

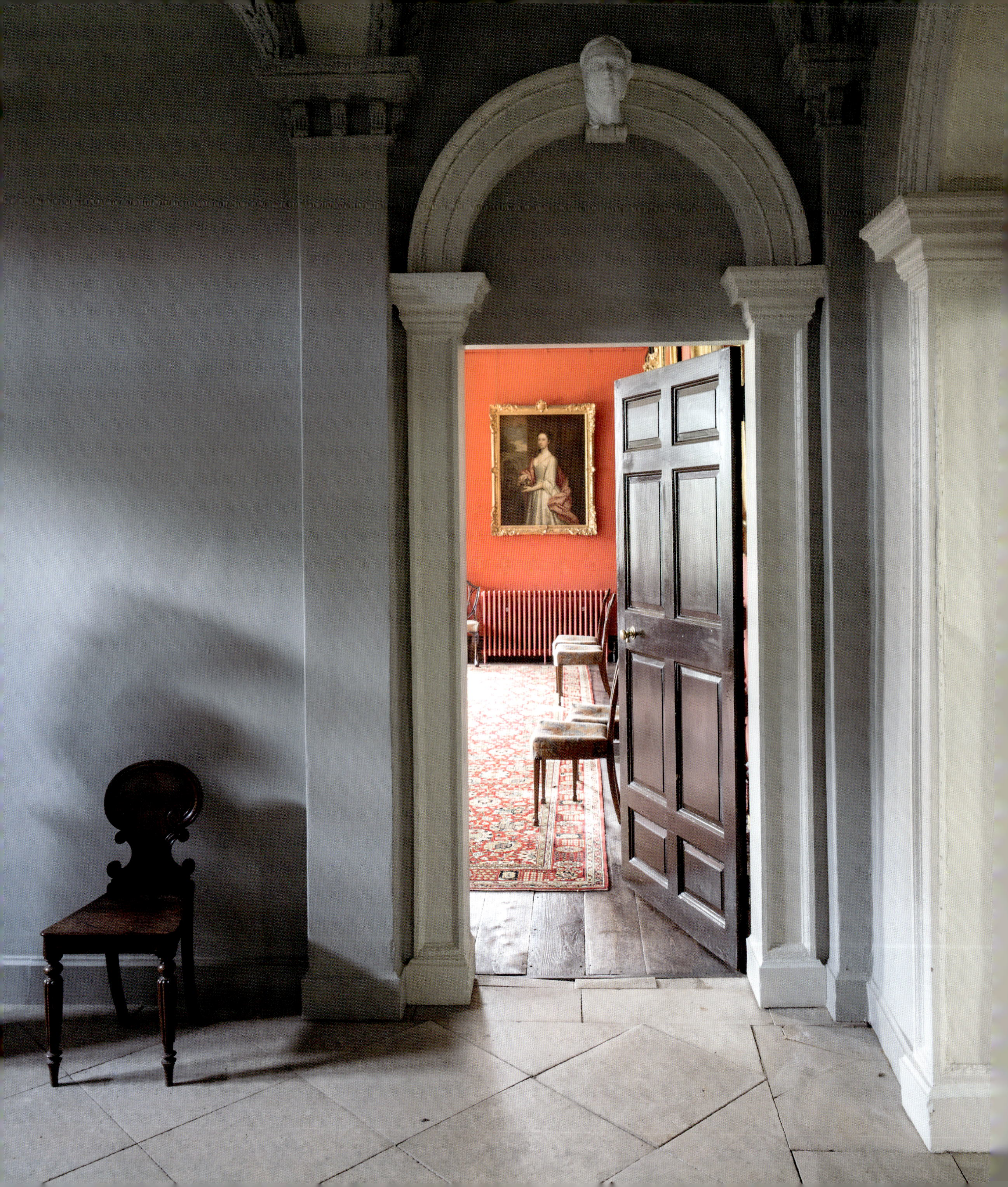

CASE STUDY 9

QUINTESSENTIALLY COUNTRY

Deans Court in Dorset is a manor house layered with history as well as colour. With its Saxon foundations, it is a time capsule of English country life that has been home to the same family since the mid-16th century.

In many contemporary homes, it feels right to create some drama in the hall, to start with an explosion of colour. Here, restraint has instead been exercised in the choice of Hardwick White on the hall walls. The modesty of this decorative scheme, in contrast with the warm, red-brick façade, lets the building speak for itself. Submissive in nature, Hardwick White works particularly well as a foil to the richly coloured reception rooms that adjoin the hall and was also chosen on account of its chameleon-like quality – the colour positively dances as the light changes through the day. This encourages you to take time to appreciate the classical statues, which were a major consideration in the colour choice. In order to highlight them, the architraves and ceiling were picked out in Wimborne White, similar in tone to their stone, while the skirting has been "lost" in the wall colour and the doors remain in their original, unpainted state. Many people worry about using different trim colours in one space, but this illustrates that there are no rules when it comes to decorating.

FACING PAGE
Modest Hardwick White makes every room off the hall feel important — the dining room painted in Blazer glows in contrast. Hardwick White is particularly susceptible to change in different light conditions, so the walls never feel flat or lifeless.

INSET ABOVE
The beautifully aged red-brick façade, dating from the 16th century, creates a warm welcome to Deans Court.

ABOVE
Although the decoration of the serene hall appears simple, much thought went into getting the tones correct. Hardwick White walls sit seamlessly with the floor, while the soft Wimborne White trim draws attention to the classical statues.

BELOW
In very different light from the front hall, Hardwick White takes on another guise in the stairwell. It has a much softer feel in contrast to the original panelling. Taking the colour over the moulding gives extra height.

FACING PAGE
Richly saturated Blazer on the dining room walls was chosen for its fiery quality during the day and warmth at night. It also makes a fine backdrop for the owner's collection of portraits. With an unpainted trim, it was important to use a darker, more complementary white on the ceiling to prevent it from defining the space and feeling too modern. Joa's White was the perfect choice, giving a low-impact contrast between the walls and ceiling.

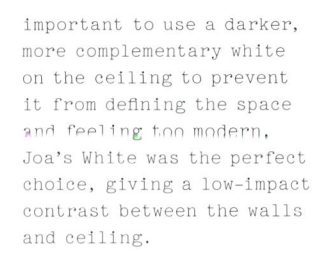

From the calm and cool oasis of the entrance hall come two very fiery spaces – rooms packed with sumptuous colour that instantly nourish the soul. In the magnificent dining room, Blazer, a richly saturated shade, is eye-catching without being overpowering. This timeless colour creates the perfect backdrop for impressive family portraits and furniture that have all been lovingly handed down from generation to generation. When combined with the richness of the dark wood, Blazer emits a visual warmth that entices you into the room and is as enchanting during the day as it is opulent at night. The combination of the strong wall colour and lustrous woodwork is complemented by sympathetic Joa's White on the ceiling and mouldings. A bright white ceiling would have deprived this scheme of its timeless feel.

From the dining room you can either pass back into the hall for an intake of neutral calm or go straight through to the first of many sitting rooms. Here, Hague Blue has been used to add some gravitas and maintain the grandeur so evident in the dining room. Passing between rooms painted in colours of a similar depth feels fantastically seamless, despite them being such different hues. The design of the sitting room pays homage to a bygone era, and although recently decorated, it still feels timeless and comforting in equal measure. As in all the rooms that are mostly used at night, the deep, dramatic colour on the walls doesn't feel oppressive but rather enhances the intimate feel, while the choice of a fairly light white, Wimborne White, on the woodwork and ceiling creates a crisp contrast that gives the room a lift during the day, making it feel animated and lively.

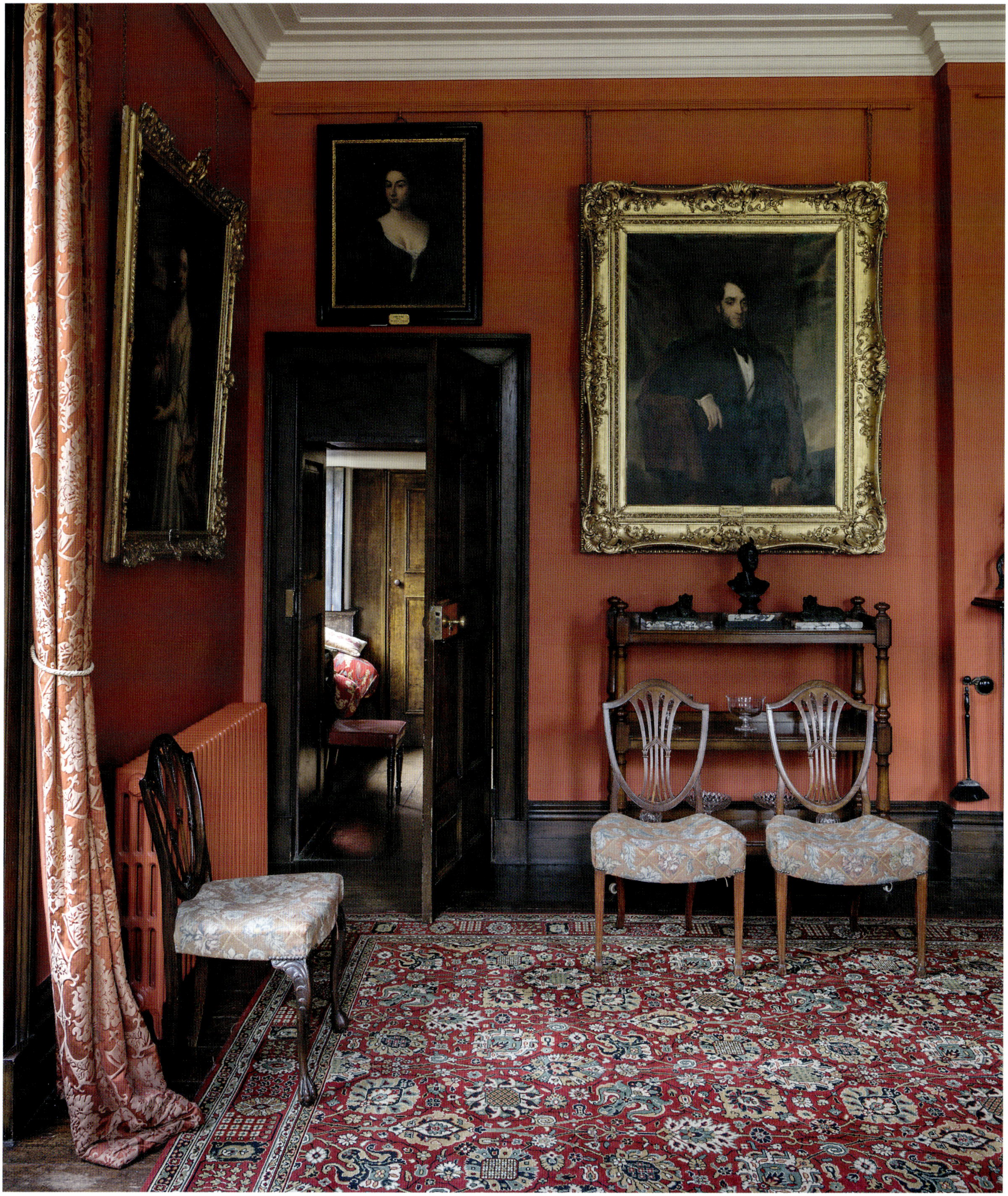

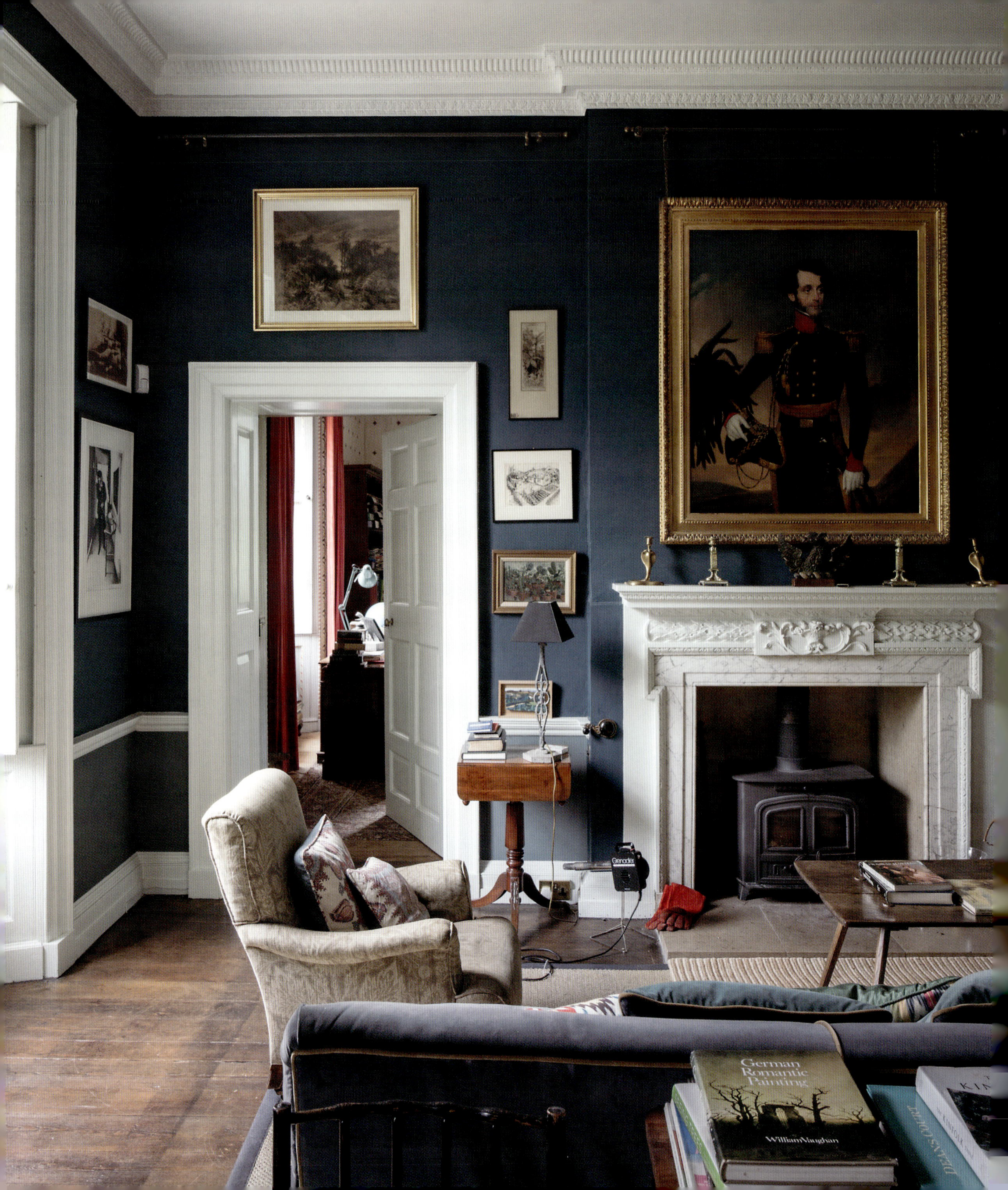
German Romantic Painting
William Vaughan

CASE STUDY 9

FACING PAGE AND BELOW
In this sitting room, Hague Blue has a strong impact in natural daylight, especially with Wimborne White on the trim. This high contrast brings energy to the room, making it feel fresh but with an old-world feel. Hague Blue reacts in a different way with darker tones, such as the bookcase and floor, where it feels a little moodier yet still easy to live with. It is clear to see why this has become a favourite colour for sitting rooms in traditional and contemporary homes.

BELOW
The high-gloss walls in the passageway to the kitchen have remained unchanged for many years but have stood the test of time. They sit happily with their Farrow & Ball counterparts in the adjoining rooms.

On the other side of the hall there is a passageway to the kitchen where the colours have remained untouched for many years. These colours are not from the Farrow & Ball range but sit fantastically alongside those that are. The fabulous combination of sunshine yellow and deep aqua blue fill one's heart with joy and all the more so because of their high-gloss finish that bounces light around this compromised space (for a similar look try Babouche and Stiffkey Blue in Full Gloss). They also do a fine job of making the kitchen at the end of the passageway feel huge and light in comparison.

CASE STUDY 9

BELOW AND FACING PAGE
In the kitchen, decorating wizardry bridges the gap between practical and traditional. An ancient portrait hangs alongside units painted in Railings, a colour much loved in contemporary kitchens, as is Strong White, which feels here as if it has been on the walls forever. The lightest colour on the largest surface makes the room feel big and bright. Slightly darker Lamp Room Gray on the woodwork makes the colour selection look more considered.

The overall mood in the family kitchen is one of calm. A farmhouse table is juxtaposed with a regal portrait, while a relaxed sofa softens the space between the Lamp Room Gray window frames. This slightly darker tone on the woodwork, in contrast to the Strong White walls, makes the room feel large and light while maintaining some decorative heft. The cheeky addition of Railings on a couple of kitchen units completes the scheme. It is fascinating to see how these colours, which are staples of many contemporary kitchens, hold up in a house of such venerable history.

The bedrooms in this house all have a softness that is apparent only at second glance. They are tinged with a delightful nostalgia, as if each past occupant has left their own mark on the house. The bedroom shown on page 130 is suitably lacking in colour, as if the strong tones have been reserved for rooms where one entertains, while whimsical neutral shades are for those that nurture. Shaded White on the panelling feels as if it might have been there for decades. The ability of a colour to sit comfortably like this in a historic setting is something unique to Farrow & Ball.

The Shaded White panelling continues in the bathroom (shown on page 131), where it sits alongside another age-old Farrow & Ball favourite. This time it is a lively and stimulating colour. In spite of having a name derived from the poison rumoured to have been in the wallpaper that poisoned Napoleon, Arsenic is an unexpected but fun choice. By being used only on the lower panelling, below one's eyeline, it doesn't overwhelm this overall restful scheme.

This is a sublime example of timeless country house decoration, with many rooms left untouched since the 1930s. Previous custodians obviously took their decorating very seriously and their choices have certainly stood the test of time. The present owners have been successful in preserving the past, while weaving in colours that suit their own lifestyle. The result is a relaxed, happy place, with a sense of deep contentment expressed in its unique combinations of colours both old and new.

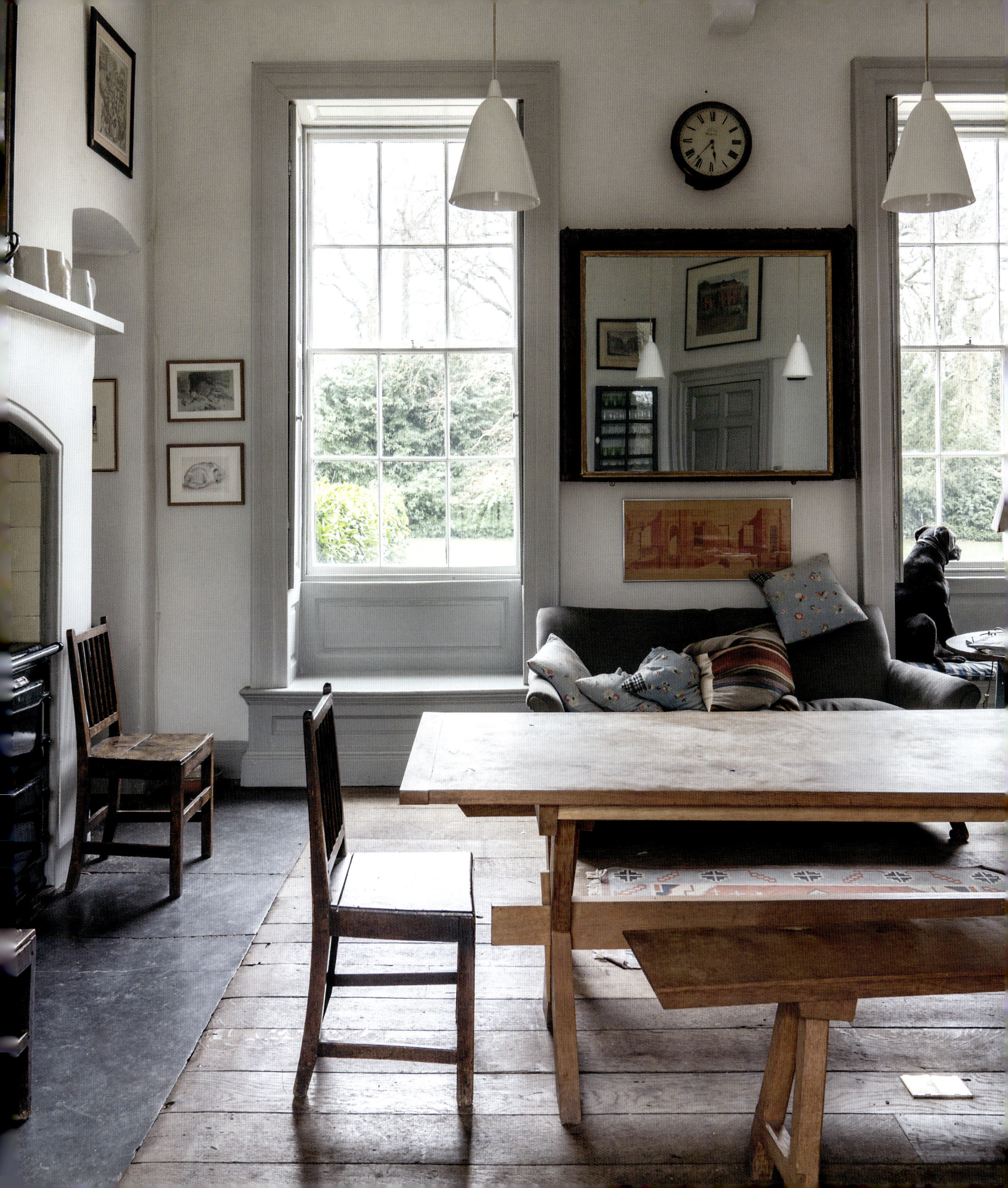

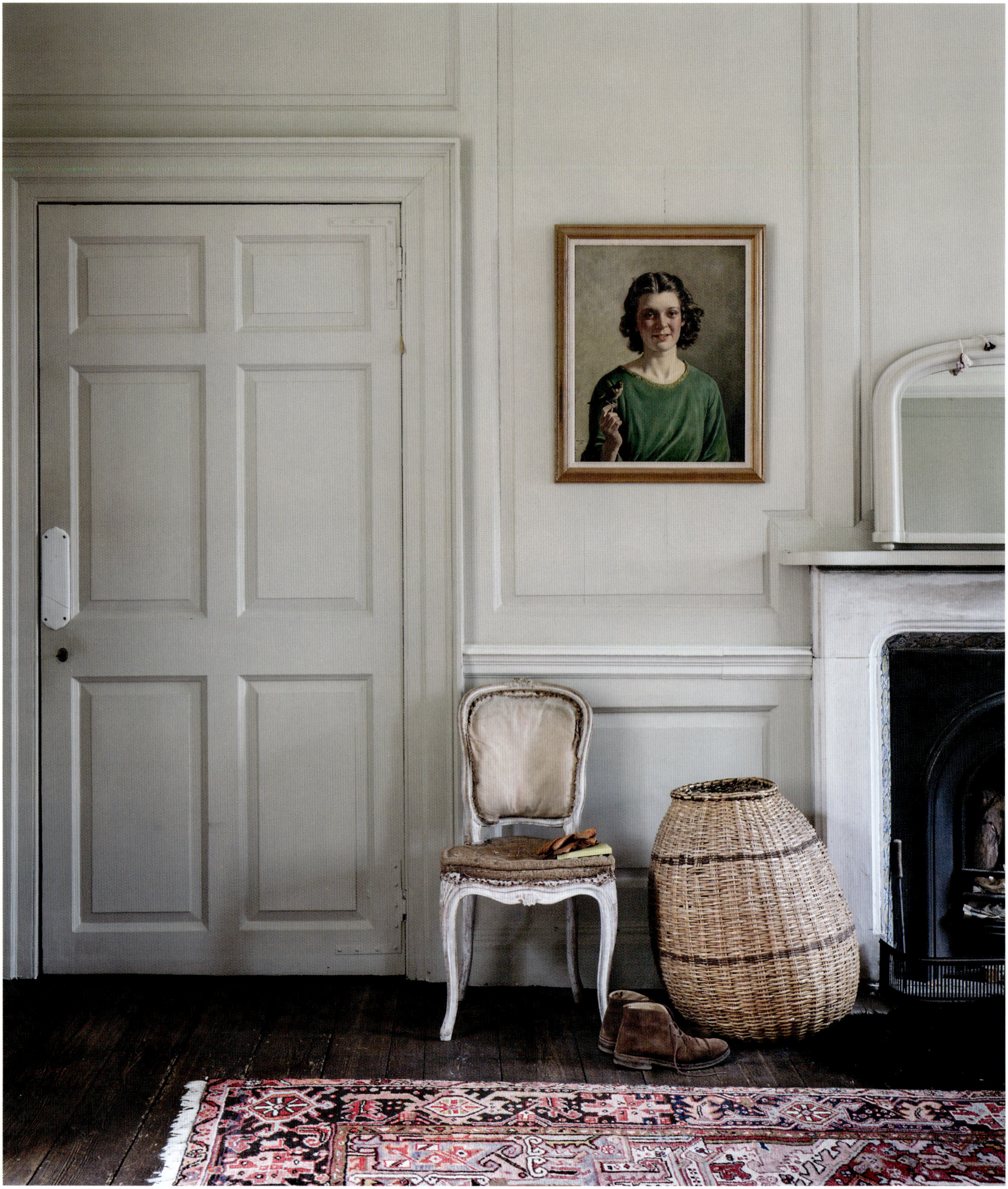

CASE STUDY 9

FACING PAGE
Both the paint colour and the paint finish render this bedroom timeless. Shaded White is a neutral tone that feels neither too warm nor too cool. It takes its name from the soft tone created when white is used in deep shade, and it has a gentle greyness that results in restful spaces with a relaxed feel. The Dead Flat finish is the modern answer to "flatted lead", used in the second quarter of the 18th century. Here, it replicates the traditional look of this historic property.

RIGHT
Shaded White has also been used on the panelling in the bathroom but this time it is teamed with Arsenic. This lively green changes the room's atmosphere but is not overwhelming because it has been kept well below the eyeline. The Estate Eggshell finish is robust, smooth and silky — making it perfect for a bathroom.

QUINTESSENTIALLY COUNTRY

CASE STUDY 9

QUINTESSENTIALLY COUNTRY PALETTE

RECIPE TIPS

* A light hall gives licence to use rich colours in the rooms off it. Here, Hardwick White is the perfect foil for Blazer and Hague Blue.
* Strong colours feel more relaxed when matched with a strong trim, as in this dining room.
* White trim used with saturated colours, as in this sitting room, creates a lively atmosphere.
* Deep colours enhance rooms used to relax in at the end of the day.
* Darker corridors make the rooms at the end of them feel lighter.
* Neutral bedrooms, like this Shaded White one, feel restful in a house packed with colour in other areas.

HALL

HARDWICK WHITE
walls/skirting

WIMBORNE WHITE
ceiling

SITTING ROOM

HAGUE BLUE
walls

WIMBORNE WHITE
cornice/ceiling

KITCHEN

STRONG WHITE
walls

LAMP ROOM GRAY
woodwork

RAILINGS
units

DINING ROOM

BLAZER
walls

JOA'S WHITE
cornice/ceiling

BATHROOM

ARSENIC
lower panelling

SHADED WHITE
upper panelling

BEDROOM

SHADED WHITE
panelling

132

CASE STUDIES

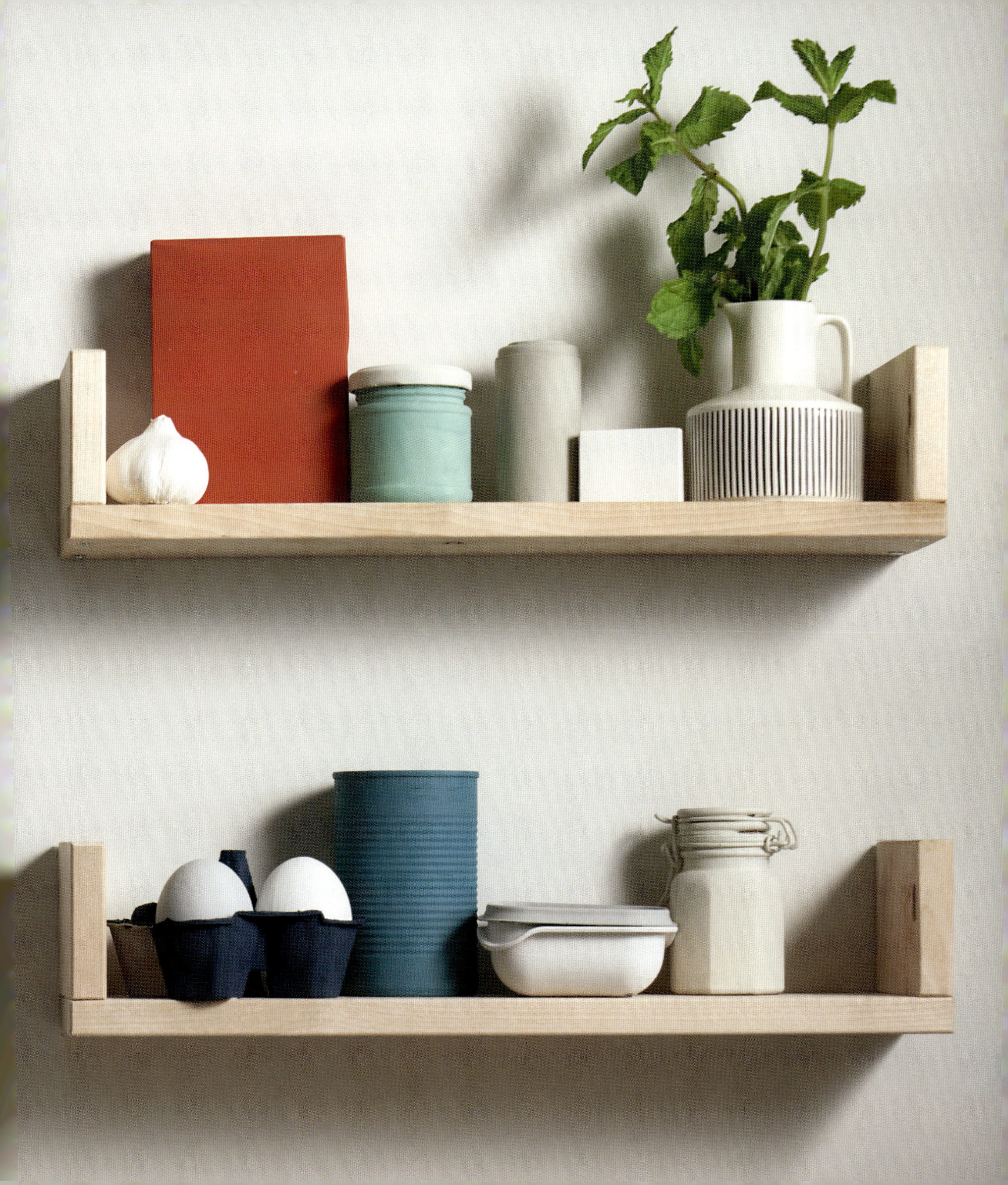

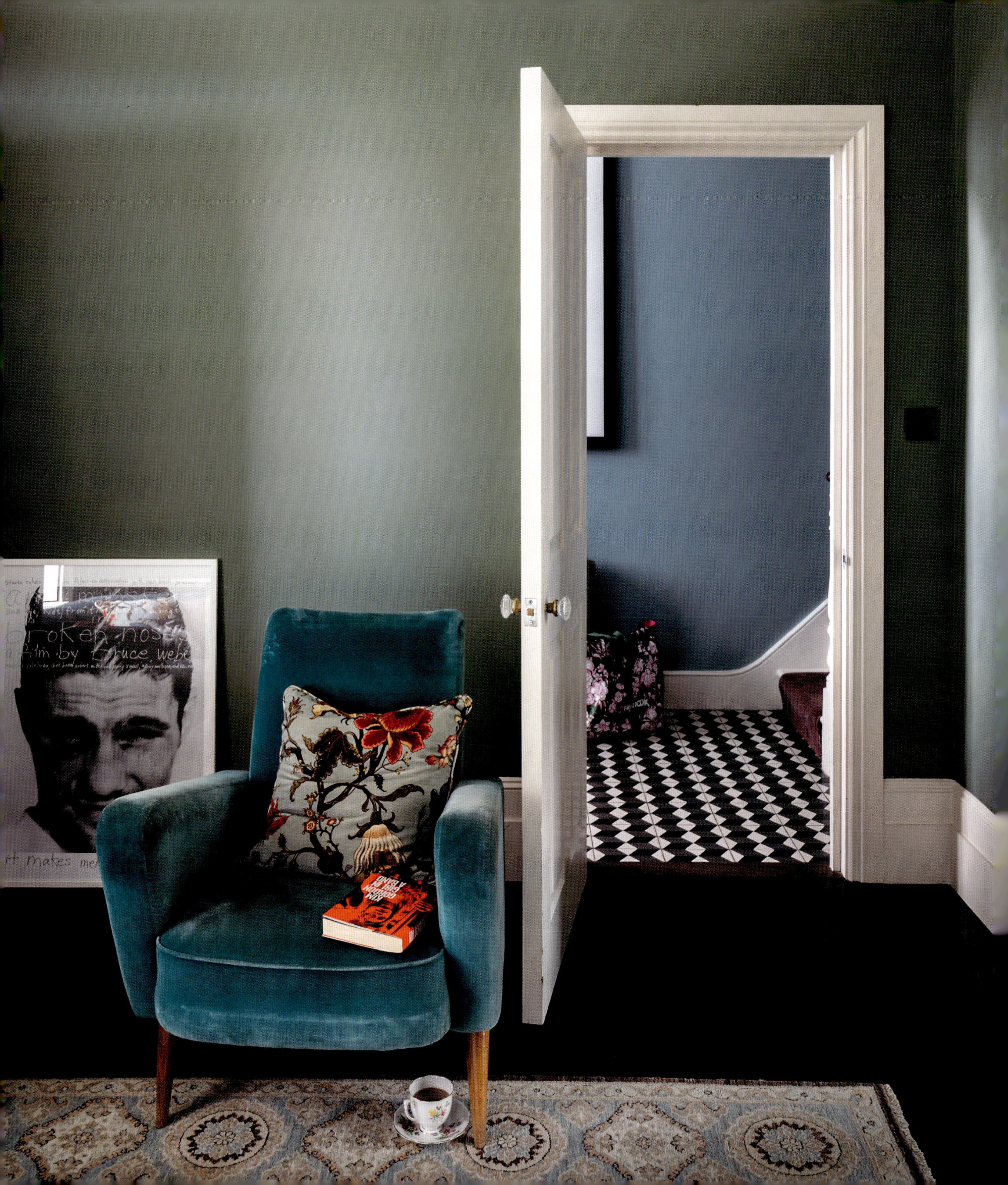
broken noses
a film by

CASE STUDY 10

EASY MODERN

For most of us, our homes are a constant arena for experimentation. That is certainly true of this house, which belongs to a long-time stylist, recently turned designer. Located in an achingly fashionable area of London, it is full of quirky personal objects and cutting-edge art. It is also packed with colour, but not those that shock or jolt, rather ones that feel eclectic while being comforting.

This sense of warmth is first evident in the front entrance, painted Charleston Gray, the strongest colour in our Contemporary Neutrals group of paints. Its warm undertone means it sits seamlessly with the brick, the perfect choice for making the house stand out from the crowd but not shout "look at me". The colour of the front door has been taken over its full frame, making the entrance appear bigger and more welcoming, while the same tile design on the garden path and in the hall lures you into the house.

Once inside, a purple stair runner brings warmth and a whimsical twist to a hall that is predominantly white, while the Oval Room Blue wall that runs from the ground floor up on to the first floor gives the space character. The most blackened of Farrow & Ball blues, this colour has a subtly aged feel that creates depth and balance in this typically compact entrance hall.

FACING PAGE
The hall is painted in Strong White, with one contrast wall in Oval Room Blue. This continues onto the next floor, adding a feeling of solidity to the house and, when viewed from the front living room, provides a fun contrast with the Green Smoke on its walls.

INSET ABOVE
The warm tones of Charleston Gray sit perfectly alongside the brick and create a warm and welcoming entrance.

ABOVE
Green Smoke has an inviting quality and works well on walls in shadowy corners, as in the internal living room. The kitchen feels lighter when approached from this smoky tone, which has taken over from charcoal as the colour for fashionable homes.

135

EASY MODERN

CASE STUDY 10

BELOW RIGHT AND FACING PAGE
The Green Smoke walls feel less mysterious when seen in the front living room, which benefits from more natural light than the internal living room. The original mouldings, window shutters and boxes are picked out in Strong White. This classic way of decorating, with a colour on the walls and white on the woodwork, feels both comforting and familiar. Despite the strong contrast, this scheme still manages to evoke a sense of calm. Art by Peter Blake.

PAGES 138-9 AND PAGE 140, TOP
The kitchen has been kept as light and bright as possible, with Strong White on the walls and ceiling, to disguise the break between the two planes, and cooler Pavilion Gray on the skirting, for contrast and definition. The stars of the show are, without doubt, the bespoke brass cabinets and the contemporary window seat — an irresistible place for sitting and relaxing. All of the decoration in this room complements the clean lines of the space.

The owner has chosen Strong White for the remaining hall walls and all the woodwork, which then acts as a common denominator throughout the house. Using white on trim fluctuates in and out of fashion, but here in this house it enhances the colours of the rooms and acts as a visual palette cleanser to help balance the bolder shades. With its understated urban feel and light grey undertones, Strong White adds a contemporary twist to this period home.

Green Smoke has been used on all of the walls in the living room. In the internal area of the living room, which lacks natural light, the colour takes on a delightfully mysterious quality and feels calming and therapeutic. People often shy away from using stronger shades in darker spaces, but it is much more effective to embrace the darkness and create a space that is irresistibly inviting.

In the front area of the living room, which benefits from more natural light, the same wall colour retains its depth but appears softer and has a weathered familiarity that sits perfectly with the Oval Room Blue in the adjacent hall. It is somehow comforting to see blue and green together; they are nature's colours, after all, and always feel embracing. This is a particularly clever use of colour because the living room, with its view of the feature wall in the hall, feels snug and intimate, while the light kitchen and the rest of the hall have a more functional feel. The spaces sit together seamlessly on account of the same white — Strong White — being used in all of them, whether on the walls or trim.

Strong White has been taken through to the kitchen (see pages 138–9 and 140, top), to make the most of the light in this largely glazed space, where the focal point, visible all the way from the front door, is a contemporary window seat, ideal for sitting and soaking up the midday sun. The green of the garden is neatly echoed in both the vintage fabric and the rich green metro tiles, while the brass units add another contemporary design flourish. Pavilion Gray on the trim in the kitchen brings a little more structure to this new extension and prevents the room from feeling under decorated.

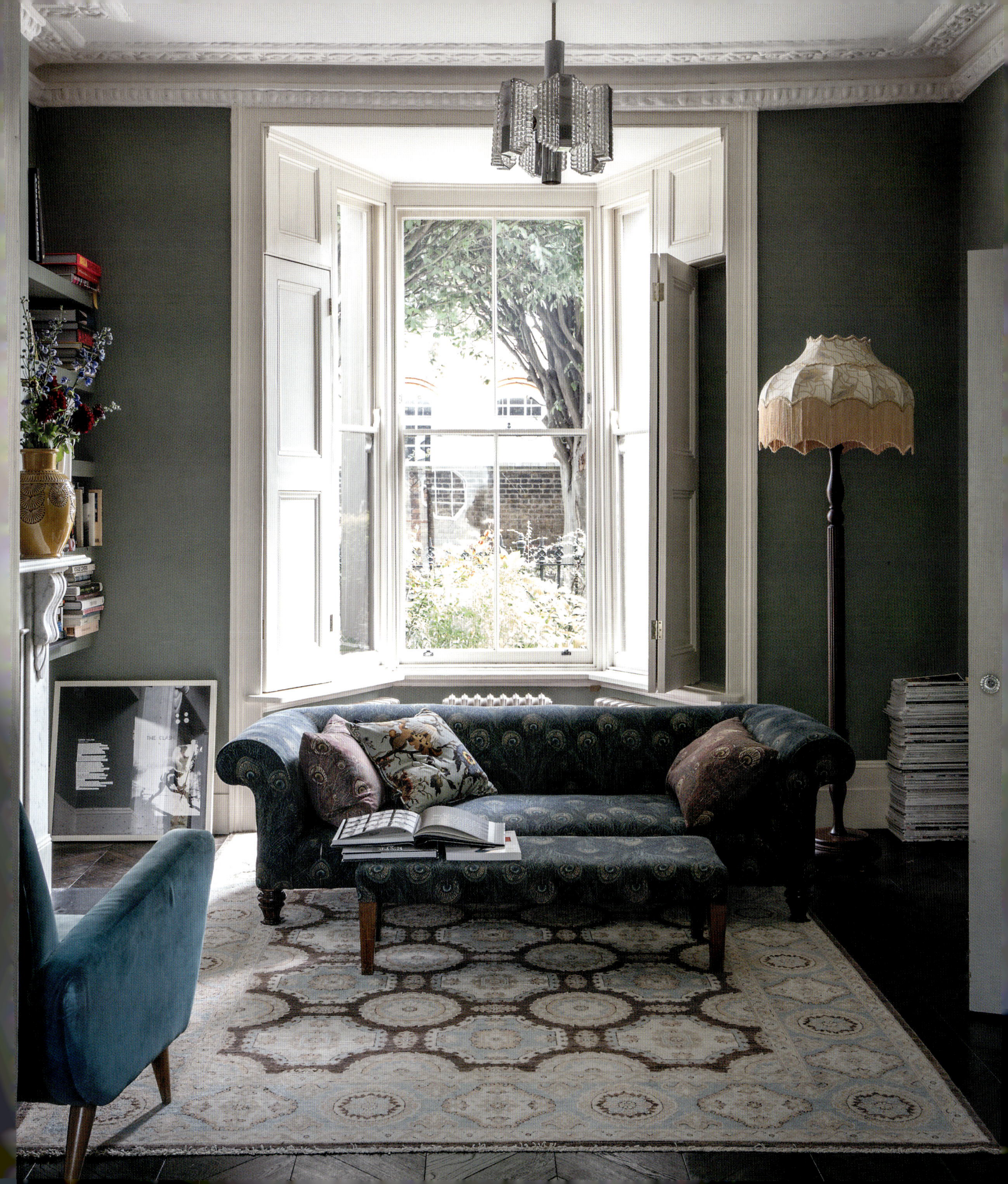
THE CLASH

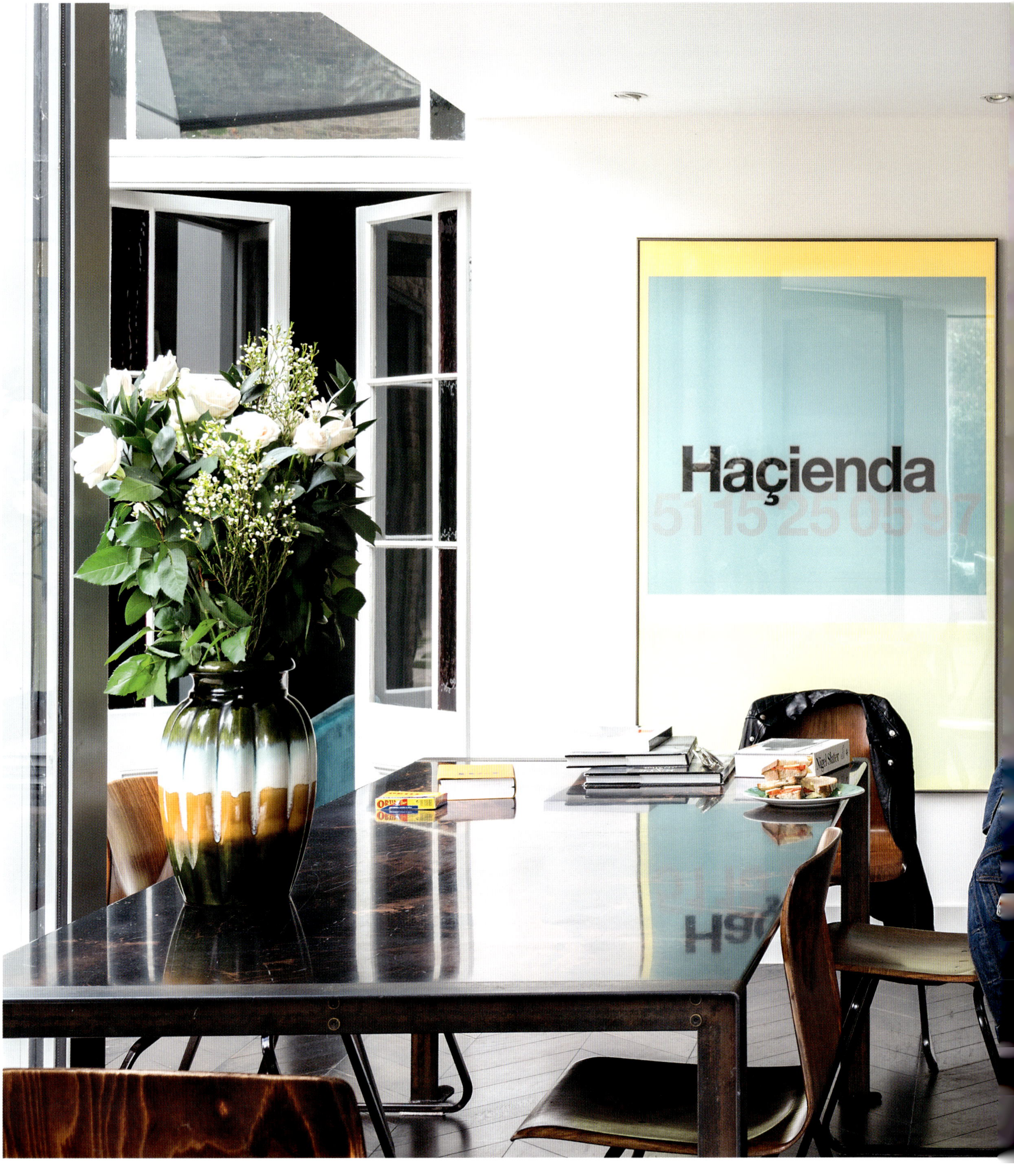
Haçienda
51 15 25 05 97

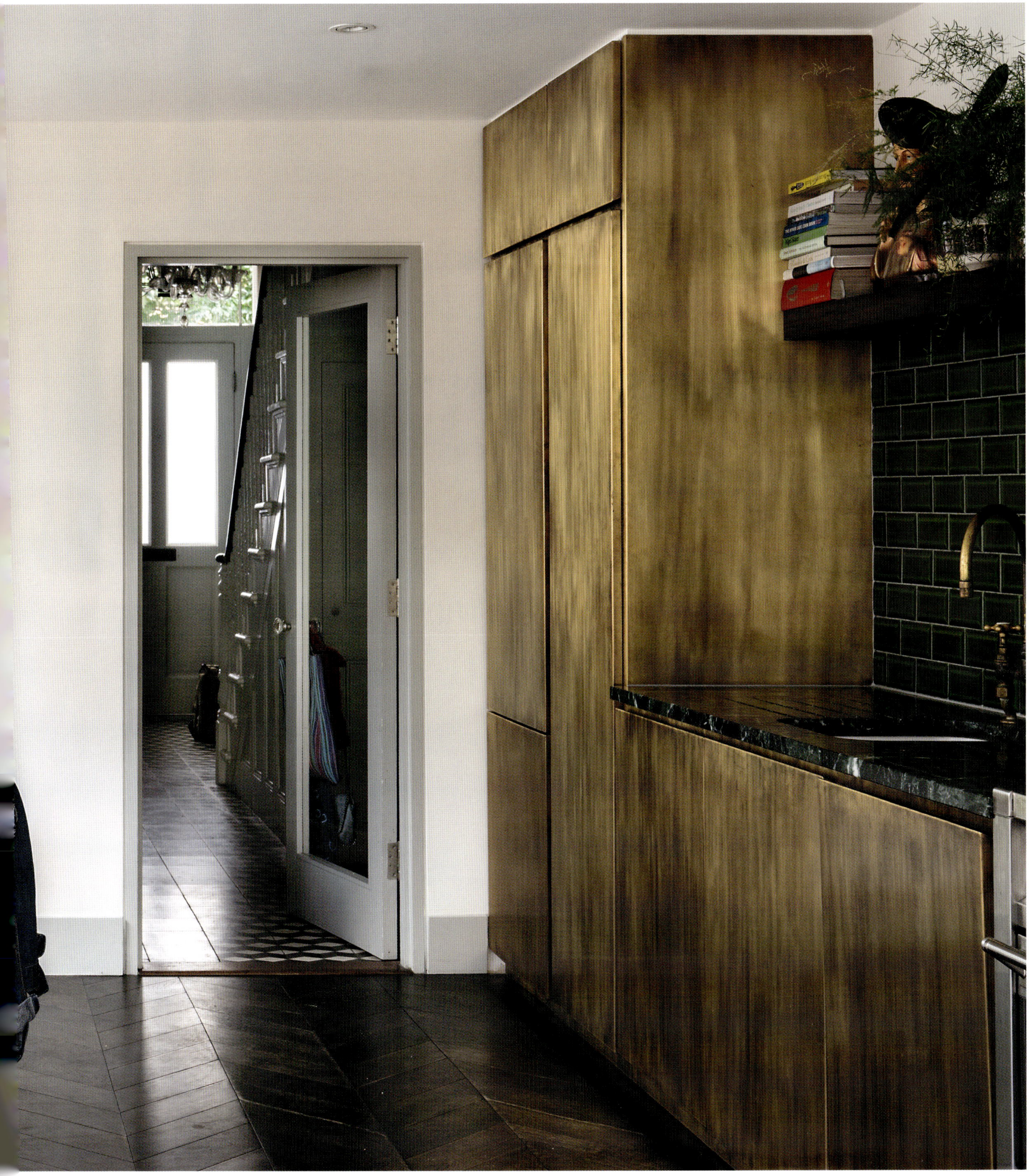

CLYDE
BEATTY-COLE BROS.
COMBINED
CIRCUS
MUNCIE
29
WORLDS
LARGEST
CIRCUS
ON. JUNE

FACING PAGE, BOTTOM
Similar colours have been used in the bathroom and bedrooms to link them. Often regarded as a very "girly" pink, Nancy's Blushes on the underside of the bathtub feels almost graphic when counterbalanced with the blue tiles. Peignoir on the wall, however, retains its special dusty grey tone, while Middleton Pink, our prettiest and most delicate pink, feels fresh and gently playful in this child's bedroom.

BELOW
The summerhouse colours echo those of the main house. Middleton Pink creates an enchanting interior that sits harmoniously with Dove Tale on the exterior cladding. Strong White has again been used on all the trim.

PAGES 142-3
Blue Gray walls and trim in the master bedroom create an oasis of calm, where the colour will shift as the light conditions change through the day. Charleston Gray on the radiators gives them a vintage presence.

Upstairs, clever colour touches in the somewhat vibrant bathroom create a link between the softer Middleton Pink child's bedroom and the Blue Gray master bedroom (on pages 142–3). Sophisticated pink Peignoir has been used on the walls. The greyest of pinks, with a big dose of black, this colour feels romantic but not sugary, so perfect, if unexpected, alongside the soft blue tiles. As is customary in this house, an extra twist has been introduced by using attention-grabbing Nancy's Blushes on the underside of the Victorian bathtub.

In the master bedroom, Blue Gray has been used on both the walls and the trim, to create the most relaxing of rooms. This colour's subtle mix of blue, green and black pigments makes it feel as if the room has been this colour forever. It also has the almost magical quality of gently shifting between blue and grey, depending on the light and the time of day – here, it is more upbeat and blue in the morning and cosier towards the end of the day. The owner's decorating flair is evident once more in the Charleston Gray-painted radiators, which also appear to have always been this colour.

More soft tones have been used in the summerhouse, making it feel like a natural extension of the house. Middleton Pink reappears to create a charming and warm interior, while the Dove Tale exterior complements the slightly darker Charleston Gray used on the exterior woodwork of the house.

Every colour in this home has been carefully considered, yet it feels as if it has been showered with buckets of love rather than being over designed. The kitchen is light and vibrant while the living rooms are intimate and the bedrooms relaxed. It is, however, the colour that nourishes this home and creates a sense of security.

EASY MODERN

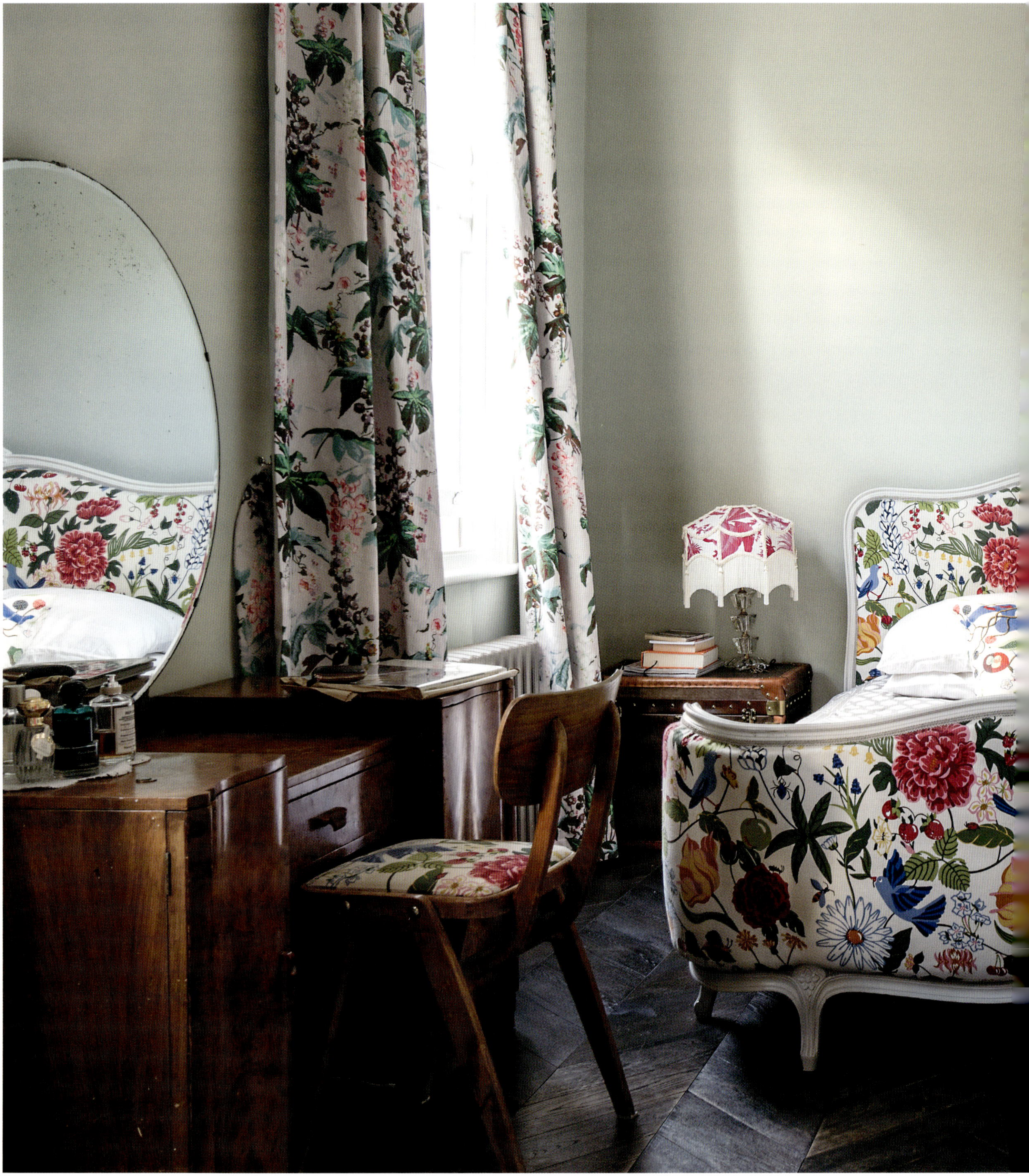

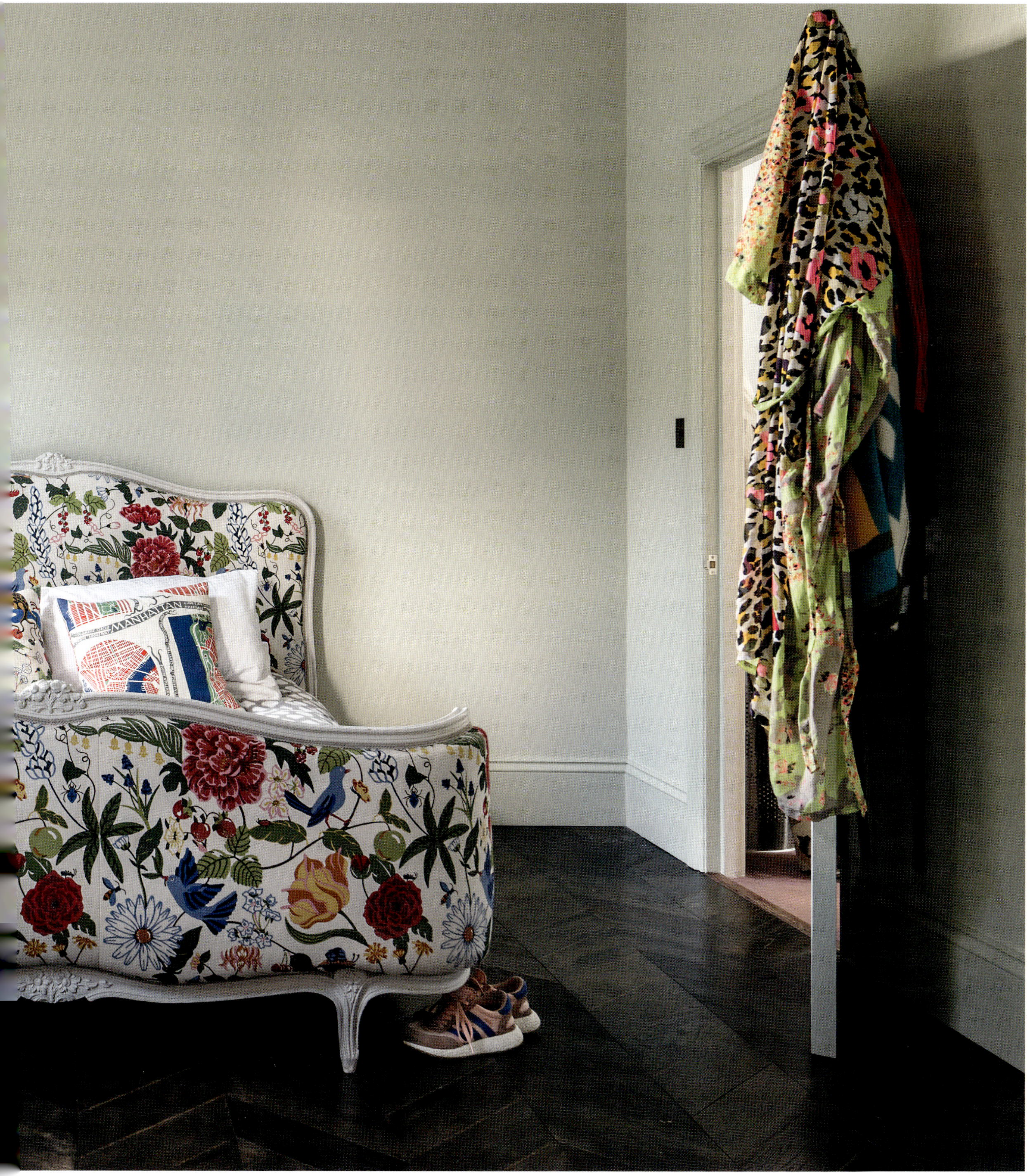
MANHATTAN

CASE STUDY 10

EASY MODERN PALETTE

RECIPE TIPS

* Create a crisp look by contrasting the walls and trim, as with the use of Strong White throughout this house.
* Use the same rich tone, such as Green Smoke, to add interest on walls in adjoining rooms where light conditions vary.
* Choose tones from the same colour family, in this case Charleston Gray and Dove Tale, on the front and back of the house to define a natural axis.
* Repeat an interior colour in an exterior garden room to unite the two.

HALL, STAIRS AND LANDING

STRONG WHITE
walls/woodwork/ceiling

OVAL ROOM BLUE
feature wall

KITCHEN

STRONG WHITE
walls/ceiling

PAVILION GRAY
woodwork

CHILD'S BEDROOM

MIDDLETON PINK
walls/woodwork

STRONG WHITE
ceiling

MASTER BEDROOM

BLUE GRAY
walls/woodwork

CHARLESTON GRAY
radiators

STRONG WHITE
ceiling

LIVING ROOMS

GREEN SMOKE
walls

STRONG WHITE
woodwork/cornice/ceiling

BATHROOM

PEIGNOIR
walls

NANCY'S BLUSHES
bath

SUMMERHOUSE

DOVE TALE
exterior

MIDDLETON PINK
interior

EXTERIOR

CHARLESTON GRAY
front door/frame

CASE STUDIES

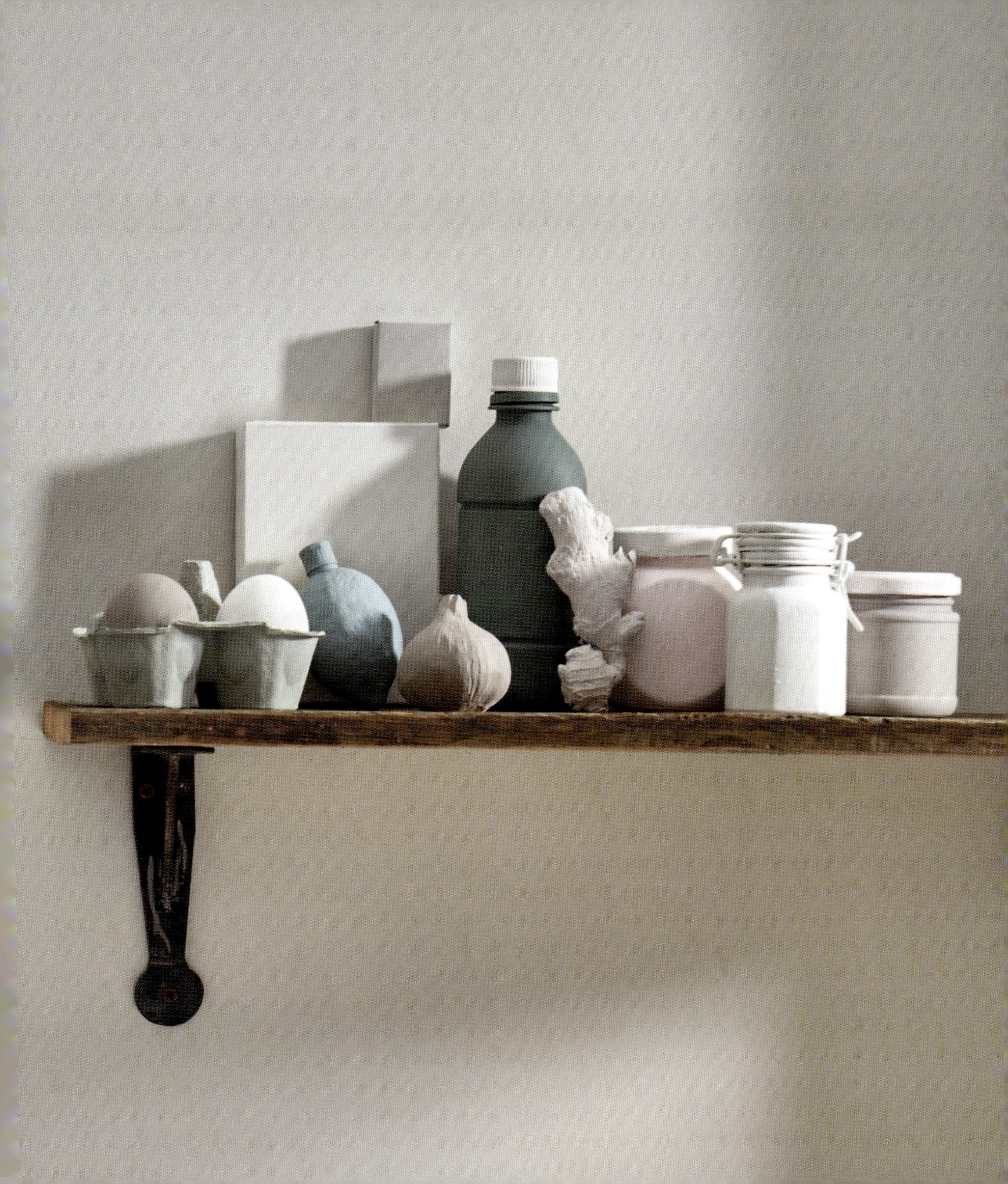

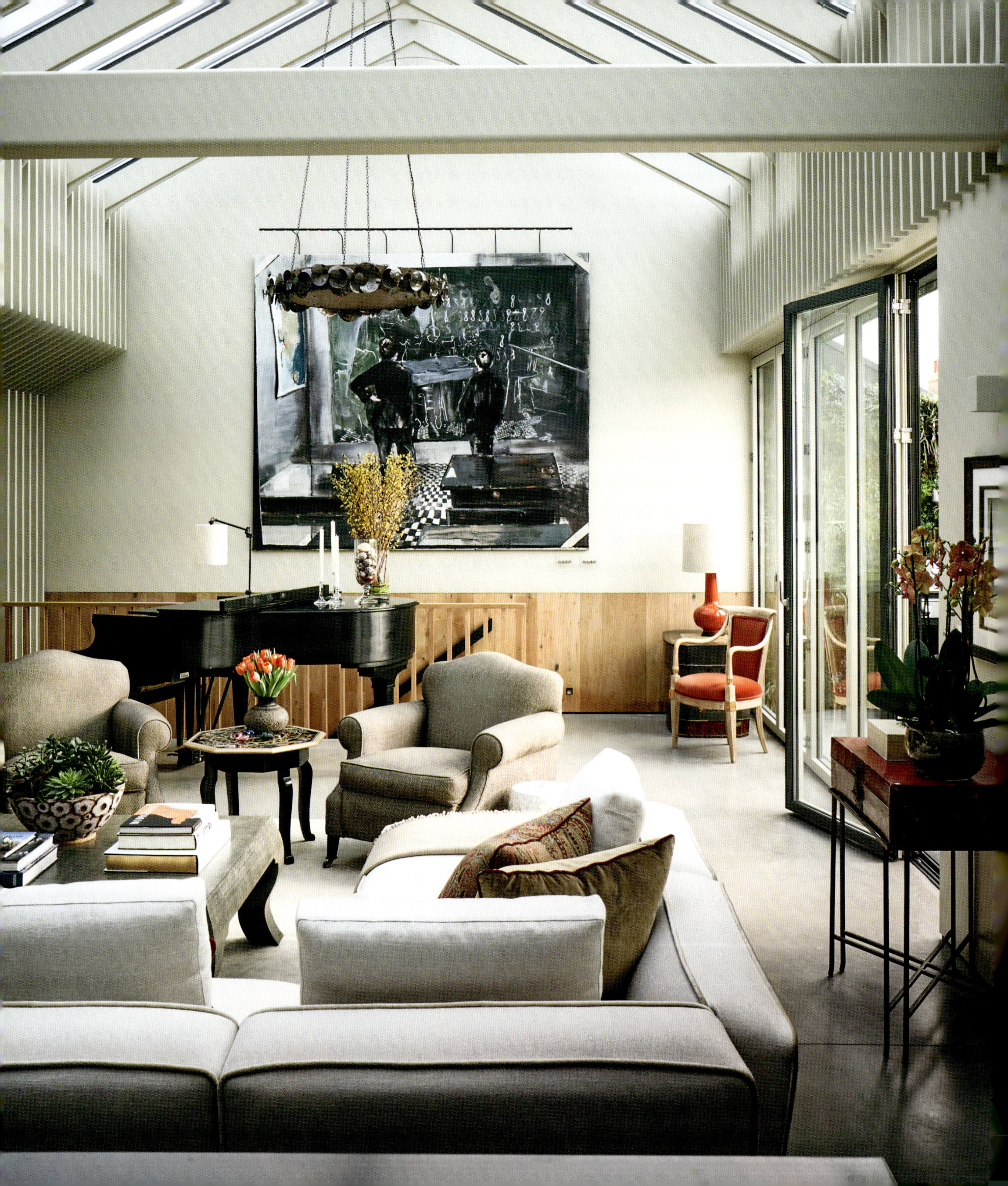

CASE STUDY 11

INDUSTRIAL REBORN

This stylish home has had many lives. Originally a Victorian industrial laundry and then a film studio, it has now been completely refurbished to truly exacting standards. Its latest incarnation is as an "upside-down" house, with the living areas on the light-drenched first floor and the bedrooms and bathrooms on the darker ground floor. A little overwhelmed by the acres of white paint they were initially faced with, the owners embarked on softening the somewhat severe joinery and demanding aesthetic with colour.

The period façade of this house gives no indication of the cutting-edge design within but, by way of a clue, the front door has been redecorated in Biddulph Bronze (A), an extraordinary colour that is neither black, brown or grey. Its roots are firmly in the past – it was discovered at Biddulph Grange, a landscaped Victorian garden in Staffordshire – but somehow it fits perfectly here.

Adding colour to the interior of the house was a particularly brave thing to do because the building had been designed to remain an architect-friendly pure white. In addition, the two 12-metre (39-ft) walls running the length of the living area, which are covered in fin-like, rhythmic panels that are bathed in light, required nothing less than a perfect finish, making it a painstaking job for the decorators.

FACING PAGE AND RIGHT
The architectural lines in this living area have been softened with Old White. A colour that you could never tire of, it has a discreet grey–green undertone. Despite feeling a little unexpected, it sits comfortably with the oak, creating the perfect background for antiques and giving the fins spanning the building a restrained air. Here, the quality of the paint is seen at its very best and, at varying times of the day, it feels as if the colour is evolving and reflecting nature's dappled shades. Art by Simon Lucas.

INSET ABOVE LEFT
Glamorous Biddulph Bronze (A), an Archive colour that was created for the National Trust many years ago, makes for a dramatic entrance.

CASE STUDY 11

BELOW
Painting the TV room darker than Old White was irresistible. Archive colour Olive (A) creates an intimate space in contrast to the living area. As the door between these spaces is always open, the colours had to sit flawlessly together.

FACING PAGE
In the main living area, soft furnishings provide a contrast to the architectural kitchen, with its dark oak units and concrete floors. The shelves at each end of the dining table repeat the Olive (A) of the TV room on the opposite side of the space.

After much consideration, Old White, the darkest colour in our Traditional Neutrals group of paints, was chosen to create the inviting atmosphere that was desired. The colour makes the space feel restrained, while imparting a richness and depth. This is as a result of the unmatched quality of the paint and the fact that no compromises are made in the ingredients used – which really shows. The complex underlying grey-green tone has a certain softness, which generates a decorative scheme that feels as if it might have been there forever, despite the cutting-edge architecture. With its roots firmly in the past, this inimitable colour was one of the first whites created by Farrow & Ball and yet it sits perfectly in this super-modern house.

Small colour adjustments can make huge changes in homes with a neutral palette and creating a scheme that is right for your space is not as simple as you may think. Light conditions play an important role, especially in a building such as this, which is flooded with light in the day but needs to feel snug at night. Old White provides just enough colour for the owners to feel comfortable, but is sufficiently neutral to sit sympathetically with the huge expanse of concrete flooring and smoked oak joinery.

The kitchen, dining and living area is open-plan and the fin-like panels also front the bookshelves built into the walls and the doorways leading to the adjacent pantry and TV room. These smaller spaces offered up the opportunity to add some extra colour. However, it was important that this darker tone should relate strongly to the main room. With a Farrow & Ball Colour Consultant on site, the owner and her designer had access to Archive colour Olive (A). Its calm tone is perfect in the cosier TV room, creating a cocooned escape from the main room while echoing the colour of the greenery from the "living wall" on the balcony. Olive (A) was also reprised on the two bookshelves at either end of the dining table, to create a more intimate atmosphere for eating, and used on the shelving in the pantry, but this time purely to raise a smile.

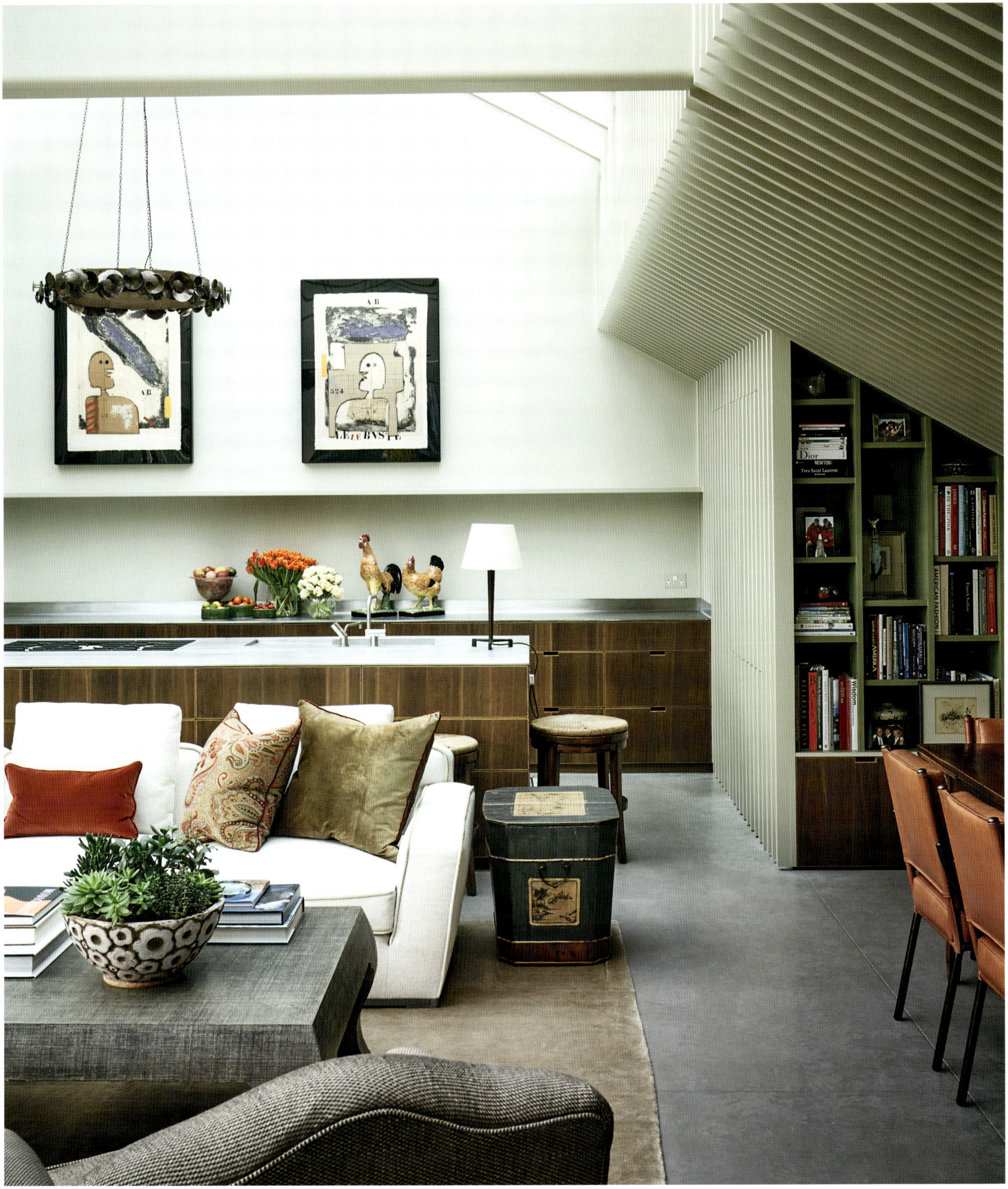
Dior
AMERICAN FASHION

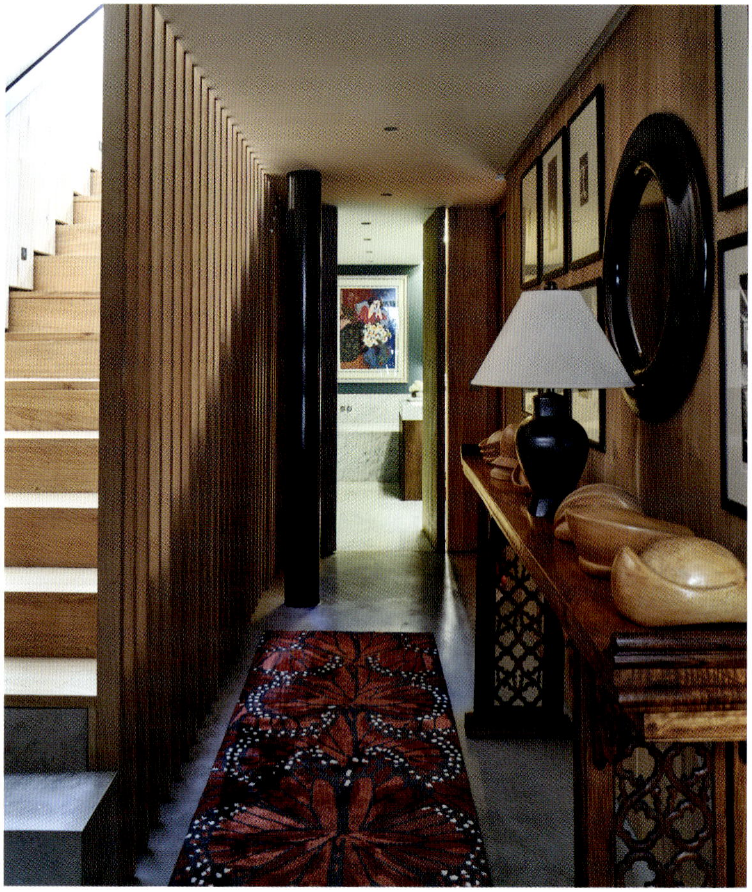

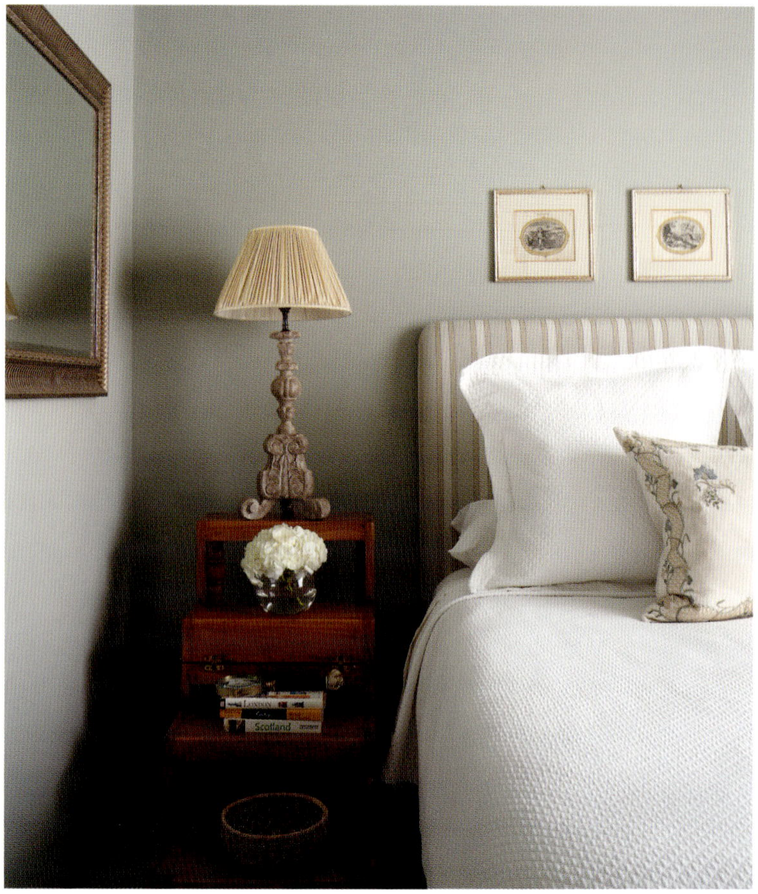
Scotland

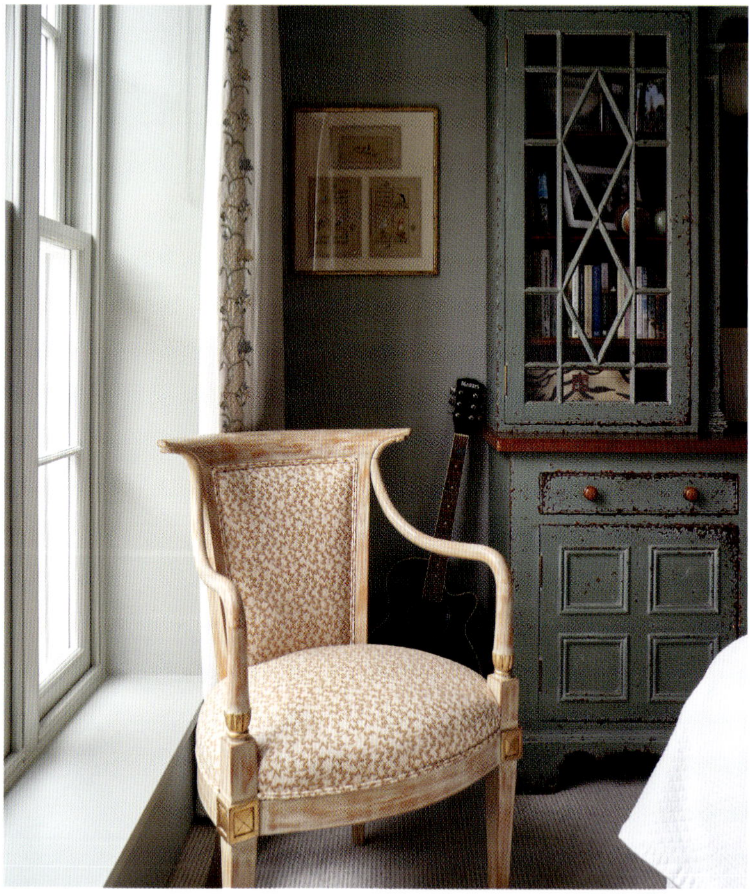

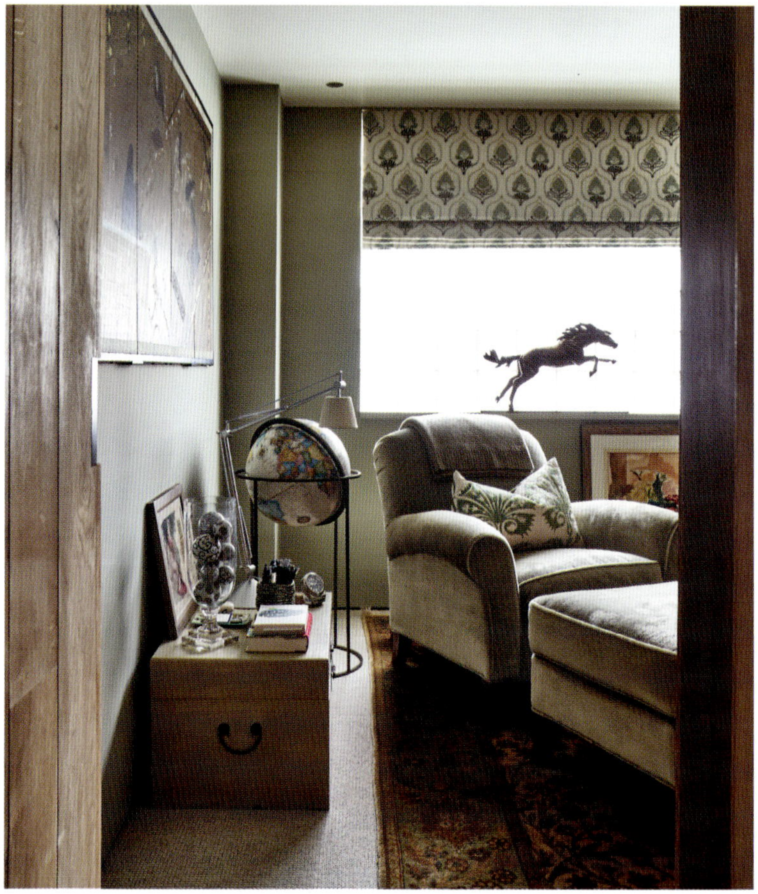

FACING PAGE, TOP LEFT
A dark metal banister and pale oak staircase lead upstairs, the bottom two concrete steps providing continuity with the rest of the flooring. This corridor has a reserved tone that makes the upstairs level seem all the more enticing.

FACING PAGE, TOP RIGHT AND BOTTOM LEFT
The bedrooms provide respite from the contemporary shapes upstairs. Soft Blue Gray on the walls and ceiling in the guest bedroom creates a tranquil haven for visitors.

FACING PAGE, BOTTOM RIGHT
Stony Ground was used in this study to complete the quietly cohesive scheme on this floor. Its classic stone colour has an underlying red that adds warmth and creates a soft, beige finish, which feels restful by night and nourishing by day.

BELOW
In the bathroom, the white marble is complemented by a mix of dark wood, mirror-clad cabinets and moody Inchyra Blue on the walls. Each of these adds substance and texture, but it is the wall colour that makes the room feel so inviting.

Downstairs, an altogether darker and more brooding oak-lined corridor serves all the bedrooms. It certainly would have been wrong to paint the beautiful wood, but in order to add some much-yearned-for colour, the bathroom, which sits at the end of the corridor opposite the front door, has been transformed with moody Inchyra Blue walls. This, along with the pillars in Biddulph Bronze (A), make the entrance to the house feel much more inviting and promise treasures to come.

All the bedrooms are decorated simply to make the best use of limited natural daylight. The guest bedroom is a serene sanctuary painted in Blue Gray, the strongest of the colours used downstairs, but not one that the owners have to live with every day. This has been taken over all the woodwork and the ceiling to make it harmonious. In the master bedroom, the lighter and softer Shaded White has been used to great effect, creating a timeless space that induces sleep. Stony Ground and classic Bone felt perfect for the two studies, so one can drift seamlessly from room to room, barely noticing that the colours change. This adds to the understated elegance of the ground floor.

This house is indeed a fabulous melange of things both old and new. Its use has been changed from industrial to residential, its layout has been reconfigured so the living space and bedrooms are flipped, and the décor designed to suit the present owners and make it their home. In principle it might not have worked, but it turns out to be a comfortable modern masterpiece.

CASE STUDY 11

INDUSTRIAL REBORN PALETTE

RECIPE TIPS

* Your home should be an extension of yourself – use colours that make you feel comfortable.
* A restrained palette of colours, such as Shaded White, Bone and Stony Ground, which are used downstairs in this house, will make light-deprived spaces feel bigger.
* Carry an accent colour through the space, as Olive (A) has been here.
* Use dramatic colour on the front door to signal the treasures that are to come.
* Make a feature of architectural elements, such as pillars, rather than trying to disguise them.

HALL

SLIPPER SATIN
ceiling

BIDDULPH BRONZE (A)
pillars

BATHROOM

INCHYRA BLUE
walls

SLIPPER SATIN
ceiling

STUDY 1

STONY GROUND
walls

SLIPPER SATIN
ceiling

MOUSE'S BACK
sill/reveals

STUDY 2

BONE
all

LIVING AREA

OLD WHITE
walls/woodwork

OLIVE (A)
shelves

PANTRY

OFF-WHITE
walls/ceiling

OLIVE (A)
shelves

GUEST BEDROOM

BLUE GRAY
all

MASTER BEDROOM

SLIPPER SATIN
ceiling

SHADED WHITE
walls

TV ROOM

OLIVE (A)
all

EXTERIOR

BIDDULPH BRONZE (A)
door/window frames

CASE STUDIES

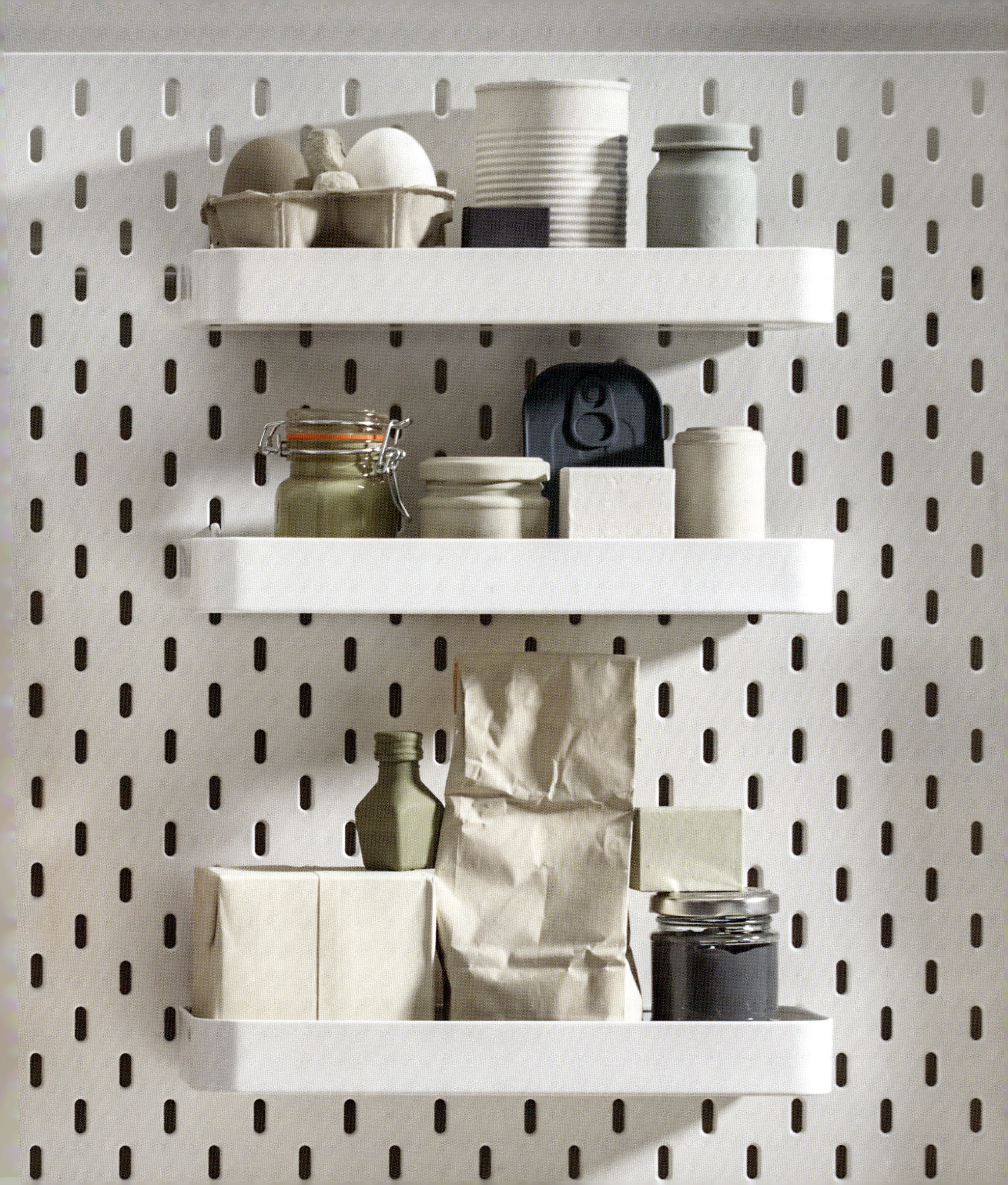

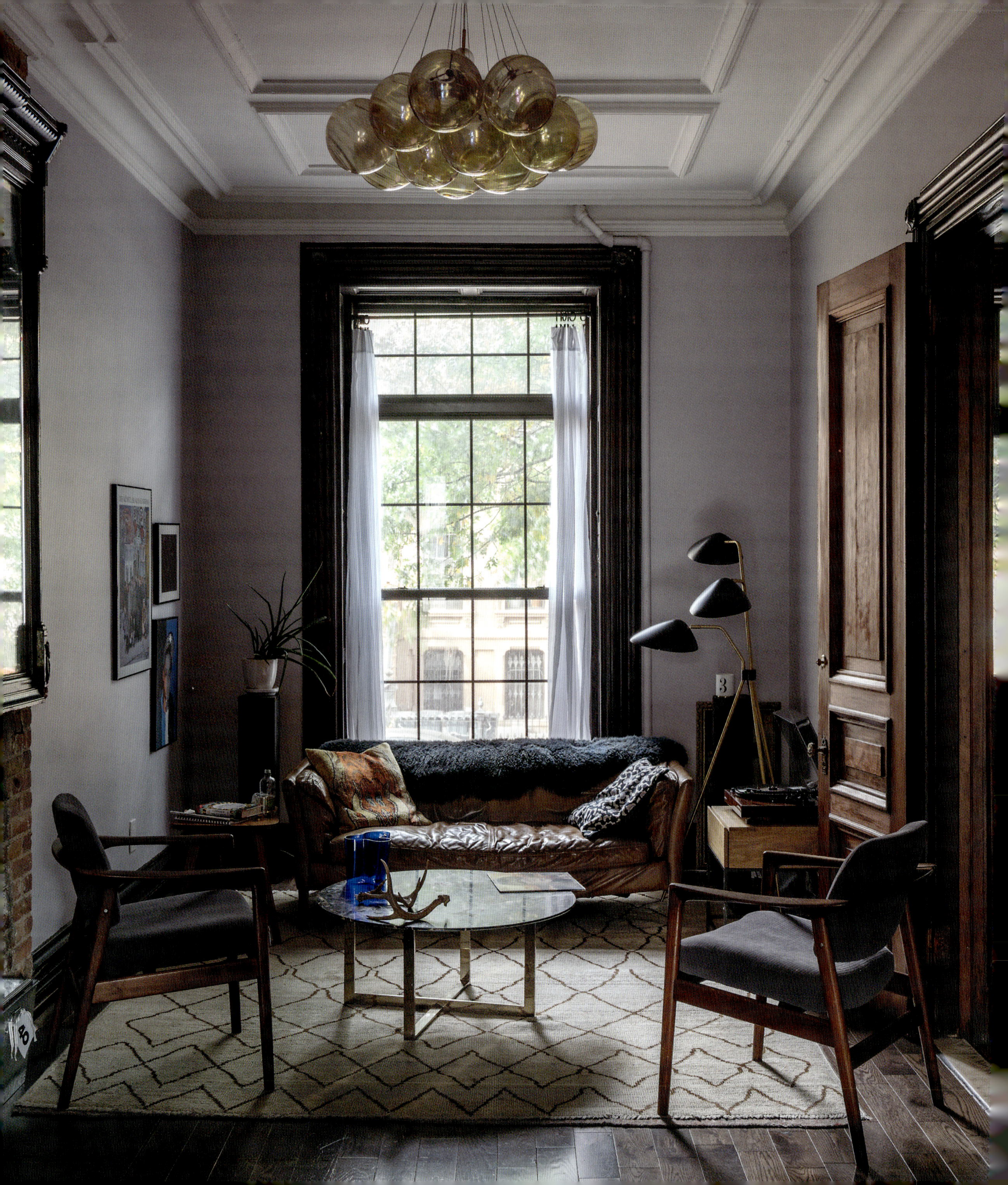

LIGHT-FILLED BROWNSTONE

The owners of this three-storey brownstone in Brooklyn were drawn to its weathered exterior and original architectural details, all of which have been saved for posterity. This is not a house begging for colour but one much better suited to a stripped-back style that allows the authentic features to dominate. There is an overriding sense of light here, even though some of the rooms are illuminated by only a constant north light and others are tucked in the shadowy corners at the back of the house.

Original mahogany panelling and doors greet you in the ground floor hall. The rich wood brings warmth to this space and has been left to take centre stage. Having such strongly coloured features needn't mean that there is no choice when selecting a wall colour – Wevet feels restrained yet wholly considered here. The subtle urban feel of its light grey undertone adds a contemporary twist to this period home and shows off the original plasterwork to its best. The spindles on the stairs remain unpainted, preserved as much by economic necessity as by desire, while the stairs themselves rejoice in the dramatic tones of Hague Blue. On the upper landing, the rich mahogany gives way to an All White trim, the perfect pairing with Wevet for an effortlessly cohesive and stimulating scheme.

FACING PAGE
The sitting room in Calluna feels sophisticated and intimate. There is an eclectic dialogue between the wood, brick, wall colour and ceiling, showing that mixing materials can be just as important as using a range of colours.

INSET ABOVE
Like many doorways in Brooklyn, this one, painted in Charleston Gray, remains anonymous.

ABOVE
The authentic features of this interior influenced the choice of neutral tones, such as delicate Wevet on the walls in the hall. The unpainted panelling, newel post and handrail give an insight into how the house may have looked originally.

CASE STUDY 12

BELOW
Lighting can be a real game-changer for neutrals, making them appear calm or tantalizingly bright. When looking through from the Calluna dining area, Blackened on the kitchen walls appears to sing in the brighter light.

BELOW RIGHT
With a reined-in palette you can afford to add pattern and texture. In the open-plan hall, the combination of Wevet walls and All White window surrounds is made instantly more comfortable with Mahogany on the window frames and a patterned rug.

FACING PAGE
Blackened, a favourite in industrial spaces, is perfect in this kitchen alongside the steel cabinets, marble island, exposed brick and highly patterned tiles. Each component is as important as the next in creating the colour recipe for this room.

Minimal Blackened has been chosen for the light-filled kitchen walls, where its industrial feel is a fitting backdrop to steel cabinets and a marble-wrapped island. To overcome the problem of a very uneven top to the walls, so common in older houses, the colour has been stopped below the ceiling to match the line of the boxing over the hob. This introduces a contemporary twist and makes the wall colour feel stronger in contrast to the All White ceiling above it. Cool in nature, Blackened counterbalances the wood floor, exposed brickwork and original mahogany window surrounds. The window frames have been painted in the dark drab Mahogany, which sits sympathetically alongside the original wood while making no attempt to mimic it. This is echoed on the other side of the room, where the giant sliding doors lead to an expansive space that now acts as both the sitting room and dining area. The decision to use Calluna on the walls here was not taken lightly in a house that is resolutely netural, but it was a risk worth taking. Who would have thought that a colour inspired by the heather so prolific across the moors of Scotland would do so much to enhance the walls of a dining area in Brooklyn? It is the inclusion of a touch of black in Calluna that ensures it appears more lilac than pink. This makes it soft and tranquil yet strangely sophisticated, perfect for a room such as this, where so much entertaining takes place.

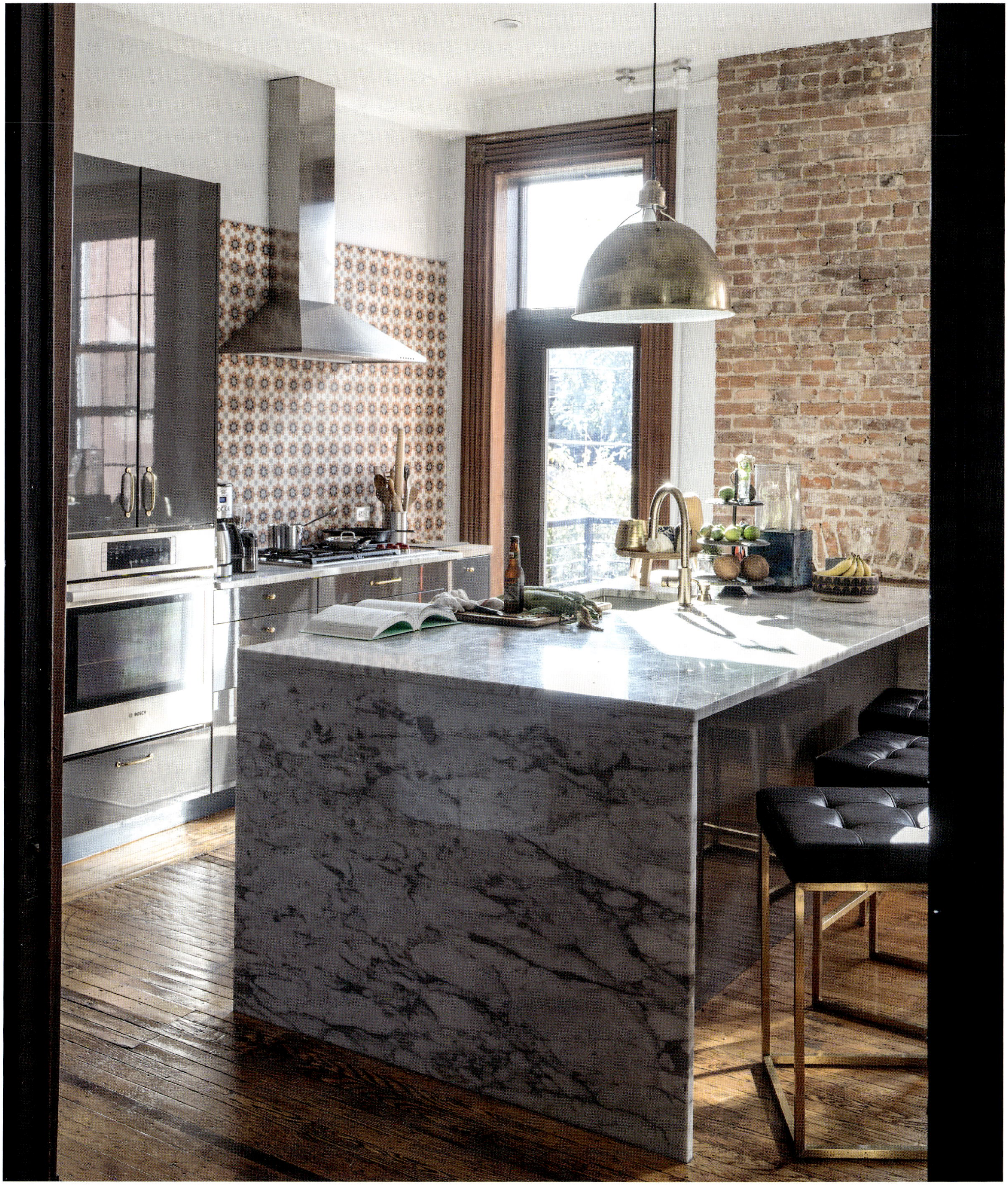

FOR BEGINNERS AND EXPERTS...
ANNETTE FUNICELLO
MICKEY ROONEY

FACING PAGE, TOP LEFT
Wevet, the most delicate of whites, gives a barely-there, almost translucent feel to the walls of the hall and landing, and forms the perfect foundation for the house. The stairs in deep, dark Hague Blue are a real treat, both grounding and dramatic.

FACING PAGE, BOTTOM LEFT
There could be no other choice for this bathroom than All White, whose colour is exactly as described. Unusually for white paint, it contains no other pigment except white, which creates the softest, most sympathetic colour without the colder, blue undertones of a brilliant white.

FACING PAGE, TOP RIGHT
Lively Blue Ground cannot help but raise the spirits in this children's bedroom, which is clean and uncomplicated without being cold. The All White window surround and Mahogany frames give an extra urban twist.

FACING PAGE, BOTTOM RIGHT
A master bedroom for colour-phobes. Delicate Pointing on the walls is easy on the eye. Proof that neutral rooms do not have to be boring.

RIGHT
Neutrals can be versatile. In this shadier corner of the master bedroom, Pointing feels warmer when contrasted with the cool blue sofa.

The master bedroom upstairs is an oasis of calm. Delicate Pointing, with its warmer undertone, has been layered on the walls, with fresh and uncomplicated All White on the trim, creating a really soft space. Pointing is the perfect colour in which to greet the day, and it has just enough warmth to feel relaxing and protective. As in the kitchen, the subtle nature of the wall colour becomes more prominent when contrasted with a "whiter" white on the trim.

In the adjoining bathroom, the trim colour of the bedroom becomes the wall colour, to make the transition to a more modern space a little more seamless. Subway tiles were much in evidence on the walls of original Brooklyn brownstones, but here they were too damaged to be able to salvage. However, contemporary replacements feel right at home.

At the top of the house, the neutral tones are laid to rest and the children have been indulged in their bedroom with some upbeat and happy colour. Although a comparatively clean blue, Blue Ground is never cold, which makes it perfect for creating a friendly atmosphere in which to grow up.

Timeless may be a hackneyed expression to use about this architectural gem but it is accurate. The owners have been extremely successful in retaining the old-world feel of their brownstone while making a modern family home. The original mahogany doors may create grand entrances, but the decoration throughout feels effortless. There is an innate honesty to this house, and that is not an easy thing to achieve.

CASE STUDY 12

LIGHT-FILLED BROWNSTONE PALETTE

RECIPE TIPS

* Don't feel compelled to have colour on every wall – neutrals still create the most relaxed of homes.
* Using All White on the trim will help you to see any colour alongside it on the walls, even the lightest of neutrals, such as Wevet or Pointing.
* When painting old woodwork alongside existing unpainted trim, choose a colour that is sympathetic to the original wood, as Mahogany is in this home, rather than trying to mimic it.
* Paint the treads and risers of a staircase in a bold feature colour, such as Hague Blue, to create a thread that runs throughout the house.

HALL

HAGUE BLUE — *stairs*
ALL WHITE — *ceiling/trim*
MAHOGANY — *windows*
WEVET — *walls*

KITCHEN

BLACKENED — *walls*
MAHOGANY — *windows*
ALL WHITE — *ceiling*

SITTING ROOM AND DINING AREA

CALLUNA — *walls*
MAHOGANY — *trim*
ALL WHITE — *ceiling/cornice*

CHILDREN'S BEDROOM

BLUE GROUND — *walls*
ALL WHITE — *ceiling/trim*
MAHOGANY — *windows*

BATHROOM

ALL WHITE — *all*

EXTERIOR

CHARLESTON GRAY — *all*

MASTER BEDROOM

POINTING — *walls*
ALL WHITE — *ceiling/trim*

CASE STUDIES

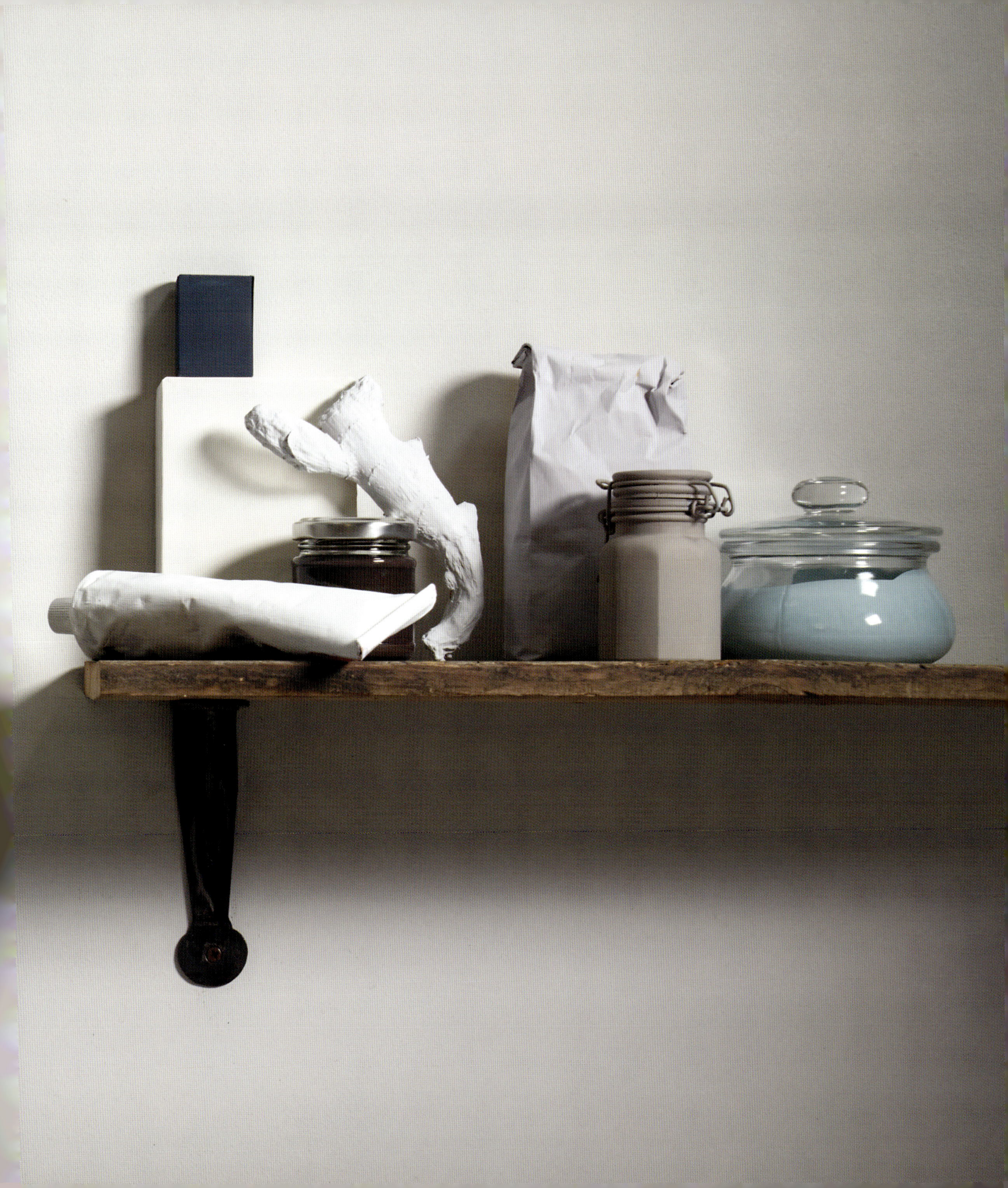

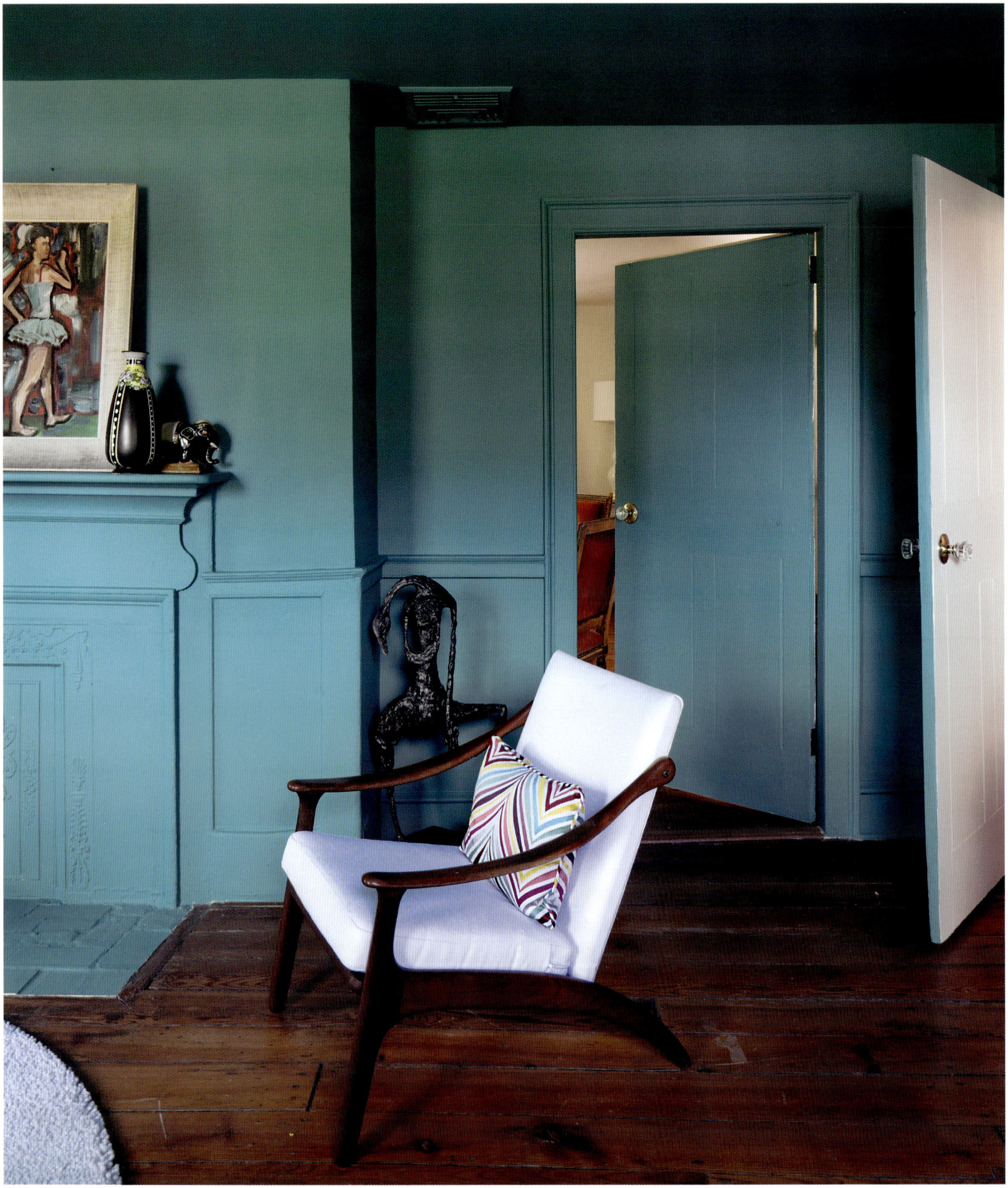

CASE STUDY 13

UPSTATE OASIS

Only 145km (90 miles) from New York City, this cottage feels a world away. Its position gives it a sense of light and perspective that is breathtaking, so when you arrive from the city, you can't help but forget your worries. This is a happy house. The sense of informality makes your shoulders drop and your face break into a smile the moment you walk through the door.

The designer who lives here always brings personality to her projects, but for this one the desire was to create a really relaxed home. This didn't mean that the colours needed to be understated. Quite the opposite. Some of the richest Farrow & Ball colours adorn these walls, but the cottage still feels like a tranquil retreat. Much of this is achieved because the decoration feels utterly uncontrived.

Simple Wevet greets you in the hall, its hushed tone giving no clues to the colourful delights to come. This almost translucent colour, which aptly shares its name with the old Dorset term for a spider's web, makes for a quiet moment, perfect when you have been transported from the hustle and bustle of the city. One of the reasons that this space feels so effortless is because one colour has been used on every surface. With no boundaries and little definition, the simple architecture can speak for itself.

FACING PAGE
What a joy it is to see Vardo in this vibrant drawing room, which is accessed from two much more neutral spaces, making it feel all the more flamboyant. As in all rooms in this house, the colour is taken over every feature. It is this single-mindedness that makes the schemes so successful. Had this form of decoration not been used here, it would have been easy to end up with the uncomfortable effect of a stripe of colour on the walls inbetween a white ceiling and panelling.

INSET ABOVE LEFT AND ABOVE
When you enter this light-filled hall, the Wevet walls have a barely visible grey tone to them, which might lure you into the false belief that this is going to be a neutral home. How wrong could you be?

163

UPSTATE OASIS

CASE STUDY 13

BELOW AND FACING PAGE
Entering a room painted in a single colour from one painted in a single contrasting colour, as with the Slipper Satin living room and Vardo drawing room, packs a punch. The effect is enhanced here by the mix of styles in the rooms. In the chalky living room, an alchemic blend of colour, texture and light, along with the layering of classic elements with modern pieces, creates a timeless interior.

PAGES 166-7
Few would dare to choose Off-Black for a dining room but here it flatters the architecture and creates a mood of refined tranquillity. Its honest simplicity, matches that of the hall and links the spaces together.

The equally restrained living room off the hall is painted in slightly warmer Slipper Satin. This chalky off-white always feels subtle and is the perfect choice here because it complements both the red tones of the floor and the grey of the sofas. The resulting timeless space somehow expresses a nostalgia for a simpler way of living and feels all the more heavenly for it.

A totally contrasting atmosphere has been established in the drawing room next door. By being painted in Vardo, a rich teal inspired by the colours used to decorate traditional horse-drawn Romany wagons, this room exudes joy and a lust for life. Despite its flamboyant nature, the space still manages not to shout, partly because, like most Farrow & Ball colours, Vardo has a slight black undertone, which has a softening effect and makes it feel as if it might have come from a bygone era. More importantly, only one colour has been used in the room, and it even goes over the fire surround and hearth (see page 162). The thought of taking such a strong colour onto the ceiling would terrify most people, but this is a fabulous example of how successful it can be, especially in a room where the ceiling height is slightly compromised. Next door, in the library, wildly romantic Cinder Rose has been used on every surface. This technique, as used in all the rooms in this cottage, makes it impossible to read where the walls end and the ceiling begins, so blurring the confines of the spaces.

An important aspect when decorating in this way is the transition in colour between adjoining areas. When there is no picking out of features in another colour, nothing diminishes the impact when two different plain colours in adjacent rooms collide. Doors left open between such rooms that are decorated in highly contrasting colours are an exciting invitation to pass from one space to the other.

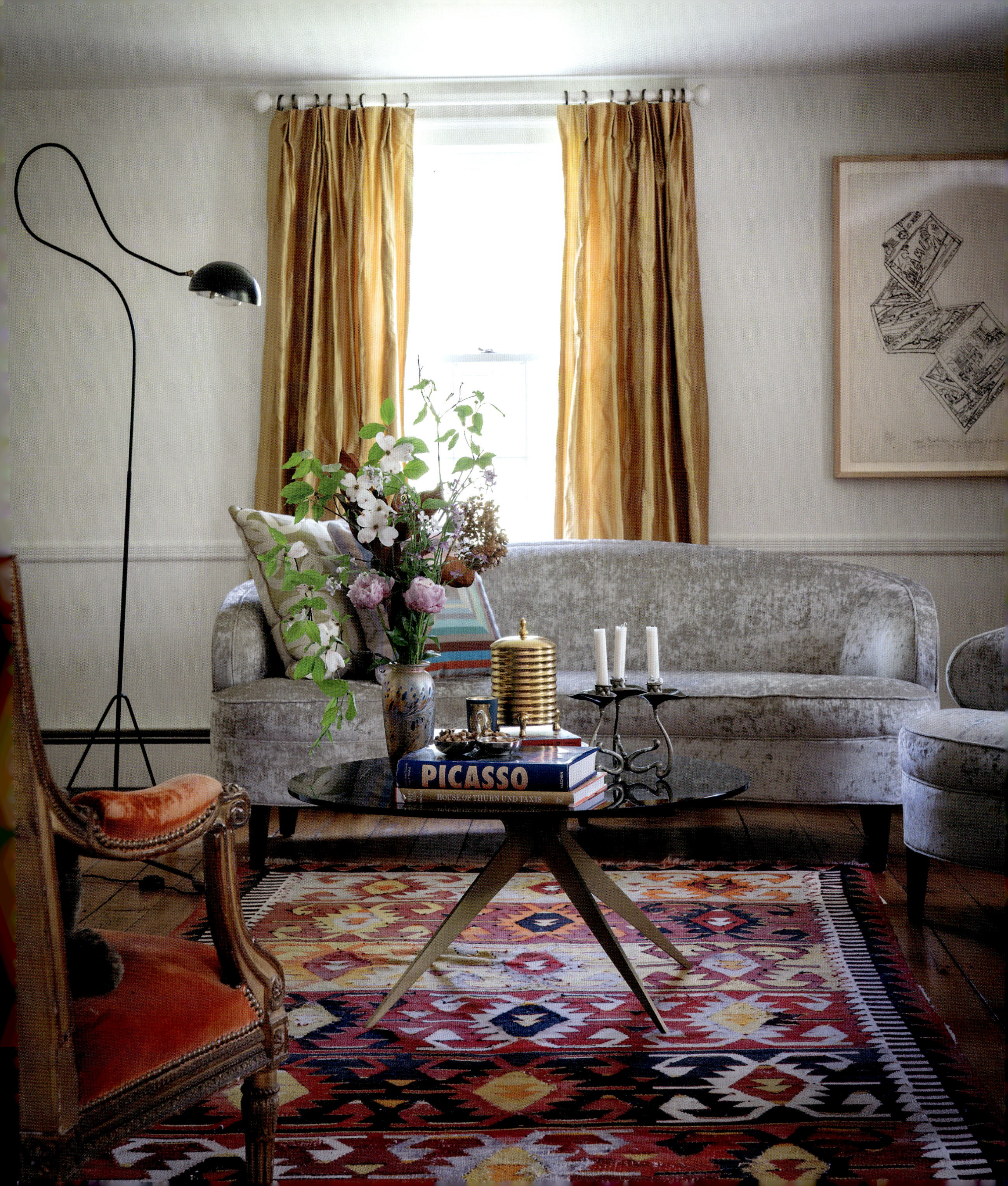
PICASSO
HOUSE OF THURN UND TAXIS

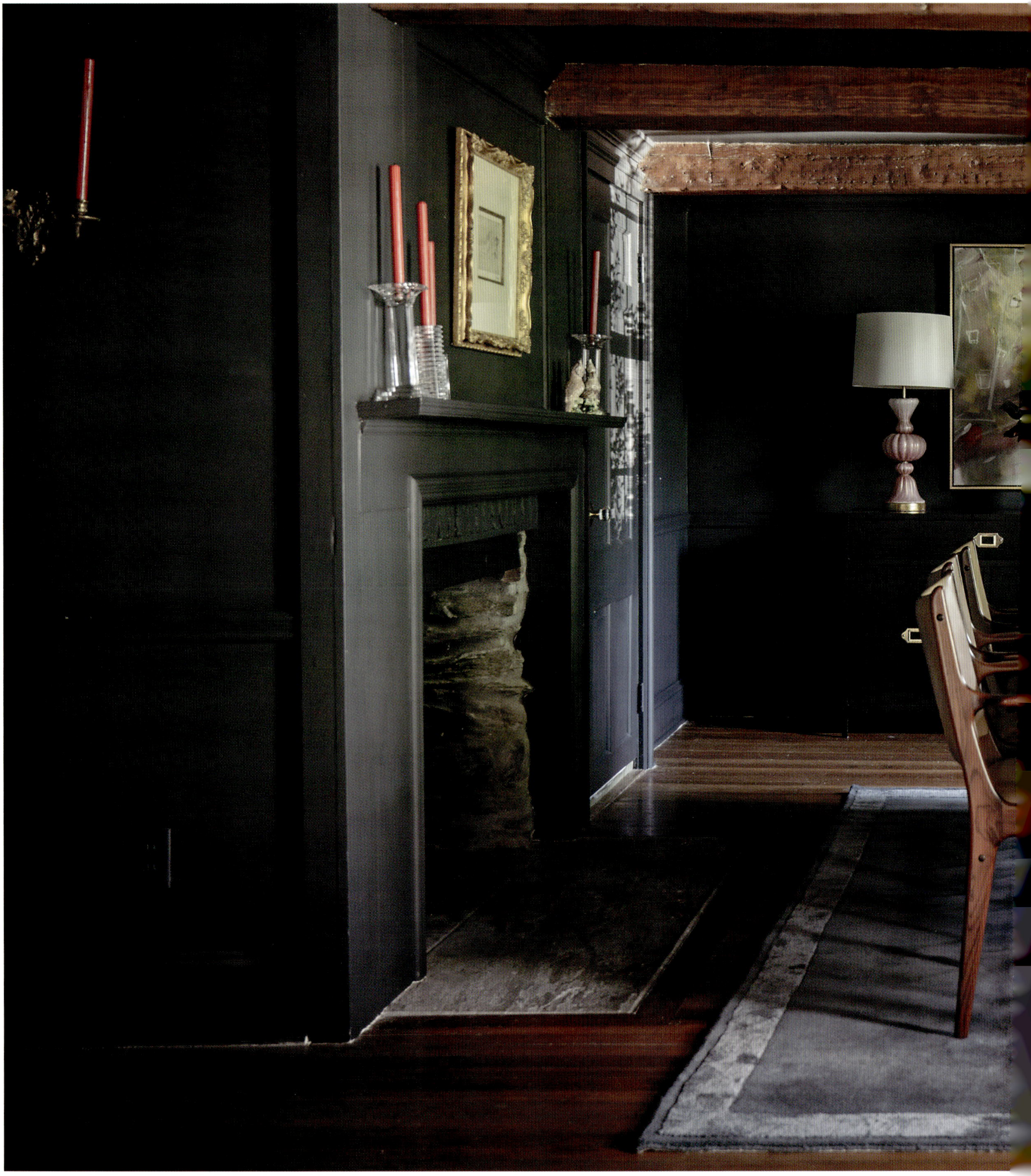

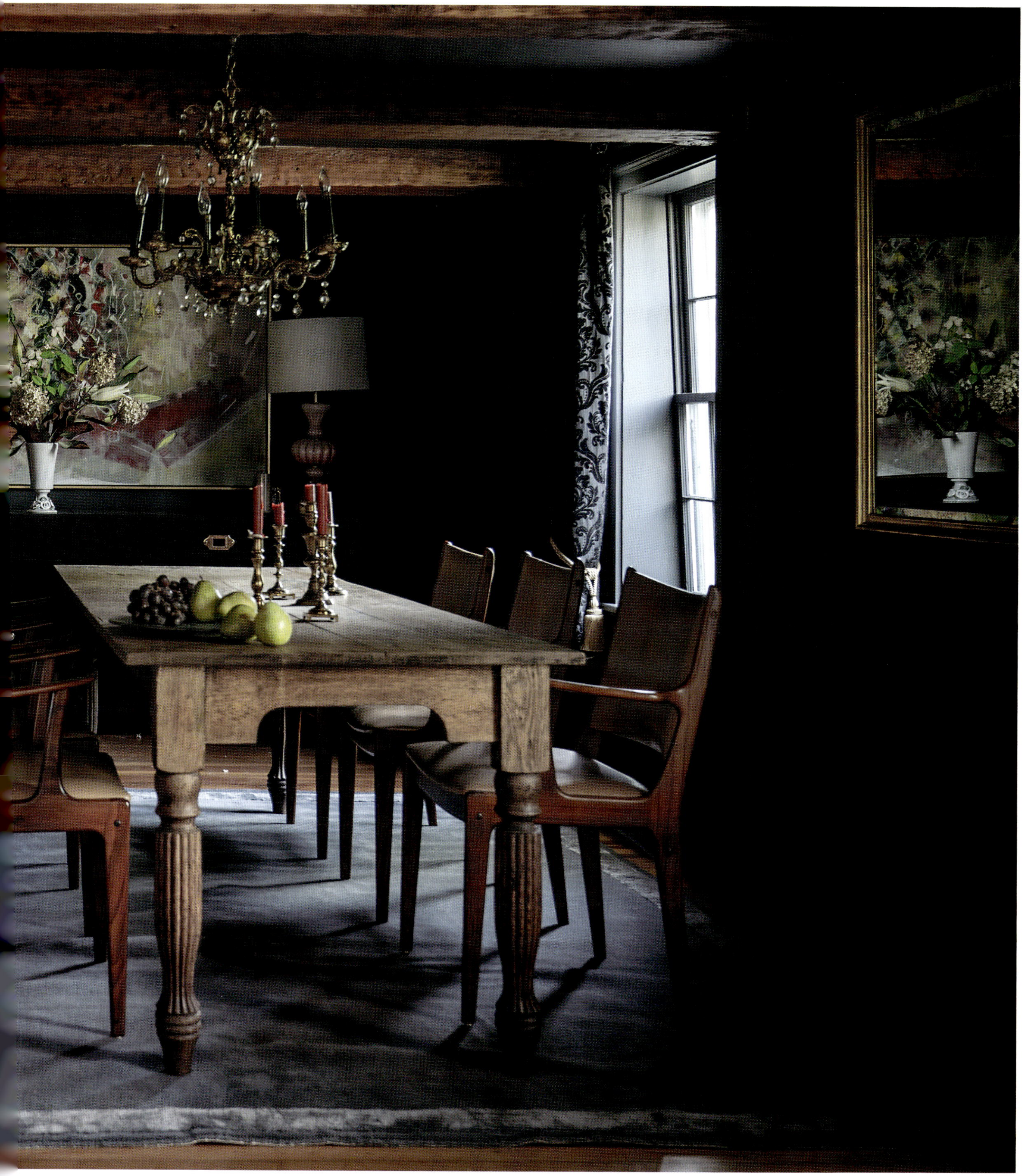

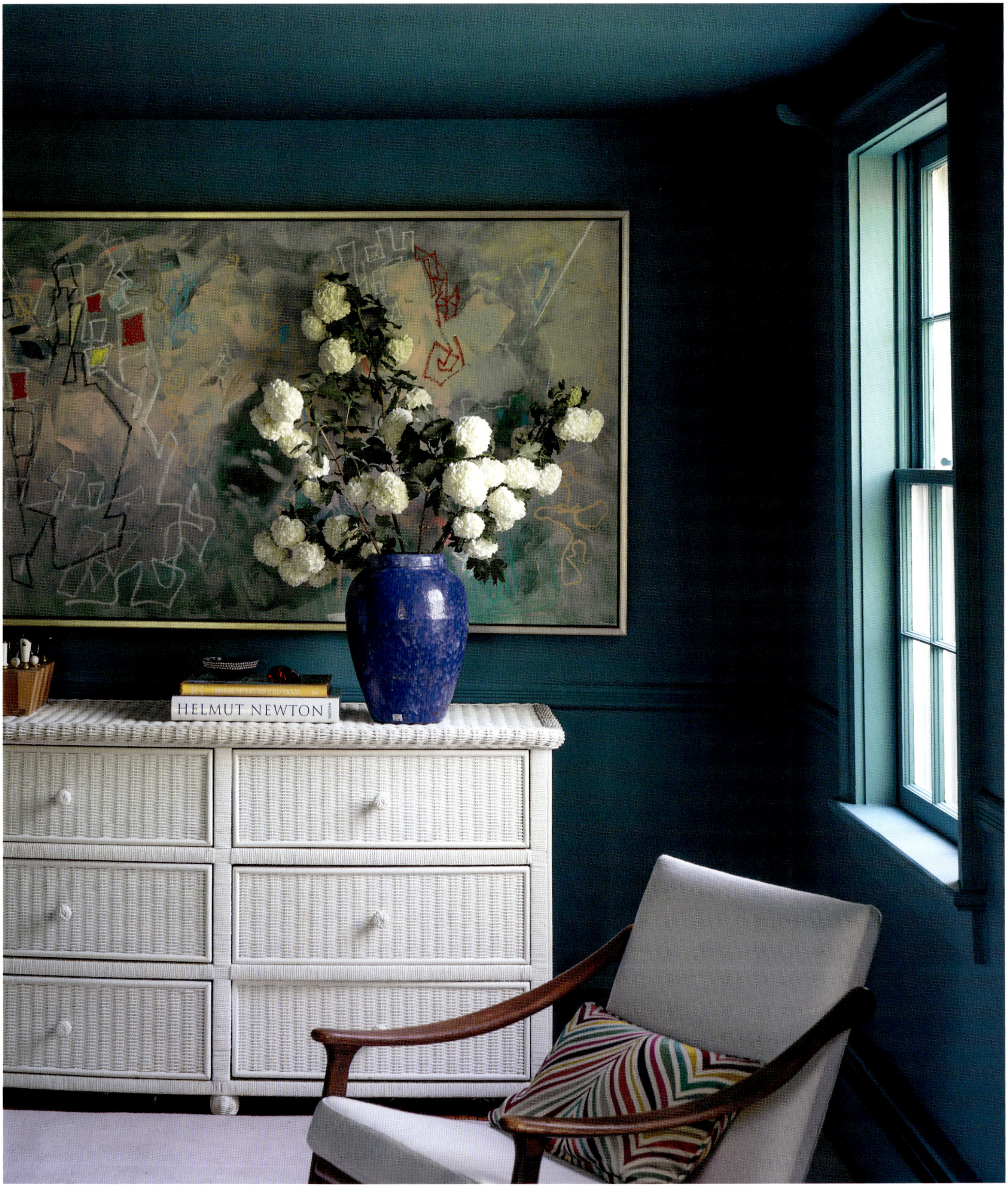
HELMUT NEWTON

CASE STUDY 13

FACING PAGE
Vardo in the drawing room alongside white becomes even more flamboyant. High contrasts with furniture or art compound the strength of a monotone palette. Painting all architectural elements the same makes objects pop.

BELOW
Using strong tones is not the only way to invigorate our homes. The simplicity and lack of colour in Wevet is its strength. The interior of this kitchen becomes subservient to the exterior in a captivating way.

BELOW
Many of the colours in this home make your heart sing but all is calm in the bedroom. Purbeck Stone on all the surfaces creates a neutral cocoon in which to relax.

There are many, very good reasons for sticking to one colour in each room, including, of course, that your painter will love you for it. Choosing this form of decoration in the dining room, especially with Off-Black paint, was certainly a brave choice but the room looks magnificent and has a truly magical quality. The softest of Farrow & Ball blacks, Off-Black flatters the rich beams and makes the space feel purposeful but, more important, livable. This is the choice of someone who understands colour and texture to perfection, and knows that had any light tones been introduced into the space, it would have only made the walls feel darker in comparison. Although the room makes a powerful statement, it remains relaxed and harmonious.

Should such drama be unwanted, there is a light-filled kitchen on the other side of the house. Here, there is such a strong connection to nature that you almost feel as if you are sitting in the canopy of the surrounding trees. The return to Wevet on both walls and the window frames means that there is a blurring of the interior and exterior, creating an alluring ambiguity – you might well be living in the landscape.

This cottage is a masterclass in using vivid colours alongside classic neutrals – the strong tones may not be to everyone's taste but you can make almost any colour work as long as it truly suits your personal style. The love and affection lavished upon it has culminated in the creation of a unique and enchanting space.

UPSTATE OASIS

CASE STUDY 13

UPSTATE OASIS PALETTE

RECIPE TIPS

* Take even very strong colours, such as Vardo or Off-Black, over the ceiling in rooms where the ceiling height is compromised – it's daring but it works.
* In areas where you want to blur the lines between the interior and exterior, make sure you don't put a contrasting colour on the window frames – in this kitchen, Wevet provides a perfect seamless link to the outside.
* By not picking out the trim, you can create real impact where two colours meet, as seen in the transition from the drawing room to the living room in this cottage.

BEDROOM

PURBECK STONE
all

HALL AND KITCHEN

WEVET
all

DRAWING ROOM

VARDO
all

LIBRARY

CINDER ROSE
all

LIVING ROOM

SLIPPER SATIN
all

DINING ROOM

OFF-BLACK
all

CASE STUDIES

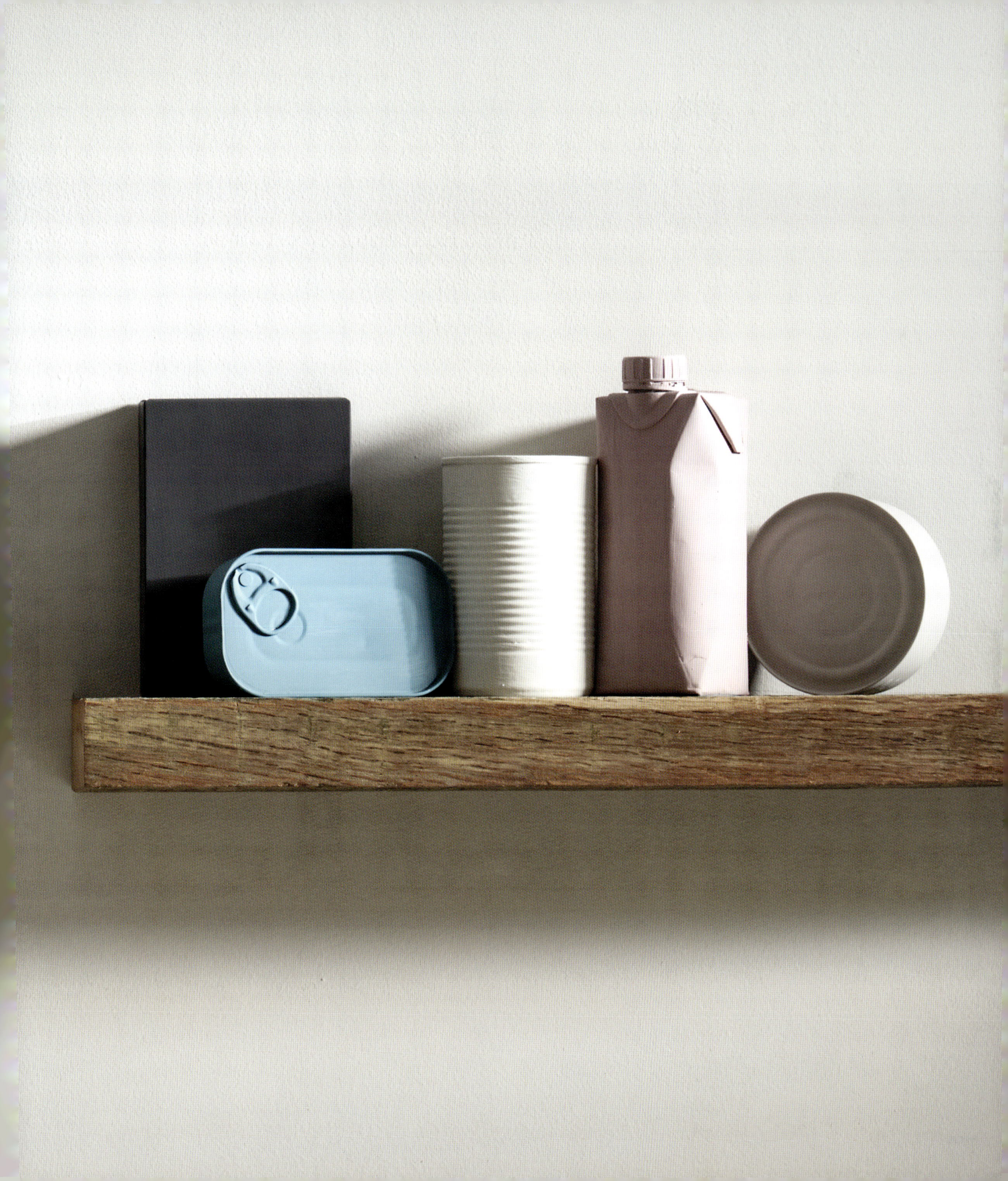

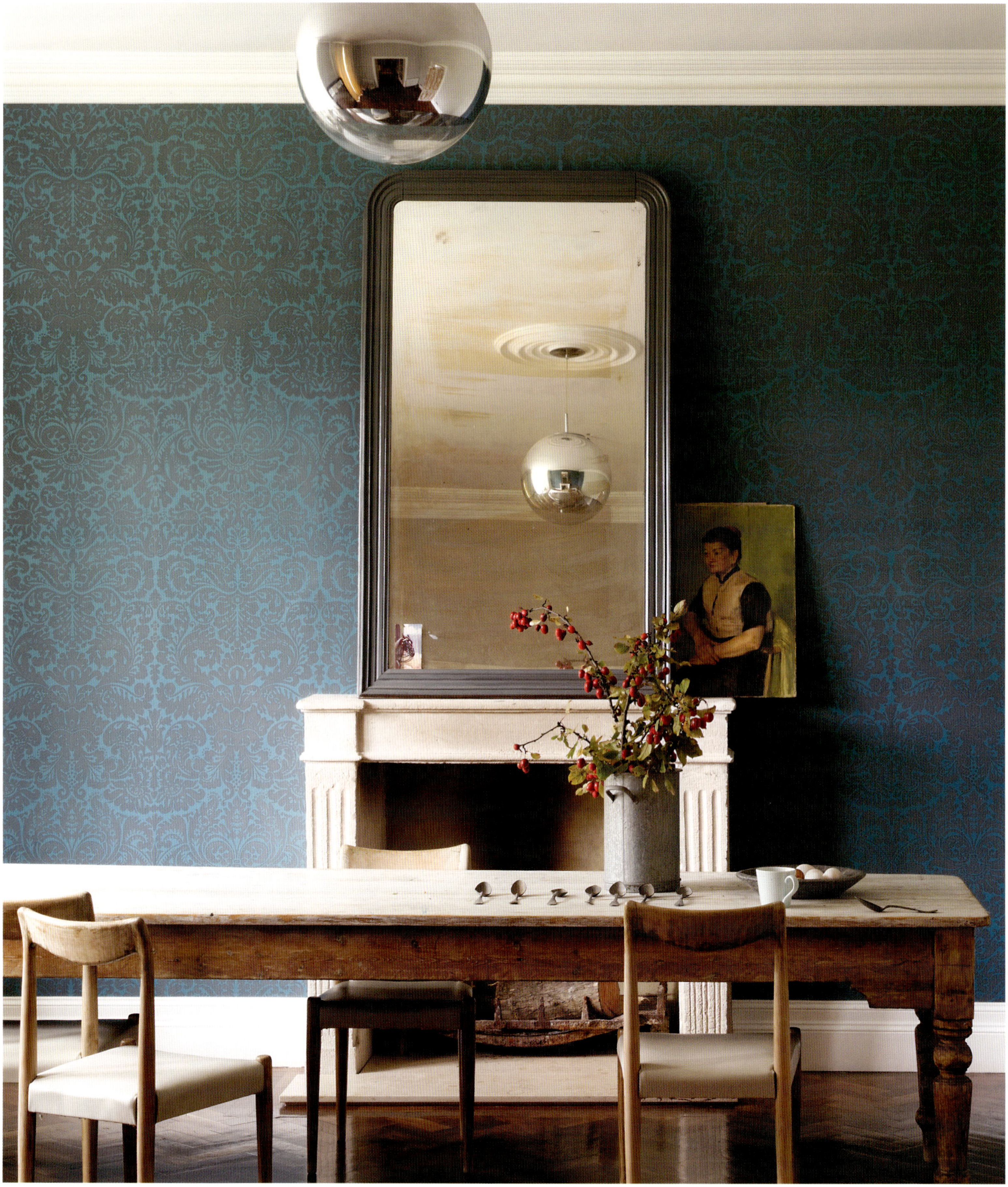

PART TWO

—

ROOM RECIPES

FACING PAGE
Occasionally at Farrow & Ball we take an established wallpaper and "reimagine" it in a different colourway. This 18th-century English damask is sensational with a Vardo background and Inchyra Blue pattern, creating an on-trend mix of old and new.

STORE CUPBOARD

Every kitchen has a store cupboard of essentials: ingredients that we can reach for without thinking too hard about what to do with them; seasoning that will work every time; and combinations we know we can rely on. Here are some suggestions for your store cupboard of paint colours, to give you the comfort of knowing that the colours you put together will be harmonious.

Many of our whites will work with the majority of our colours, but the combinations outlined below can be used with absolute confidence. Under each colour, we have given a "light" white for creating a fresh feel and a "strong" white for a subtler, more muted scheme, together with an accent colour that could be used as a darker addition on woodwork.

ALL WHITE
Strong White/School House White/Worsted

AMMONITE
Wevet/Cornforth White/Mole's Breath

ARSENIC
All White/Bone/Railings

BABOUCHE
House White/Old White/Railings

BALL GREEN
James White/Old White/Studio Green

BANCHA
James White/Off-White/Inchyra Blue

BLACKENED
All White/Pavilion Gray/Off-Black

BLAZER
Wimborne White/Joa's White/Paean Black

BLUE GRAY
School House White/Shaded White/Pigeon

BLUE GROUND
Pointing/Old White/Off-Black

BONE
Slipper Satin/Lime White/Preference Red

BORROWED LIGHT
All White/Shadow White/Stiffkey Blue

BRASSICA
Great White/Skimming Stone/Paean Black

BREAKFAST ROOM GREEN
James White/Old White/Studio Green

BRINJAL
Great White/Skimming Stone/Paean Black

CABBAGE WHITE
All White/Drop Cloth/Mole's Breath

CALAMINE
Great White/Skimming Stone/Paean Black

CALKE GREEN
Slipper Satin/Old White/Studio Green

CALLUNA
Wimborne White/Cornforth White/Paean Black

CARD ROOM GREEN
James White/Off-White/Tanner's Brown

CHARLESTON GRAY
Strong White/Skimming Stone/Paean Black

CHARLOTTE'S LOCKS
All White/Pavilion Gray/Pitch Black

CHURLISH GREEN
James White/Cornforth White/Mole's Breath

CINDER ROSE
Great White/Skimming Stone/Sulking Room Pink

CITRON
House White/Lime White/Mouse's Back

COOKING APPLE GREEN
James White/Off-White/Salon Drab

COOK'S BLUE
All White/Bone/Off-Black

CORD
White Tie/Matchstick/Tanner's Brown

CORNFORTH WHITE
Wevet/Ammonite/Mole's Breath

CROMARTY
Wimborne White/Shadow White/Pigeon

DAYROOM YELLOW
Wimborne White/Slipper Satin/Green Smoke

DEAD SALMON
Dimity/Joa's White/Paean Black

DE NIMES
School House White/Shaded White/Inchyra Blue

DIMITY
Pointing/Joa's White/Tanner's Brown

DIMPSE
All White/Pavilion Gray/Down Pipe

DIX BLUE
School House White/Shaded White/Railings

DORSET CREAM
White Tie/Off-White/Tanner's Brown

DOVE TALE
Strong White/Skimming Stone/London Clay

DOWN PIPE
Blackened/Pavilion Gray/Railings

DROP CLOTH
School House White/Shaded White/De Nimes

EATING ROOM RED
Dimity/Joa's White/Paean Black

ELEPHANT'S BREATH
Strong White/Skimming Stone/London Clay

FARROW'S CREAM
White Tie/Slipper Satin/Tanner's Brown

FRENCH GRAY
Slipper Satin/Old White/Treron

GREAT WHITE
All White/Skimming Stone/Sulking Room Pink

GREEN BLUE
Pointing/Shaded White/Mahogany

GREEN GROUND
James White/Shadow White/Studio Green

GREEN SMOKE
Slipper Satin/Old White/Off-Black

HAGUE BLUE
Wevet/Drop Cloth/Pitch Black

HARDWICK WHITE
School House White/Shadow White/Off-Black

ROOM RECIPES

HAY
James White/Old White/
  Studio Green

HOUSE WHITE
All White/Wevet/India Yellow

INCARNADINE
Wimborne White/Jitney/Off-Black

INCHYRA BLUE
School House White/Drop Cloth/
  Off-Black

INDIA YELLOW
House White/Matchstick/
  Mahogany

JAMES WHITE
All White/Lime White/Bancha

JITNEY
Pointing/Slipper Satin/Pelt

JOA'S WHITE
Wimborne White/Dimity/
  Preference Red

LAMP ROOM GRAY
All White/Strong White/Off-Black

LICHEN
Slipper Satin/Off-White/
  Studio Green

LIGHT BLUE
School House White/Shaded
  White/De Nimes

LIGHT GRAY
Slipper Satin/Old White/
  Mouse's Back

LIME WHITE
Slipper Satin/Old White/
  Treron

LONDON CLAY
Strong White/Skimming Stone/
  Paean Black

LONDON STONE
Dimity/Joa's White/London Clay

LULWORTH BLUE
All White/Cornforth White/
  Hague Blue

MAHOGANY
Dimity/Joa's White/Pitch Black

MANOR HOUSE GRAY
Blackened/Pavilion Gray/
  Down Pipe

MATCHSTICK
Wimborne White/New White/
  Mouse's Back

MIDDLETON PINK
All White/Cornforth White/
  Paean Black

MIZZLE
School House White/Shaded
  White/Pigeon

MOLE'S BREATH
Wevet/Cornforth White/
  Railings

MOUSE'S BACK
Slipper Satin/Old White/
  Salon Drab

NANCY'S BLUSHES
Great White/Drop Cloth/
  Railings

NEW WHITE
White Tie/Matchstick/
  Salon Drab

OFF-BLACK
Strong White/Purbeck Stone/
  Pitch Black

OFF-WHITE
Slipper Satin/Old White/
  Mouse's Back

OLD WHITE
Slipper Satin/Off-White/
  Mouse's Back

OVAL ROOM BLUE
Shadow White/Drop Cloth/
  De Nimes

OXFORD STONE
Dimity/Joa's White/London Stone

PAEAN BLACK
Great White/Dimpse/Railings

PALE HOUND
Wimborne White/Bone/
  Mouse's Back

PALE POWDER
Pointing/Shaded White/
  Light Gray

PARMA GRAY
Pointing/Bone/Off-Black

PAVILION BLUE
All White/Cornforth White/
  Mole's Breath

PAVILION GRAY
Blackened/Dimpse/Railings

PEIGNOIR
Great White/Skimming Stone/
  Paean Black

PELT
Great White/Skimming Stone/
  Pitch Black

PICTURE GALLERY RED
Dimity/Joa's White/Mahogany

PIGEON
Shadow White/Shaded White/
  Treron

PINK GROUND
Wimborne White/Tallow/Mahogany

PITCH BLACK
All White/Blackened/Rangwali

PITCH BLUE
Blackened/Pavilion Gray/
  Pitch Black

PLUMMETT
Blackened/Pavilion Gray/
  Down Pipe

POINTING
All White/Slipper Satin/Pelt

PREFERENCE RED
Dimity/Joa's White/
  Tanner's Brown

PURBECK STONE
Wevet/Cornforth White/
  Mole's Breath

RADICCHIO
Dimity/Joa's White/
  Tanner's Brown

RAILINGS
Ammonite/Cornforth White/
  Pitch Black

RANGWALI
All White/Wevet/Paean Black

RECTORY RED
Wimborne White/Skimming
  Stone/Railings

RED EARTH
Dimity/Joa's White/Mahogany

SALON DRAB
Dimity/Joa's White/Pitch Black

SAVAGE GROUND
White Tie/Matchstick/
  Salon Drab

SCHOOL HOUSE WHITE
All White/Shaded White/
  De Nimes

SETTING PLASTER
Tallow/Off-White/Paean Black

SHADED WHITE
School House White/Drop Cloth/
  De Nimes

SHADOW WHITE
All White/Shaded White/
  Drop Cloth

SKIMMING STONE
Strong White/Elephant's Breath/
  Charleston Gray

SKYLIGHT
All White/Cornforth White/
  Mole's Breath

SLIPPER SATIN
Pointing/Old White/Mouse's Back

ST GILES BLUE
All White/Dimpse/Down Pipe

STIFFKEY BLUE
Strong White/Cornforth White/
  Railings

STONE BLUE
School House White/Drop Cloth/
  Off-Black

STONY GROUND
Wimborne White/Slipper Satin/
  Brinjal

STRING
White Tie/Matchstick/
  Mouse's Back

STRONG WHITE
All White/Ammonite/
  Mole's Breath

STUDIO GREEN
Slipper Satin/Old White/
  Off-Black

SUDBURY YELLOW
White Tie/New White/
  Salon Drab

SULKING ROOM PINK
Strong White/Skimming Stone/
  Paean Black

TALLOW
Pointing/Matchstick/
  Mahogany

TANNER'S BROWN
Dimity/Joa's White/
  Off-Black

TERESA'S GREEN
Slipper Satin/Lime White/
  Mouse's Back

TRERON
Slipper Satin/Old White/
  Studio Green

VARDO
School House White/Shaded
  White/Pitch Black

VERT DE TERRE
Slipper Satin/Off-White/
  Studio Green

WEVET
All White/Ammonite/
  Mole's Breath

WHITE TIE
Wimborne White/New White/
  Cord

WIMBORNE WHITE
All White/Pointing/
  Green Smoke

WORSTED
Strong White/Ammonite/
  Mole's Breath

YEABRIDGE GREEN
James White/Lime White/
  Studio Green

YELLOW GROUND
Wimborne White/House White/
  Plummett

NEUTRAL RECIPES

The other essentials in our store cupboard are six different groups of neutrals, carefully balanced and understated colours that make few demands on the eye. The neutral recipes given below are not set in stone but you will find that you can use the four colours in each group in any combination on your walls and trim to create calm, tranquil rooms that have a certain lucidity. However, each group of neutrals will result in a very different look. Which is your dish of choice?

TRADITIONAL NEUTRALS

Old White/Off-White/Lime White/Slipper Satin

These historic whites contain an underlying green, ideal for restrained, traditional rooms. The softness of these colours makes rooms feel as if they have been painted in that way forever.

YELLOW BASED NEUTRALS

String/Matchstick/New White/White Tie

Pretty and uncomplicated neutrals with their roots in the country, these charming traditional colours have a naturally reflective quality that is comfortable and easy to live with.

RED BASED NEUTRALS

Oxford Stone/Joa's White/Dimity/Pointing

These warm, friendly tones are particularly suited to contemporary, classic homes, as well as to underlit spaces, where they create serene and welcoming interiors.

CONTEMPORARY NEUTRALS

Elephant's Breath/Skimming Stone/Strong White/All White

All the colours, bar All White, in this group of neutrals has an underlying lilac tone, which brings a warm edge to grey decorative schemes, making them feel stony rather than cold.

EASY NEUTRALS

Purbeck Stone/Cornforth White/Ammonite/Wevet

With their gossamer appearance, these are perfect if you prefer an understated look. Natural and quiet, with a quality that is hard to pin down, they are the perfect greys for the modern family home.

ARCHITECTURAL NEUTRALS

Manor House Gray/Pavilion Gray/Dimpse/Blackened

Originally designed to give a modern, industrial feel, these are cooler than the other neutral groups. With a blue undertone, they create a more hard-edged look that is conducive to minimal living.

TIMELESS NEUTRALS

School House White/Shadow White/Shaded White/Drop Cloth

A slightly under-the-radar group of Farrow & Ball neutrals, which are neither too grey to be edgy and uncomfortable, nor too creamy to feel out of date. This timeless group is my personal favourite.

FACING PAGE
Arsenic-painted doors in a Full Gloss finish bring sheer glamour to this stylish Wevet kitchen.

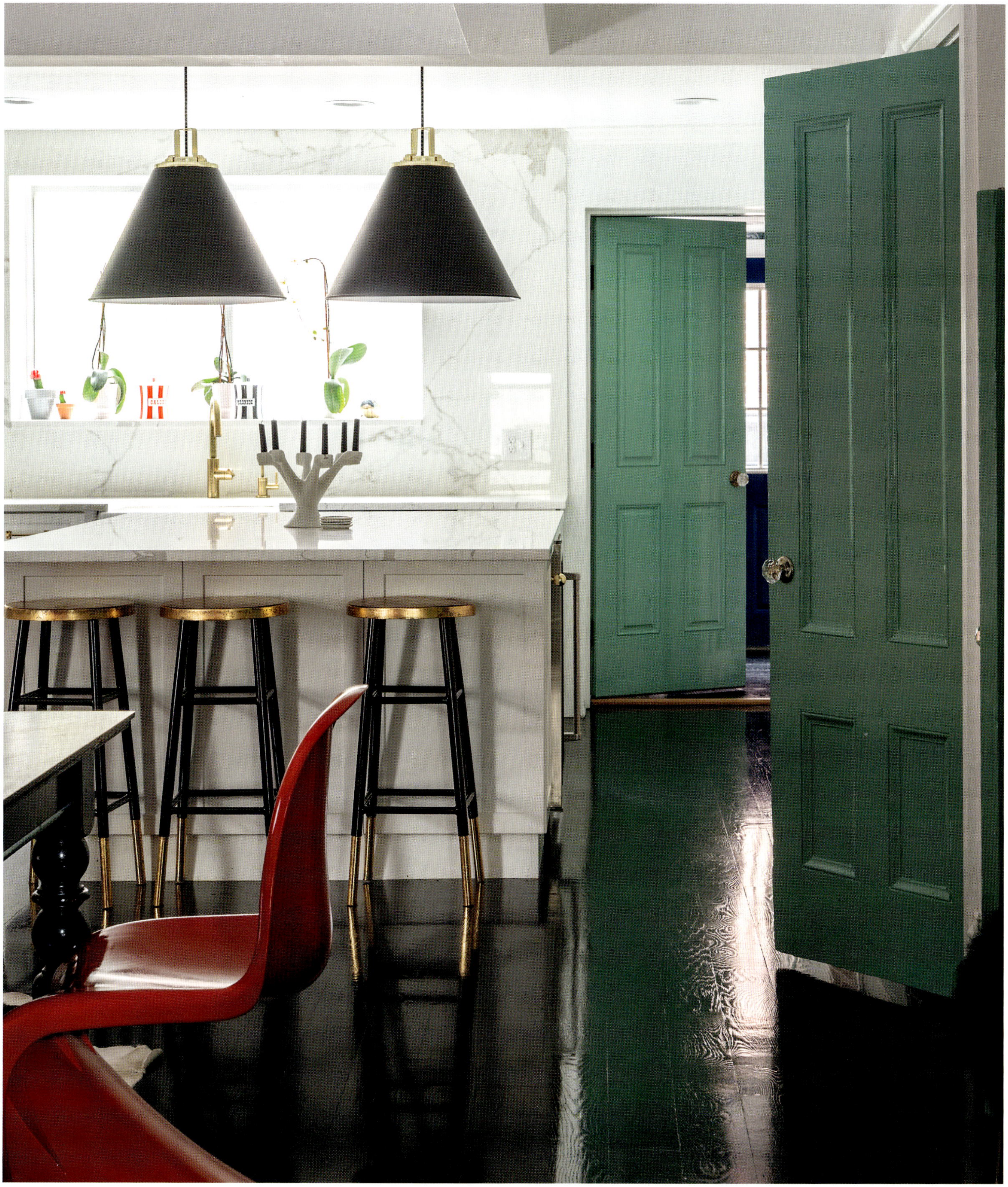

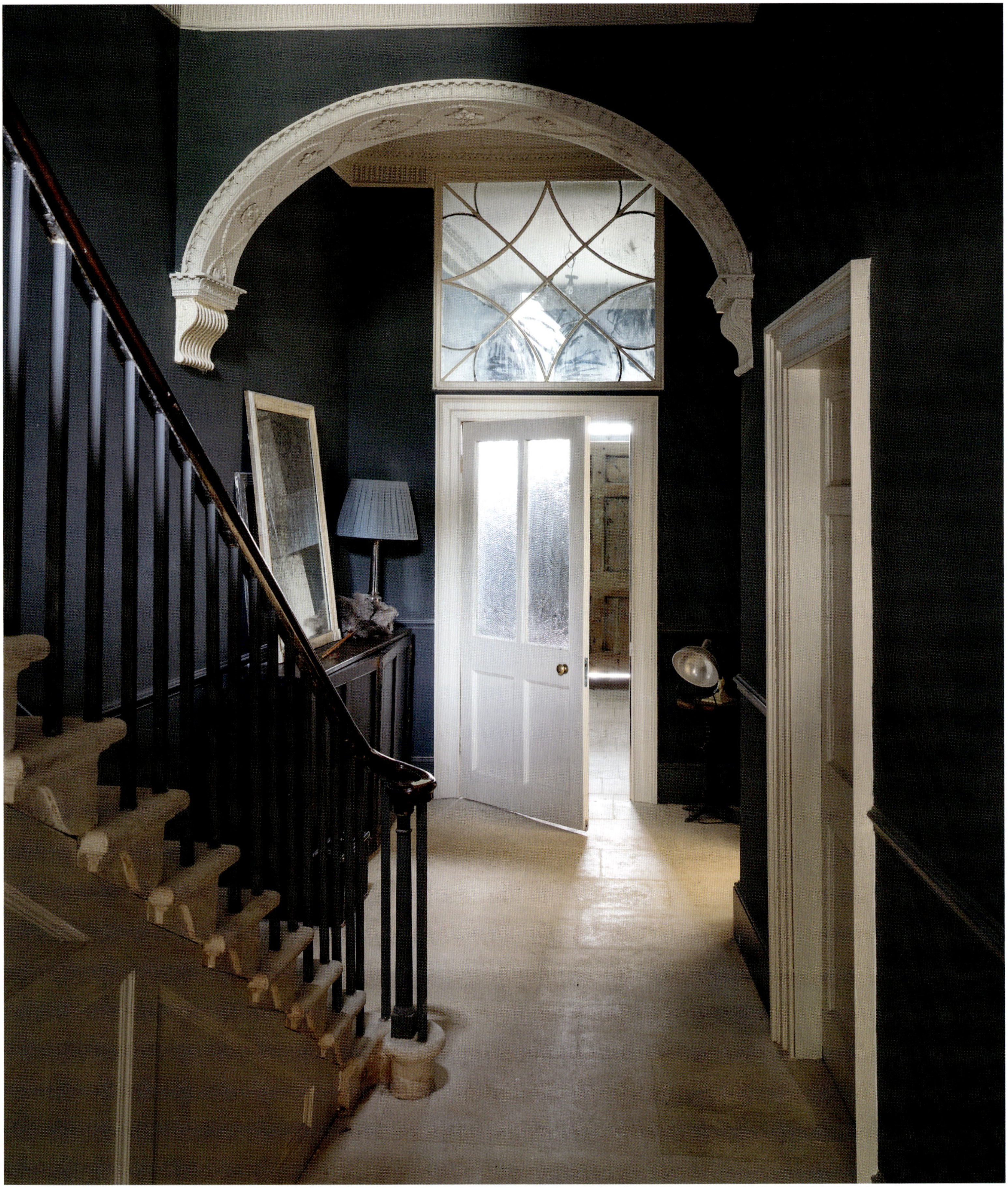

HALLS

If you have the luxury of decorating a whole house, then it is always best to start with the hall. The colour used here will obviously create the first impression of your home and set the tone for what is to follow. The way we react to colours that we come into contact with constantly is often instinctive and emotive, so the choice of colour for the hall, which we pass through all the time, should be instinctive, too. First and foremost, it must be welcoming and reflect your personality. Your visitors will also appreciate the most exuberant decoration, as long as it's true to your style, even if they shy away from such bold choices in their own homes.

Let the amount of natural light help inform your colour choices, and always bear in mind the colour of your front door – having a visual link to the interior is essential. Halls in rural areas tend to have a lot of natural light, while those in towns and cities are often starved of it. Choose your colours accordingly.

Start by deciding what you want to achieve. Would you like your hall to appear as big and light as possible, or would you prefer to make it feel intimate and dramatic?

FACING PAGE
Inchyra Blue on the walls, with contrasting Strong White on the doors and architraves, makes for a dramatic hall. Choosing not to pick out the skirting and dado rail but painting them the same colour as the walls prevents the scheme from looking too busy.

BELOW
Gentle James White, with its underlying green tone, creates an airy feel in a light-starved hall. The lack of contrasting colours enhances the space, set off by warm Smoked Trout in the sitting room beyond.

BELOW RIGHT
In this bohemian Brooklyn home, the colour is confined to the rooms leading off the hall, while the hall itself is kept completely neutral with both the walls and the panelling painted in delicate, barely-there Wevet.

FACING PAGE
Railings creates a dramatic entrance to this chic French apartment. The same colour has been taken through to the inner hall bookcase, but here the walls and panelling are in the much lighter, and more welcoming, Elephant's Breath.

LIGHT COLOURS

A light colour in the hall evokes calm and serenity, but be wary of creating a bland or uninviting space. The best way to avoid this is to contrast light walls with a darker tone on the trim. Since the walls are the largest surface, they will give a sense of space, while the darker trim will add a decorative element. A subtle contrast like School House White on the walls and Drop Cloth on the woodwork feels calm and gentle, while a stronger, contrasting colour such as Railings on the woodwork will create a more dynamic space.

Using a sober colour such as Tanner's Brown or Studio Green on the spindles of a staircase is an extremely effective way to add a small splash of bold decoration, at the same time creating a grounding dark backbone through the centre of the house.

In a mostly neutral home, a light hall will create an uninterrupted visual flow from room to room, retaining a sense of unity. In this case, it is often worth considering a marginally stronger and more welcoming tone for the hall than for the other rooms.

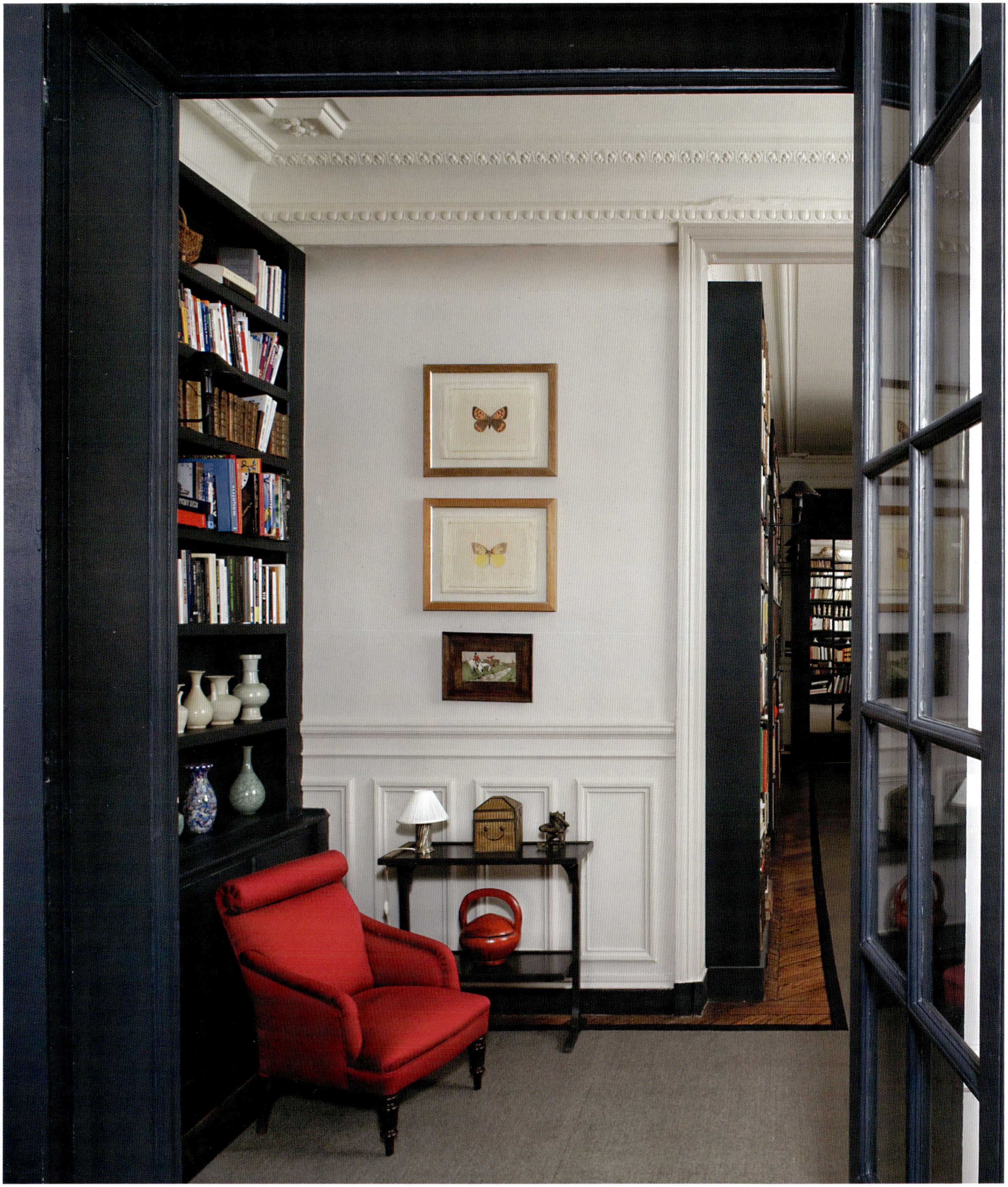

BELOW
A deliciously deep purple, Pelt creates a dramatic entrance, especially in dark areas where it appears almost black. It is an exciting choice for this light-starved space where a white would have felt bland.

BELOW RIGHT
The rooms off this hall, painted in Railings, feel extraordinarily light in contrast. It is a brave choice, as well as witty, with Yellowcake (A) used on the back of the front door and its frame.

FACING PAGE, LEFT
This charming and playful Bumble Bee wallpaper, inspired by a fabric found in Joséphine Bonaparte's bedchamber, sets the scene and tone for the rest of the house, despite its sober Calke Green background.

FACING PAGE, RIGHT
Tourbillon wallpaper is composed of segmented circles that blend for a graphic look. Here, where the pattern and background are so close in colour, it softens what might have seemed a flat and uninteresting wall.

STRONG COLOURS

If your hall is deprived of natural light, it may be advisable to paint it a warm, enveloping colour – you are not going to win the battle with nature to create a light and airy space, so it makes sense to embrace what you have and use it to your advantage.

Don't be frightened of using a stronger colour in your hall. It is not a place where you spend a significant amount of time, but rather just pass through it on your way to another room. A strong colour in a hallway has the instant effect of making rooms leading off it appear bigger and brighter. And a dark hall will create a distinct viewpoint, drawing your eye to a natural focal point such as a light-filled kitchen. If you want to break up a strong colour, then think about using two different finishes to create some interest. For a contemporary feel with only one colour, try a Full Gloss finish on the bottom half of the walls and a Modern Emulsion finish above. This works particularly well with deep tones, such as Inchyra Blue and Paean Black, and is the perfect practical solution for disguising inevitable scuff marks on the walls.

PATTERNS

Nothing feels more inviting than a strongly coloured or patterned entrance to a house. By filling your hall with a bold design, you will, in effect, have decorated your whole home because every time you pass from one room to another by way of the hall, it will lift your spirits. An additional bonus is that a highly decorated hall gives you licence to be much more neutral with your decorating in all the other rooms, where you spend most of your time.

Pattern certainly makes life more interesting, and a rich hall delivers a shot of energy to the soul without impacting on the rooms we actually live in. To create a smooth visual transition, the pattern or background colours of the wallpaper can be used in adjacent rooms (remember that all Farrow & Ball wallpaper is made with our actual paint, which makes this super-simple to do).

If you are lucky enough to have a panelled hall, then a certain purity is retained by using one colour from floor to ceiling, letting the intrinsic dignity of the architecture speak for itself. However, a combination of paint and wallpaper, divided by a dado rail, can feel just as elegant. It is best, from both an aesthetic and a practical point of view, to use a stronger coloured paint below the rail and a lighter wallpaper above.

ELEGANT HALL

I have had the privilege of working in many different houses all over the world for the past 20 years and it is not often that a property makes me gasp. On entering this hall, however, it would have been hard not to show some sort of emotion. It is truly breathtaking – opulent and crazy yet tranquil and totally authentic. Built in the second half of the 19th century, in the style of the French Renaissance, the building has a long and rich history as part of two symmetrical terraces that stand proudly atop a hill in the centre of Glasgow. Originally lived in by a shipbuilder and philanthropist, the home is being lovingly restored by the present owner.

Unusually, the hall is not at the entrance to the building but at its centre, where the light from the magnificent dome permeates all the rooms around it. This space is all about symmetry, and the choice of a palette of three blues was inspired not only by the windows and the mosaic floor but also by the huge amount of sky so evident during the day. These colours make the space feel amazingly tranquil, despite the decorative embellishment.

Good decoration is a matter of opinion and there can be no rules. Many rooms that we admire flout every rule in the book, and this is certainly one of them. The walls have been painted in simple Off-White, which has a naturally recessive feel in this space, allowing the pillars and dado rail in Inchyra Blue to have more importance. This colour has a suitable gravitas, as does Mouse's Back, which has been used to emphasize the arch surrounding the curved recess, now home to a new-found treasure. Stone Blue enhances the window frames and is the near-perfect match to areas of the beautifully preserved stained glass, which makes them positively gleam. The third colour is the slightly more upbeat Teresa's Green (which most people read as blue), artfully placed on the inner rim of the dome to reflect the tones of the moody Scottish skies.

This hall is not merely for crossing from one room to another – it begs you to stop and sit in it. But if you do happen to be just passing through, it cannot fail to be an awe-inspiring experience.

ABOVE
Stone Blue window surrounds bring extra life to this historic room. Painting both the walls and skirting in Off-White ensures that it is more difficult to read the size and shape of the space.

FACING PAGE
This colour combination is subtle and considered. Inchyra Blue, the strongest tone, looks regal on the pillars, Teresa's Green on the ceiling reflects the colour of the sky, and Mouse's Back frames the central sculpture.

PALETTE

TERESA'S GREEN® 236	MOUSE'S BACK® 40
ceiling	*central alcove arch*

INCHYRA BLUE® 289	STONE BLUE® 86
pillars	*window surrounds*

ROOM RECIPES

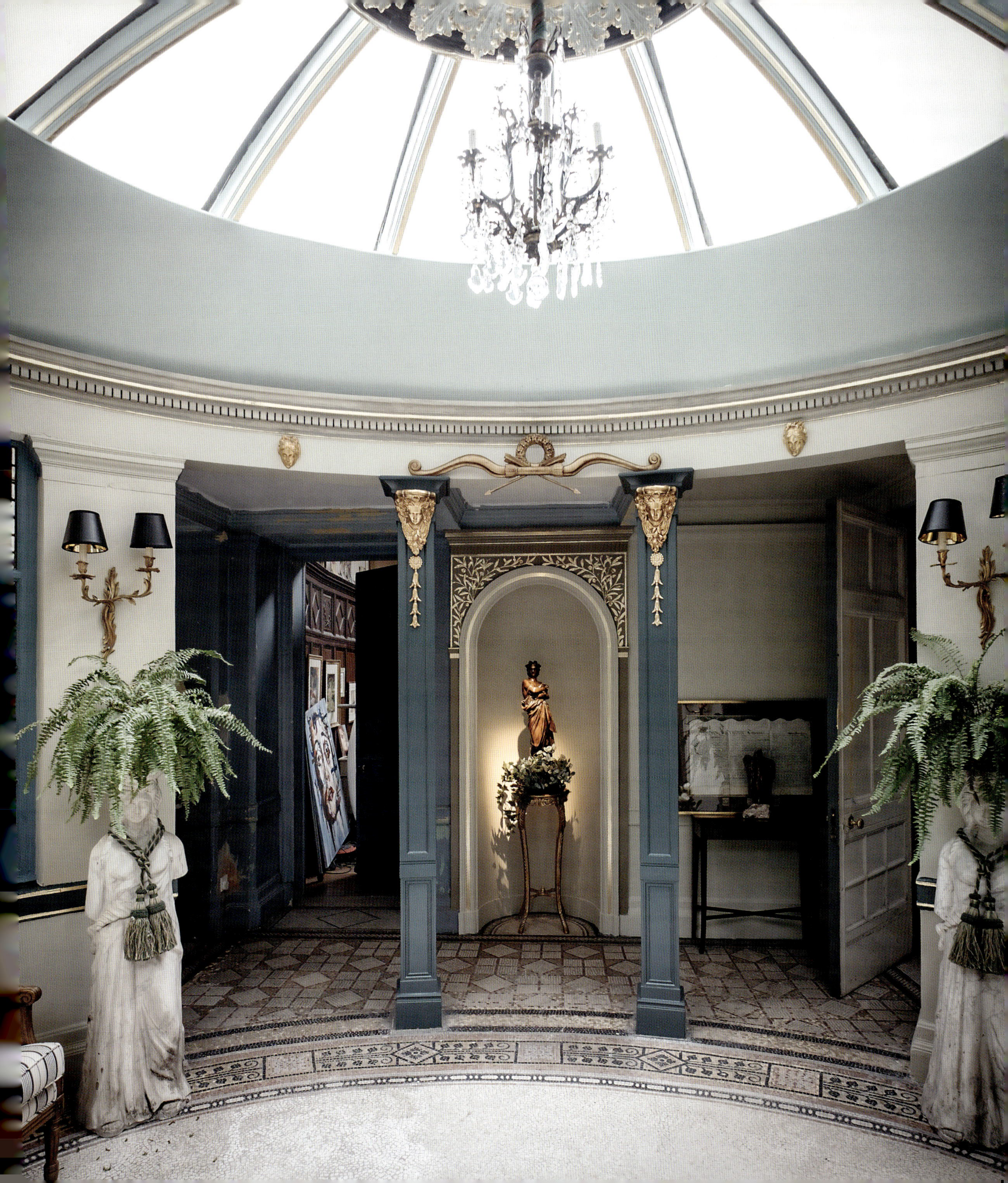

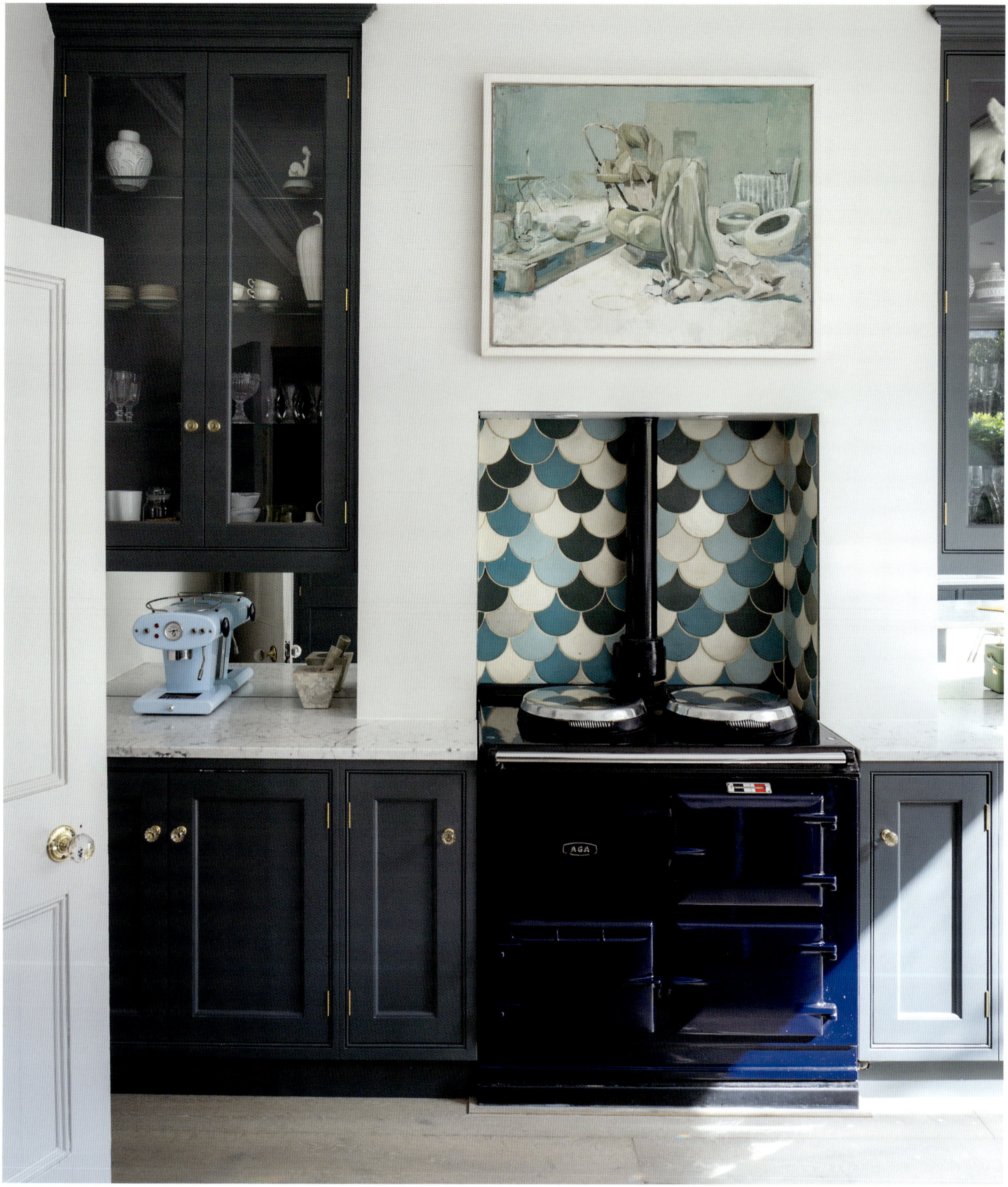
AGA

KITCHENS

The way that we use the kitchen has changed dramatically over the past couple of decades. No longer is it just a place for preparing food for our families, it is somewhere to nurture them, too. For many of us, it is the heart of the home and where we spend most of our time. The way that we decorate the room has changed accordingly. Most of us crave light, and the kitchen often benefits from being the brightest space in the home. It is somewhere that beckons and welcomes and, like a moth to a flame, we are drawn to it.

These are my favourite tips that you can consider applying in your kitchen: use the same colour on both the walls and the woodwork to give the space more flexibility and make it feel bigger; make your kitchen the lightest room in the house – it is probably where you will end up spending the most of your time; add colour to normally hidden or unexpected places such as the back of dressers or the inside of larder cupboards.

FACING PAGE
This kitchen is bang on trend. Ammonite's hushed tone lends an understated grey to the walls, while the soft black-blue undertone in Railings makes it the perfect choice for cabinets. Both colours feel more relaxed than pure white/black. Here you see the true nuances of Farrow & Ball colours.

Whether you are an uncompromising minimalist or have a profound reverence for tradition, having just one colour in the kitchen on both the walls and the woodwork makes for an easier and more relaxed space. Starting with a simple palette also gives you greater flexibility when you come to add colour to kitchen units, dressers and islands, all of which are subject to the whims of fashion and your taste.

Dark tones on floor-standing units creates a modern look with a nod to tradition, but it pays to be wary of using strong colour on wall-hung units because they can make the kitchen claustrophobic. Darker units against lighter walls is the easiest way to add impact, but it is essential to get the balance correct.

If you crave a little extra colour, add some to the back of a dresser, behind a glass splashback or to the inside of a larder cupboard – simple ways to brighten up your life as you go about your chores.

ABOVE LEFT
Just one colour has been used in this pared-down country kitchen. Drop Cloth, which is neither too warm nor too cool, is timeless here, enhancing both the ancient walls and the newly built joinery.

FACING PAGE
The geometric Tessella wallpaper in this dining area really enhances the parquet floor. Strong White, the background colour, has been used on the walls, with Purbeck Stone, the pattern colour, on the units. The effect is perfect harmony.

ABOVE
A combination taken from both ends of our palette. All White, a pure white, on the walls and ceiling is contrasted with Pitch Black, a pure black, on the cabinets for a clean, almost graphic scheme. The flooring, chairs and lights all follow suit.

ROOM RECIPES

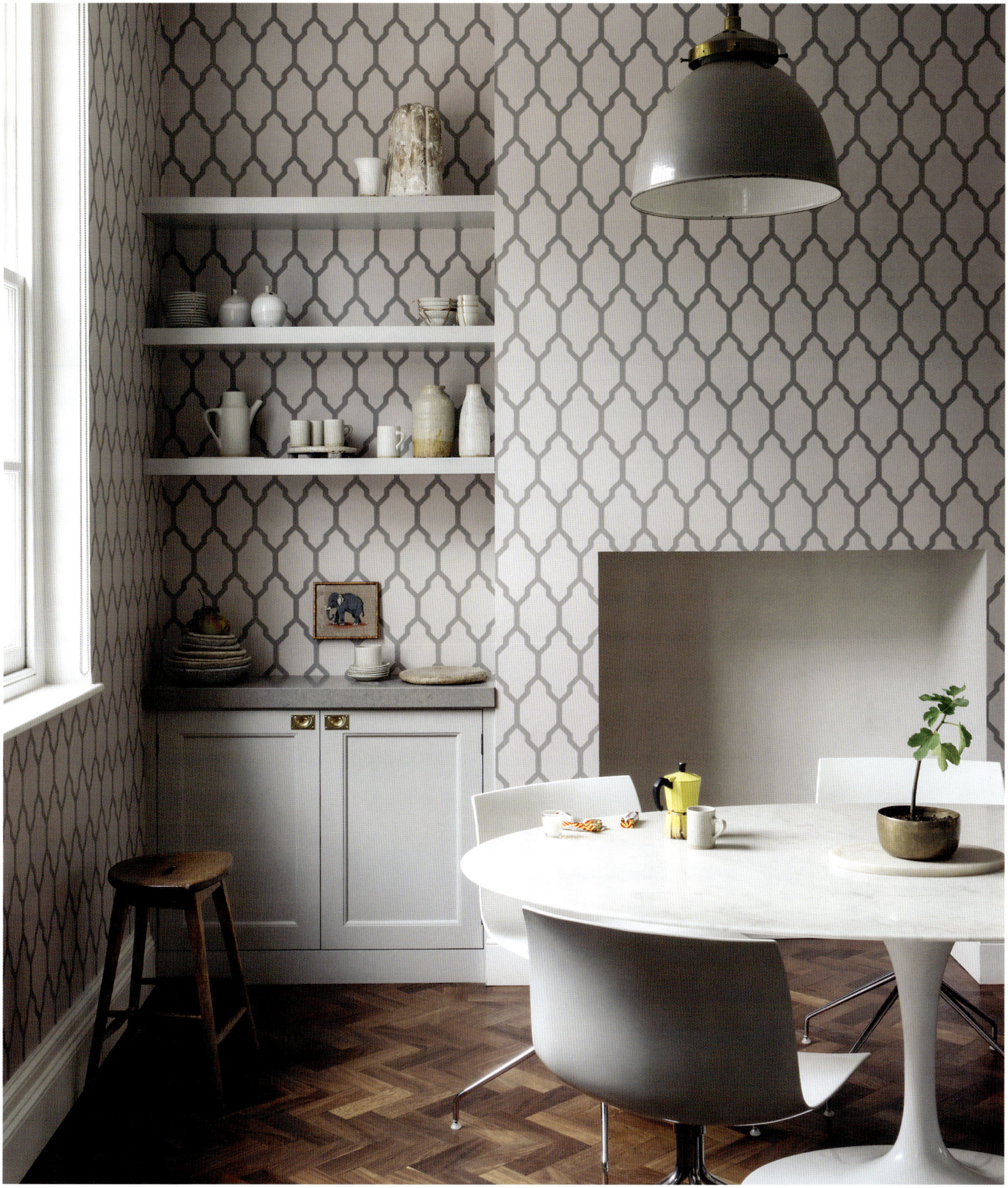

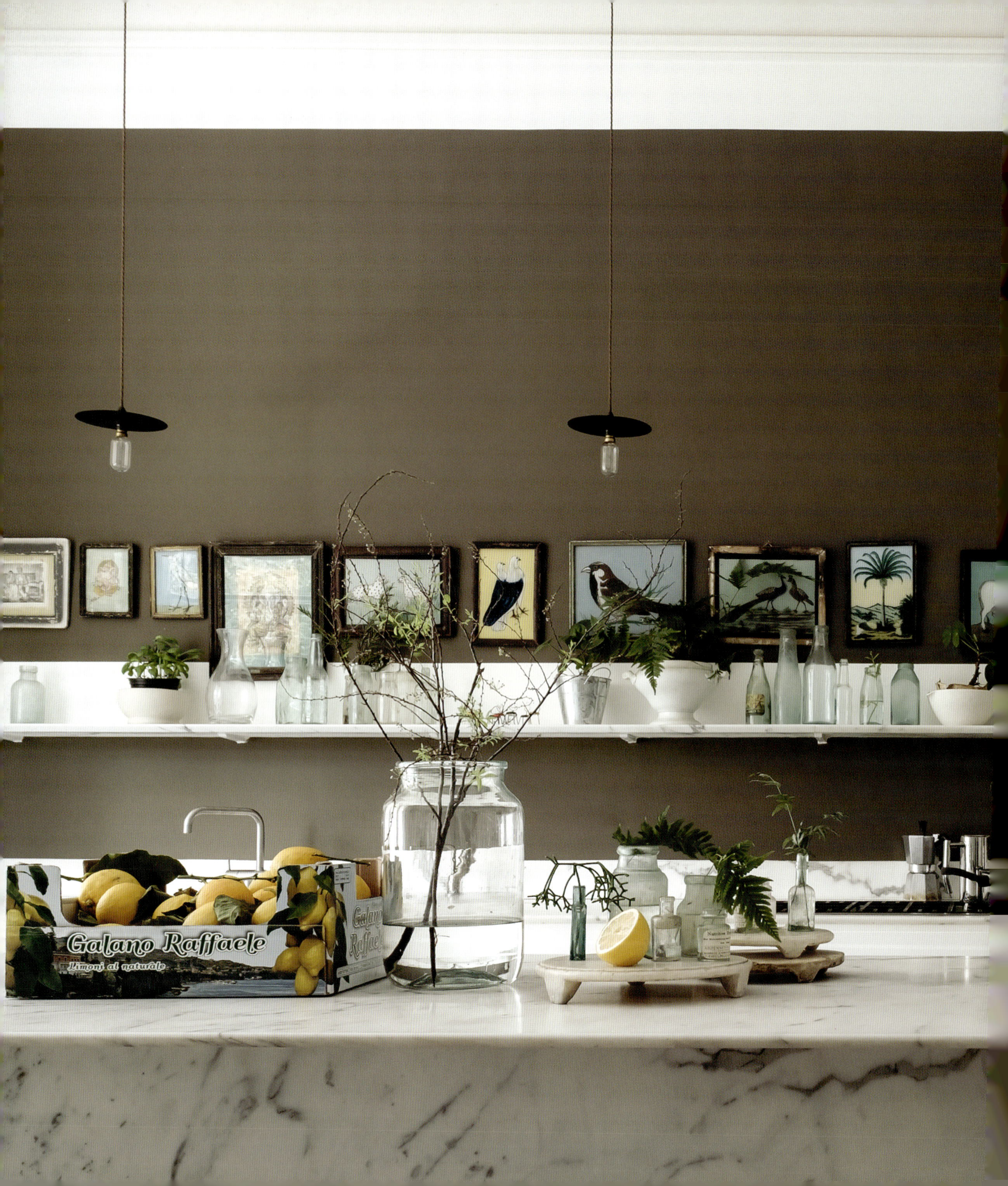
Galano Raffaele
Limoni al naturale

THIS PAGE
Natural materials can be unpredictable in their coloration, which means that particular care must be taken when choosing paint colours for the room. The markings in this marble island and worktop tend towards brown, which has been echoed in the chocolatey Salon Drab walls. Instantly appealing, this colour makes the kitchen feel more than just a room devoted to the preparation of food.

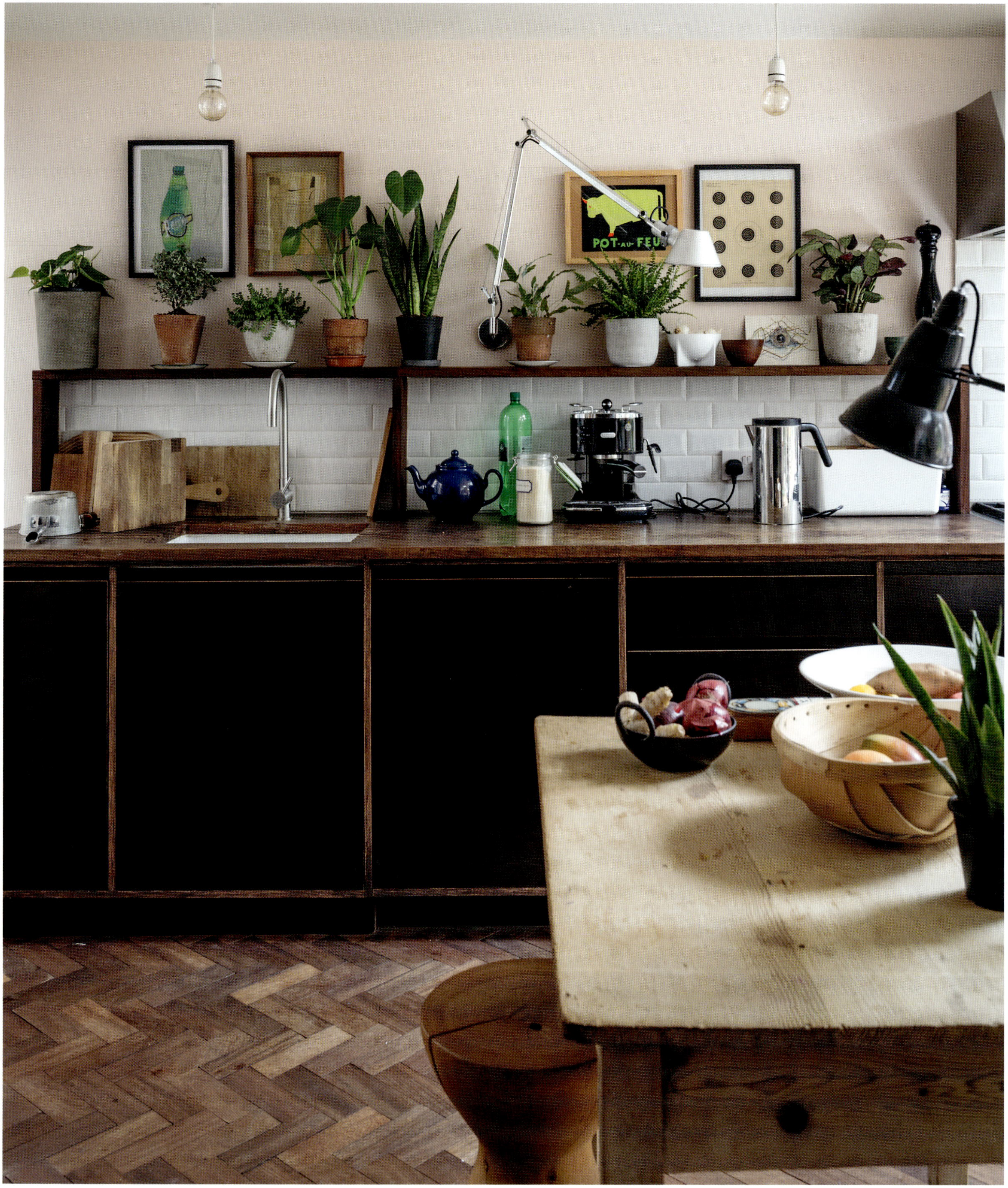
POT-AU-FEU

FACING PAGE
The dusty blush of Pink Ground is delightful on the walls of this contemporary kitchen and the perfect accompaniment to the floor and bespoke units. With its large dose of yellow pigment, it creates the softest glow.

BELOW
This kitchen is the relaxed heart of a historic house. Chinese Blue (A), on the window frame, and Print Room Yellow (A), on the units, bring a smile to one's face. Clunch (A) lends a chalky finish to the neutral walls.

BELOW
Deep mustard India Yellow is strong and moody in this kitchen, where it has been used on the walls, floor, trim and cupboard. However, it is not overwhelming due to the lack of contrast with a lighter tone, which would have made it look darker. Its intensity makes the room a fun-filled space to eat and live in. A carefully orchestrated stripe of Inchyra Blue crosses the floor, giving an effective respite from the yellow.

KITCHENS

COUNTRY KITCHEN

This fabulous rambling house is packed full of colour, except for the intentionally cool and neutral kitchen, reached through a traditional Mizzle hall and a surprising Calamine corridor. The walls are painted in Blackened, one of our Architectural Neutrals, an ideal choice for those who want a slightly modern, industrial feel but are keen to avoid a blindingly stark pure white.

The kitchen is where the family spend most of their time, so the owners have chosen to make it their lightest, brightest space. Taking advantage of the fact that the room is south-facing, the perceived cool tones of Blackened are softened somewhat and the kitchen works as a perfect counterbalance to the bucolic view. The room was originally the dining room in the house, but modern-day living meant that converting it to a kitchen was the obvious choice. Now the family can spill out into the garden direct from the kitchen, and with the trim on all the doors and windows painted the same colour as the walls, that journey feels seamless.

The units at either end of the room are painted in Pavilion Gray, so the contrast with the walls is very slight, making the space feel even bigger, while the island is painted in Pitch Black, to add an amazing dash of drama. Having such a large, dark object in the centre of the room makes everything around it feel bigger and lighter, and the fact that this strong colour sits below the eye line means it is much easier to live with than if it had been used on wall-hung cabinets. The addition of an old French cupboard painted in Oval Room Blue softens the overall look and prevents the room from having an unforgiving or clinical feel. Despite its cool palette, this room has the warmest of atmospheres and is the perfect neutral backdrop to a highly colourful family.

ABOVE
This pastoral view from the kitchen is the perfect outlook for this modern kitchen. Blackened has been used on the walls, doors and shutters, to create a seamless link to the outside.

FACING PAGE
The Pavilion Gray units are only very slightly darker than the walls, which helps to create a sense of space. The daring use of Pitch Black on the monumental island gives the rest of the room a feeling of spaciousness.

PALETTE

PAVILION GRAY* 242 — units
OVAL ROOM BLUE* 85 — cupboard
BLACKENED* 2011 — walls/woodwork
PITCH BLACK™ 256 — island

ROOM RECIPES

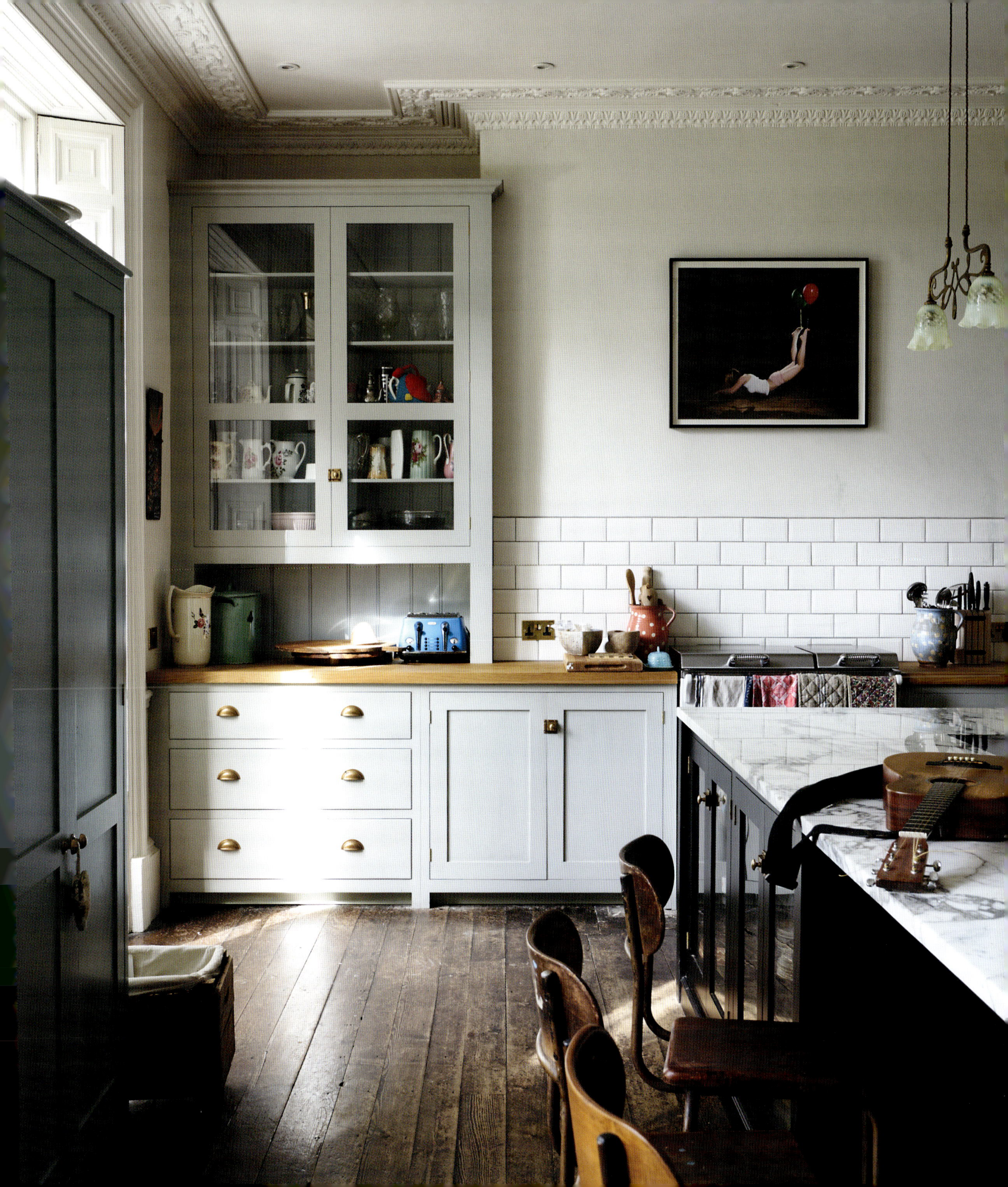

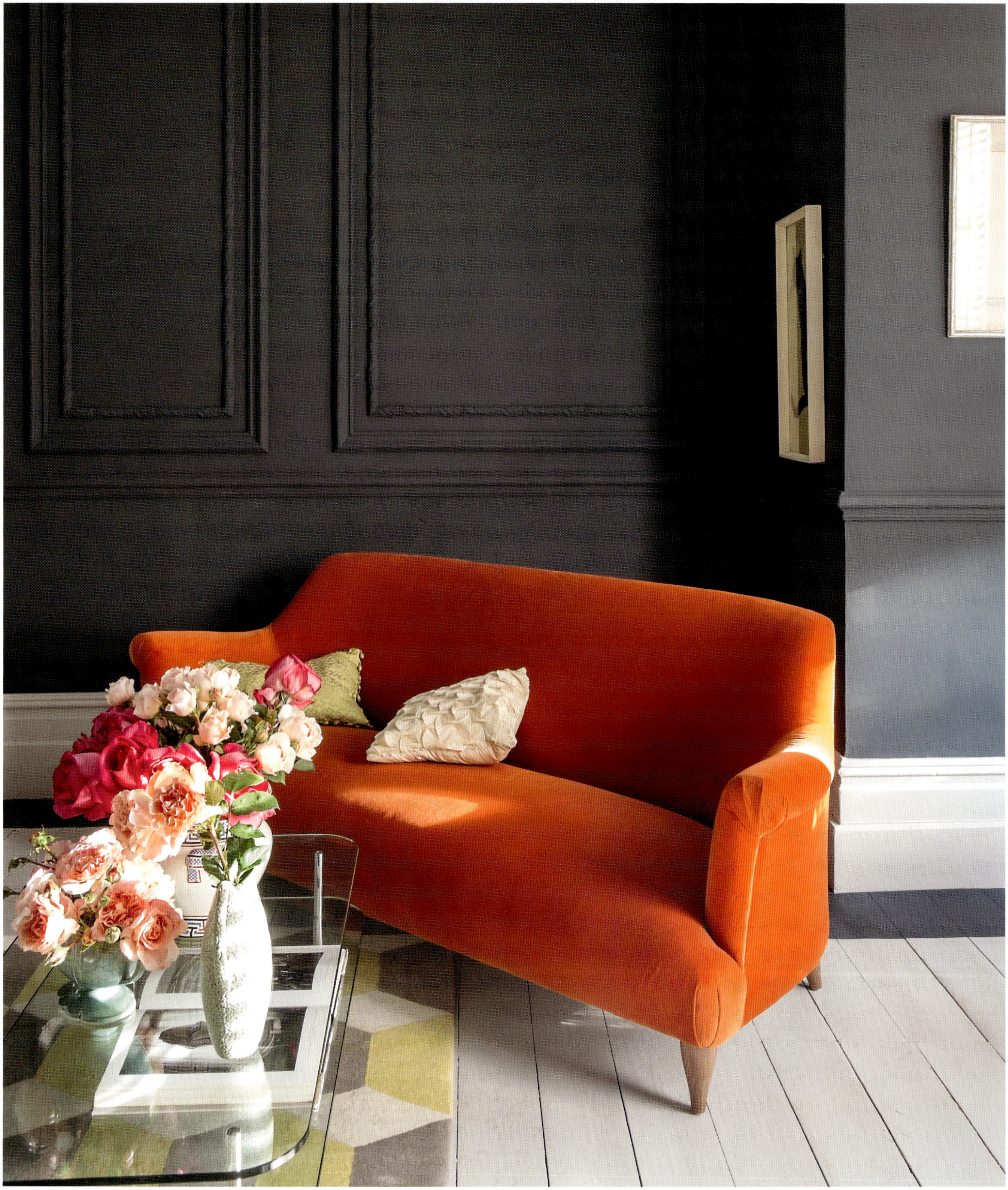

SITTING ROOMS

Your sitting, or living, room is where you unwind and enjoy the comforts of home, making it deserving of your full decorating attention. Many sitting rooms are used primarily at night, either when entertaining guests or simply relaxing in front of a screen. In such cases, darker tones may be more suitable. But if your sitting room is used in the day and at night, you will need chameleon-like colours that will work with both natural and artificial light.

Rich colours have an amazing ability to fuse elegance with comfort, creating rooms that feel exciting and inviting, as well as being a million miles away from the everyday work environment. There is something pleasingly indulgent about leaving a bright, functional office or kitchen to end the day in an enveloping room of saturated colour. Sulking Room Pink and Card Room Green both have enough colour in them to feel luxurious, and they also exude calm and serenity, making them perfect for an evening retreat.

FACING PAGE
Although the Farrow & Ball neutral groups and graduated colour combinations are tailor-made to pick out different planes in panelling, many people choose to use just one colour. This creates a stronger look and allows the architecture to speak for itself. For the contemporary twist in this sitting room, Down Pipe has been used on the walls and also as a border around the Strong White wood floor, which echoes the skirting.

BELOW
My favourite wallpaper Tessella was "reimagined" here with a vibrant Yeabridge Green background and an All White pattern for a fresh, upbeat feel. The pattern colour has also been used on the ceiling and trim.

BELOW RIGHT
This sitting room feels extraordinarily relaxed because it is painted in just one colour, Blue Gray, which appears pleasingly blue during the day in natural light but is much more muted and grey at night.

FACING PAGE
There is a striking freshness to this modern sitting room, painted in the time-honoured combination of Pavilion Gray on the walls and Wevet on the ceiling and trim — a crisp contrast that accentuates the simplicity of the decoration.

DAY TO NIGHT

For sitting rooms used at all times of the day, tones such as Mizzle and French Gray work particularly well. Their complex make-up means that they are pleasingly blue or green in natural light but more muted in the evening, creating the best of both worlds.

If your wish is to retreat to a neutral sea of calm at the end of the day, a warm wall colour such as Elephant's Breath will result in a relaxed sitting room, while cool Pavilion Gray will add a certain formality and help to balance the warmer tones of wood flooring and furniture. Remember that a pared-back wall colour will mean that the tactile elements, such as a sofa, will take centre stage.

When choosing wall colours, always take your artwork into consideration. The paint or wallpaper should either complement or echo pictures, to create a sense of harmony and make the room comfortable and relaxing.

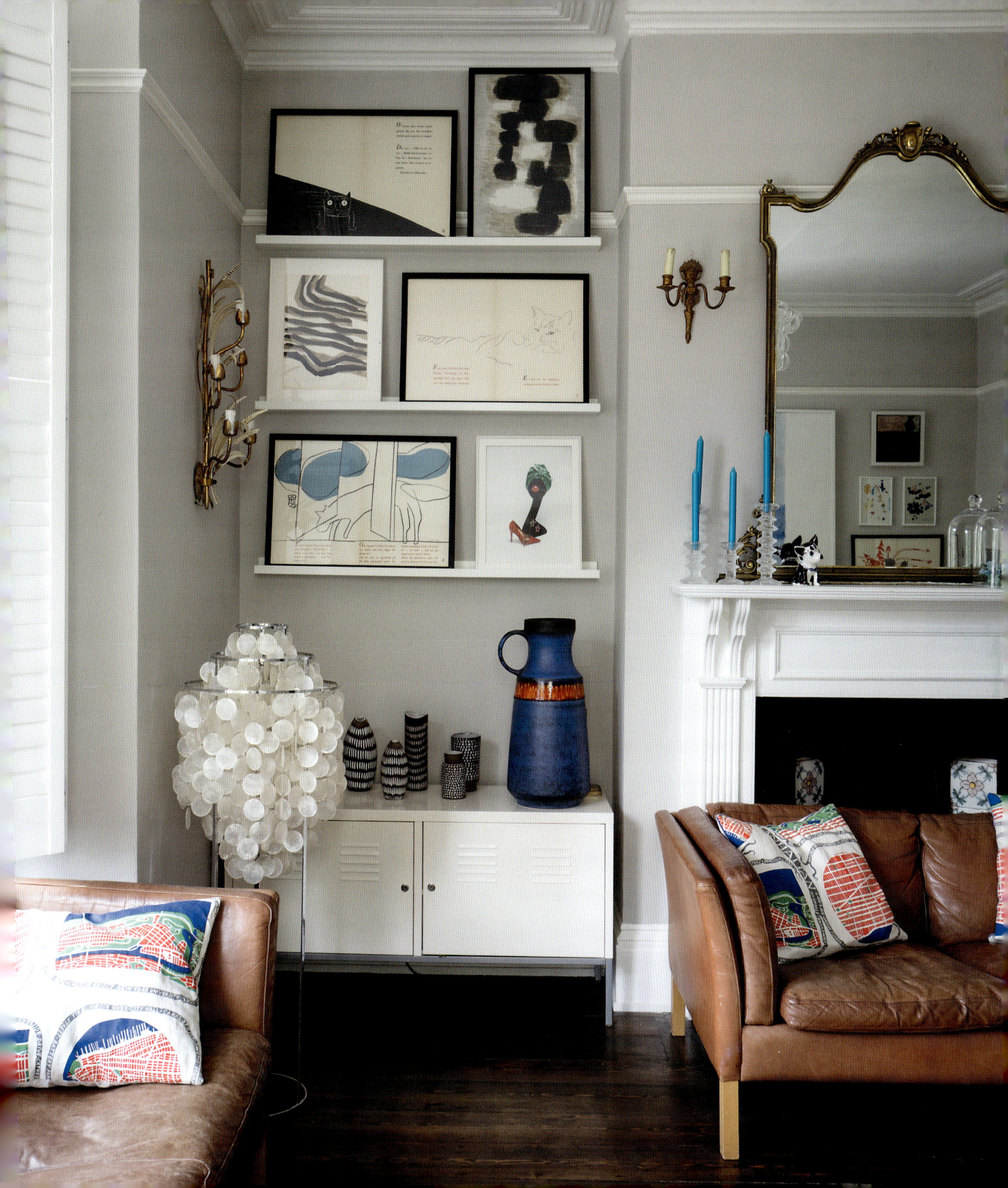

ABOVE
Bumble Bee wallpaper always delights and, with its background in dusty grey-pink Peignoir and the pattern in Skimming Stone, it feels positively peaceful in this laid-back sitting room. Both colours are muted and complex, so work together seamlessly, especially when the pattern colour is also used on the ceiling and trim.

ABOVE
Old meets new as the early 19th-century damask wallpaper Silvergate is used in a contemporary home. In uncomplicated Yeabridge Green and muted Cromarty, the wallpaper is satisfyingly subtle and feels atmospheric but not busy. Complementary James White, with its slight green undertone, is perfect on the walls and trim.

ABOVE
With its Arts and Crafts-style flower in clean Parma Gray and an Off-Black background, the Lotus wallpaper is an audacious choice when teamed with a neon sign and brightly coloured sofa. This is a joyful room, designed to be used by teenagers who might not appreciate the subtler things in life.

ABOVE
Tessella wallpaper in the rich colourway of Vardo and Inchyra Blue was chosen for this sitting room, which is used mostly at night so needs to feel atmospheric. During the day, the All White trim and ceiling not only ensure the room feels crisp but also connect it to the softer kitchen space glimpsed through the open door.

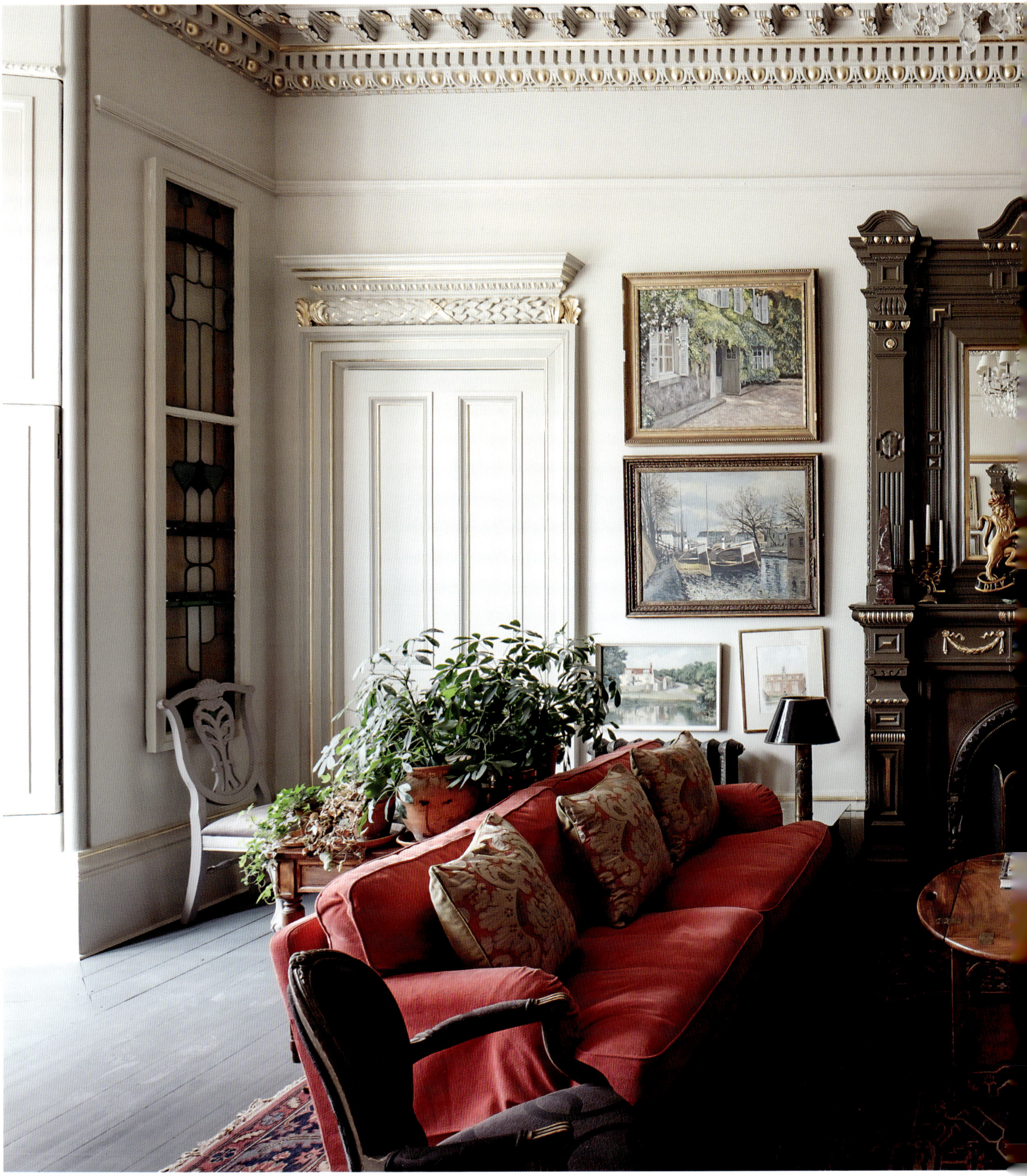

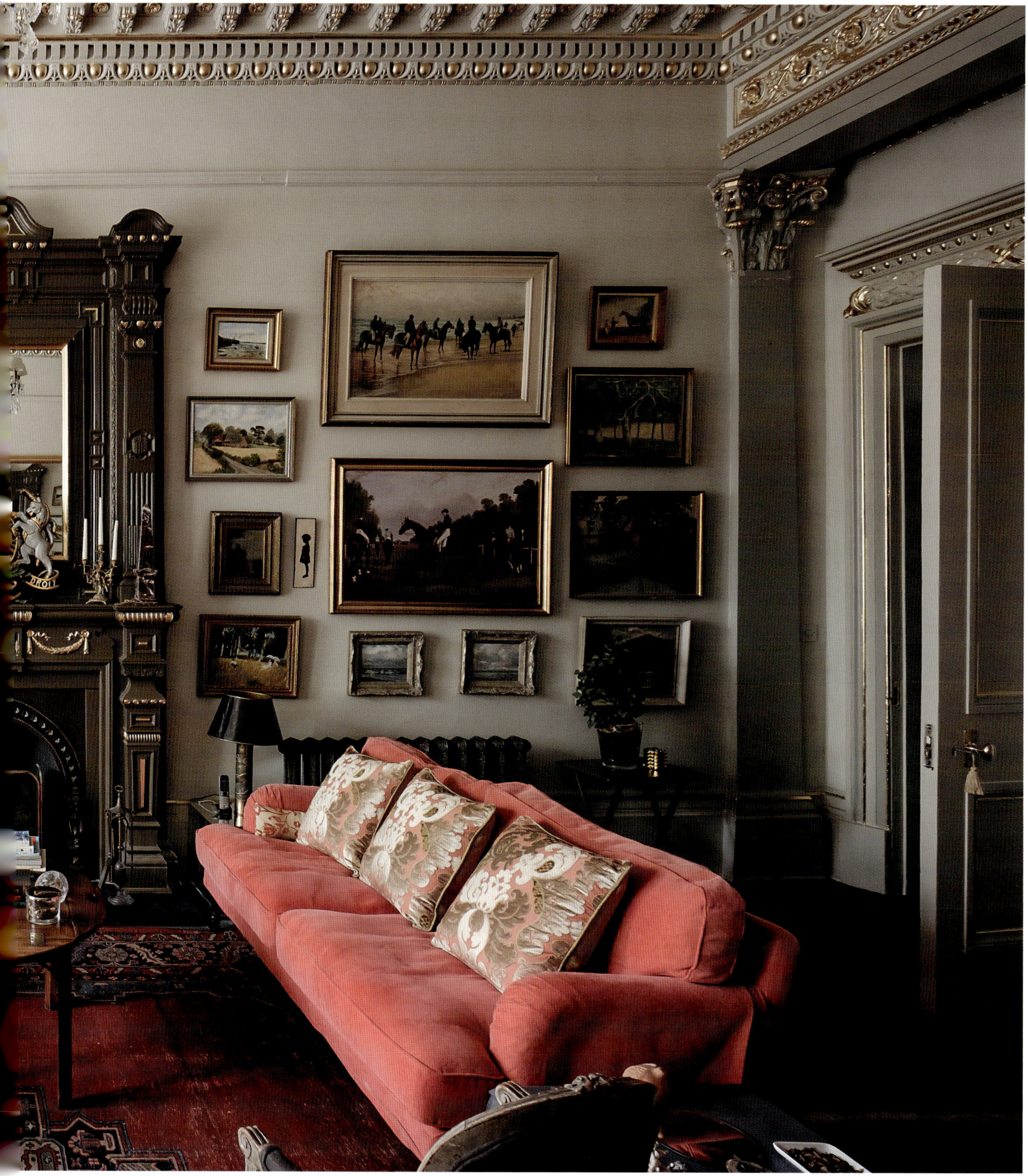

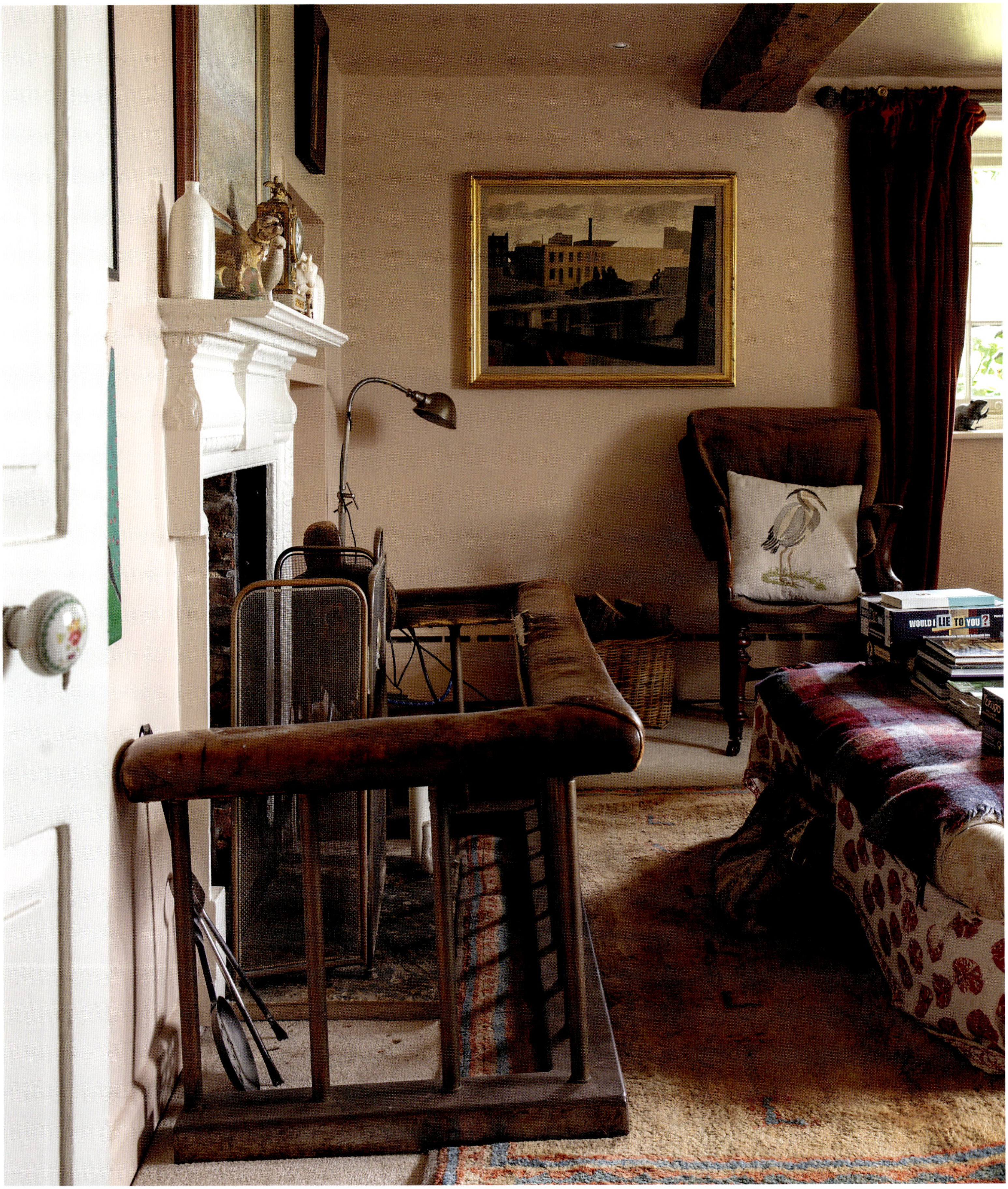
WOULD I LIE TO YOU?

PAGES 202-3
Although recently decorated, this room looks as if it is from a past time. Exceptional gilding complements the paint colours: Shadow White, Shaded White, Drop Cloth, Hardwick White, Railings and Salon Drab.

FACING PAGE
It took a while to convince the owners of this relaxed sitting room to paint it in Setting Plaster, and even longer to get them to agree to using it on the ceiling as well. However, they are thrilled with the result.

BELOW LEFT
Pavilion Gray walls flow up the stairs, so the shelving unit has been painted Pitch Black to make the seating area feel more intimate. This dramatic colour also appears on the doors and staircase for consistency.

BELOW
Spending time in this room gives you a burst of energy. All White on the skirting, moulding, ceiling and fire surround creates a rigid formality, but Vardo in a Full Gloss finish on the walls is nothing other than fun.

FOCAL POINTS

A stronger tone can be used in a small area to create a focal point. Paint a chimney breast in a different tone from the walls, for example, but remember to wrap the colour around the whole breast, not just on the front. The look can be very subtle, such as when using Treron on the chimney breast against a French Gray wall. Although the overall effect is restful, the contrast creates just enough tension to wake up an otherwise sleepy space.

Using a darker tone on the interior of shelves results in an element of sophistication and depth. By painting the three vertical surfaces of a bookcase, you will highlight special ornaments without the stronger colour stealing the show. Preference Red used in this way in a sitting room painted in Skimming Stone will keep the room feeling classic, but with a little decorative twist.

Make paint colour one of the last things you consider. Furnishings must take priority because it is much easier to match a paint colour to a sofa than vice versa. Paint is also one of the smallest investments you will make in a room, so it is best to choose the more expensive items first, then decorate around them. It's worth remembering that if you wish to make your sitting room feel larger, choosing similar colours for the walls and furnishings works best.

SITTING ROOMS

BOLD SITTING ROOM

Although it might not appeal to the faint-hearted, this exuberant decorative scheme has been perfectly tailored to the occupant's taste. Some of the most vibrant Farrow & Ball tones have been used throughout this super-stylish Boston home, including Stone Blue in the lively sitting room. Many feel timid about using blue because of its perceived cold tones, but Stone Blue is a saturated, timeless colour that, with its green undertones, always creates a really inviting space. It can have a slightly vintage look, but here, contrasted with near-black accents, it feels cleaner and more contemporary. The real drama of this room, however, comes from having just one colour from the bottom of the skirting to the top of the cornice.

The walls are painted in Estate Emulsion, with the mouldings accentuated in Full Gloss, which creates dynamism, as well as being ultimately durable. If the trim had been picked out in a contrasting white, the room would be fussy and uncomfortable, while light frames for the windows and glazed doors would create a barrier between the interior and exterior. Using just one colour unifies the room and links it perfectly to the balcony.

Colour is a quick way to transform an entire room. Another warm blue, Dix Blue, has been used to great effect on the ceiling. With its touch of black pigment, the paint introduces a slightly aged and relaxed feel and makes it difficult to read the confines of the room. Had the ceiling been a conventional white, you would immediately be able to ascertain the size of the room, which would make it seem smaller. It would also make the walls look darker.

There is an age-old decorating belief that there should be an element of black in every room. Nothing could be truer here. The Pitch Black bookcase reflects the dark of the fire surround and the TV, and is picked up in the cushions and rug. This makes the bookcase feel like the ultimate black accessory.

This is unconventional decoration with a kick – brave but sound choices have resulted in a room seemingly perfect for entertaining.

ABOVE
Black is by far the best colour against which to display artefacts and family treasures. Here, Pitch Black on the joinery creates a naturally more intimate corner in the darkest part of the room.

FACING PAGE
The bold decision to use Stone Blue on the walls, panelling and trim has enormous impact and connects the interior to the outside. Dix Blue on the ceiling was an unconventional but effective choice in this light-filled room.

PALETTE

STONE BLUE® 86
walls/panelling/trim

PITCH BLACK™ 256
joinery

DIX BLUE® 82
ceiling

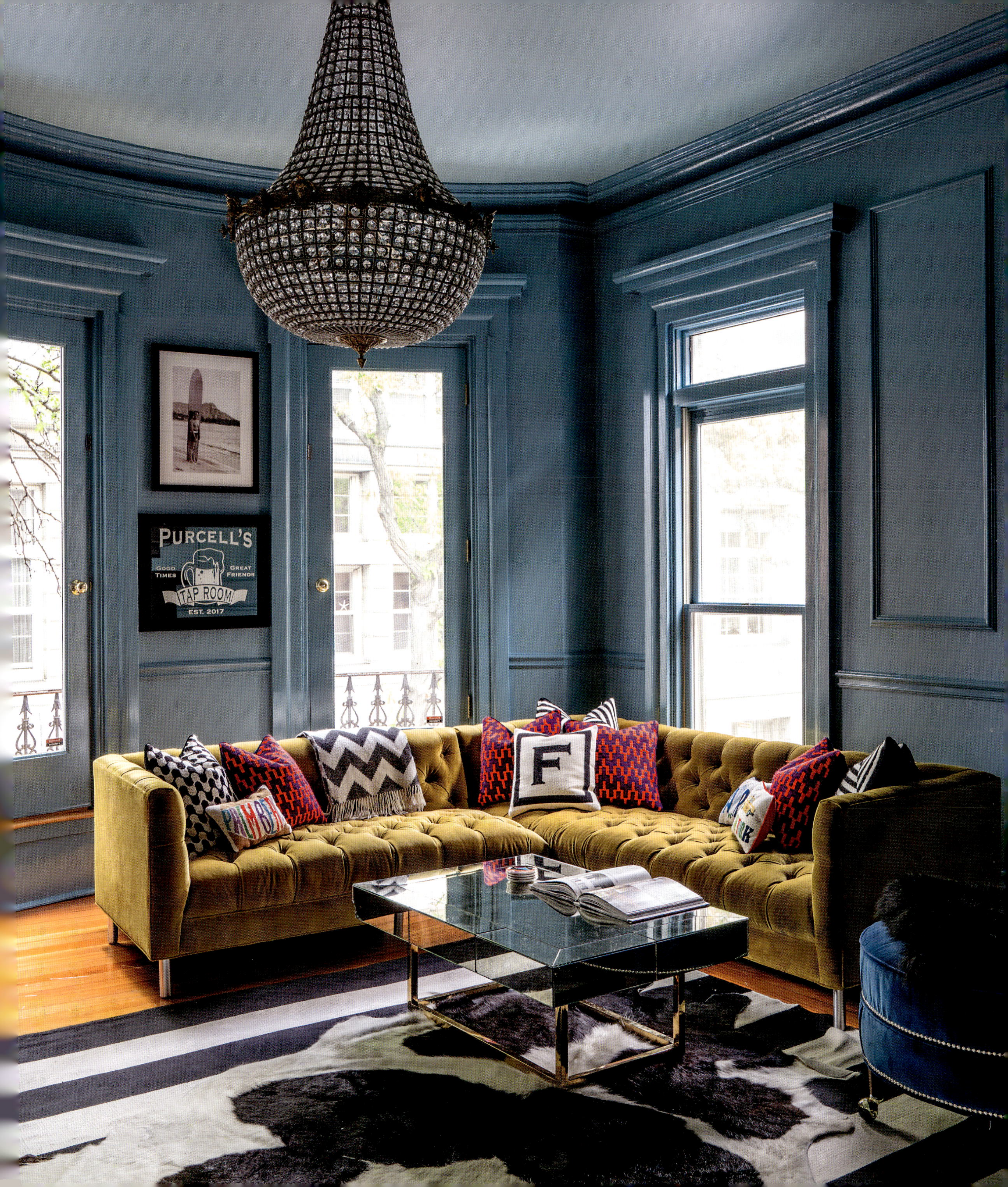
PURCELL'S
GOOD TIMES
GREAT FRIENDS
TAP ROOM
EST. 2017
F

HIPPIE DICTIONARY
smashed
KINGDOM OF FEAR
HUNTER S. THOMPSON
CHARLES BUKOWSKI
THE PLEASURES OF THE DAMNED
BARRY REIGATE
ONE CANNOT GET FINGERPRINTS FROM A ROCK

BEDROOMS

Bedrooms are deeply personal spaces and should be decorated accordingly. If you are a morning person who likes to jump out of bed and attack the day first thing, then you are probably more suited to having a clean, light colour on the walls, such as Pavilion Blue. Evening people will more likely embrace the dark, womb-like shades of London Clay or Dead Salmon. For a bedroom used purely for sleeping, serene colours such as Light Blue and Setting Plaster will induce a good night's rest and a sense of calm. Alternatively, you might prefer to create a dreamy, ethereal feel with the use of James White or Skimming Stone.

FACING PAGE
This room has the smallest of windows, so it is lucky that its occupant likes to feel wrapped in a cocoon of colour. Brinjal, a sophisticated aubergine colour, looks warm and nourishing, especially when taken over every surface, except the floor. On this, Pointing in a Modern Eggshell finish bounces any available light back onto the walls.

BELOW
Capturing the innocence of simpler times, the Gable wallpaper used behind the bed as a feature wall seems to ground the room. The Green Blue of the wallpaper has been used on the other walls for a cohesive look.

BELOW RIGHT
The 18th-century French damask wallpaper St Antoine has a feminine feel, but the Green Ground and Pointing colouring stops it from being sugary. Pointing on the trim and ceiling makes the pattern as unobtrusive as possible.

FACING PAGE
For those who like their lives calm and serene, this bedroom is the ultimate haven. The understated combination of Skimming Stone on the walls, slightly darker Elephant's Breath on the walls of the en suite bathroom and Strong White on the trim and ceilings never fails. Strong White in a Modern Eggshell finish on the floor maintains a truly relaxed feel.

WALLS

When you consider how much more time you spend looking at the architectural elements of a bedroom while lying in bed, you could decide to treat yourself to really sumptuous walls by using a Dead Flat finish. However, it is very matt and only suited to rooms with little traffic. To introduce an extra element to lift the space, use an accent colour or flamboyant wallpaper on a feature wall behind the bed. This grounds the room and feels nurturing.

TRIM

Bedrooms feel much more restful if all the trim and the walls are painted in the same colour, so that your eyes aren't distracted by the contrasts. Alternatively, choose a white for the trim that is sympathetic to the colour used on the walls in order to keep the difference between the two muted.

ROOM RECIPES

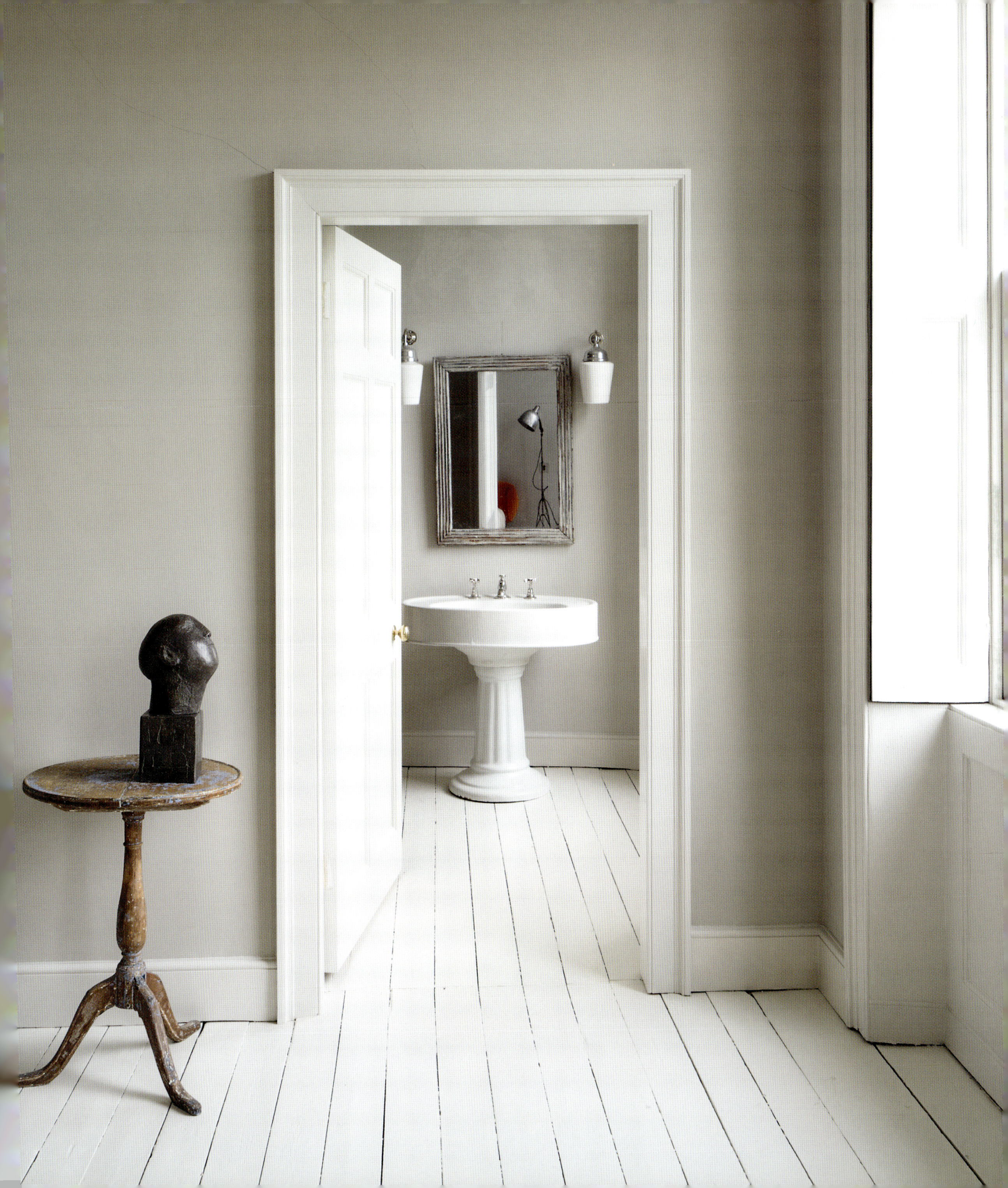

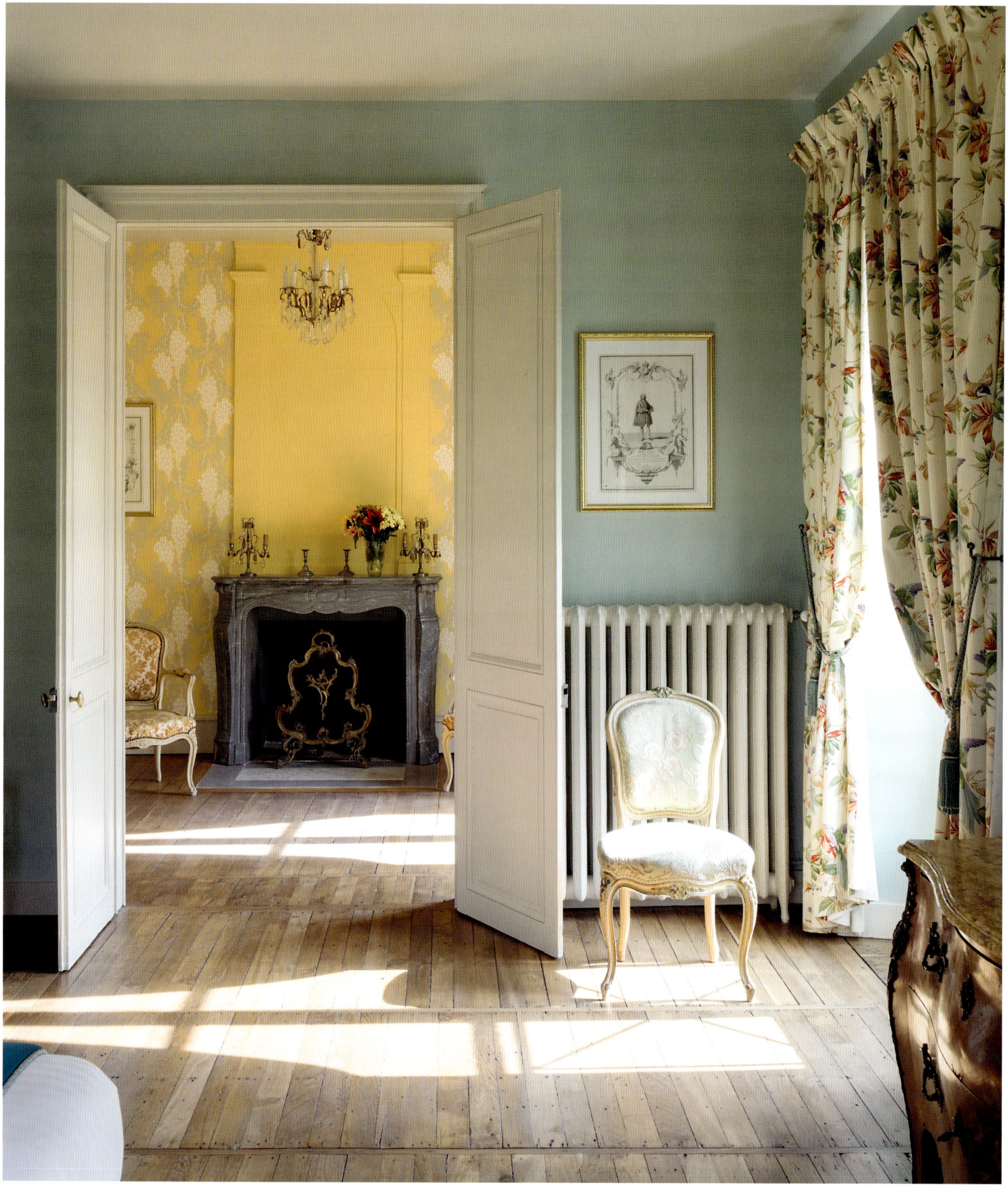

FACING PAGE
Two very different colours have been used in this bedroom and dressing room for a look of pure opulence. Aqua-coloured Teresa's Green has a calming and therapeutic effect in the bedroom, while the classic English floral pattern of Wisteria in the dressing room is altogether more energizing. Although the lively Yellow Ground background of the wallpaper is the antithesis of the serene bedroom, the two spaces are united by Pointing on the trim in both areas.

BELOW LEFT
With its hint of black, warm Brassica is sophisticated and a little grey by night but more feminine and charming by day. Stopping the colour below the Great White ceiling brings a certain intimacy to the room.

BELOW
Giving a bedroom ceiling due consideration is important because we spend a lot of time looking at it. Here, Middleton Pink has been taken onto the ceiling, coving and beams, creating the ultimate space in which to unwind.

CEILINGS

Bedroom ceilings garner more attention than those elsewhere. For the ultimate in calm, use the same colour on the ceiling as the walls, thus increasing the perceived room height. This may sound alarming, but the result is a wonderfully cocoon-like space and you probably won't even notice that the ceiling isn't white.

If you want a bedroom to feel more snug and you have a picture rail, then carry the ceiling colour down to the rail, reducing the ceiling height and creating an intimate atmosphere.

GUEST BEDROOMS

If you are wary of having strong colours and flamboyant patterns in your own bedroom, use them in a guest room. Your guests will undoubtedly be thrilled and made to feel very special.

ATTIC BEDROOM

Of all the layers that make up an interior, colour is perhaps the most versatile. Colours can be chosen for myriad reasons – to highlight areas, change the perceived shape of a room, create warmth, intimacy or drama – but, hopefully, they will always bring delight and solace to the occupant.

The bold choices made in this attic bedroom not only bring the space to life but also create a more evenly proportioned room, together with a warmer atmosphere. Down Pipe on the two end walls makes the room feel squarer in shape, particularly when used in sharp contrast with the much lighter Dimpse on the long walls and ceiling. Meanwhile, the beams in Eating Room Red warm up the space and make it feel a little more intimate.

The architecture of the room, tucked into the eaves of the house, demands that the sloping walls are kept as light as possible. Dimpse, with its almost imperceptible amount of grey pigment, works brilliantly in architectural spaces like this. It is cool without being cold and is the perfect companion for daringly dramatic Down Pipe, chosen to reflect the colour of the steel beams and simple iron banister. To limit the number of colours and keep the look simple and graphic, the desk matches the colour of the wall it sits behind, which helps to expand the feeling of space.

When beams are such an integral part of a room, one can either try to disguise them by painting them the same colour as the walls, or embrace them fully, turning them into a flamboyant feature. Red is an inspired choice for the beams here because the colour reflects its warmth onto the walls. The black pigment in rich Eating Room Red gives a look that is far from modern, so that although the room is graphic in feel, it still feels relaxed, whereas a cleaner red tone may well have felt hard and uninviting.

In this compromised space, colour has been used not only to be visually pleasing, but also as a powerful, transformative tool. The result is a decoratively exciting and inviting bedroom.

ABOVE
Long, thin rooms can benefit from having a darker colour on their shorter walls in order to make the space feel more square. Here, Down Pipe contrasts with Dimpse on the longer walls to create exactly this effect.

FACING PAGE
How wonderful to have embraced the beams in this contemporary loft space. Rather than being incidental (and possibly in the way), they are now the main event on account of being painted in striking Eating Room Red.

PALETTE

EATING ROOM RED* 43
beams

DIMPSE* 277
long walls

DOWN PIPE* 26
short walls

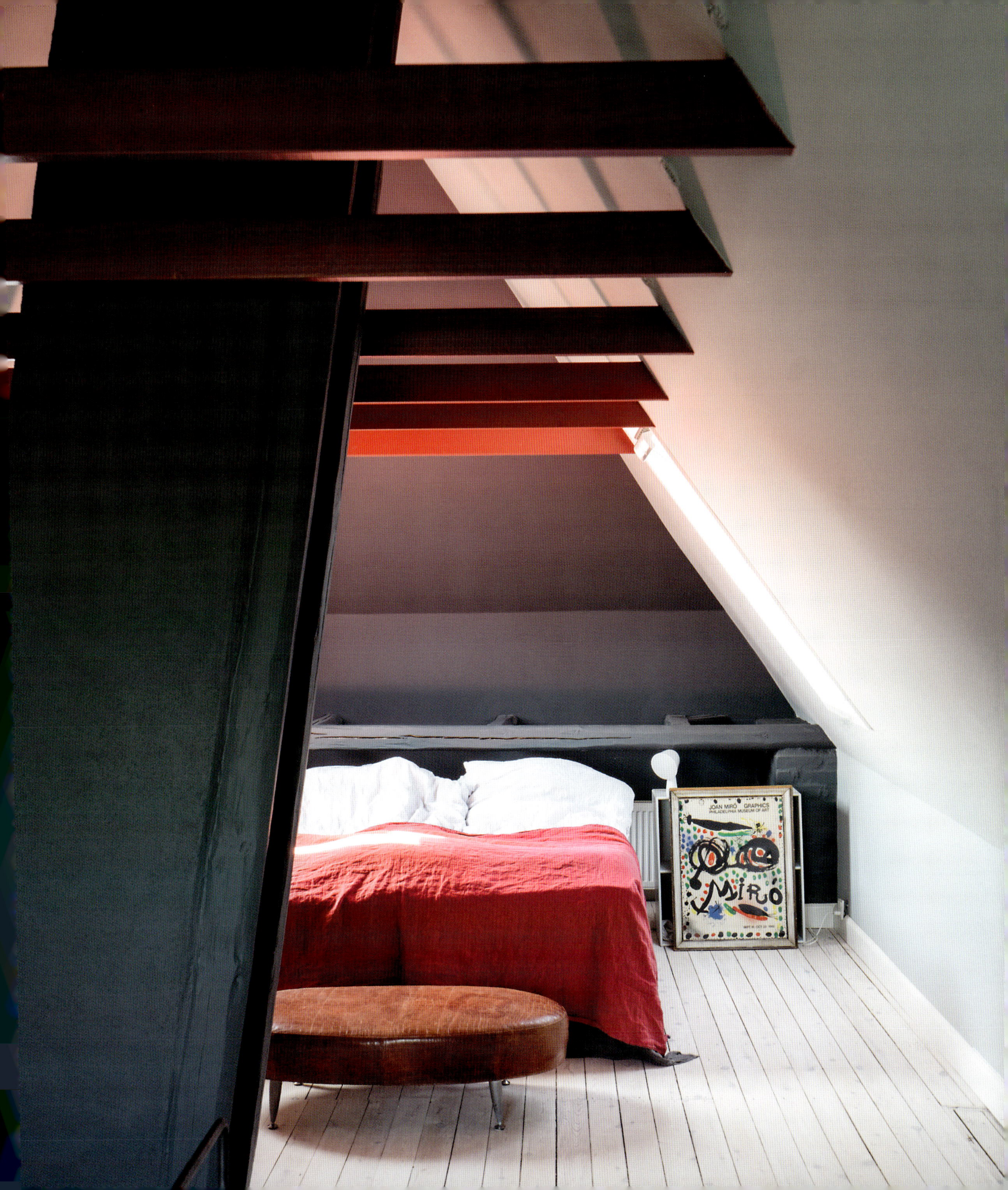
JOAN MIRÓ GRAPHICS
PHILADELPHIA MUSEUM OF ART
MIRÓ

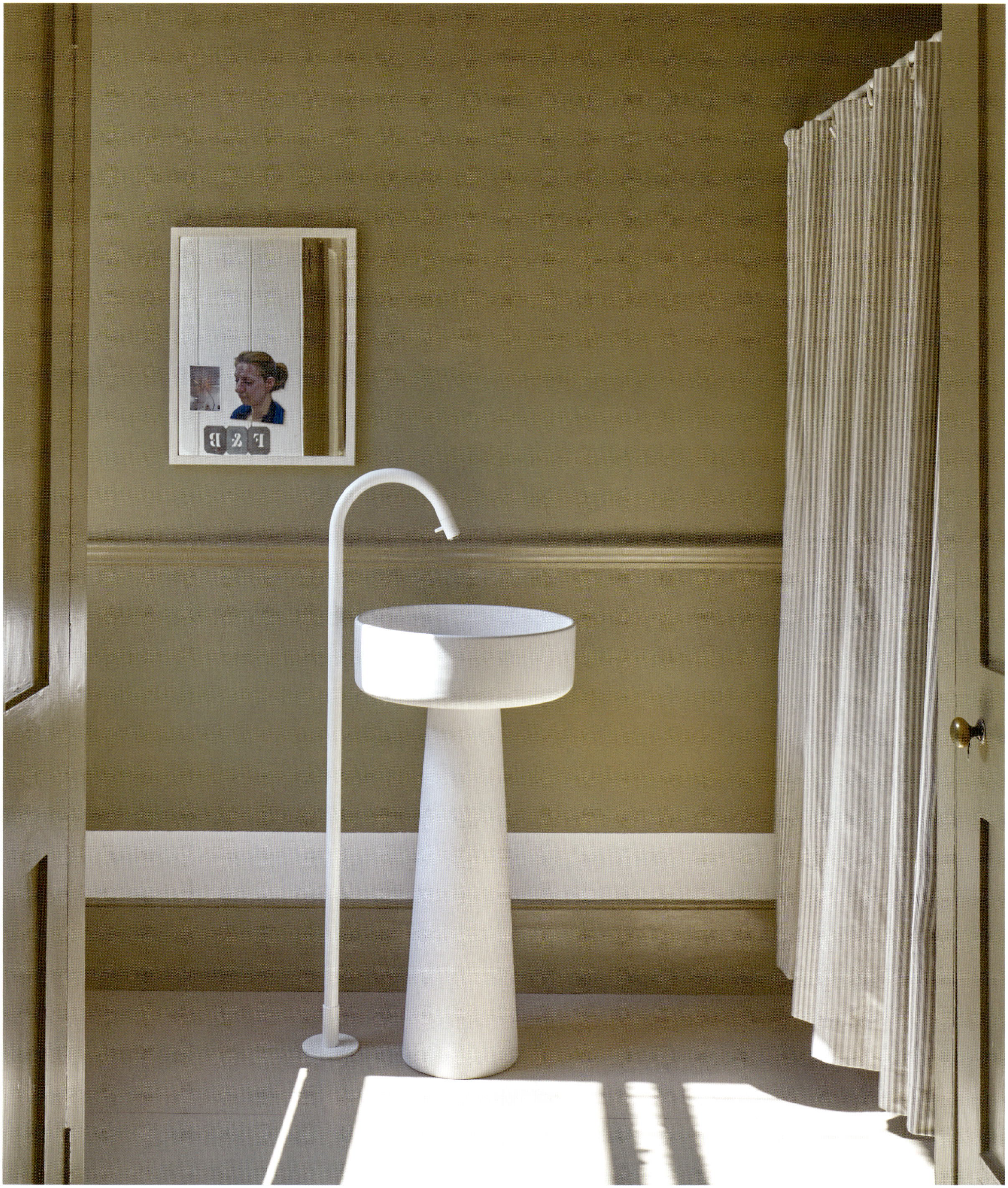

BATHROOMS

Unless you are extremely fortunate, your bathroom is probably the smallest space in your home, which means that every square centimetre matters. But never let size limit your colour choices. Whether you opt for a tranquil, holistic feel or a striking, stimulating design, bathrooms are full of decorating potential.

FACING PAGE
Who could resist the simplicity of this design? The contemporary pedestal basin and floor-standing tap are shown to their very best advantage against the walls painted in Mouse's Back. The same colour serves to disguise the dado rail and skirting, while an All White graphic stripe at the bottom of the wall provides a modern twist.

BELOW
The background and pattern of Farrow & Ball wallpapers are often similar colours, promoting a sense of calm. What could be gentler in a country bathroom than this classic Silvergate 804 in Pointing and Joa's White?

FACING PAGE
Sulking Room Pink is sublime in this bathroom. Dusty in bright daylight, it looks warmer in the evening. The skirting is chic in London Clay, while the radiator is the same colour as the wall, so as not to be distracting.

THE LIGHT, SERENE BATHROOM

If you wish to create your own personal oasis, then varying shades of the same colour provide depth and visual interest, while keeping the room cohesive and soothing. Pick light colours for the largest surfaces, such as the walls, and save the richer tones for accents.

You may want your bathroom tiles or stone to take centre stage, so just let the walls relax into a pale shade of one of their colours. Choose the tiles or stone first – it will then be easy to find a complementary paint tone in our extensive collection.

Skimming Stone works seamlessly with many types of stone for a warm grey colour scheme, while Cornforth White is clean, calm and very versatile, making it perfect with marble. Sophisticated and subtle, both these neutrals have a chameleon-like quality, taking on endless shades of grey.

Bathrooms with large expanses of white, whether in the tiles or sanitaryware, may benefit from a calm grey to soothe the palette and bring a sense of cohesion to the entire space. Cool Blackened or the slightly stronger Dimpse have the beautiful light-reflective qualities that are crucial to a spa-like bathroom. All White is also an important colour to consider because it always feels fresh and clean. In a bathroom where everything, from the towels, to the tiles, to the walls, is white, it can be a good idea to make All White the crux of your scheme. But to prevent an all-white palette from feeling too crisp or cold, introduce some panelling for texture.

For a more soothing scheme, pair an off-white, such as timeless Shaded White or School House White, with white tiles. But if you crave a small amount of colour, try a light blue. Borrowed Light feels effortless in a bathroom, like a breath of fresh air, while the slightly warmer Pale Powder contains enough grey to give it depth and prevent it from looking too pastel. And don't forget your "fifth wall" – it is wonderful to contemplate a coloured ceiling while lying in the tub. Cabbage White on the ceiling will enhance an All White bathroom and, if you're feeling brave, paint it in Full Gloss.

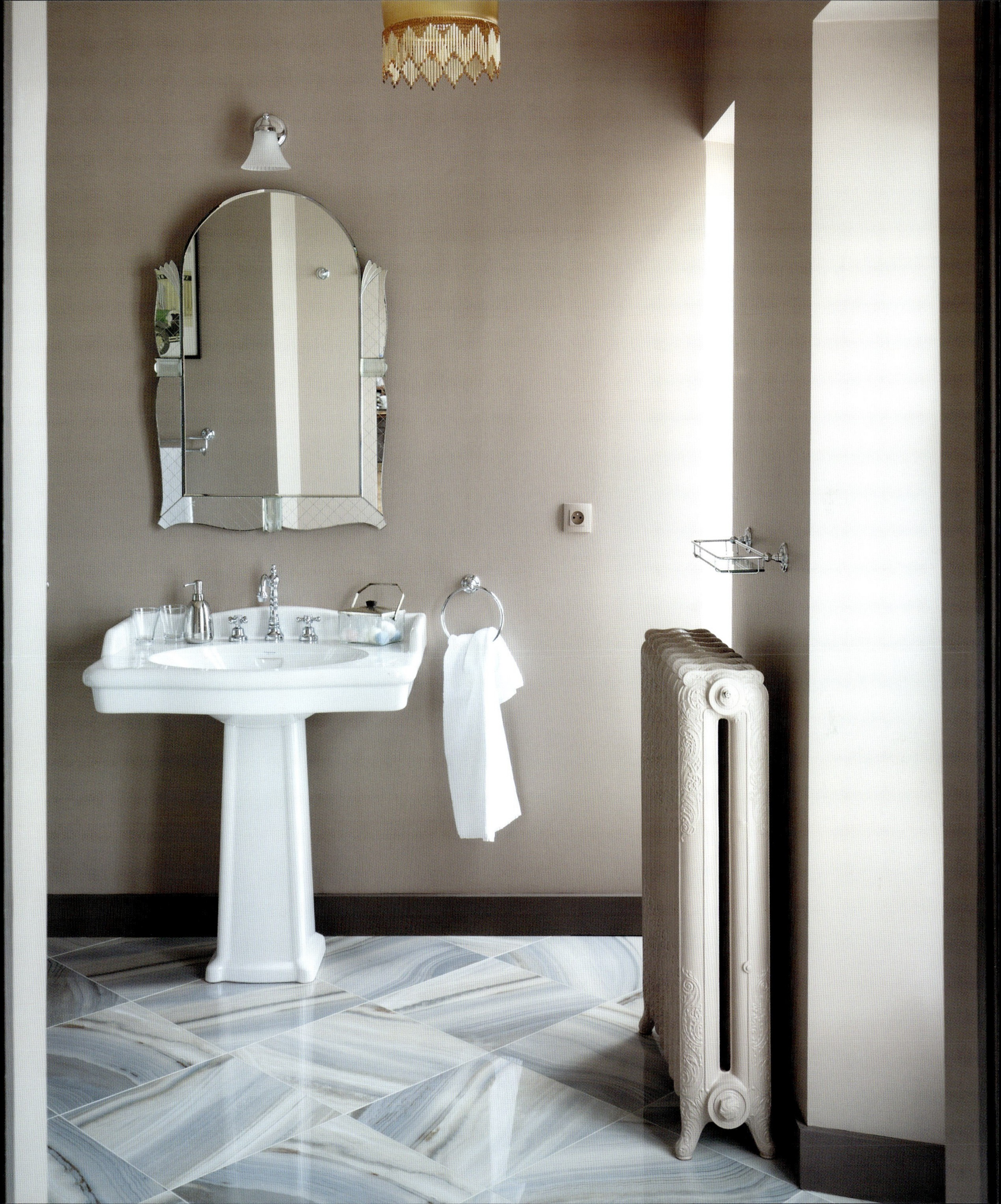

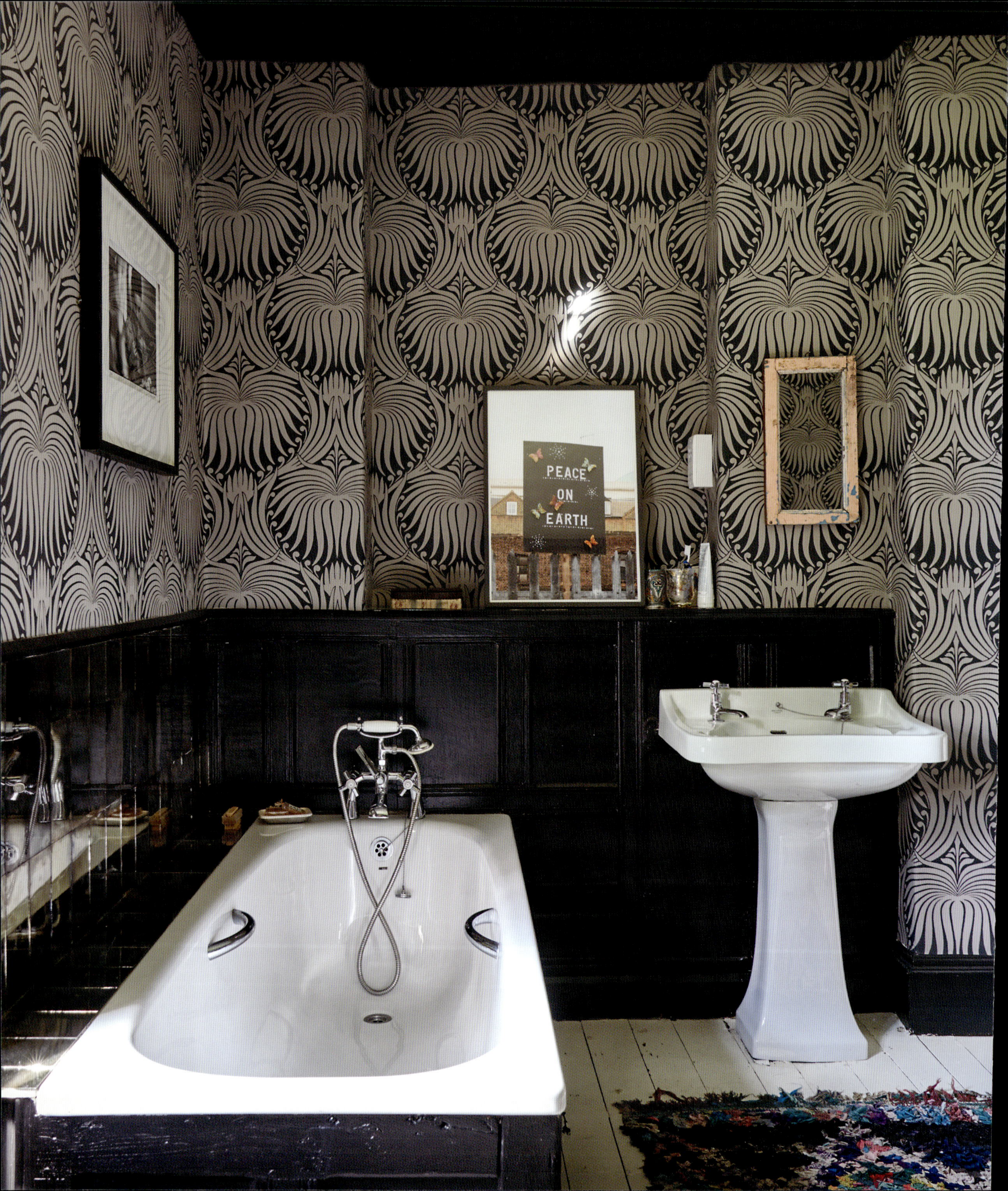
PEACE
ON
EARTH

FACING PAGE
In this glamorous bathroom, the Off-Black background colour of the Lotus wallpaper has been carried over in paint onto the panelling and the ceiling for an added sense of drama. The underlying red in the Charleston Gray of the pattern has a softening effect and prevents the room from looking too cold.

BELOW
The vintage copper bathtub is the star of this bathroom. To give the space an intimate feel, the French Gray Estate Eggshell on the walls stops well below the ceiling — a simple but very effective decorating trick.

THE DRAMATIC BATHROOM

Strong colours are best suited to small, internal bathrooms where electricity provides all the light you need. Guest cloakrooms see limited use, so put form over function and embrace your lack of space. Chic Hague Blue can work miracles in turning a small, dull room into something special, while the harder-to-read but equally refined Inchyra Blue feels a little softer. Tanner's Brown is simultaneously snug and luxurious, Railings is undeniably sleek and urban, while Rangwali will result in a fun-filled, quirky space. Although the thought of using strong colours may be a little scary, they don't make a room feel smaller. Instead, they cause the boundaries to disappear, creating an illusion of space.

Dark walls are an invitation to display art or photographs, and it's always easier to see how you look in a mirror if you're against a dark background. To make an even grander statement, use wallpaper to turn a small space into a piece of artwork itself. Contained spaces expand when covered in a large pattern, particularly when it is taken over the ceiling. Although it might seem counterintuitive to fill a small room with a lot of busy pattern, it makes it feel more luxurious. Our Enigma wallpaper, with its bold geometric design, will invigorate a small, dark space, especially in its metallic colourway, which will bounce any available light around the room.

If you want to temper opulent colours with something a little calmer, use panelling or boarding to dado height. Conventional wisdom dictates that when using two colours, the lighter one should be on the panelling and the other overhead. But in a small bathroom, it is best to keep the stronger colour below the eye line, to open out the room. Even the most neutral bathroom will benefit from a little sumptuous colour, such as Brinjal or Pelt, on a vanity unit and bath panel. Or let your imagination run wild and pick your favourite colour for the underside of a freestanding bath. The added benefit of this approach is that such a small area is very easy to change on a whim.

BATHROOMS

BELOW
Sophisticated Brinjal has been stopped at the top of the panelling in this cheerful bathroom, leaving the Wevet wall and ceiling to reflect the colour of the sanitaryware and bounce light around the room.

FACING PAGE
When combining a bathroom and bedroom space, zone the areas by colour. The basins behind the screen sit on an All White wall, which flows down from the ceiling, while the bath radiates against Chinese Blue (A) bedroom walls.

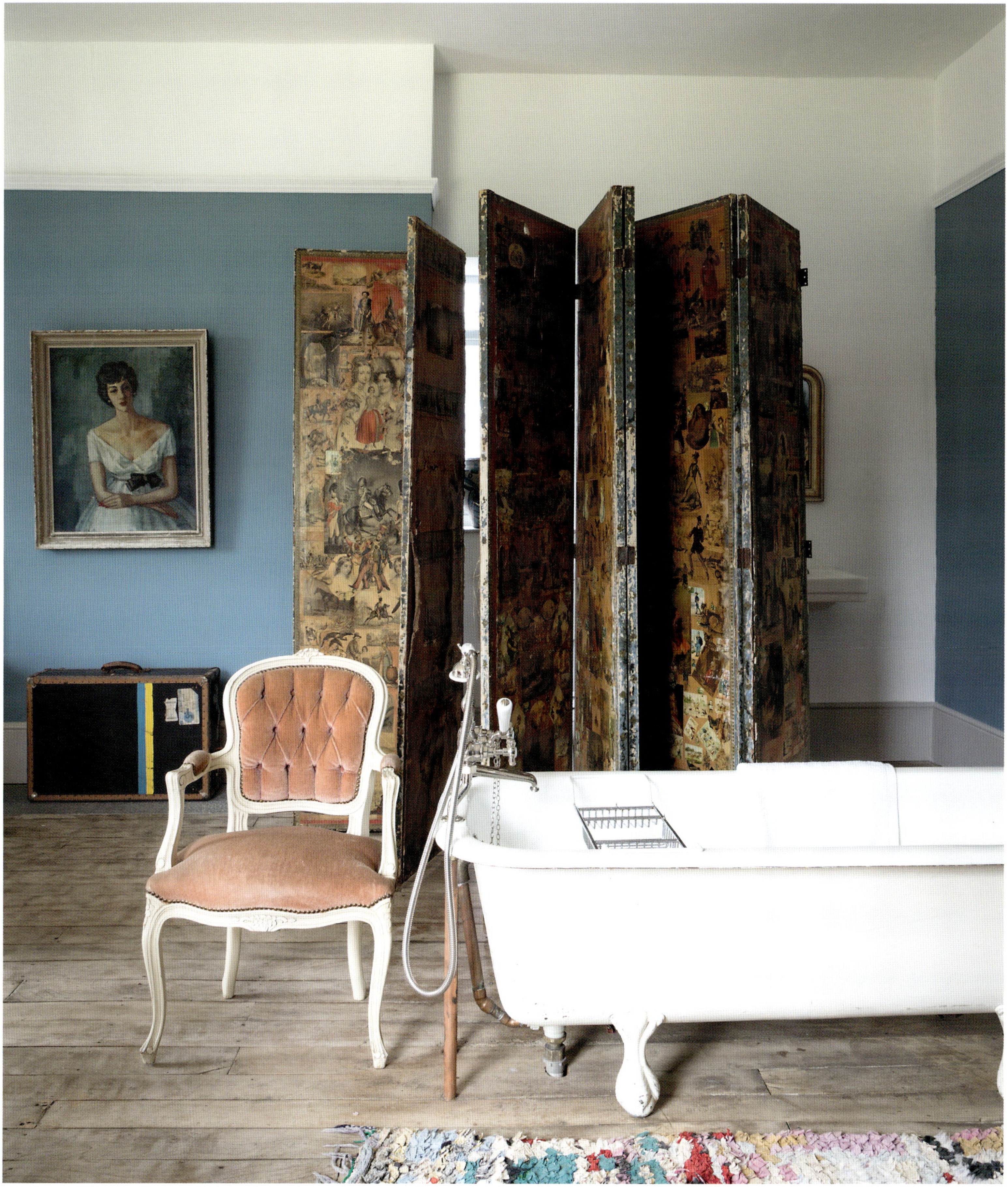

LUXE BATHROOM

The treatment of this elegant bathroom, which is restricted to just two colours, ignores many decorating beliefs, but it is perhaps all the more special because of that.

In such a large, light-filled space, it is often advisable to keep the walls light, but here the high contrast between the Paean Black walls and the Wevet woodwork works to perfection, creating a room that manages to be dramatic as well as light and serene. The outsize window means that the room is bathed in natural light during the day, allowing the Wevet floor to bounce the light back onto the rich, velvety walls. Because the window frame goes down to the floor, it has also been painted in Wevet, to avoid any uncomfortable meeting of different whites. Wevet was also chosen to match the trim in the adjoining bedroom, where it is the perfect foil for Cornforth White, which is just as easy to live with. When you pass from the intentionally very neutral bedroom into this stunning bathroom, it feels like a shot of colour to the soul.

So often when a strong colour is used on the walls above a lighter tone, it feels as if the walls are falling in on top of you. However, because the panelling in this bathroom is only on one wall and is painted the same colour as the floor, this is not the case. The effect is to help make the room feel bigger by tricking the eye into thinking that the floor is larger than it actually is. Repeating the wall colour on the outside of the bath, in Modern Eggshell, draws the eye downwards and cleverly grounds the whole space. The genius of this room, however, is in the use of the horizontal line – in the wall panelling, the highlighted bath base and the stripe on the towel, which falls just at the top of the skirting line.

It takes a special touch to create such a stylish room with two very different colours – Wevet, a delicate white that has an almost translucent feel to it, and Paean Black, a saturated black-red intended to create glamorous and intimate rooms. In this bathroom they sit together perfectly.

ABOVE AND FACING PAGE
The ceiling of this bathroom is very high, so the cornice has been included in the ceiling colour, Paean Black, to reduce the vastness of the walls. Wevet on the panelling and the floor exaggerates the feeling of space.

PALETTE

PAEAN BLACK® 294
walls/ceiling/bath

WEVET® 273
floor/panelling

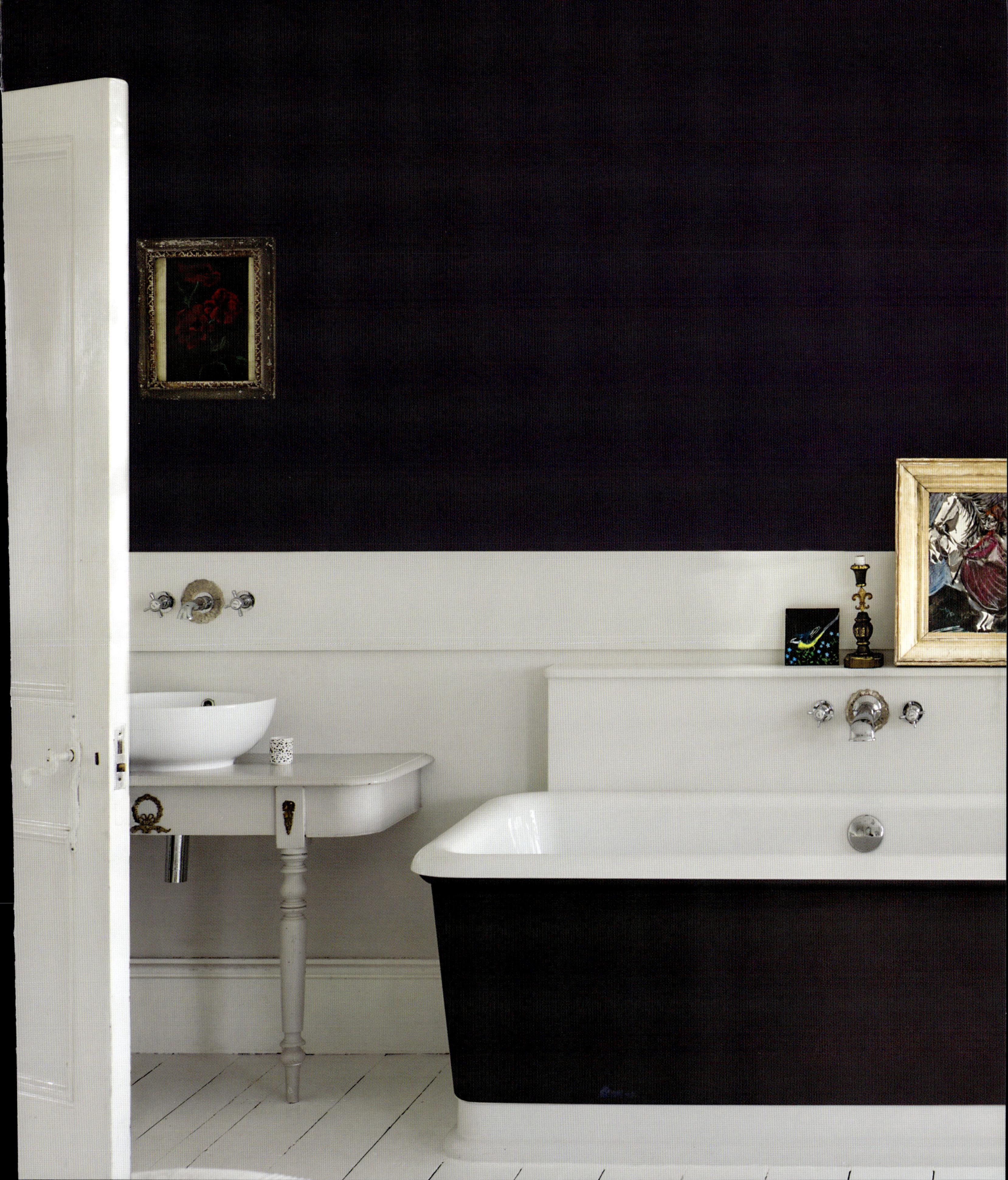

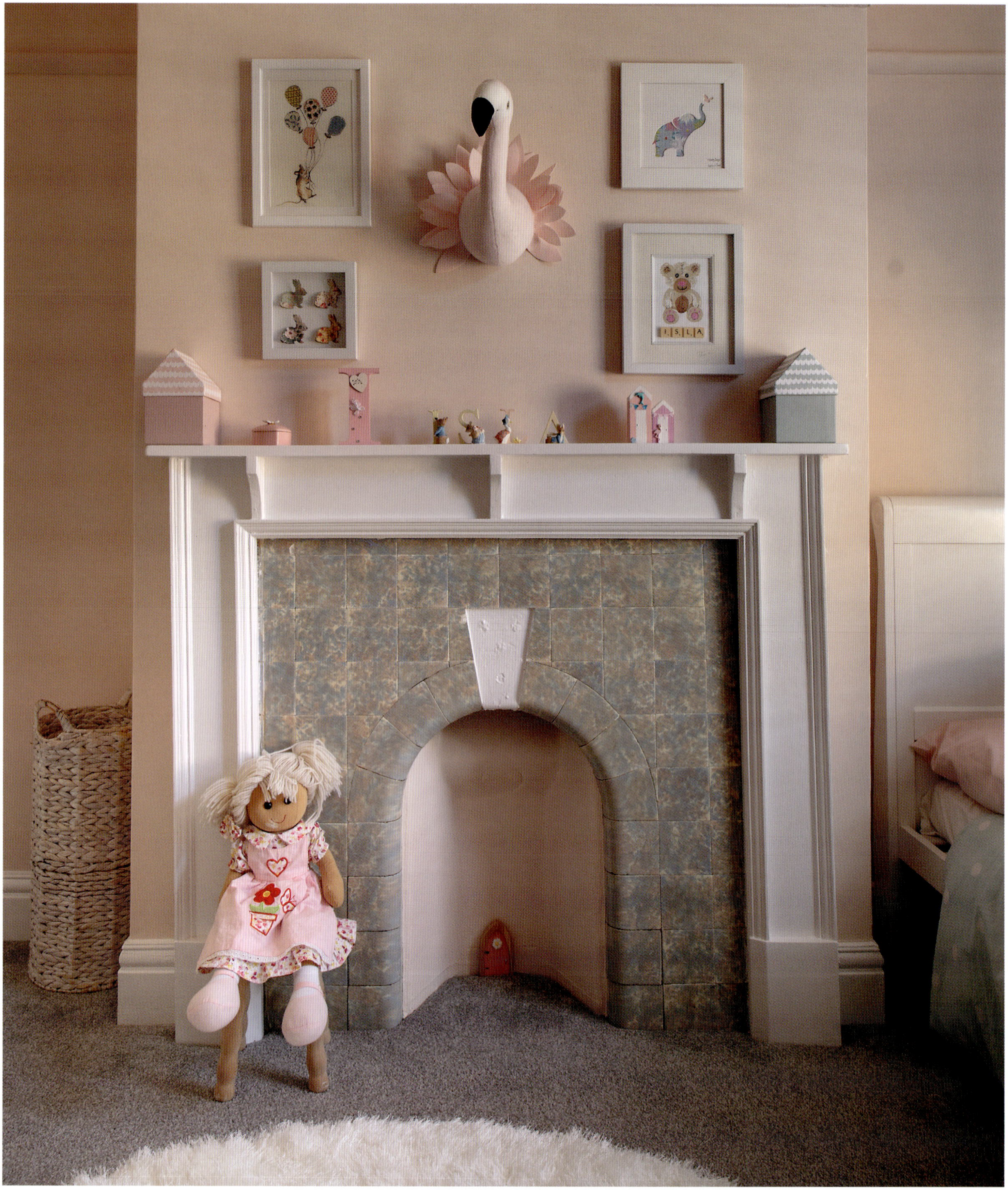
ISLA

CHILDREN'S BEDROOMS

The first thing to establish is whether you want your children's bedrooms to flow with the colour palette of the rest of your home or you are happy for them to stand alone – rooms where teenagers can make their own mark or nurseries where you can indulge in pastel fantasies.

If you feel strongly about making your entire home a cohesive space, then choose a neutral colour sympathetic to your established colour palette and use strong colour in small amounts on furniture or woodwork. If you want to create a flow between two children's rooms, it is best to match the depth of colour – Borrowed Light and Middleton Pink, for example – in adjacent spaces, rather than having one light and one dark room.

FACING PAGE
Pink Ground provides the softest blush of colour, but without any sugary sweet overtones, while Wevet on the woodwork gives this scheme a slightly modern twist.

BELOW
Versatile Cornforth White is popular for teenager's bedrooms. Here, it creates a calming retreat, its grey qualities enhanced by the All White ceiling. The Hague Blue window adds a little drama.

BELOW
Blackboard paint on one wall of this Dutch teenager's bedroom serves as a creative outlet. Adding crisp All White to the walls, trim and ceiling makes the ultimate colour contrast – a timeless and graphic combination.

WOODWORK COLOUR

The simplest way to inject some character into a child's neutral bedroom is to use a strong or fun colour, such as Stiffkey Blue or Teresa's Green, both of which work well with most neutrals, on the woodwork. If the amount of colour that involves still concerns you, consider painting just the back of the door (but not its frame), which can only be seen from inside the room when it's closed. A door in Charlotte's Locks, St Giles Blue or Arsenic will excite any child or teen – especially if it's in a dramatic Full Gloss finish.

WALLS

Modern Emulsion paint is best suited to a child's bedroom because its durable and washable finish will be able to stand up to the inevitable rash of stickers and posters, favoured from all ages from toddler to teen, that will end up decorating the walls.

There is no reason at all why paint colour should always have to fill a wall. To give a room a super-modern feel, stop the colour at any height, rather than take it all the way to the ceiling. Treating the walls in this way has the added benefit of making the ceiling height

BELOW
Jolly crayons, from left: Babouche and Yellow Ground; Cinder Rose and Pink Ground; Stone Blue and Lulworth Blue; Breakfast Room Green and Cooking Apple Green. Wimborne White provides the backdrop; Purbeck Stone the shadows.

BELOW
The smallest amount of colour, when cleverly placed, can achieve fabulous results. An Incarnadine oblong and a stripe of the Archive colour Drawing Room Blue have transformed the desk area in this teenager's bedroom.

appear lower and the room feel cosier. Alternatively, leave a gap or frame around the wall colour on all four sides to create a really graphic space. If you want to keep the room as light as possible, think about using the same colour but in two different finishes on the walls. Full Gloss or Estate Eggshell finishes on the bottom half of the wall (including the skirting) and a Modern Emulsion above is particularly effective when used with cooler neutrals, such as Strong White or Blackened.

HIDDEN COLOUR

Involve your child in the decorating of their bedroom by allowing them to choose an incidental colour, such as for the interior of a cupboard. It will not only please them to be greeted by a favourite colour each time they open the door but you will also have the option of shutting the door and blocking out their choice, which may well be somewhat garish. Choosing a surface that remains hidden for much of the time means that the colour can be very easily changed as the child grows in age and sophistication.

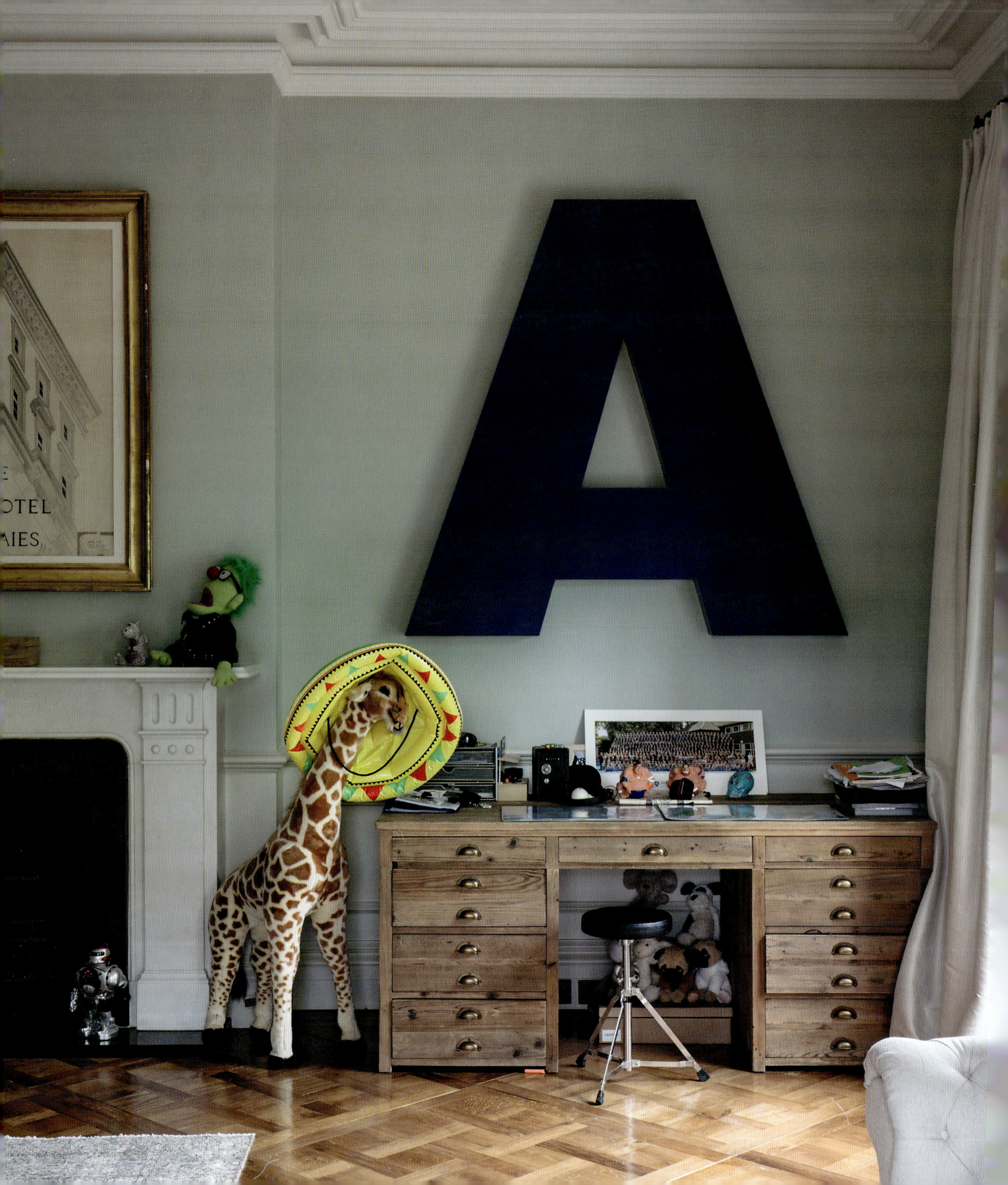

FACING PAGE
Many parents prefer the colour of their children's bedrooms to be in line with the rest of the home. Soft, grey-green Mizzle walls in this child's bedroom appear understated against Shaded White on the panelling and trim, perfectly complementing the decoration employed elsewhere.

BELOW
For the sake of versatility, you may prefer to paint your child's bedroom walls in a simple neutral, such as Strong White. You could then paint a piece of furniture, such as this wardrobe, in charming Peignoir.

FURNITURE

Painting furniture is the easiest way to introduce interest in a child's room. Upcycle an old chest of drawers by painting each drawer in a different colour or in a sophisticated gradation of just one colour. Bear in mind that the legs of tables or chairs don't need to be the same colour as the tabletop or chair seat. Bedheads can be personalized or painted directly onto the wall – a favourite, not to mention, inexpensive solution for children. Shelves cry out for contrasting colours, and the back of bookcases are enhanced with really bright tones, such as Yellowcake (A) or Vardo.

CEILINGS

The ceiling in a child's bedroom deserves more thought than those in other rooms, so why not make the most of this "fifth wall" by using colour or even wallpaper. Farrow & Ball Yukutori wallpaper has the magical effect of birds flying overhead, while a graphic stripe taken over the ceiling and down the walls seems to thrill every teenager. Alternatively, create a jewel-like, glistening effect on the ceiling with Full Gloss paint.

FLOORS

As well as feeling informal and relaxed, painted floors are extremely practical in a child's room. A white, such as Wevet, will bounce light around a small space, while India Yellow or Cook's Blue will make it feel playful. Have fun with colour on the floor of a children's bathroom – Parma Gray is a great choice – and experiment with making and colouring classic diamond patterns or stripes.

CHILDREN'S BEDROOMS

BELOW
A lucky little girl has lively Atacama wallpaper in Vardo and Churlish Green on the interior of her wardrobe, to make her smile every day.

FACING PAGE
A curved wall with Block Print Stripe wallpaper makes for an intriguing mix. This colourway has a Pointing background to add warmth to the room, while stripes in Railings and bespoke silver add glamour.

WALLPAPERS

Incorporating wallpaper brings an extra dimension to the bedrooms of children of any age. For the very young, Brockhampton Star is an enchanting design that is warm and welcoming, especially in a neutral colourway. Slightly older children will appreciate our Gable wallpaper, which depicts a charming rural scene of ploughed fields, picket fences and farmyard animals. Meanwhile, playful Atacama 5805, a tropical print with prickly cacti in Vardo and Churlish Green, is the ultimate in teenage escapism.

And if you don't want to wallpaper the whole room, why not line the inside of a cupboard for a discreet decorative touch?

POPULAR COLOURS FOR CHILDREN'S BEDROOMS

Here are some tried-and-tested colours that have been used successfully in rooms of children of all ages. Each one can be paired with fresh All White on the ceiling and trim.

Traditional Nursery	**Tallow or Borrowed Light**
Contemporary Nursery	**Strong White or Peignoir**
Young child	**Calamine or Skylight**
Teenager	**Brassica or De Nimes**

ROOM RECIPES

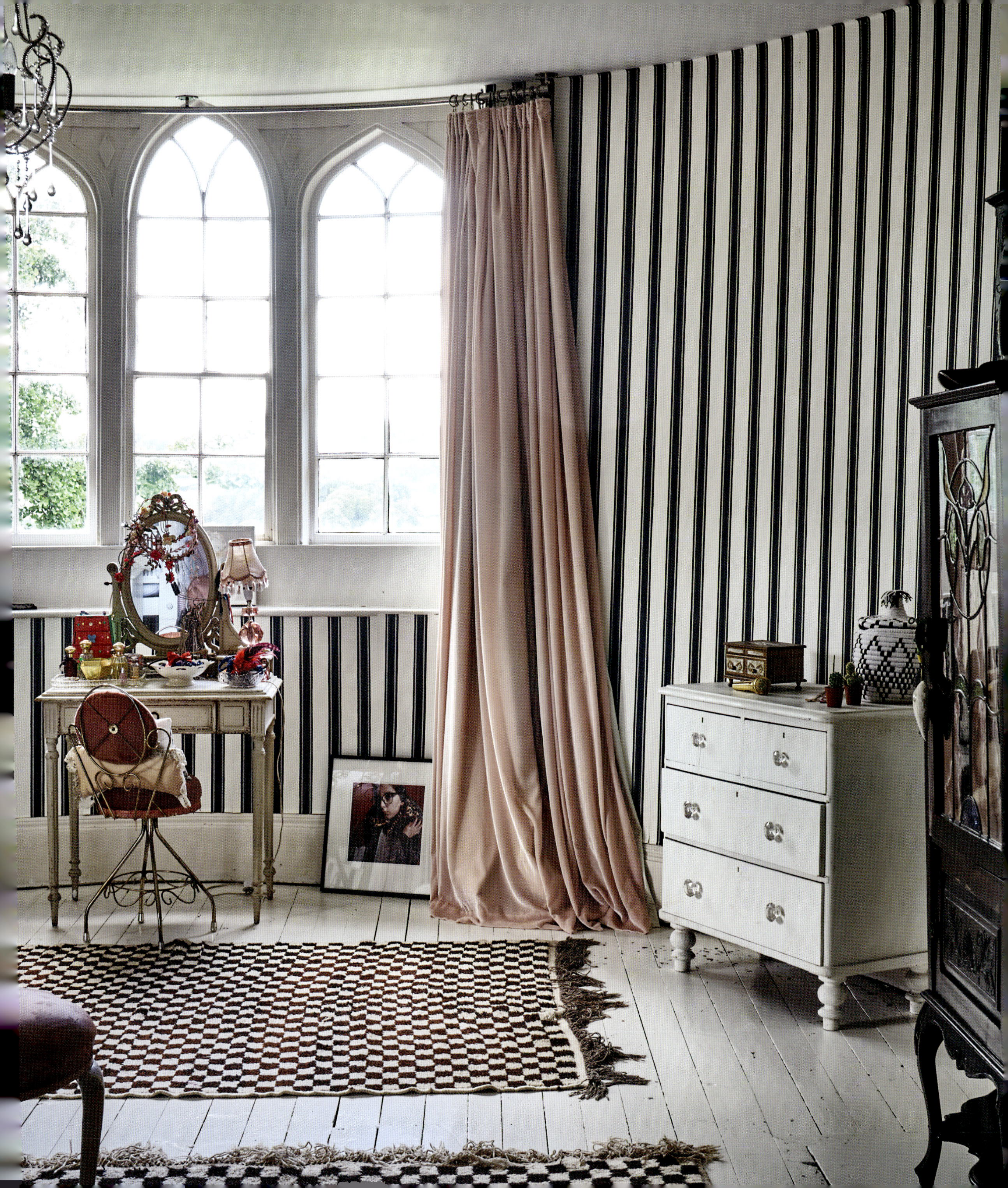

FUN-FILLED BEDROOM

Roll up! Roll up! Come and spend some time in this little, enchanting, private haven, decorated like a circus big top and so vibrant and full of energy. It would have been all too easy to have defaulted to white in this diminutive bedroom, mistakenly thinking that this would make it look bigger and lighter. However, I doubt that this was ever considered in this very stylish London home, and rightly so.

When decorating a child's room, it's a good idea to sit on the floor so you can appreciate the dimensions of the room from a similar height as that of its occupant. Considerable thought has gone into making this room as intimate as possible, taking into account the hours that the child might spend gazing at the ceiling from their bed. Luckily, the proportions of this room make it almost a square and so it is ideal for creating the illusion of a circus tent, but you need to make absolutely sure that the room you have in mind is suitable for such a design – it won't work in a long, thin room.

Daringly wide stripes of Blazer have been painted directly onto the crisp Wevet walls and ceiling, deliberately ignoring the coving (I particularly love that about this room and the fact that there is so much attention to detail, such as matching the colour of the ceiling light flex to the Blazer stripes). Thin stripes have a bigger impact on the eye, while thick stripes, as here, are more suitable for a child's room because they are more relaxing. For an extra twist, fresh Lulworth Blue Modern Emulsion has been painted on the walls up to a height that will make the room feel more intimate for a child. This colour is a particularly good choice as, despite its brightness, in low light it promotes peaceful sleep. Note that the radiator is the same colour, although painted in Estate Eggshell, to make it disappear into the wall. However, the window frame and door remain unpainted, bringing an extra element of warmth as well as keeping the look true to the rest of the house.

This is a magical room, and the perfect modern interpretation of a circus big top for a little one.

ABOVE AND FACING PAGE
Clean and bright Blazer, fresh Lulworth Blue and delicate Wevet, with its hint of grey, are a classic combination that have been playfully combined in this small bedroom.

PALETTE

BLAZER® 212
ceiling

LULWORTH BLUE® 89
walls

WEVET® 273
ceiling/walls

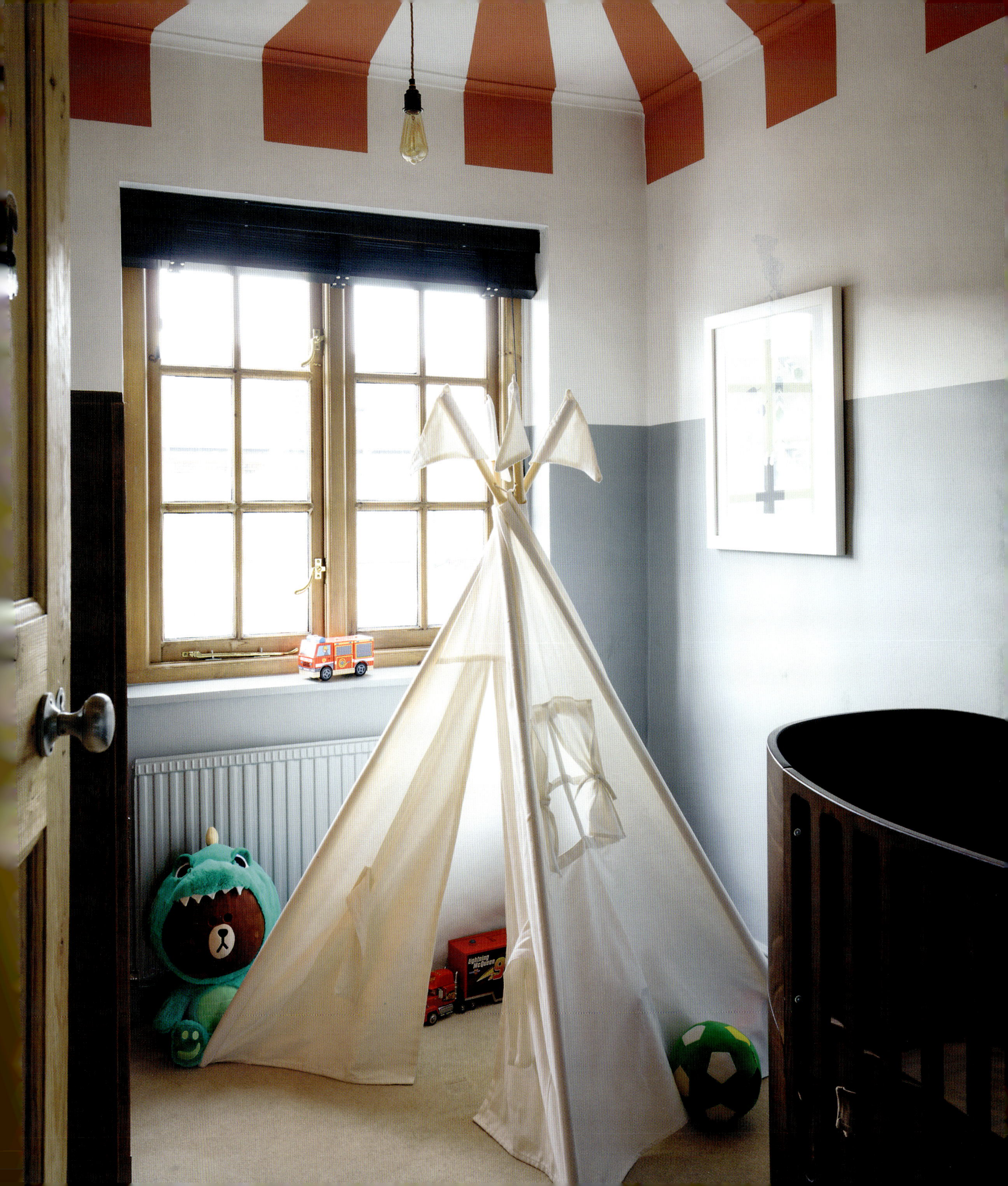

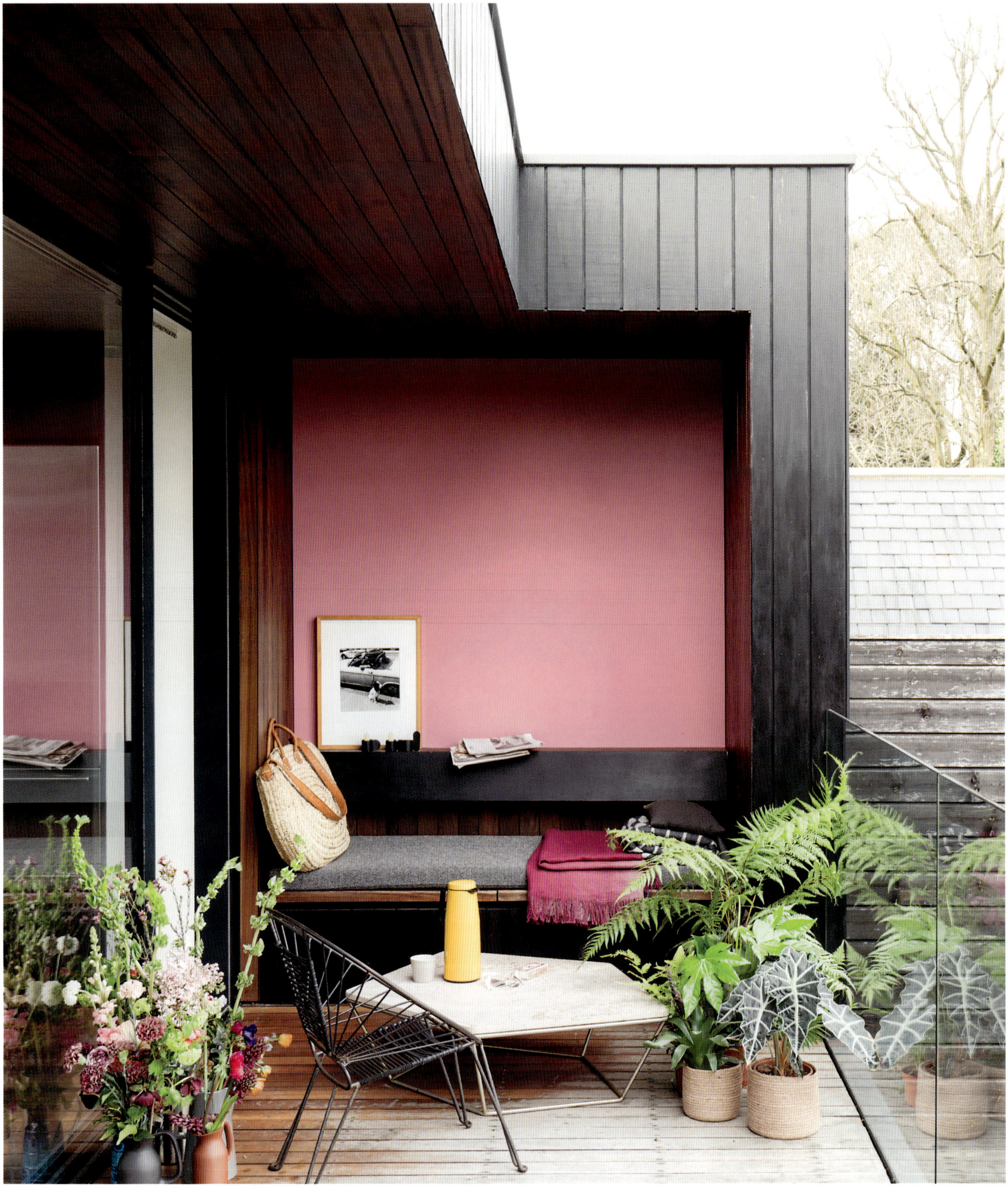

EXTERIORS

Approach the decoration of the outside of your home in exactly the same way as you would a room. Think about every element that needs to be painted – from the walls and window frames to the ironwork and front door – and the impact that the colour of each one may have on the others.

FACING PAGE
Rangwali, an exotic and adventurous pink, has transformed this exterior space on the balcony of a contemporary home. Bright and vital during the day, the colour becomes rich and exciting at night. Although it is not an obvious colour choice to use outside, the contrast with the dark cladding of the house is an utter triumph.

FACING PAGE, TOP LEFT
The woodwork on this coach house is painted in Pigeon to match the exterior colour throughout the estate. Its slightly nostalgic blue-grey tone makes it feel as if it might have been used over many centuries.

FACING PAGE, TOP RIGHT
Studio Green is the perfect choice for both the interior and exterior of this charming West Country hardware store.

FACING PAGE, BOTTOM LEFT
I wonder if this camouflage door design of many different Exterior Eggshell colours came about as a result of indecision regarding the choice of colour, or an admirable desire to stand out from the crowd?

FACING PAGE, BOTTOM RIGHT
This unembellished garden shed looks suitably understated painted in Card Room Green in Exterior Eggshell, contrasting with the walls of the house painted in Drop Cloth Exterior Masonry.

FRONT DOORS

Make a feature of your front door. Choose a colour that not only enhances the wall colour but reflects your personality – the front door speaks volumes about you to visitors.

Painting the complete frame and the door in a single colour will make it look bigger and more imposing, as well as much more contemporary. It is interesting that this technique has been used in every one of the case studies in this book.

Think about the relationship between the colour of the door and the colours used inside. The door colour is a prelude to what is to come, and it's a good idea to establish a visual connection between the exterior and interior.

Consider the paint finish as well as the colour. Exterior Eggshell gives a relaxed feel in soft colours and a more contemporary look in strong colours. Full Gloss, meanwhile, has a classic, more traditional look and is especially effective in strong colours, making them appear both chic and discreet.

MASONRY AND WALLS

You will be amazed by how much stronger your colour choices for exterior walls can afford to be. Subtle colours can appear bland and lifeless in bright sunshine, but be wary of very vibrant tones, as these can look garish in a northern light.

In an unspoiled rural setting, you may want the house to recede into the landscape. Using muted, green-based tones on the masonry and a sympathetic colour on the woodwork will minimize the impact of the house.

WINDOWS AND FRAMES

If you have neighbours close by, look at the colours they have used and decide if you want a complementary or contrasting scheme. Remember that subtle off-whites can look dirty compared to bright whites on adjacent buildings. Strong colours on windows and frames add definition to a façade, making it feel modern and impactful but not dark. For a totally classic look, any of the colours in our six neutral groups can be layered on exteriors, with the darkest on the walls and the lightest on the windows and frames.

FINISHES

Different finishes give added interest. Painting the front door and any other woodwork (excluding the windows) – such as garage doors, window boxes and garden gates – in the same colour, using Full Gloss on the door for gravitasx and the slightly more relaxed-looking Exterior Eggshell for everything else, works especially well.

FAVOURITE FRONT DOOR TREATMENTS

These are my personal favourite colours and finishes for front doors to suit different decorating styles.

Style	Colour	Finish
Urban classic	Railings	Full Gloss
Industrial	Off-Black	Exterior Eggshell
Handsome	Hague Blue	Full Gloss
Quirky	Babouche	Full Gloss
Traditional	Studio Green	Full Gloss
Modern	Calke Green	Exterior Eggshell
Contemporary	Mole's Breath	Exterior Eggshell
Relaxed	French Gray	Exterior Eggshell
Country classic	Treron	Exterior Eggshell
Grand	Preference Red	Full Gloss
Pretty	Teresa's Green	Exterior Eggshell
Charming	Calamine	Exterior Eggshell

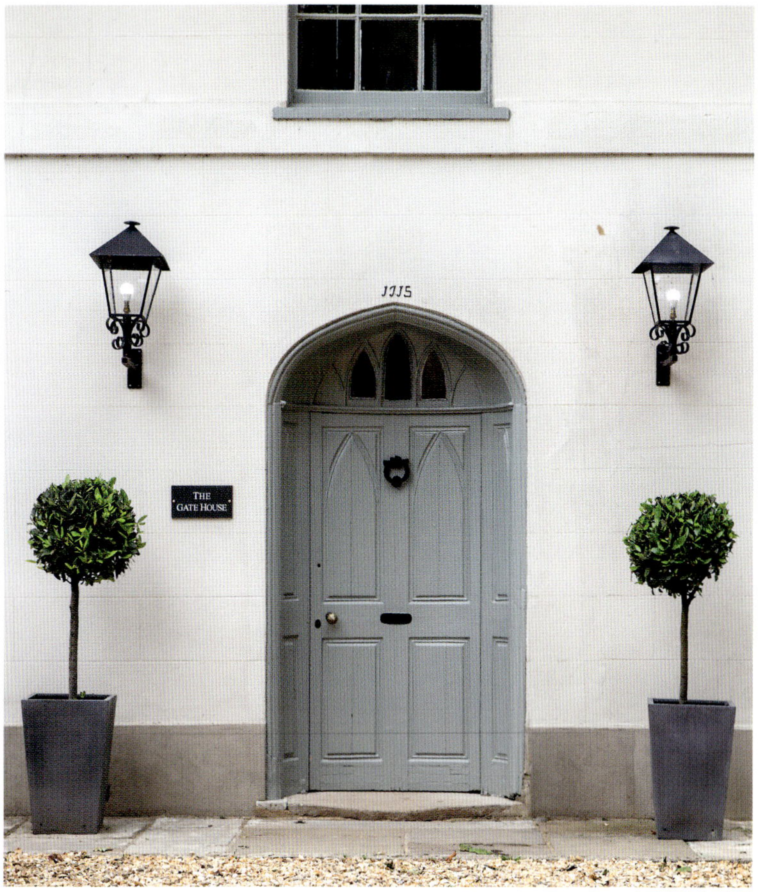
THE
GATE HOUSE

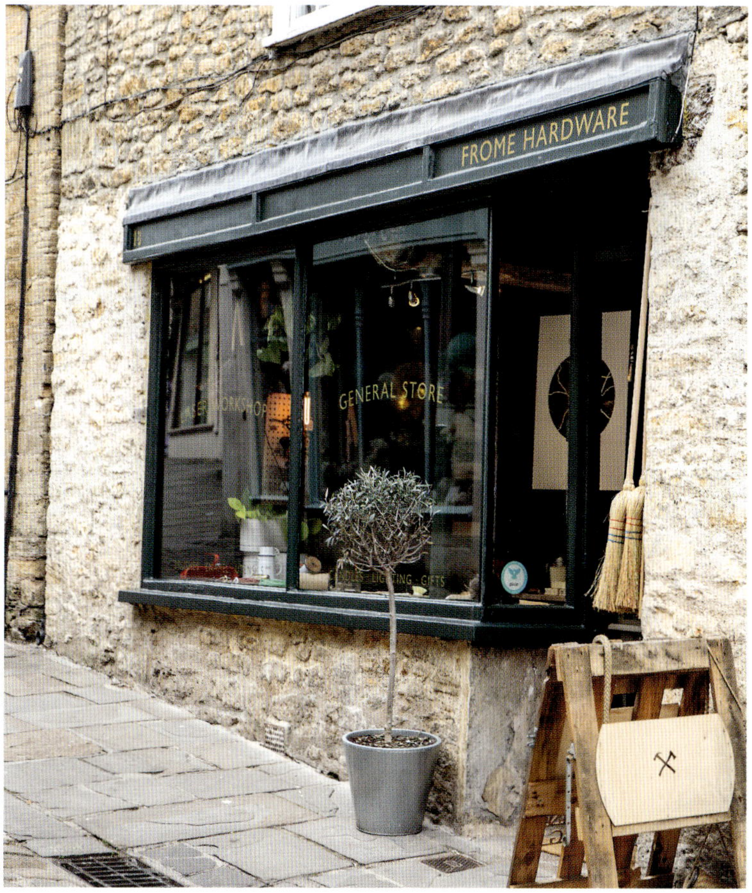
FROME HARDWARE
GENERAL STORE

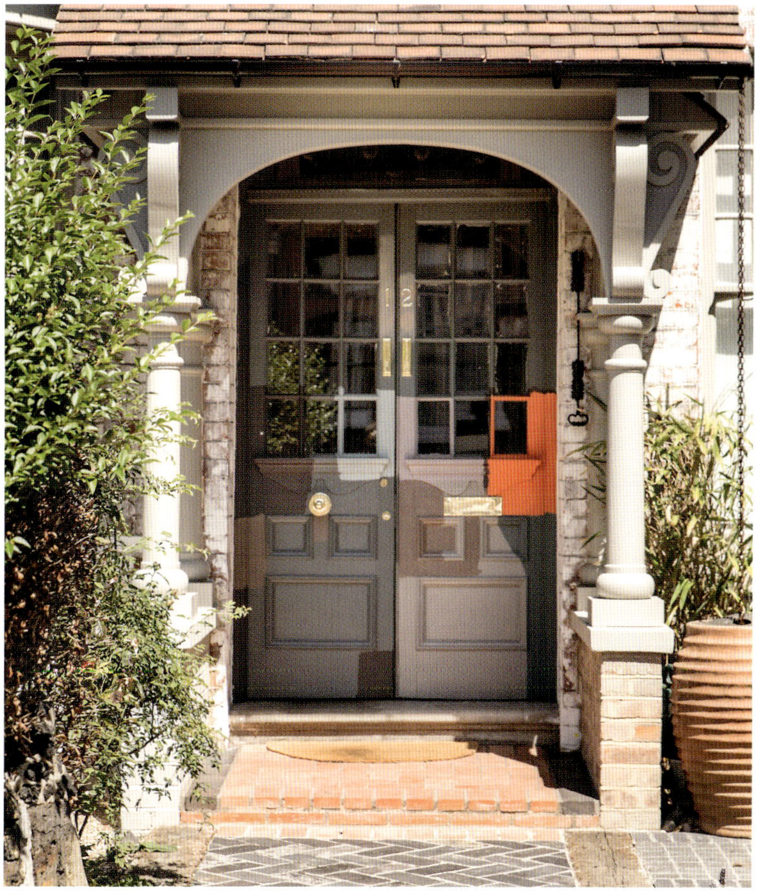

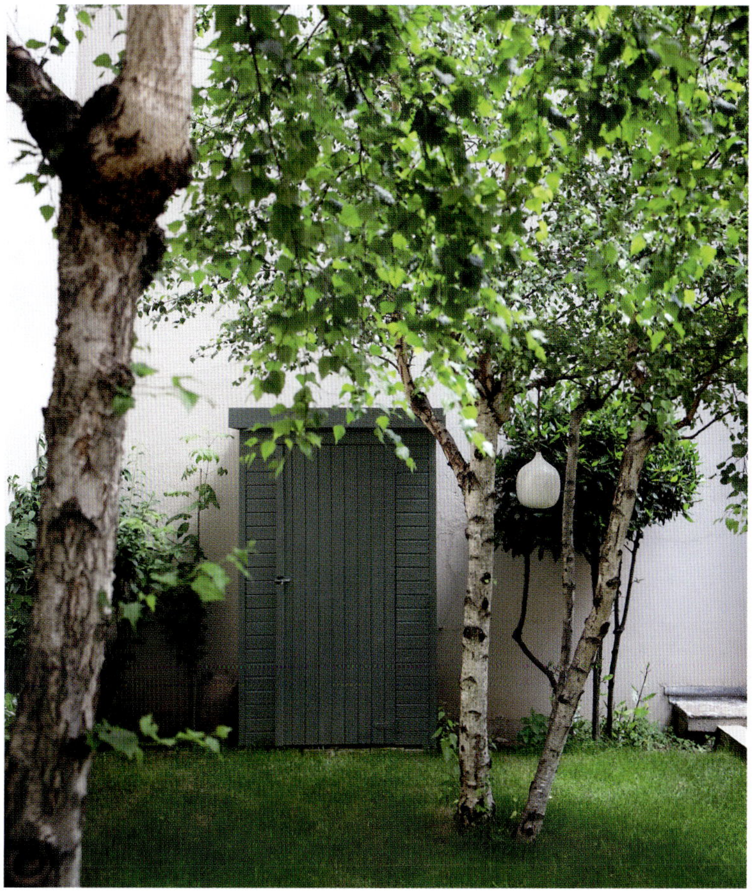

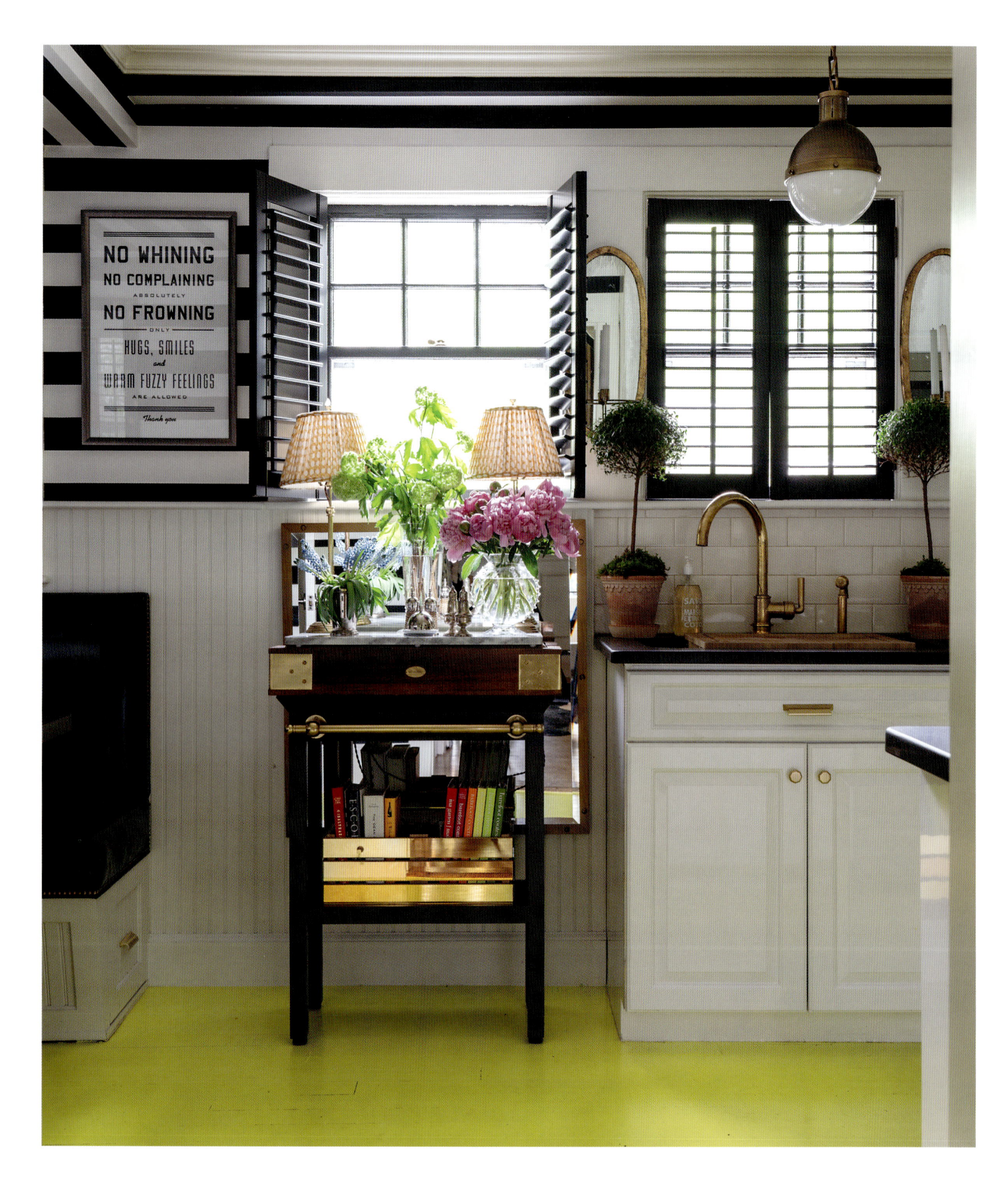

NO WHINING
NO COMPLAINING
ABSOLUTELY
NO FROWNING
ONLY
HUGS, SMILES
and
WARM FUZZY FEELINGS
ARE ALLOWED

Thank you

PART THREE

—

COLOUR SOLUTIONS

FACING PAGE
Colour can be introduced to
a room in myriad ways. In
this kitchen, the Yellowcake
(A) floor grabs the attention,
with the monotones of All
White and Pitch Black playing
supporting roles on the walls
and trim,

WHICH FINISH?

Choosing the most suitable paint finishes for the different areas of your home can be overwhelming. This simple menu of Farrow & Ball finishes and their suitability for every surface should help to make your decisions easier and more informed.

WALLS

Estate Emulsion
Our original chalky, very matt finish, Estate Emulsion is responsible for the signature Farrow & Ball look. Carefully crafted to give a flatter finish, which responds extraordinarily to all types of light.

Modern Emulsion
Tailored to the busiest areas of the home, Modern Emulsion is washable and wipeable, as well as stain and scrub resistant. This robust matt finish is ideal for children's bedrooms, hallways and high-moisture areas such as kitchens and bathrooms.

WOODWORK AND FURNITURE

Estate Eggshell
As robust as it is beautiful, this is our most popular choice. Highly resistant to a wide variety of stains, Estate Eggshell is a subtle finish that will stand the test of time.

Modern Eggshell
Most often used on floors and kitchen cabinetry, this is the toughest product in our range.

Full Gloss
A traditional high-gloss finish that is extremely versatile and robust.

CEILINGS

Estate Emulsion
Used for most ceilings.

Modern Emulsion
Good for steamy bathrooms and kitchens.

Casein Distemper
This is the chalkiest of our finishes and generally used only by specialist decorators on highly decorative or historic mouldings (see facing page).

RADIATORS

Estate Eggshell
Perfect for radiators to make them "disappear" into the wall. The formula is made specifically to withstand heat.

Modern Eggshell
Combining exceptional durability with an unrivalled depth of colour.

Full Gloss
Noted as the glossiest water-based finish on the market, Full Gloss creates a striking design statement with a wonderfully reflective sheen.

COLOUR SOLUTIONS

EXTERIORS

Exterior Masonry
This classic matt finish creates the most elegant finish for your masonry. Resistant to flaking, peeling and colour fade for up to 15 years.

Exterior Eggshell
This silky eggshell adds lasting colour to almost anything in your outdoor space – from wooden window frames and cladding to railings and metal guttering. It brings a more relaxed look and is resistant to flaking, peeling and fading for up to six years.

Full Gloss
A traditional high-gloss finish that looks extremely chic and handsome, while being robust enough to resist flaking, peeling and fading for up to six years.

SPECIALIST FINISHES

For the sympathetic decorating of historic properties.

Dead Flat
A delicate coating designed to draw interest, this completely flat matt finish can be used on any surface. It is inclined to mark, which makes it unsuitable for kitchens and bathrooms, on furniture or for areas of heavy wear.

Soft Distemper
An exquisitely powdery finish for fine interior plasterwork, this blend of natural resin and minerals can be easily removed from detailing and cornices.

Casein Distemper
This strengthened distemper has added casein, making it suitable for interior plastered walls and ceilings. It has a superb flat finish and allows the surfaces to breathe.

Limewash
A historical finish for walls and ceilings, both inside and out, Limewash bonds to the building itself to protect your home from the elements. Professional application recommended.

QUANTITIES AND COVERAGE

An average size room measuring about 12 × 12m (39 × 39ft), with two doors and two windows, will need approximately 10 litres for the walls, 2.5 litres for the ceiling and 2.5 litres for the trim. However, as each finish has a slightly different coverage, it's a good idea to refer to this table for more precise quantities.

Estate Emulsion
Sample pot 1m²
2.5 litres 35m²
5 litres 70m²

Modern Emulsion
2.5 litres 30m²
5 litres 60m²

Estate Eggshell
750ml 9m²
2.5 litres 30m²
5 litres 60m²

Modern Eggshell
750ml 9m²
2.5 litres 30m²
5 litres 60m²

Full Gloss
750ml 9m²
2.5 litres 30m²

Exterior Masonry
5 litres 40m²

Exterior Eggshell
750ml 10m²
2.5 litres 32m²

For specialist finishes, please refer to www.farrow-ball.com

For readers in North America requiring imperial measurements, please refer to www.farrow-ball.com

FACING PAGE
I am very lucky to have a gallery in my sitting room. The light changes little here through the day, which makes it the perfect place to sit and develop new colours — and to write this book.

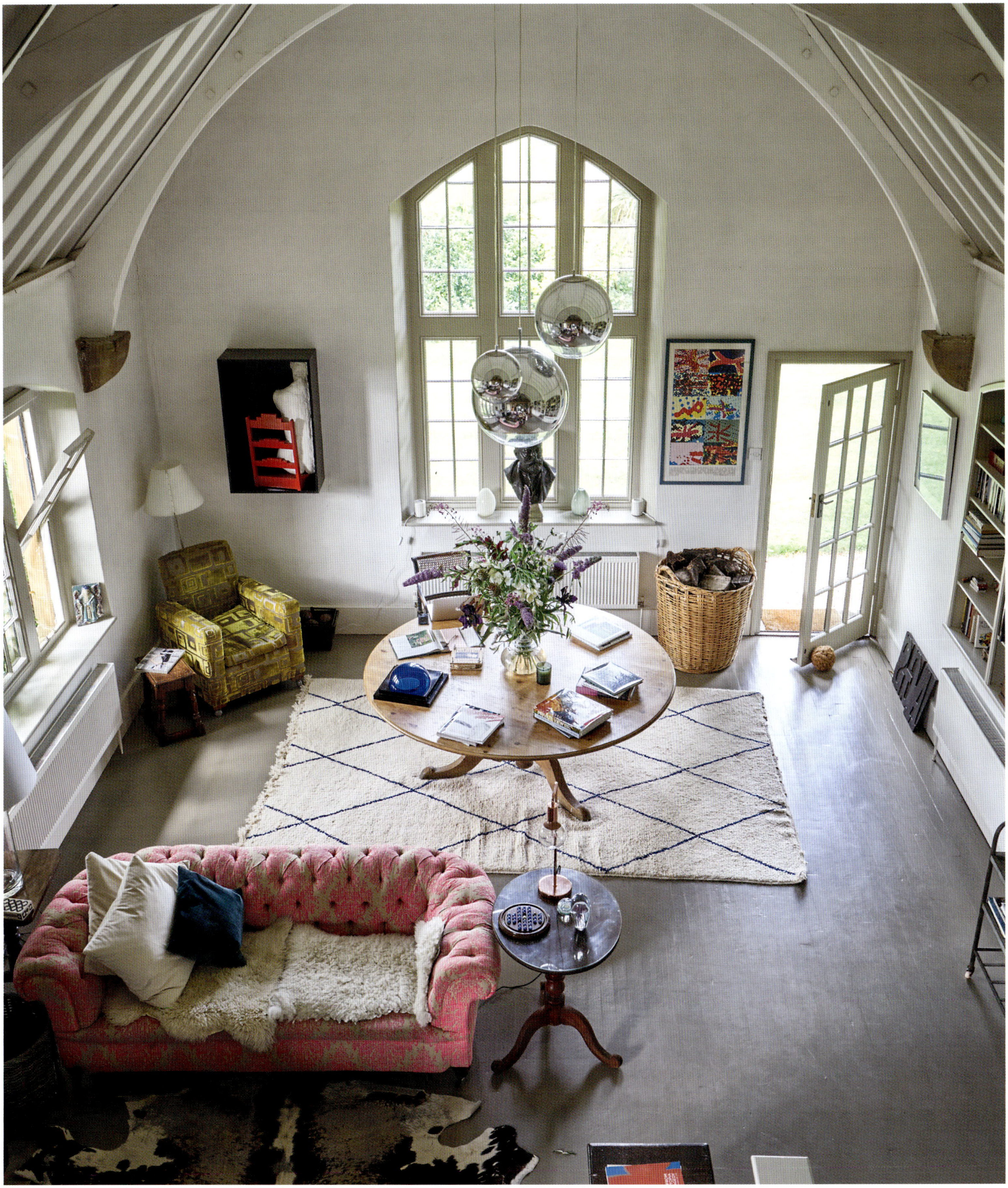

SMALL ROOMS

The successful decoration of a small room revolves around tricking the eye into making it appear larger, transforming a cramped and claustrophobic space into somewhere aesthetically pleasing. It is the most common misconception in the use of colour that dark walls shrink a room. Dark colours really don't make a room appear smaller, and neither will a light colour make a room look any more spacious.

Most people want to maximize the amount of light and space in their homes, but using white certainly isn't the only answer. Small rooms painted in strong colours have a magical quality, and dark tones often disguise the corners of the room so that you can't read the boundaries of the space, which in turn makes it feel larger.

USING LIGHT COLOURS

If, in your quest for a calming environment, you are determined to use neutral colours, a palette of different off-whites on the walls may appear to push the walls back, increasing the sense of space, and illuminate the room by reflecting light. However, it is all too easy with light colours to end up with a bland room void of personality. To prevent this, it is essential to layer neutrals with different textures and white-on-white patterns. But remember that when you choose a neutral palette for a small space, the walls are close to one another, so unexpected and unwanted undertones will be immediately obvious. Our six neutral groups (see page 176) are tailor-made for decorating small rooms successfully, their complex mix of pigments changing in different light conditions to keep a space full of vitality and life. Just because a room is small doesn't mean it has to be dull.

ABOVE
The space in this sitting room is fairly compromised, with the walls and furniture in close proximity to each other. Dimpse, with its slight blue undertone, was chosen to complement the sofa, while All White on the ceiling enhances the colour on the walls.

FACING PAGE, LEFT
Off-Black is a great backdrop for a collection of art. It doesn't matter that this room is dark, as the light will always be on when it is used.

FACING PAGE, RIGHT
The background colour of the Oriental-style Shouchikubai wallpaper dominates here, so that the intricate pattern doesn't overwhelm.

USING DARK COLOURS

Dark colours are far from off limits when decorating a small room. In fact, a saturated hue can be completely appropriate, providing warmth and depth, as well as making a small space look luxurious and classy. But to achieve that depth, it is best to use just one colour. A strong contrast between walls and trim tends to break up the room into small areas, meaning that the overall size of the room appears reduced and the walls look dark in comparison to the trim. Using a single colour over every surface in a small room is strongly recommended – you will end up with something quite magical. Complex blues such as Inchyra Blue and Oval Room Blue create moody spaces, while the cleaner Hague Blue will feel more chic. Rich Railings, Tanner's Brown, Studio Green and Paean Black also work perfectly. Generally, blacks will appear too hard, and reds may be too overwhelming.

USING WALLPAPER

It is generally assumed that wallpaper will make a room look smaller and more cluttered, but it does just the opposite if you use the right pattern. It may seem counterintuitive, but a large-scale pattern in a small room works much better than a small, busy one. Being able to read plenty of the background of a wallpaper will make a room feel more airy, while a wall overloaded with an intricate pattern immediately shrinks the space. Wallpapers such as our free-flowing Hegemone or Ringwold, abundant Wisteria, intriguing Enigma and geometric Tessella work wonders in small rooms. They envelop you with a beguiling dynamism, but don't make the space feel any smaller. If you would prefer to use wallpaper on just one wall it is best to paint the rest of the walls the same colour as the background of the paper. This will mean that the proportions of the room remain the same.

BIG ROOMS

Although often coveted, big rooms present their own challenges. They can appear cavernous, cold and uninviting, so it is essential to use exactly the right amount of colour on the walls. Don't default to using a strong tone in a big room just because you think its size means that it can "take it" – sometimes light colours are far more appropriate.

USING LIGHT COLOURS

If you have a big room that is full of light, then it really is best to keep it that way – cherish the light you have. A dark colour on the walls will counterbalance the light, resulting in a nondescript, boring space, while patterns and strong colours can be overwhelming in very large doses. Neutrals such as Cornforth White and Skimming Stone are light enough to feel airy, but sufficiently rich to have the depth and soul that a large space requires. Peignoir, with its underlying pink and unique pigmentation, is a great favourite in large, light rooms, where it will soften the walls and prevent the space from feeling clinical. Strong White seems to be the colour of choice in many large kitchens because it provides the perfect contemporary backdrop for busy family life, as well as sitting happily with the industrial materials popular in today's kitchens.

USING DARK COLOURS

Painting the walls in a warm, rich colour will create an instant cosiness, which can sometimes be lacking in big rooms. A strong colour will help to absorb light and move the focus away from the room's size. Use colours that provide a sense of intimacy – that are soothing like Green Smoke, restful like Oval Room Blue or rich and chic like Hague Blue or Preference Red. They all have the unique Farrow & Ball look characterized by their underlying black undertone, which prevents them from looking too bright and garish when used over large surfaces. However, clean colours, such as St Giles Blue and Charlotte's Locks, tend to be a little overwhelming in large rooms. If you have the unusual conundrum of needing to make your room look smaller, then a strongly contrasting trim colour, whether lighter or darker than the walls, will help to define the space so that it doesn't feel endless.

FACING PAGE
The intriguing combination of the Stiffkey Blue walls and the Brassica trim brings a sense of intimacy to this enormous room.

BELOW, TOP
A feature wall papered in Helleborus, with its large-pattern design, transforms this Mouse's Back room into a warm and wonderful retreat.

BELOW, BOTTOM
How very wise to keep this big, bright room in a light colour. All White enhances every aspect of this irresistible workspace.

USING WALLPAPER

Wallpaper can enhance any big space because the pattern will distract you from noticing the surface area of the walls. Proportion is key here. Smaller patterns, such as tantalizing Ocelot, create an intimate feel in any size of room, while the elegant 18th-century damask St Antoine has the ability to make even the most cavernous room feel loved. It is particularly effective when used above a dado rail and partnered with the same enveloping shade of background colour on the walls below. To truly celebrate the size of your room, Helleborus, with one of the largest motifs in our collection, is perfect. The organic pattern hints at growth and rejuvenation, transforming big rooms into warm and wonderful retreats.

CHANGING THE SHAPE OF A SPACE

* Feature walls often cause havoc by playing with the proportions of a room – use them with care.
* A bold wallpaper pattern will work in a bedroom if it is on the wall behind the bed and paired with the background colour on the other walls. This will ground the room and add interest.
* Painting a strong colour on the longest walls in a room will make them appear to squeeze together.
* A dark wall at either end (or both ends) of a long, thin corridor or room will have the effect of bringing it closer, making the space seem more square in shape.
* Painting the trim in a colour that contrasts strongly with the walls creates a focal point, which is useful for defining and containing a space.
* If you want to make a space feel bigger, be restrained with the number of colours you use.

BIG ROOMS

LIGHT AND DARK

As humans, we crave natural light. It is a basic need and the absence of it adversely affects our physical wellbeing and our state of mind. For this reason, it is best to ensure that the rooms in which we spend most of our time during the day, and this is often the kitchen, are the lightest rooms in our homes.

COLOURS FOR LIGHT ROOMS

Light is the most important thing to consider when choosing paint colours. Start by taking into account which direction the room faces, as this will have a significant impact on the appearance of a colour during the day. Then consider the artificial lighting. Table lamps, downlighters, chandeliers and even candles all play a significant part in achieving the desired look and mood in a room, so have them to hand when sampling paint colours. If you are lucky enough to have a room that runs from east to west, the colours will change during the day in accordance with the movement of the sun. This is when the heavy pigmentation of Farrow & Ball colours really comes into its own – the colours are brought alive and have a movement that delights all day long, adding enormous depth and character to a scheme.

A light-filled room really should be kept that way – light. The temptation to use a strong colour in a light room should definitely be avoided. Why fight nature? Painting the walls in a dark tone will act as a counterbalance to all the available natural light and the room will become flat and lifeless.

FACING PAGE
If you are fortunate enough
to have a large room that
is bathed in natural light,
like this Georgian gem,
I would advise you to keep
the colour scheme neutral.
The extraordinary nuances
of Skimming Stone mean that
these walls feel "alive"
whatever the time of day.

ABOVE
A Down Pipe bookcase set
against a wall and ceiling
in Manor House Gray could
not be more fitting in
this dark area of a Dutch
industrial conversion.

ABOVE, RIGHT
Glimpsing this rich Radicchio
games room while wandering
around an otherwise very
neutral home is guaranteed
to lift the spirits.

COLOURS FOR DARK ROOMS

When looking to decorate a room that doesn't have an abundance of natural light, the temptation is to paint it bright white to force it to feel brighter. Sadly, this just results in a flat, dull room. Instead, using a warm, darker colour or a wallpaper will result in a room that feels opulent and interesting. Bold, intense colour is often one of the most defining features of a home. When you create richly coloured rooms, it makes the lighter spaces feel even brighter in contrast. A glance into an intensely coloured room en route from the front door to a light-filled kitchen promises intimate evenings to come and creates real impact. Strong colour feels luxurious and nurturing and can't fail to introduce a little passion to your home.

HIGH AND LOW

Although the ceiling is often overlooked in a decorative scheme, it can have a huge impact, and there are many different ways to help create the illusion of either raising or lowering the perceived ceiling height.

INCREASING THE CEILING HEIGHT

Using colour
Don't default to a bright white ceiling. This will only highlight where the walls end and the ceiling begins. Conversely, having the same colour on the ceiling as the walls makes it difficult to tell where the walls end and the ceiling begins, and the perceived ceiling height is raised. Choosing a white for the ceiling that is complementary to the wall colour makes it feel as if the walls are simply gradating into the ceiling. To camouflage an oddly angled or slanted ceiling, take the colour up the wall and over the ceiling.

Cornices and coving
Paint the moulding the same colour as the walls, rather than the ceiling, to give the illusion of additional height. Avoid moulding with a deep profile, which will shorten the wall's expanse.

Trim
Increase the sense of space between the floor and the ceiling by using just one colour from the bottom of the skirting to the top of the moulding.

ABOVE
A frieze of Card Room Green has been added to the Shadow White walls, lowering the ceiling height above this intimate desk area.

COLOUR SOLUTIONS

LEFT
This unusual decorating device, in which Green Smoke has been painted on the wall behind the bed and slightly onto the ceiling, immediately tricks the eye into thinking that the wall is taller than it really is.

BELOW
To disguise the low ceiling in this busy pantry, both the ceiling and the walls have been painted in the same colour, Joa's White, making it difficult to tell where the walls end and the ceiling begins.

LOWERING THE CEILING HEIGHT

Using colour
There are occasionally drawbacks to having very high ceilings. Usually they impart a grand and luxurious feel to a room, but they can also make a room feel cold, unfriendly and empty. In this case, it is best to use a darker colour on the ceiling than on the walls. This can be as subtle as an Oxford Stone ceiling against Joa's White walls. The warmer the tone on the ceiling, the friendler the room becomes, while a darker tone on the ceiling, such as London Stone, will give the room a more intimate feel. To be a little more adventurous, use pattern on the ceiling. Wallpaper on a high ceiling brings it closer to the viewer.

Cornices and coving
Paint the moulding the same colour as the ceiling, to make the walls appear shorter, especially if the moulding has a really deep profile.

Trim
Always use a contrasting colour on the skirting, which will decrease the expanse of the wall, thereby reducing the height of the ceiling. If there is a dado rail, paint it, the walls below it and the skirting the same colour, and then paint the walls above it and the ceiling in a darker colour. This will create a strong horizontal line that draws your attention away from the height of the ceiling. If you have a picture rail, your life has been made easy – taking the ceiling colour all the way down to this level will lower the height of the room.

TRIED-AND-TESTED RECIPES

Here are some favourite Farrow & Ball recipes for different rooms in three different styles: traditional (Classic), modern (Nouvelle Cuisine) or family (Fusion). They are all tried and tested but probably need your own personal seasoning. It's up to you if you want to try just one recipe in a single room or all the recipes of a particular style throughout your home.

HALLS

This is usually the first part of your home that you or any guest will see, making it a great place to start. Large patterns, as on the Tessella wallpaper in the Nouvelle Cuisine recipe, are good at making small spaces feel bigger, whereas a grand, airy entrance using the Classic recipe will be timeless. The Fusion recipe will add a touch of drama to any hall, big or small, and make adjoining rooms feel spacious and light in comparison.

CLASSIC

walls: Sudbury Yellow
trim: New White
ceiling: Pointing
wallpaper: Toile Trellis 683

NOUVELLE CUISINE

walls: Cornforth White
trim: Strong White
ceiling: Wevet
wallpaper: Tessella 3604

FUSION

walls: Inchyra Blue
trim: Inchyra Blue
ceiling: Shadow White
wallpaper: Silvergate 883

SITTING ROOMS

All these schemes are intentionally stronger than those suggested for kitchens (see facing page), in order to create rooms that feel more intimate. In each case, the wallpaper could be used on a carefully chosen feature wall or as an accent on the interior of painted cupboards or shelves, for a decorative twist.

CLASSIC
walls: French Gray
trim: Slipper Satin
ceiling: Pointing
joinery: Treron
wallpaper: Brocade 3208

NOUVELLE CUISINE
walls: Worsted
trim: Mole's Breath
ceiling: Wevet
joinery: Railings
wallpaper: Enigma 5501

FUSION
walls: Oval Room Blue
trim: Inchyra Blue
ceiling: Shadow White
joinery: Inchyra Blue
wallpaper: Lotus 2053

COLOUR SOLUTIONS

KITCHENS

Most people would like their kitchens to feel as big and light as possible, so these schemes are suitably neutral, with little or no contrast between the walls and trim in order to increase the sense of space. For all three schemes, I have suggested two colours for the joinery, one of which could be for the kitchen units and the other for an island, or the stronger tone could be used on the insides of cupboards.

CLASSIC
walls: Slipper Satin
trim: Lime White
ceiling: Pointing
joinery: Blue Gray/Pigeon

NOUVELLE CUISINE
walls: Strong White
trim: Strong White
ceiling: Wevet
joinery: Purbeck Stone/Railings

FUSION
walls: Peignoir
trim: Peignoir
ceiling: Peignoir
joinery: Strong White/Rangwali

TRIED-AND-TESTED RECIPES

BEDROOMS

The Renaissance wallpaper in the warm Classic colourway is enchanting and understated and will create a tranquil bedroom, while tropical Atacama in the Nouvelle Cuisine recipe is more playful and individual. In the Fusion scheme, Samphire is delicate but tantalizing, to give an intimate space where the light will be reflected off the metallic pattern. If using wallpaper on just one wall, it is always best placed behind the bed.

CLASSIC

walls: Setting Plaster
trim: Dimity
ceiling: Pointing
joinery: Mahogany
wallpaper: Renaissance 2804

NOUVELLE CUISINE

walls: Sulking Room Pink
trim: Skimming Stone
ceiling: Strong White
joinery: Pigeon
wallpaper: Atacama 5802

FUSION

walls: Light Blue
trim: Shaded White
ceiling: Shadow White
joinery: Stiffkey Blue
wallpaper: Samphire 4005

COLOUR SOLUTIONS

BATHROOMS

These Classic and Nouvelle Cuisine recipes are intended to create serene bathrooms by using varying shades of the same colour. The stronger accents should be restricted to the underside of bathtubs or vanity units, to give just a pop of colour. For an altogether more exhilarating bathing experience, adopt the Fusion scheme, which has been plucked straight from my own bathroom.

CLASSIC
walls: Joa's White
trim: Pointing
ceiling: Pointing
joinery: Oxford Stone
wallpaper: Jasmine 3901

NOUVELLE CUISINE
walls: Great White
trim: Great White
ceiling: All White
joinery: Pelt
wallpaper: Arcade 5301

FUSION
walls: De Nimes
trim: Light Blue
ceiling: Shadow White
joinery: Light Blue
wallpaper: Shouchikubai 4502

TRIED-AND-TESTED RECIPES

CLOAKROOMS

There's no reason to rein yourself in when choosing colours for a small cloakroom. Strong colours and bold patterns create jewel-like rooms. You will be amazed at how the boundaries of the room disappear, creating an illusion of space. The trim and vanity units can be even stronger in colour than the walls, especially if you are using panelling, because the darker tone at the base of the walls will ground the room and make it look bigger.

CLASSIC
walls: Eating Room Red
trim: Mahogany
ceiling: Joa's White
joinery: Mahogany
wallpaper: Orangerie 2510

NOUVELLE CUISINE
walls: Paean Black
trim: Pitch Black
ceiling: Skimming Stone
joinery: Pitch Black
wallpaper: Ocelot 3704

FUSION
walls: Bancha
trim: Studio Green
ceiling: Shaded White
joinery: Studio Green
wallpaper: Feather Grass 5106

CHILDREN'S BEDROOMS

Go powder-soft, as in the Fusion recipe, or unleash your fun streak with the Classic scheme and a wall of Bumble Bee. Feeling adventurous? Use Full Gloss paint for any of these ceilings or the Brockhampton Star wallpaper in the Nouvelle Cuisine recipe. Exceptionally durable Modern Emulsion is best for the walls.

CLASSIC
walls: New White
trim: Skimming Stone
ceiling: Pointing
joinery: Teresa's Green
wallpaper: Bumble Bee 555

NOUVELLE CUISINE
walls: Pavilion Blue
trim: All White
ceiling: All White
joinery: Vardo
wallpaper: Brockhampton Star 506

FUSION
walls: Teresa's Green
trim: Elephant's Breath
ceiling: Strong White
joinery: Charleston Gray
wallpaper: Gable 5406

TRIED-AND-TESTED RECIPES

FARROW & BALL SHOWROOMS

UK

Bath
124 Walcot Street
Bath
Somerset BA1 5BG
+44 (0) 1225 466700

Battersea
146 Northcote Road
Battersea
London SW11 6RD
+44 (0) 20 7228 6578

Beaconsfield
39 London End
Old Beaconsfield
Buckinghamshire
HP9 2HW
+44 (0) 1494 677700

Blackheath
48 Tranquil Vale
Blackheath
London SE3 0BD
+44 (0) 20 8852 9836

Bristol
16 Princess Victoria Street
Clifton
Bristol BS8 4BP
+44 (0) 1179 733900

Cambridge
14 Regent Street
Cambridge
Cambridgeshire CB2 1DB
+44 (0) 1223 367771

Chelsea
249 Fulham Road
Chelsea
London SW3 6HY
+44 (0) 20 7351 0273

Cheltenham
15-17 Suffolk Road
Cheltenham
Gloucestershire GL50 2AF
+44 (0) 1242 230898

Edinburgh
20 North West Circus
Place
Stockbridge
Edinburgh EH3 6SX
+44 (0) 131 226 2216

Esher
15 High Street
Esher
Surrey KT10 9RL
+44 (0) 1372 477129

Glasgow
470 Great Western Road
Glasgow G12 8EW
+44 (0) 141 337 7043

Guildford
11 Tunsgate
Guildford
Surrey GU1 3QT
+44 (0) 1483 511365

Hampstead
58 Rosslyn Hill
Hampstead
London NW3 1ND
+44 (0) 20 7435 5169

Harrogate
18-22 Albert Street
Harrogate
North Yorkshire HG1 1JT
+44 (0) 1423 522 552

Henley-on-Thames
21 Thameside
Henley-on-Thames
Oxfordshire RG9 2LJ
+44 (0) 1491 636128

Hove
31b Western Road
Hove
East Sussex BN3 1AF
+44 (0) 1273 774640

Islington
38 Cross Street
Islington
London N1 2BG
+44 (0) 20 7226 2627

Leamington Spa
82 Regent Street
Leamington Spa
Warwickshire CV32 4NS
+44 (0) 1926 424760

Manchester
270 Deansgate
Manchester M3 4JB
+44 (0) 161 839 5532

Marylebone
64-65 Paddington Street
Marylebone
London W1U 4JG
+44 (0) 20 7487 4733

Notting Hill
21-22 Chepstow Corner
Notting Hill
London W2 4XE
+44 (0) 20 7221 2328

Oxford
225 Banbury Road
Summertown
Oxford OX2 7HS
+44 (0) 1865 559575

Richmond
30 Hill Rise
Richmond
Surrey TW10 6UA
+44 (0) 20 8948 7700

Solihull
36 Mill Lane
Mell Square
Solihull
West Midlands B91 3BA
+44 (0) 121 709 3360

St Albans
36 Market Place
St Albans
Hertfordshire AL3 5DG
+44 (0) 1727 847155

Sunningdale
5 Broomhall Buildings
Sunningdale
Berkshire SL5 0DU
+44 (0) 1344 876615

Tunbridge Wells
4 High Street
Tunbridge Wells
Kent TN1 1UX
+44 (0) 1892 512121

Wilmslow
19 Church Street
Wilmslow
Cheshire SK9 1AX
+44 (0) 1625 415102

Wimbledon
90 High Street
Wimbledon
London SW19 5EG
+44 (0) 20 8605 2099

Wimborne
Uddens Estate
Wimborne
Dorset BH21 7NL
+44 (0) 1202 890905

Winchester
32 The Square
Winchester
Hampshire SO23 9EX
+44 (0) 1962 843179

Windsor
9 High Street
Windsor
Berkshire SL4 1LD
+44 (0) 1753 840663

EUROPE

Dublin
14 Cornmarket
Dublin D08 TN6P
IRELAND
+353 1 67 70 111

Cologne
Pfeilstrasse 20
Cologne 50672
GERMANY
+49 221 277 36761

Düsseldorf
Hohe Straße 37
Düsseldorf 40213
GERMANY
+49 21 12 10 73 561

Frankfurt
Kaiserstraße 25
Frankfurt am Main 60311
GERMANY
+49 69 24 24 62 69

Hamburg
Neue ABC-Strraße. 2–3
Hamburg 20354
GERMANY
+49 40 21 98 22 35

Munich
Rumfordstraße 48
80469 Munich
GERMANY
+49 89 21 26 94 16

Paris Marais
111 Bis Rue de Turenne
75003 Paris
FRANCE
+33 1 44 61 18 22

Paris Neuilly
2 Bis Rue du Château
Neuilly-sur-Seine
92200 Paris
FRANCE
+33 1 47 22 98 28

Paris Rive Gauche
50 rue de l'université
75007 Paris
FRANCE
+33 1 42 22 65 94

Paris St Germain en Laye
7 Rue du Docteur Timsit
St Germain En Laye
78100 Paris
FRANCE
+33 1 39 10 46 50

Strasbourg
1 Rue de la Nuée Bleue
67000 Strasbourg
FRANCE
+33 390 20 08 40

NORTH AMERICA

Berkeley
1813 Fourth Street
Berkeley
CA 94710 USA
+1 510 848 8153

Boston
One Design Center Place
Suite 208
Boston
MA 02210 USA
+1 617 345 5344

Brooklyn
383 Atlantic Avenue
Brooklyn
New York
NY 11217 USA
+1 718 858 8840

Chicago
449 North Wells Street
Chicago
IL 60654 USA
+1 312 222 9620

Greenwich
32 East Putnam Avenue
Greenwich
CT 06830 USA
+1 203 422 0990

Los Angeles
741 N. La Cienega Blvd
West Hollywood
Los Angeles
CA 90069 USA
+1 323 655 4499

NY Flatiron
32 East 22nd Street
New York
NY 10010 USA
+1 212 334 8330

NY Midtown
D&D Building Suite 1519
979 Third Avenue
New York
NY 10022 USA
+1 212 752 5544

NY Upper East Side
142 East 73rd Street
New York
NY 10021 USA
+1 212 737 7400

Orange County
3323 Hyland Avenue
Suite C
Costa Mesa
CA 92626 USA
+1 714 438 2448

Paramus
160 Route 17 North
Paramus
NJ 07652 USA
+1 201 265 4030

Pasadena
54 West Green Street
Pasadena
CA 91105 USA
+1 626 796 1459

Santa Monica
1016 Montana Avenue
Santa Monica
CA 90403 USA
+1 310 857 5811

Toronto
1128 Yonge Street
Toronto
ON M4W 2L8 CANADA
+1 416 920 0200

Washington
5221 Wisconsin Avenue
NW
Washington DC
DC 20015 USA
+1 202 479 6780

For the most up-to-date list of showrooms and stockists please visit www.farrow-ball.com

INDEX

Page numbers in *italic* refer to captions; **bold** to recipe tips; ***bold italic*** to colour charts. Quote marks have been used to signify names of Farrow & Ball paints and wallpapers

A

accent colours 26, *53*, 152, 174, 210
adding depth and balance 22, 205, 218, 227, 242, 247, 248, 250
"All White" *11*, *16*, 174, 175, 176, *188*, *198*, *201*, 205, *217*, 218, *222*, 228, 232, *241*, *246*, *249*, *259*, *261*
all-white palette 218
"Ammonite" 44, ***50***, 94, *94*, ***96***, 111, *111*, *114*, 117, *117*, 120, ***120***, 174, 175, 176, *187*
aqua blue 127
architectural details 15, 155, 210, 214
Architectural Neutrals 67, *67*, 176, 194
architrave and coving 58, 65, 94, 100, *111*, 123
Archive colours 12, 21, 86, 93, *147*, 148, *148*, 229
"Arsenic" 128, *131*, ***132***
art, choosing colours to aid display of 221
art, decorating as 8
art, wallpaper as 221
"art gallery" white 58
artificial light (*see also* light/lighting; natural light) 197, 221, *246*, 250
Arts and Crafts *201*
aspect, effect on colour *249*
attic rooms 214–15

B

"Babouche" 102, 105, ***108***, 127
balance 8, 16, 27, *32*, 37, 41, 44, 135, 136, 176, 188, 198
Ball, Richard 21
"Ball Green" 174
banisters 65, *70*, **74**, *151*
Baroque 61
baseboards *see* skirting/baseboards
bathroom tiles 218
bathrooms 8, 44, *49*, **50**, *50*, 61, *61*, **62**, 70, 73, **74**, 82, *82*, 85, *85*, ***86***, *93*, 94, *94*, ***96***, 128, *131*, ***132***, 141, *141*, ***144***, 147, 151, *151*, ***152***, 159, *159*, ***160***, 210, 216–225, *218*, *221*, *222*, *224*, 231, 242, 243, 259
bathtubs 70, 73, 85, *117*, 141, *141*
bedrooms 209–13, *210*, *213*
below stairs *32*
Bevilacqua, Michael *58*
"Bible Black" 21
black (*see also* black paints by name) 21, 182, *187*, 188, 206, *206*, *213*, 214, 248
"Black Blue" 77, *77*, ***86***, 99, *99*, ***108***, *117*
blackened 44, 135
"Blackened" *70*, **74**, 156, *156*, ***160***, 174, 175, 176, 194, *194*, 218, 229
Blake, Peter *136*
blandness 246
"Blazer" *123*, 124, *124*, **132**, ***132***, 174, 234, *234*
"Block Print Stripe" wallpaper *232*
blue (*see also* blue paints by name) 37, 44, 58, 61, 67, 89, 105, 114, 117, 127, 135, 136, 141, *141*, 159, *159*
"Blue Gray" 20, *198*, *257*
bold decoration 14, 22, 179, 180, 183, 206–7, *206*, 214, 221, 251, 260
Bonaparte, Joséphine 85
Bonaparte, Napoleon 128
"Bone" 151
"Book Room Red" 77, *77*, 82, ***86***
bookcases *24*, 99, *99*, *100*, ***108***, *127*
borrowed light *90*
"Borrowed Light" 174, 218, 227, 232
boudoir (*bouder*) 20
"Brassica" 94, *94*, ***96***, 174, *213*, 232, *249*
"Breakfast Room Green" 82, *82*, ***86***
"Brinjal" 174, 175, *209*, 221, *222*
"Brocade" wallpaper 256
"Brockhampton Star" wallpaper 232, 261, *261*
brushes 18
buff 118
"Bumble Bee" wallpaper *182*, *200*, *261*

C

cacti prints 232
"Cabbage White" 14, 175, 221
"Calamine" 174, 194, 232, 238
"Calke Green" *16*, 61, *61*, **62**, 82, *82*, ***86***, 174, *182*, 238
"Calluna" *155*, 156, *156*, ***160***, 174
camouflage *238*, 252
candlelight 22, *41*, 250
"Card Room Green" 174, 197, *238*, 252
case studies 24–171
Casein Distemper 77, 242, 243
cavernous spaces 248, 249
ceiling height 8, 213, 228–9, 252, *252*, 253
ceiling light (*see also* light/lighting) 234
ceilings (*see also* "fifth wall") 8, 22, **38**, 42, **50**, *50*, 58, 61, **62**, *62*, 67, **74**, 82, ***86***, 90, 93, *93*, 94, ***96***, *96*, 99, 105, ***108***, 114, ***120***, 123, 124, ***132***, ***144***, 151, ***152***, 156, ***160***, 164, 170, 183, ***184***, ***206***, 213, 214, 218, 221, 228, 231, 232, ***234***, 242–4 *passim*, 252–3, *255–1 passim*
central colours *184*, ***184***
chairs *188*, 231
chandeliers 250
"Charleston Gray" 135, *135*, 141, *141*, ***144***, *144*, *155*, ***160***
"Charlotte's Locks" *11*, 22, 61, *61*, **62**, 174, 228, 248
children's bathroom 227–33, 231, 242, 261
children's bedrooms (*see also* bedrooms) 37, *37*, **38**, 94, *94*, ***96***, 118, *118*, 120, ***120***, *159*, ***160***
"Chinese Blue" *193*, 222
choosing colours 8, *16*, 22, 27, 41, 53, 242, 246, 248, 255
Churchill room 42, *42*, ***50***
"Churlish Green" 174, 232, *232*
"Cinder Rose" 164, ***170***
circus-tent design 234, *234*
"Citron" 174
classic neutrals 169
Classic (traditional) style 254
claustrophobic spaces, choosing colours to avoid 188
"Claydon Blue" 93, *93*, ***96***
cloakrooms 221, 260
"Clunch" *193*
colour cards/charts 12–13, 20, **38**, **50**, **62**, **74**, **86**, **96**, **108**, **120**, **132**, **144**, **152**, **160**, **170**, **184**, **194**, **206**, **214**, **224**, **234**
colour combinations 11, *184*, *197*
colour, as a transformative tool 214
colour wheel 13
colours, linking by name 20
complementary colours *14*, 17, 26, 28, 44, 58, 67, 70, 89, 93, *99*, 124, *124*, 141, 164, 198, *200*, *205*, 218, *231*, *238*, *246*, *252*
computer-generated tones 12
Contemporary Neutrals *41*, 135, 176
continuity 37, 65, *81*, 151
"Cooking Apple Green" 229
"Cook's Blue" 231
cool colours 176, 194, 198, 214, 218, 229
corbels *100*
"Cord" 20, 77, *77*, ***86***
"Cornforth White" 44, *44*, ***50***
cornicing and moulding 42, 44, ***50***, *50*, 65, 67, 77, *77*, ***86***, *94*, ***96***, 124, *124*, ***132***, 136, ***144***, ***160***
corridors 41, *57*, *58*, 61, 105, *106*, ***108***, ***132***, 151, *151*
counterbalancing 141, 156, 248
country kitchens (*see also* kitchens) *193*, 194–5, *194*
coverage 244
coving and architrave 58, 65, 94, 100, *111*, 123
craving for light (*see also* light/lighting) 187, 250
cream 176
"Cromarty" 37, *37*, **38**, ***38***
cupboards, colours inside 22, *22*, *187*, 188, *193*, 194, ***194***, 229, 256, 257
cupboards, wallpaper-lined 232

D

dado rails *179*, 183, 184, *217*, 221, 249, 253
Dalsgaard, Sven *61*

damask wallpapers *200, 210*, 249
dark colours 32, 50, 58, 86, 246, 247, 248, 251
"Dayroom Yellow" 174
"De Nimes" 21
Dead Flat 77, 86, *131*
"Dead Salmon" 26, 41, *41*, 42, 50, 118, *118*, **120**
Deans Court 123, *123*
decorating, as art 8
decorating styles 238, 254
decorating tips (*see also* recipe tips) 22
depth *28*, 32, 37, 44, 53, 77, 82, 86, 124, 135, 136, 148
"Dimity" *41*, **50**
"Dimpse" *89, 90*, **96**
displays, black best for 206, 221
distemper 77, 242, 243
"Dix Blue" 174, 206, *206*
door finger plates *80*
doors 22, 26, *31, 41*, 77, *77*, **86**, *89, 99*, 111, *111*, **120**, 135, 136, **144**, 147, 151, 152, *176*, 179, *179, 182*, 194, *194, 201, 205*, 206, 228, 229, 234, 237, 238, *238*, 244, 251
Dorset 21, 123, 163
"Dorset Cream" 174
"Dove Tale" 42, **50**, 70, *73*, **74**, 141, *141*, **144**, *144*
"Down Pipe" 32, *32*, 37, *37*, **38**, 65, 67, *67*, 70, *73*, **74**, *74*, 174, 175, *197*, 214, *214*, *251*
downlighting (*see also* light/lighting) 250
drawing rooms 42, *163*, 164, *164, 169*, **170**, *170*
"Drawing Room Blue" 229
"Drop Cloth" **50**, 100, *100*, **108**, 174, 175, 176, 180, *188, 205, 238*
Duus, Matilde *61*

E
earthy hues/tones 111, 118
east-facing rooms 111
Easy Neutrals 70, *93*, 176
"Eating Room Red" *28*
Eggshell 22, 31, *31*, *90, 99, 131, 209, 210, 221*, 224, 229, 234, 242, 244
18th-century style 61, 131, *173*, *210*, 249
"Elephant's Breath" 21, 41, *42*, **50**
Elmgreen & Dragset *53*
emulsion 22, 53, *70*, 89, *90*, 182, 206, 228, 229, 234, 242, 244, 261
English kitchens (*see also* kitchens) 32
entrance halls (*see also* halls/hallways) 41, 105, **108**, 124, 135
environment, living 16, 42, 58, 118, 246
environment, working 93, 197
Escobar, Darío *57*
Estate Eggshell 22, *131, 221*, 229, 234, 242, 244
Estate Emulsion 22, 53, *70*, 89, *90*, 206, 242, 244
exotic design 20
Exterior Eggshell 31, *31*, *90, 99*, 238, *238*, 243, 244
exterior to interior, interconnecting 206, 238
Exterior Masonry 238, 243, 244
exteriors 31, *31*, **50**, 77, *77*, **86**, 99, *99*, 105, *106*, **108**, 111, **120**, *120*, 141, *141*, 144, **144**, **152**, 155, **160**, 169, *169*, 170, 237–9, *238*, 243

F
family (Fusion) style 254
Farrow & Ball decorating book 8, 28
Farrow & Ball recipes 254–61
Farrow & Ball, story of 8–11
Farrow, John 21
"Farrow's Cream" 174
"Feather Grass" wallpaper *260*
feature walls *37*, **38**, *38*, 94, *94*, 136, **144**, 210, *210*, 249, 256
Festival of Colours 20
"fifth wall" (*see also* ceilings) 218, 231, 253
finger plates *80*
finishes 12, 22, *176*, 182, *193, 205, 209*, 210, *210*, 228, 238, 242–5
fire surrounds 164
flamboyancy 210, 213, 214
floor tiles 89, *89*, 94, *94*
floors/flooring *11*, 17, 42, 67, *148, 183, 188, 193, 197*, 198, *209, 210*, 224, *224*, **224**, 231, 234, *241*, 252
floral patterns *201, 213*
flow 26, 49, 53, 58, 65, 67, 86, 90, *93, 94*, 96
flow of light (*see also* light/lighting) 16
flower patterns *see* floral patterns
"French Gray" 20, 105, *106*, **108**, 174, 198, 205, *221*, 238, *256*
front doors 26, *31, 41*, 77, *77*, **86**, *89, 99*, 111, *111*, **120**, 135, 136, **144**, 147, 151, 152, 179, 182, 237, 238, 251
Full Gloss 22, *176*, 182, *205*, 206, 218, 228, 229, 231, 238, 242, 243, 244, 261
furniture (*see also* kitchen units) *18*, 44, 67, 70, *169*, 198, 227, 231, *231*, 242, 243, *246*
Fusion (family) style 254

G
gardens 194, 238, *238*,
garage doors 238
geometric tiles 22
geometric wallpaper *188*, 221, 247, 249
Georgian houses 21, 41, *42*, 44, 77–85, **86**, 251
Georgian windows 44
glazed doors 206
Gloss *see* Full Gloss
Gordillo, Guy *53*
"Great White" 177, 207, *213*, 221
green (*see also* green paints by name) 26, *32*, 42, 99, *99*, 105, *106*, 114, *131*, 136, 141
"Green Blue" 210
green-blues 42
grey-green *147*, 148
grey (*see also* grey paints by name) 89, *147*
guest cloakrooms 221
guest rooms 213

H
"Hague Blue" 70, *73*, **74**, 124, *127*, **132**, *132*, 155, *159*, **160**, *160*, 174, 175, 221, 228, 238, 247, 248
halls/hallways 8, *14*, 17, *18*, 26, 27, *28*, *31*, 32, **38**, 41, *41*, **50**, 65, *65*, 67, **74**, 77, *77*, **86**, 89, *89*, 90, *90, 93*, *93*, 94, **96**, *96*, 99, *99*, 105, *105*, **108**, 111, *111*, 114, *114*, 117, *117*, **120**, 123, 124, *124*, **124**, 127, **132**, *132*, 135, *135*, 136, **144**, **152**, 155, 155, *156*, *159*, **160**, 163, *163*, 164, *164*, **170**, 179–85
hardware store 238
227, 231, *231*, 242, 243, *246*
Fusion (family) style 254

"Hardwick White" 32, *32*, **38**, 123, *123*, 124, **132**, *132*
harmonious colours 26, 37, *37*, *57*, 61, 74, *141*, 151, 169
"Hay" 175
hearths 164
Hindu ceremonies 20
historic houses 8, 20, 184–5, *193*
historic style 77
history of Farrow & Ball 8–11
Holi 20
"House White" (*see also* "School House White") 174, 175
How to Decorate (Farrow & Ball) 8, 28

I
"Incarnadine" 58, 201, 209
"Inchyra Blue" 22, *28*, 49, **50**, *50*, 53, *57*, 58, 61, **62**, 89, *89*, 90, *93*, *93*, 94, **96**, *96*, 105, *105*, *106*, **108**, *108*, 111, 114, *114*, **120**, 151, *151*, **152**, *173*, 174, 175, *179*, 182, 184, *184*, *193, 201*, 221, 247, *255*, *256*
"India Yellow" *37*, *37*, **38**, *38*, 175, *193*, 231
indigo 21
inspiration 8, 20, 21, *21*, 22, 182, 184
inspired choices *11*, *14*, 214
interconnecting rooms *201*
interconnecting, interior to exterior 206, 238
internal windows 85, *90*, *90*

J
"James White" 174, 175, *180*, *200*, 209
"Jasmine" wallpaper *259*
"Joa's White" *41*, 42, **50**, 124, *124*, **132**, 174, 175, 176, 218, 253, *253*, *259*, *260*

K

kitchen/dining room 37
kitchens 8, *16*, 17, 26, 31, 32, **38**, 44, *44*, *57*, **62**, 70, *70*, **74**, *74*, 80, 81, 82, **86**, 89, 90, *90*, *96*, *102*, 105, *105*, **108**, 114, *114*, 117, *117*, **120**, 127-8, *127*, *128*, **132**, *135*, 136, *136*, 141, **144**, 148, *148*, 156, *156*, 159, **160**, 169, *169*, **170**, *170*, 174, *176*, 182, 187-95, *187*, *188*, *191*, *193*, 197, 201, *241*, 242, *243*, 248, 250, 251, 256, 257
kitchen islands 44, *44*, **50**
kitchen units 28, *32*, 44, *44*, **50**, *57*, 58, 70, *70*, 82, *102*, *117*, *148*, *156*
Kjeldbæk, Bentemarie *31*
Krokatsis, Henry *53*

L

lack of light (*see also* light/lighting) 17, *180*, *182*
"Lamp Room Gray" 128, *128*, **132**
landings **50**, 58, **96**, **120**, **144**, 155, *159*
large patterns 221, 225
large rooms 248, *251*
Laval, Karine *67*
leather-clad furniture and artefacts *21*, *67*, 70
libraries *67*, 67, **74**, 90, 164, **170**
"Lichen" 20
lifestyle 26, 128
light absorption 248
"Light Blue" 57
"Light Gray" 77, *77*, **86**, 175
light/lighting (*see also* natural light) 17, *188*, 229
light reflection 218, 246, 258
light rooms 248, *249*, 250, 257
lighter colours 12, 14, 180, 188, 193, 209, *209*, 214, 218, 221, *222*, 231
lighter wallpapers 183
lilac 176
"Lime White" 42, **50**, 80, 82, **86**, 174, 175, 176, *257*
limestone 28
Limewash 243
living environment 16, 42, 58, *118*, 246

London 41, *44*, 49, 77, 111-120, 135
"London Clay" 111, *111*, **120**, *120*, 174, 175, 209, *218*
"London Stone" 175, 253
long walls 214, **214**
"Lotus" wallpaper *201*, *221*, 256
low lighting, to aid sleep (*see also* light/lighting) 234
Lucas, Simon *147*
"Lulworth Blue" 175, *229*, 234, *234*
luxe bathrooms (*see also* bathrooms)&&& 224-5, *224*

M

magenta 42, 111
"Mahogany" 77, *77*, 82, **86**, *86*, 156, *157*, **160**, *160*, 174, 175, *258*, *260*
mahogany doors/panelling/windows 155, 156, 159, *159*
"Manor House Gray" 65, 67, **74**
manor houses 123
masonry 238, 243
Exterior Masonry *238*, 243, 244
"Matchstick" 174, 175, 176
metallic 22, 221, 258
metro tiles 136
"Middleton Pink" 141, *141*, **144**, 175, *213*, 227
minerals 243
"Mizzle" 14, 18, 44, **50**, 203
Mitchell Beazley 8
Modern Eggshell *209*, 210, 224, 242, 244
Modern Emulsion 70, 182, 228, 229, 234, 242, 244, 261
modern (Nouvelle Cuisine) style 254
"Mole's Breath" 44, **50**, 174, 175, 238, *256*
monotone (*see also* one-colour) 169
moody colours 184, *193*, 247
mouldings 44, 65, *94*, **96**, *124*, *124*, *136*
"Mouse's Back" 26, **50**, 100, **108**, *152*, 174, 175, 184, *184*, *217*, *249*
mosaic 184

N

names of colours (*see also* paints by name) 20-1
"Nancy's Blushes" 19, 100, *100*, **108**, *108*, 141, *141*, **144**
Napoleon I, Emperor 128
National Trust (NT) 147
natural light (*see also* light/lighting) 18, *41*, 44, 58, 67, *118*, 136, *136*, 179, 182, 198, *198*, *218*, 224, *244*, 248, 250, 251, *251*
nature, embracing 20, 182, 250
near-black (*see also* paints by name) 206
Neutrals 27, 37, 41, *41*, 42, 44, **50**, 67, 74, 94, 114, *114*, 118, 124, 128, *131*, **132**, 148, 155, *156*, 159, *159*, **160**, *163*, *169*, 176
"New White" 175, 176, *255*, *261*
19th-century style *32*, 184, *200*
Nîmes, France 21
north-facing rooms 26, 94
northern light (*see also* light/lighting) 238
Nouvelle Cuisine (modern) style 254, 261

O

"Ocelot" wallpaper 249, *260*
"Octagon Yellow" 25, 77, *77*, 82, **86**
"Off-Black" 80, 81, 82, 85, *85*, **86**, *164*, 169, **170**, *170*, 174, 175, *201*, *221*, 238, *246*
"Off-White" (*see also* "Shaded White"; "School House White") 42, **50**, *152*, 174, 175, 176, 184, *184*
off-whites 218, 238, 246
old schoolhouse 99-109, *108*
"Old White" 42, **50**, 77, 81, 82, *82*, **86**, *147*, 148, *148*, **152**, 174, 175, 176
old world *85*, *127*, 159
"Olive" 69
one-colour 14, 15, 44, **50**, 82, **96**, 105, 163, 164, 169, 182, 183, 188, *188*, *197*, *198*, 206, 231, 247, 252
open-plan 37, 74, 100, 114, 148

orange (*see also* paints by name) 61
"Orangerie" wallpaper *260*
Oriental-style *246*
outdoor spaces 243
"Oval Room Blue" 20, 44, *44*, **50**, *94*, **96**, *102*, 105, **108**, 135, *135*, 136, **144**, 175, 194, 247, 248, *256*
"Oxford Stone" *41*, **50**, *118*

P

"Paean Black" 21, 174, 175, 182, 224, **224**, 247, *260*
paint colours (*see also* paints by name) 8, 17, 22, 174-6, 191, 205, *205*, 228, 250, 254-61
paint factory, Richard Ball and John Farrow start 21
paint coverage 244
paints, history of 8-11
painting techniques 8, 22, 238
Pettibon, Raymond *67*
printing wallpapers 251
paintbrushes 18
"Pale Hound" 175
"Pale Powder" 42, **50**, 175, 218
"Parma Gray" 175, *201*, 231
parquet flooring 28, *42*, *188*
passageways *127*, *127*
past, as inspiration 8, 21, 182, 184, 187, 205
pastels 218, 227
pastoral view *194*
patterns 22, 183, 213, 231, 246, 248, 249, 255, 260
"Pavilion Blue" 44, **50**, 61, *61*, **62**, 65, *65*, 67, 70, **74**, *74*, 93, **96**, 136, *136*, **144**, 175, 209, *261*
"Pavilion Gray" 44, **50**, 61, *61*, **62**, 65, *65*, 67, 70, **74**, *74*, 93, **96**, 136, *136*, **144**, 174, 175, 176, 194, *194*, 198, *198*, 205
"Pea Green" 85, *85*, 86, **86**
"Peignoir" 14, 44, *44*, **50**, 90, *90*, **96**, 141, *141*, **144**, 175, *200*, 231, 232, 248, *257*
"Pelt" 175, 182, 221, *259*
period houses (*see also* case studies) 136, 155
personality 8, 16, 179, 238, 246

photographs, choosing colours to aid display of 221
"Picture Gallery Red" 175
picture mounts 58
picture rails 213, 253
pictures (*see also* portraits) *11*, 17, 58, 61, 114, 198
"Pigeon" 12, 20, 174, 175, *238*, *257*, *258*
pigments 17, 37, 53, *53*, 58, 111, 141, *159*, *193*, 206, 214, 246, 248, 250
pink (*see also* pink paints by name) *41*, 42, 44, 58, *61*, 90, *90*, 94, 118, 141, 156, *200*
"Pink Ground" 175, *193*, 227, *229*
"Pitch Black" 65, *67*, 70, **74**, *74*, 174, 175, *188*, 194, *194*, 205, 206, *206*, *241*, *260*
"Pitch Blue" 175
plasterwork 14, *41*, 42, *42*, **50**, 58, 155, 243
playrooms 81, 90
"Plummett" 175
"Pointing" *159*, 159, **160**, *160*, 174, 175, 176, 209, 210, 213, 218, 232, 255-9 *passim*, *261*
portraits (*see also* pictures) 114, 124, *124*, 128, *128*
"Potted Shrimp" *41*, **50**
Preference Paints 21
"Preference Red" 21, 174, 175, 205, *238*, 248
"Print Room Yellow" 20, *193*
"Purbeck Stone" 22, 70, *70*, **74**, *169*, **170**, 175, 176, *188*, *229*, *257*, 236
purple (*see also* paints by name) 135

Q

Quintessential décor 123-33

R

R., Tal *32*
"Radicchio" 42, *42*, **50**, **50**, 175, *251*
"Railings" *11*, 14, 22, 31, *31*, 37, *37*, **38**, *38*, 44, **50**, 89, 90, 93, 94, **96**, *96*, 99, *99*, 100, **108**, 128, *128*, **132**, 174, 175, 180, *180*, 182, 187, 205, 221, 232, 238, 243, 247, *256*, *257*

"Rangwali" 20, 175, 221, *237*, 257
Rangwali Holi 20
"ready-weathered" look 82
receding colours 238
recipe tips 38, 50, 62, 74, 86, 96, 108, 120, 132, 144, 152, 160, 170
reading rooms 114
red (*see also red paints by name*) 28, *41*, 42, 82, 94, 151, 164
Red Based Neutrals 42, 176
red-brick façade 123
"Red Earth" 33, 58, 175, 184
Regency 61
Renaissance 184
"Renaissance" wallpaper 258
resin 243
restraint 41, 65, 123
rhythm 147
"Ringwold" wallpaper 247
Rødland, Torbjørn 53
Romany wagons 164
"room-named" colours 20
room sizes 36
rooms *see by type*

S
sage green 61
"St Antoine" wallpaper *210*, 249
"St Giles Blue" *16*, 175, 228, 248
"Samphire" wallpaper 258, *258*
sampling paints *41*, 58
"Savage Ground" 175
"School House White" (*see also* "House White") 99, *102*, 105, *105*, *106*, **108**
Scottish Regency 61
sculptures 58, *184*
serge de Nîmes 21
"Setting Plaster" 14, 58, *58*, 61, *62*, 94, *94*, **96**, 106, *106*, **108**, 118, *118*, *120*, 175, *205*, 209
"Shaded White" 20, 44, **50**, 77, 77, *86*, 128, 131, **132**, *132*, 151, **152**, *152*, 174, 175, 176, *205*, 218, *231*, *258*, 260
"Shadow White" 20, **50**, 174, 175, 176, *205*, *252*, *255*, *256*, *258*, *259*
short walls, **214**

showrooms 12, 26, 27, *86*, 262–3
Shrigley, David 53
shutters *194*
signature Farrow & Ball look 242
"Silvergate" wallpaper *200*, *218*, *255*
sitting rooms *16*, *180*, 197–208, *197*, *198*, *200*, *201*, *205*, *244*, *246*, 256
"Skimming Stone" *41*, 44, **50**, 174, 175, 176, *200*, *205*, 209, *210*, 218, 248, *251*, *258*, *260*, *261*
skirting/baseboards *14*, 58, 77, 80, 82, *86*, **86**, 123, **132**, *136*, *179*, *184*, *197*, *205*, 206, *217*, *218*, *224*, *229*, *252*, *253*
"Skylight" *94*, **94**, **96**, 175, *232*
skylights 93
"Slipper Satin" **50**, *152*, 164, *164*, **170**, 174, 175, 176, *256*, *257*
small rooms 221, 246–7
"Smoked Trout" *180*
Soft Distemper 243
south-facing rooms 26, 82, 194
spa-like bathroom 218
splashbacks 188
stair runners 135
stair spindles 77, *77*
stair treads 65, *70*, **74**, *74*
staircases 26, 27, **50**, 57, *58*, *62*, 90, **96**, 117, *117*, *120*, **144**, 151, 155, *159*, **160**, *160*
stairwell *124*
"Stiffkey Blue" *14*, 94, *94*, **96**, 117, *117*, **120**, *120*, 127, 174, 175, 228, *249*, *258*
"Stone Blue" 22, 61, *61*, **62**, *62*, 81, 82, 85, *85*, *86*, 118, *118*, **120**, 175, *184*, *184*, 206, *206*, *229*
stone colour 77, *100*, 151
stone corbels *100*
storing paint 174–6
"String" 20, 175, 176
stripes *163*, *193*, *217*, *224*, *229*, *231*, *232*, *234*, *234*
stripped-back style 155
strong colours 27, 32, **38**, *58*, *62*, 89–90, 94, **96**, 99, 106, **108**, 114, 117, *118*, **120**, *132*, *164*, **170**

"Strong White" *14*, *31*, 32, 37, **38**, *38*, 41, 42, **50**, *93*, **96**, *111*, 114, *114*, **120**, 128, *128*, *132*, *135*, 136, *136*, *141*, **144**, *144*, 174, 175, 176, *179*, *188*, *197*, *210*, *229*, *231*, *232*, *248*, *255*, *257*, *258*, *261*
"Studio Green" *31*, 32, *32*, **38**, *38*, 44, **50**, 85, *85*, *86*, *102*, 105, **108**
style 16–18, *32*, 41, 61, 77, *81*, *100*, 114, 131, 155, *164*, 169, *179*, *184*, *201*, 238, *246*, 254–61
"Sudbury Yellow" 175, *255*
"Sulking Room Pink" 20
sunshine yellow 127

T
tables 8, 18, 231, 244
table lamps 250
"Tallow" 175, 232
"Tanner's Brown" 174, 175, 180, 221, 247
"Teresa's Green" 175, 184, *184*, *213*, *228*, *238*, *261*
"Tessella" wallpaper 22, *188*, *198*, *201*, *247*, *255*, *255*
timeless colours 218
Timeless Neutrals 176
tone 12, 17, *18*, 20–2 *passim*, 176, 179, 180, *180*, *182*, *184*, *187*, *193*, 205, 214, 218, 224, *238*, 248, 250, 253, 257, 260
tone-on-tone woodwork 15
"Tourbillon" wallpaper 22, *182*
traditional (Classic) style 12, 14, 20, 176, 194, 232, 238, 242, 243, 254
Traditional Neutrals 42, *42*, 82, 148, 176
"Treron" 20
trim (*see also* woodwork) 11, 14, *14*, 15, 16, 22, 176, 180, *193*, 194, *198*, *200*, *201*, 206, *206*, **206**, 210, *210*, *213*, 224, *228*, *231*, *232*, *241*, 244, 247–9 *passim*, *249*, *252*, *253*, 255–61 *passim*
tropical prints 232
21st-century style *32*
twilight, colour of 93

U
Uddens Estate, Wimborne 10
underlighting 176
underlying colours 174, 176, *180*, *221*, 248
under-the-radar neutrals 176
undersides, colours for 221, *259*
understated colours 176, *187*, *210*, *231*, *238*, 258
undertones 176, *187*, *200*, 206, 246, *246*, 248
unifying colours 14, 17
upper landings 155
urban exteriors 31
urban interiors 70, 136, 155, *159*
urban living 65, 73
useful information 11
using wallpaper (*see also* wallpaper; *wallpapers by name*) 247, 249
utility 21, 70, **74**

V
"Vardo" 22, *163*, 164, *164*, 169, **170**, *170*, *173*, 175, *201*, *205*, *231*, *232*, *232*, *261*
vastness 224
"Vert de Terre" 20, 175
vibrancy 20, 53, 141, *163*, *198*, 206, 234, 238
Victorian houses 89, *111*, *117*, 141, 147
Victorian gardens 147
vintage look *206*, 206

W
wallpaper (*see also* using wallpaper; *wallpapers by name*) 18, 22, 22, *173*, *183*, 198, 210, 218, 221, 231, 232, *232*, 247, 249, 251, 253
wall-to-wall cupboards *94*
warm colours 176, *180*, 182, 194, 198, 206, 209, 213, 214, 218, *218*, 232, *232*, 234, 247–9 *passim*, 249, 251, 253, 258
water-based paints 242
"Wevet" 14, 16, *111*, **120**, 155, *155*, *156*, *159*, **160**, *160*, 163, *163*, 169, *169*, **170**, *170*, 174, 175, 176, *176*, *180*, *198*, *222*, *224*, *224*, *227*, *231*, *234*, *234*, 255, 256, 257

which white? 242–3
white (*see also white paints by name*) 14, *16*, 174, 176, *182*, *187*, *188*, 194, 206, 210, 213, 218, 224, 231, 234, 238, 246, 251, 252
"White Tie" 174, 175, 176
white-on-white 246
"whiter" whites 159
Wimborne, Dorset 21
"Wimborne White" *16*, 37, *37*, **38**, **50**, 123, *123*, 124, *127*, **132**, 174, 175, *229*
window frames 22, 31, **50**, 128, *152*, 156, *156*, 169, **170**, 184, *193*, 224, 234, *237*, 243
window recesses 102, 105, *105*, **108**
window seats 128, *136*
window shutters *111*, *136*
window surrounds 156, *156*, *159*
windows 31, *31*, 37, *37*, 42, 44, 82, 85, *85*, 90, *90*, *93*, **96**, 100, *100*, 105, *111*, **160**
"Wisteria" wallpaper *213*, 247
woodwork (*see also* trim) 11, 14, *14*, 15, 26, 27, *31*, 32, **62**, 77, 77, *81*, 82, *85*, *86*, **86**, 89, 94, **96**, *96*, 99, *105*, *106*, **108**, *111*, *111*, *114*, 117, 124, 128, *128*, **132**, 136, *136*, 141, **144**, 151, **152**, **160**, 174, 180, 187, 188, **194**, 224, *227*, **227**, 228, 238, *238*, 242
working environment 93, 197
work surfaces *117*
workspace 249
"Worsted" 93, **96**, *111*, 114, *114*, 117, **120**, *120*, 220

Y
"Yeabridge Green" 175, *198*, *200*
yellow (*see also yellow paints by name*) 37, 58, 127
Yellow Based Neutrals 176
"Yellow Ground" 175, *213*, *229*
"Yellowcake" *16*, *182*, 231, *241*
"Yukutori" wallpaper 231

ACKNOWLEDGMENTS

It says a lot that while writing this book each house was referred to simply by the name of the owner as it is their DNA which is imbued in the fabric of the houses. Many thanks to you all for your generosity in sharing these beautiful homes with us.

None of this could have come about without the Octopus team who have showed enormous patience and unfailing support. Particular thanks go to the brilliant Alison Starling, Jonathan Christie, Polly Poulter and Katherine Hockley.

It goes without saying that enormous thanks go to the fabulous and extremely flexible James Merrell, whose images are the backbone of this book. His calm, quiet talent knows no bounds and a day spent with him is always a treat.

Most importantly, I an indebted to the extraordinary energy of my friend and colleague Charlotte Cosby – even when busy producing the fabulous Bea, she shared an abundance of creative inspiration, masterminding the fantastic imagery for the cover and case study palettes with her usual flair and good humour, as well as creating the masterful coloured crayons on page 229! The images for this book would never have seen the light of day without the extraordinary hard work of Tracey Mack, to whom I am unfathomably grateful.

On a personal note, I would like to thank my mother for her unswerving belief in me, and the pride that both she and my father were never afraid to show. And lastly, and most importantly, to my unfailingly patient husband, who first taught me to love and treasure books and then nursed me through the process of creating one. Thank you, And.

— *Joa Studholme*

An Hachette UK Company
www.hachette.co.uk

First published in Great Britain in 2019 by Mitchell Beazley, an imprint of Octopus Publishing Group Ltd, Carmelite House, 50 Victoria Embankment, London EC4Y 0DZ
www.octopusbooks.co.uk

Text and illustrations copyright © Farrow & Ball Limited 2019

All rights reserved. No part of this work may be reproduced or utilized in any form or by any means, electronic or mechanical, including photocopying, recording or by any information storage and retrieval system, without the prior written permission of the publisher.

ISBN 978-1-78472-436-8

A CIP catalogue record for this book is available from the British Library.

Printed and bound in China

10 9 8 7 6 5 4 3 2 1

Text: Joa Studholme
Photographers: James Merrell and Robin Kitchen

Publisher: Alison Starling
Creative Director: Jonathan Christie
Senior Editor: Pollyanna Poulter
Copy Editor: Helen Ridge
Proofreader: Zia Mattocks
Senior Production Manager: Katherine Hockley

JOA STUDHOLME

Farrow & Ball Colour Curator Joa Studholme has amassed a vast wealth of experience in the 23 years she has worked with the company. When she is not developing and naming new colours, or spreading the word about how to use them, Joa delights in working with the paints and papers on design projects all over the world, some of which feature in this book.

JAMES MERRELL

London-based James Merrell is the book's photographer. James's work has been featured in *W*, *Elle Decor* (all editions), *Vogue Living*, *Town & Country*, *Domino*, *Food & Wine*, *Martha Stewart Living*, *Departures*, *Travel + Leisure*, *The Wall Street Journal* and *Living Etc*. It has also appeared in many bestselling interiors books.

Joa and James were the co-author and photographer for Farrow & Ball's *How to Decorate*, which was also published by Mitchell Beazley.